1/25 RN Soc Sc

CW01065204

JUDGING SOCIAL RIC

Countries that now contemplate constitutional reform often grapple with the question of whether to constitutionalise social rights. This book presents an argument for why, under the right conditions, doing so can be a good way to advance social justice. In making such a case, the author considers the nature of the social minimum, the role of courts among other institutions, the empirical record of judicial impact, and the role of constitutional text. He argues, however, that when enforcing such rights, judges ought to adopt a theory of judicial restraint structured around four principles: democratic legitimacy, polycentricity, expertise, and flexibility. These four principles, when taken collectively, commend an incremental-ist approach to adjudication. The book combines theoretical, doctrinal, empirical, and comparative analysis, and is written to be accessible to law-yers, social scientists, political theorists, and human rights advocates.

JEFF KING is a senior lecturer at the Faculty of Laws, University College London, where he teaches public law, human rights, and legal theory.

CAMBRIDGE STUDIES IN CONSTITUTIONAL LAW

The aim of this series is to produce leading monographs in constitutional law. All areas of constitutional law and public law fall within the ambit of the series, including human rights and civil liberties law, administrative law, as well as constitutional theory and the history of constitutional law. A wide variety of scholarly approaches is encouraged, with the governing criterion being simply that the work is of interest to an international audience. Thus, works concerned with only one jurisdiction will be included in the series as appropriate, while, at the same time, the series will include works which are explicitly comparative or theoretical – or both. The series editors likewise welcome proposals that work at the intersection of constitutional and international law, or that seek to bridge the gaps between civil law systems, the USA, and the common law jurisdictions of the Commonwealth.

Series Editors
David Dyzenhaus
Professor of Law and Philosophy,
University of Toronto, Canada
Adam Tomkins
John Millar Professor of Public Law,
University of Glasgow, UK

Editorial Advisory Board
T. R. S. Allan, Cambridge, UK
Damian Chalmers, LSE, UK
Sujit Choudhry, Toronto, Canada
Monica Claes, Maastricht, Netherlands
David Cole, Georgetown, USA
K. D. Ewing, King's College London, UK
David Feldman, Cambridge, UK
Cora Hoexter, Witwatersrand, South Africa
Christoph Moellers, Goettingen, Germany
Adrienne Stone, Melbourne, Australia
Adrian Vermeule, Harvard, USA

JUDGING SOCIAL RIGHTS

JEFF KING

University College London

CAMBRIDGE
UNIVERSITY PRESS

CAMBRIDGE UNIVERSITY PRESS
Cambridge, New York, Melbourne, Madrid, Cape Town,
Singapore, São Paulo, Delhi, Mexico City

Cambridge University Press
The Edinburgh Building, Cambridge CB2 8RU, UK

Published in the United States of America by Cambridge University Press, New York

www.cambridge.org
Information on this title: www.cambridge.org/9781107008021

© Jeff King 2012

This publication is in copyright. Subject to statutory exception
and to the provisions of relevant collective licensing agreements,
no reproduction of any part may take place without the written
permission of Cambridge University Press.

First published 2012

Printed in the United Kingdom at the University Press, Cambridge

A catalogue record for this publication is available from the British Library

Library of Congress Cataloguing in Publication data
King, Jeff, 1973–
Judging social rights / Jeff King, University College London.
pages   cm. – (Cambridge studies in constitutional law)
Includes bibliographical references and index.
ISBN 978-1-107-00802-1 (hardback) – ISBN 978-1-107-40032-0 (paperback)
1. Social rights–United States.   2. Judicial power–Social aspects–United
States.   3. Constitutional law–United States.   4. Political questions
and judicial power–United States.   5. Social justice–United States.
6. Social rights–Philosophy.   I. Title.
KF4749.K557 2012
342.08′5–dc23
2012002123

ISBN 978-1-107-00802-1 Hardback
ISBN 978-1-107-40032-0 Paperback

Cambridge University Press has no responsibility for the persistence or
accuracy of URLs for external or third-party internet websites referred to in
this publication, and does not guarantee that any content on such websites is,
or will remain, accurate or appropriate.

CONTENTS

DETAILED TABLE OF CONTENTS

ACKNOWLEDGMENTS

This book is the culmination of many years of academic interest in the topic of social rights. I have incurred several extraordinary debts along the way. The book began as a doctoral dissertation completed at the University of Oxford, Keble College. I would like therefore first to thank my various supervisors. Timothy Endicott brought much greater depth and precision to my writing, and clarified some crucial issues in the early stages of the work. Simon Halliday broadened my understanding of the accountability landscape, a turn in both my thinking about social rights and my long-term research agenda. Yet I worked with Paul Craig for the longest period. The breadth of his understanding of so many disparate fields, and depth of his attention to detail, was an inestimable contribution to this book, just as his mentorship has been to my work outside of it. I also owe a weighty debt of gratitude to my two examiners, Denis Galligan and Jeffrey Jowell, and their helpful comments made both during and after the viva.

The dissertation was substantially revised during my time as a Fellow and Tutor in law at Balliol College, Oxford, and university lecturer for the Faculty of Law. I would thank the Master and Fellows of Balliol College, and my colleague Dr Grant Lamond, for a period of sabbatical leave and other support that proved instrumental for completing the manuscript. The Oxford Law Faculty provided numerous small grants that facilitated research assistance on various topics covered in the book. I would also like to thank Keble College, Oxford, and Edwin Peel and James Edelman in particular, for the congenial research and work environment provided there during my year as Research Fellow and Tutor. Lastly, I thank University College London for providing an office and other valuable support prior to the commencement of my teaching.

Prior to coming to Oxford, I benefitted from the guidance of a number of people whose influence can be traced in the pages of this book. I thank in particular Roderick MacDonald, Ashfaq Khalfan, Sandra Liebenberg, René Provost, and especially Bruce Porter and Malcolm Langford for their time and insights. Bruce was and remains an inspiration in many ways, and Malcolm not only taught me much about social rights, but was gracious enough to part with the title of this book when we discovered that we had both come to it separately.

The following individuals read drafts or engaged in extended conversations with me about the ideas in this book: T. R. S. Allan, J. W. F. Allison, Nigel Balmer, Anne Carter, Cathryn Costello, Alice Donald, James Edelman, Richard Ekins, Cécile Fabre, Brian Flanagan, Sandra Fredman, Octavio Ferraz, Judith Freedman, Dennis Galligan, Graham Gee, Tarunabh Khaitan, Tom Hickman, Richard Kirkham, Dimitrios Kyritsis, Jan Luba, Kirsty McLean, Kai Möller, James Nickel, Aoife Nolan, Colm O'Cinneide, Justice Catherine O'Regan, Dan Priel, Gavin Phillipson, Roger Shiner, Adam Swift, François Tanguay-Renaud, Lisa Vanhalla, Mila Versteeg, Paul Yowell, Alison Young, and Jan van Zyl Smit (who I also thank for drawing my attention to Tom Hunter's work, *Woman Reading a Possession Order*, which graces the cover of this book). The following people also made important clarifications in conversation or correspondence: Nicholas Bamforth, Varda Bondy, Alan Bogg, Trevor Buck, Anne Davies, David Dyzenhaus, Pavlos Eleftheriadis, Jennifer Erkulwater, Leslie Green, Mitu Gulati, Murray Hunt, Michael Klarman, Grant Lamond, Martin Loughlin, Virginia Mantouvalou, Christopher McCrudden, Stephanie Motz, Aoife Nolan, Ellie Palmer, Larry Sager, Martin Shapiro, Maurice Sunkin, Victor Tadros, Adam Tomkins, Adrian Vermeule, and Murray Wesson. Hayley Hooper, Arghya Sengupta, and Rachel Sheppard provided helpful research assistance on various substantive matters. Marya Shabir's help with the final manuscript was nothing short of extraordinary.

I would like in particular to thank Graham Gee, Cathryn Costello, Nick Barber, and Aileen Kavanagh for contributions that exceeded the call of friendship. Bryan Thomas, now as ever, has done more to clarify my thinking about political philosophy than have the dreamy spires of Oxford. I would also thank Cameron Russell for allowing me to shadow him at a Mental Health Review Tribunal, and for countless extended and illuminating conversations about the role of law in social work.

Chapters or portions of this book were presented to various audiences over the years: Annual Conference of the Socio Legal Studies Association (Stirling, 2006); W. G. Hart Annual Workshop (London, 2007); Society of Legal Scholars (Ireland, 2008); Foundation for Law, Justice and Society Workshop (Oxford, 2008; 2011); Oxford Centre for Socio-Legal Studies Seminar Series (Oxford, 2008); and law faculty research seminars at

Cambridge (2009), Warwick (2010), and Durham (2011), as well as at conferences at Leeds (on the HRA, 2009) and London Metropolitan (on accountability, 2010). I benefitted greatly from feedback at each.

Chapter 5 is adapted from 'Institutional Approaches to Judicial Restraint' (2008) 28 *Oxford Journal of Legal Studies* 409–41. Parts of Chapter 6 are drawn from 'The Pervasiveness of Polycentricity' [2008] *Public Law* 401–24. Adaptations from forthcoming work are noted in the text where relevant.

I received major research support funding from the following sources: McGill University (Thomas Shearer Stewart Fellowship); Canadian Council on International Law (John Peters Humphrey Human Rights Scholarship); Canadian Social Sciences and Humanities Research Council (SSHRC); and various grants from the Oxford Faculty of Law and from the Nuffield Foundation for related research.

The most important contribution of all to this book was made by my wife, Julika Erfurt. Love, support, humour, sanity, strength, perseverance, and much else were the daily fare in the years leading up to the completion of this work. Her work in government shed much light on the topics I discuss, and her discussion with me of the social minimum was a notable contribution to my understanding of it. No page of this book would look the same without her contribution. Lastly, I want to express profound gratitude to my parents. Without their love, support and encouragement from an early age, this book would never have been attempted, let alone completed. To the three of them, my holy trinity, this book is dedicated.

TABLE OF CASES

United Kingdom

xvi

United States

Canada

South Africa

European Court of Human Rights

Other cases

TABLE OF LEGISLATION

International agreements

Domestic legislation

United Kingdom

United States

Canada

South Africa

Introduction: aims and methods

I   Introduction

What is more important, having the ability to preach politics on Hyde Park Corner, or ensuring that we have a fighting chance to live past heart disease or breast cancer? In any just society we should not have to choose between them, and thankfully in most rich ones we don't. But in the Western political tradition we have tended to speak about the former issue in terms of fundamental human rights, and the latter as a matter of policy. There is something ironic in this approach, particularly when many think rights are normatively superior to policy and preferences. A generation ago, many writers were preoccupied with justifying the claim that social rights are human rights. In international law and philosophy, that debate is now largely over: few now deny that it is obvious that our right to live past cancer is as essential to our and our family's basic dignity as is a right so few of us actually choose to exercise. This book is for those who accept that social rights are human rights, or ought to be given comparable political priority, and want to know chiefly about another, more focused institutional question. That question is whether abstract social rights to housing, education, health care, and social security should be put into constitutions and judges should be given broad powers to interpret and enforce them – including by striking down legislation.

This book offers an extended argument about why doing that would be one good way among others to protect our social rights. It will shortly be seen that one cannot answer the question of *whether* to constitutionalise social rights, without saying a lot about *how* judges will enforce them. No theory can answer every question about *how* in advance. Yet a good one should say enough that, if faithfully observed by judges, it would allow us to say with some confidence that judges would avoid the key pitfalls and deliver the core benefits. At the same time, any theory of judging must be one we can reasonably expect judges to adopt. It must fit with the institutional and political constraints under which they operate, and it ought ideally to connect with the jurisprudential traditions instinct in their craft. It should not be too exotic, in other words.

The main prescription for courts in this book is hardly exotic at all: if given powers to adjudicate abstract constitutional social rights, judges should act incrementally, taking small steps to expand the coverage of existing rules and principles in a controlled fashion, learning from past experiences, and waiting for feedback on new developments. The thorny problems for the thesis in this book are why incrementalism is not too much or too little, and when it is that a judge will need considerably more than the techniques of incrementalism to wade through the thicket of difficulties presented in a typical hard case about social rights.

II   Why does it matter?

It would be naïve to think that adopting a bill of constitutional social rights would ensure their protection. A surprisingly large number of countries have adopted bills of social rights without any great reduction in inequality.[1] And all countries that provide the best current legislative protection of social rights did so without constitutional bills of social rights, and a few of them, including Britain, Sweden, the Netherlands, and France, did so in legal environments that were distinctly hostile to judicial review of any legislation. I show in Chapter 2 that the legislative and executive branches play the key role in protecting social rights, and adjudication of the non-constitutional variety already plays a substantial supporting role.

But the question of whether and how to constitutionalise social rights is nonetheless crucially important because rights-discourse is a key element in our contemporary political rhetoric, and in my view either *including* or *excluding* social rights claims from our ontology of constitutional rights has both expressive and concrete impact. Moreover, as I show in Part I of this book, constitutional adjudication offers some important instrumental benefits for protecting our rights and interests. And perhaps most importantly, many countries have already gone down the road towards constitutional social rights, and so some careful guidance at a general level is desirable.

---

[1] D. S. Law and M. Versteeg, 'The Evolution and Ideology of Global Constitutionalism' (2011) 99 *California Law Review* 101.

This last reason deserves some elaboration. Whether to constitution-alise social rights is a pressing issue in the United Kingdom, for one.[2] The European Union also has given formal recognition to social rights in its Charter of Fundamental Rights.[3] Indeed, the worldwide constitutional profusion of social rights is as remarkable as it is unknown. Of the constitutions of the countries of the world, as of 2006, 82 per cent include rights to work and to public education at state expense, 78 per cent include physical needs rights, 72 per cent the right to unionise and organise, and well over half include children's rights and a smattering of other worker's rights.[4] Some deep thinking about both whether to constitutionalise enforceable social rights, and how to interpret them, is quite obviously needed.

III   Arguments against constitutional social rights

For a long time the debate about social rights focused on whether they 'are' justiciable. Justiciability refers, roughly, to whether an issue is amenable to judicial review.[5] I once asked a constitutional law professor whether he thought social rights were justiciable, and his answer was 'they are if the constitution says they are'. That is certainly one way to answer the question. In South Africa there is no denying that social rights are justiciable, because the only reasonable reading of the constitution is that it says they are.[6] However, there are two ways of answering the justiciability question, because, as Geoffrey Marshall pointed out, the term has two senses: a fact-stating sense (i.e. that something is in fact an issue that courts *will*

---

[2] See Ministry of Justice, Rights and Responsibilities: Developing Our Constitutional Framework, Cm 7577 (2009), Chapter 3 (see pp. 57–58); see also Joint Committee on Human Rights, 'The International Covenant on Economic, Social and Cultural Rights', (Twenty-First Report of Session 2003–2004), 10 October 2004; Joint Committee on Human Rights, 'A Bill of Rights for the UK?' (Twenty-Ninth Report of Session 2007–2008), 10 August 2008. For a stronger endorsement after nearly a decade of extensive consultations, see Northern Ireland Human Rights Commission, 'A Bill of Rights for Northern Ireland: Advice to the Secretary of State for Northern Ireland', 10 December 2008, Chapter 3 (advising the Secretary of State for Northern Ireland to adopt a bill of rights that includes justiciable rights to education, health care and social services), available at www.nihrc.org/.
[3] European Union, Charter of Fundamental Rights Parts III, IV, V, 7 December 2000, OJ [2007] C303/1.
[4] Law and Versteeg, 'Global Constitutionalism', 138 (Table 2).
[5] See Chapter 5, section II.C for a discussion of the concept.
[6] *In re Certification of the Constitution of the Republic of South Africa*, 1996 (4) SA 744 (CC).

adjudicate) and a normative sense (i.e. that it is something they *ought to* adjudicate (or have no good reason not to) in view of their *institutional capacity and legitimacy*).[7] I was asking the professor about the normative sense, and his answer addressed the fact-stating sense. It is easy to trade on this ambiguity, and both critics and advocates do trade on it by appealing to either sense of the term to prove their point. The pressing issue in dispute here, of course, is whether we ought or ought not to empower courts to adjudicate constitutional social rights disputes. Once focused on this issue, one meets with a variety of arguments, some bad, some good, but none conclusive.

A   *The bad arguments*

I will start with the weaker ones first. They are as follows:

- *Social rights are not human rights*: International law has said they are for about sixty years, and even political philosophy has recently awoken from its dogmatic slumber on that issue.[8]
- *Courts cannot and will not adjudicate policy questions*: Every first-year law student knows that judges can and do base their decisions at times on policy considerations, and Ronald Dworkin's increasingly refined attempts to deny this is one of the bigger dead ends in modern jurisprudence.[9]
- *Courts cannot adjudicate positive rights*: The embarrassing fact for this argument is that they do.[10]
- *It would violate the separation of powers*: This argument is usually circular or question-begging: its advocates merely define the separation of powers in a way that excludes social rights adjudication. If a better argument lurks in the detail, it cashes out into one of the good arguments against social rights reviewed below.

---

[7] G. Marshall, 'Justiciability', in A. G. Guest (ed.), *Oxford Essays in Jurisprudence* (Oxford University Press, 1961). See Chapter 4 of this book for a discussion.

[8] See Chapter 2.

[9] See Chapter 5, section II.B.

[10] A. R. Mowbray, *The Development of Positive Obligations under the European Convention on Human Rights by the European Court of Human Rights* (Oxford: Hart Publishing, 2004); T. Harvey and J. Kenner, *Economic and Social Rights in the EU Charter of Fundamental Rights* (Oxford: Hart Publishing, 2003). See also: *Vriend* v. *Alberta* [1998] 1 SCR 493 (SCC); *R* v. *Secretary of State for the Home Department, ex parte Limbuela* [2005] UKHL 66 [920] (Lord Brown: '[I]t seems to me generally unhelpful to attempt to analyse obligations … as negative or positive, and the state's conduct as active or passive. Time and again these are shown to be false dichotomies.')

- *Social rights are too vague*: If that were the real reason not to entrench social rights, then we might need to do away with a few other legal concepts, such as reasonableness, fairness, unfair dismissal, much of regulation, most of criminal law, and all other bills of rights and much of the constitutional division of powers in federal systems.[11] And progressives beware – it is precisely this type of argument that libertarians use to oppose government regulation of the economy.[12]
- *Social rights conflict with each other*: This looks superficially true – my right to health reaches for the same resources as does your right to social security. But there are conflicts between many other rights that we accept in due course: life vs. liberty and the freedom from torture in terrorism cases; privacy vs. freedom of the press; property vs. taxation; free expression vs. the right to vote, or equality, or security of the person. Private law rights are often balanced against one another, and efficiency and justice joust for supremacy in the arena of administrative law.

People are reluctant to abandon these arguments even when they cannot explain away the counter-examples. Why so?

B   The good arguments

A better set of arguments against constitutional social rights adjudication raises four sets of concerns that are foreshadowed somewhat imperfectly above, but which can be restated more crisply:

- *Democratic legitimacy*: Resource allocation by definition implicates the interests of nearly everyone, because we nearly all pay in and take out of the public system. There could be hardly a better scenario in which the voice of each should count equally, or as close to equally as practically possible, where we can bargain and compromise, and no better institution for that than a representative legislature. The ordinary case against judicial review is thus amplified here.
- *Polycentricity*: Some issues require the comprehension of a vast number of interconnected variables in order for one to understand the likely consequences of any change of policy. Consider whether a country

---

[11] See Chapter 4, section II.C. See also C. Gearty and V. Mantouvalou, *Debating Social Rights* (Oxford: Hart Publishing, 2011), pp. 113–14.

[12] F. A. Hayek, *The Constitution of Liberty* (London: Routledge, 1960); J. O. Freedman, 'Defining Taxpayer Responsibility: In Support of a General Anti-Avoidance Principle' [2004] *British Tax Review* 332 (addressing the argument from vagueness).

should seek a foreign loan in order to cope with a financial crisis. The question is linked to a judgment about how international markets will react, the political acceptability of any repayment conditions, long-term macroeconomic stability, and all of this must be balanced against similar calculations in respect of alternative policy options. Further, all such factors change over time. This is a polycentric problem because the soundness of some proposals is dependent on the comparative merits of others, the complete comprehension of which is extremely difficult and which involves considerable guesswork. Resource allocation at the nationwide level is a polycentric activity par excellence.

- *Expertise*: Polycentric decision-making often requires expertise. However some questions are not polycentric in a strict sense but primarily require the application of expert judgment. Determining whether a drug is safe, a building structurally sound, whether a certain test is appropriate for measuring a disability, or whether some proposed procedural right will cause unsustainable problems in a modern bureaucracy are matters on which expertise must be brought to bear. Courts not only often lack that kind of expertise, but are invited to strike down expert judgments on the basis of their intuitions. Expertise, in fact, was a key rationale for limiting earlier judicial intrusions into the welfare state that most now see as having obstructed the recognition of social rights.

- *Flexibility*: On some issues the government might be shown to be essentially fumbling in the dark, and there might be no good reason to think that a judge or claimant's view on the issue is in any way inferior to the government's. But there may *still*, though, be reasons to let the executive or legislature take ownership of the issue if the possibility of changing positions in response to unforeseen information or developments is crucial. It is hard to say that there exists a fundamental right to kidney dialysis in January, but not in December, because the price spiked in June.

- *Alternatives*: No doubt there is a need for justice in the welfare state. But why look to courts first? We have over half a century of administrative justice studies and many of them have been concerned (in the common law world) with reasons why we should consider institutions that improve upon the shortcomings of courts. This led to the creation of many of those institutions.

These are strong arguments against social rights adjudication because they all contain a significant core of truth. In fact, my exploration of them in Chapter 3 and Part II of the book will show that they are critically important in public law. However, Part II also shows that these

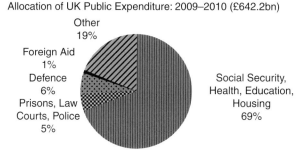

Figure 1
Source: HM Treasury, *Public Expenditure Statistical Analyses 2011* Cm 8104 (2011),
p. 69 (Table 5.2).[13]

arguments cannot justify any sweeping conclusion that social rights are
non-justiciable. Such an argument would reduce to absurdity, because
it would require us, if consistent, to abandon so much else in our legal
system. Our public and private law systems are rife with cases that are
polycentric, involve expert judgment, impose inflexibility, or raise an
issue about democratic legitimacy in some way or another (especially
modern bills of rights). These systems have adapted to take these issues
into account, without excluding adjudication altogether. So if these good
arguments against social rights do not rule out those cases, why should
they rule out social rights?

C   The best argument – the risky enterprise

A more refined argument would say, roughly, that even if courts can adjudicate some problematic cases that put a strain on the concerns mentioned
in the previous section, it may be that a bill of social rights will present a
lot more of them. We can present this type of objection a bit more graphically. It is a common riposte to arguments against social rights to say that
courts enforce positive obligations in respect of prisons, courts and the
like. Figure 1 allows us to compare the amount of the UK budget spent in
2009–2010 on areas that traditionally concern civil liberties such as law,
prisons, policing (including immigration), with that spent on the areas directly implicating social rights (with a few other familiar items thrown in

---

[13] The sums are rounded, and housing includes some funding for community development
and research and development.

for comparison). One can see that the stakes are not quite the same.[14] The aggregate number of problematic cases could be much higher, this argument goes, and thus the costs associated with all those good but rebuttable arguments against social rights would be much greater with than without constitutional social rights. Taking a few cases here and there, and showing how judges can work through them, will not convince this critic. Even less so when one takes a highly theoretical argument and applies it after the fact to a decided case, in the style of some theorists, rather than by showing how that argument can function predictably in the hands of real judges who disagree with each other and are impatient about theory. The point is, for these critics, that the whole enterprise is too risky.

IV   The case for incrementalism in a nutshell

This book seeks to give a convincing answer to all of these daunting arguments. I show first, that the four considerations set out above are best accounted for in adjudication by being restated as principles of judicial restraint. When properly understood, they function as principles to which judges can give weight when they decide cases. Part II expounds these principles, showing where the limitations of each argument lies, and why these arguments all tend to converge on one general theme, which is caution rather than abdication.

But the prescriptions aim to be more specific than suggesting mere caution. In each case, the format of the chapter is quite similar. I explain why the concern or objection addressed is insightful and important, but that it cannot be deployed (consistently) as a strong argument against justiciable social rights. In the chapter on democratic legitimacy (Chapter 6), I argue that courts can respect the idea of treating people as equals but compensate for democratic problems with the finality of legislation by addressing two key problems, namely, the absence of legislative focus on some rights issues and the failure to protect adequately those groups that are particularly vulnerable to majoritarian bias or neglect. With polycentricity (Chapter 7), I show why the argument is good but that there are a range of attenuating factors – such as the existence of a strong judicial mandate, the degree of polycentricity, role of interventions and so on – that

---

[14] Of course civil and political rights implicate more than prisons, policing and the like, but then social rights implicate other areas of the budget that I have also excluded from the tally above, such as possibly transport (£23 billion), debt servicing (£31 billion), and waste management (£7 billion).

moderate the weight that a court should attach to the polycentric character of a given legal issue. On the question of expertise (Chapter 8), I show that although the historical relationship between administrative expertise and the welfare state suggests that the idea must be given great weight, both that history and current practice point to something more nuanced than a closed door. There are trade-offs between expertise and accountability, just as there are different types of expertise calling for restraint in different ways. And then there is the problem of failures of expertise – situations where the state is inconsistent, has failed to focus on the issue, or is patently defying a substantial uniformity of expert opinion on the matter. The need for flexibility (Chapter 9), too, is acute, but courts can help to strengthen this role both by breaking up bureaucratic or political inertia, and by adopting specific techniques of adjudication that respect the need for flexibility in the welfare state. What emerges over the course of each chapter is a restatement of the argument under consideration as a principle of restraint, one that can assist the task of interpretation, and keep it within safer bounds.

These four principles of restraint are helpful when adjudicating a case that raises a particular issue in acute form (such as expertise, social science evidence, or legitimacy) but I am not suggesting that a judge sets out all four as tests and works through them mechanically in each case. Such rigour could not even be expected of the Germans.[15] It would also be unnecessary, because the four principles collectively recommend that judges take a default position of judicial incrementalism. Incrementalism is a useful heuristic, or rule of thumb, for what the principles of restraint ordinarily recommend. Incremental steps are those that require only a relatively small departure from the status quo, or which, when addressing significant macro-level policy, allow for substantial administrative or legislative flexibility by way of response. The common law has expanded incrementally over time and it typically involves expanding the coverage of a rule or principle, introducing an exception, or overruling a case after a history of problems leads to a strong case for change. The case for this approach, in a nutshell, is that judges can adjudicate social rights disputes if the range of considerations, affected parties and judicial control more generally, are ordinarily limited to a relatively localised set of issues, or, if addressing more macro-level issues, only impose finality upon the resolution of the issue to a limited degree.

---

[15] But see R. Alexy, *A Theory of Constitutional Rights*, trans. J. Rivers (Oxford University Press, 2002), pp. 120–38 (making Hohfeld's scheme of rights and duties *more* complex).

When focused in this way, the universe of relevant considerations for the judge is radically reduced. That makes the legal issue less polycentric, any deficit in expertise less of a concern, and it preserves flexibility to adjust to unforeseen circumstances or work around judicial holdings that were based on findings or assumptions that are no longer tenable. I commend a set of techniques – the techniques of incrementalism – that will at once both be familiar to judges and connected both to the idea of incrementalism and the principles of restraint set out in Part II of the book.

If we thus reconsider the good arguments against social rights, we can see that the principles of restraint explain why those arguments can be given weight in day-to-day adjudication, and the idea of judicial incrementalism gives a straightforward answer to the risky enterprise argument against social rights.

V   Background political conditions – when the argument applies

Adjudication is an institutional mechanism to help attain certain goals, and in the case addressed by this book, the implementation of social rights. I explain how this works in Chapter 2, but it should be apparent immediately that the success of constitutional adjudication is not something determined in the abstract. The attractiveness of *constitutional* social rights depends on the political conditions prevailing in the country where the case is advanced.

One way to present the case for social rights is to limit it to one jurisdiction. Another, which may be more enlightening in comparative perspective, is to identify a set of salient political conditions that are present in a particular community to which the argument is directed. I take this second approach, and the paradigm community is the United Kingdom, because of its historical centrality to the legal culture throughout the Commonwealth, similarity to other European countries, and the richness of its public law scholarship.

A   *The background political conditions*

In my view, the salient background political conditions that apply in the United Kingdom and some other Commonwealth countries are the following:

1. Courts operate on a model of common law (or institutionally similar civil law adjudication) that is not likely to change radically, and they

are unlikely to adopt the public law litigation paradigm sometimes used in the United States and India, nor a strong role for investigative judges.

2. There are reasonably independent courts that are not party political, even though the political preferences of judges may and likely will influence their judgments.

3. The legislature is elected by universal franchise, it shows a basic commitment to rights, it can pass and amend legislation competently, and committees play an important accountability function in legislative decision-making.

4. There are substantial non-judicial or specialised adjudicative accountability mechanisms for welfare rights grievances (e.g. tribunals, ombudsmen, alternative dispute resolution, complaint panels).

5. There is a good-faith political commitment to protecting social rights, manifested by a reasonably good welfare state (or in less wealthy countries, the foundations of a welfare state).

6. Disproportionate political and economic power is held by wealthy groups, whether by inherited privilege or otherwise. They own most of the major enterprises in the economy.

7. There is a reasonably independent, professional, well-functioning, mostly non-corrupt civil service and other executive agency staff.

8. The system of government respects the principle of inter-institutional collaboration. That means that there is a general rebuttable presumption that the various branches of government carry out their responsibilities in good faith, and seek to work harmoniously and respectfully with one another. Courts, respecting this idea, give weight and show deference to the good faith decisions of other institutions, and those institutions in return absorb and work in good faith with the decisions of the courts.[16]

These are not 'ideal conditions' as some might at first believe. They are broadly meant to be descriptive of the social and political conditions presently obtaining in the United Kingdom. I also believe they presently exist

---

[16] This condition is particularly important to the theory set out in this book. See Chapter 2, section IV; Chapter 3, section II; Chapter 4, section III.B; esp., Chapter 5, section III.B; Chapter 9, section III.A.3; Chapter 10, section III.A.7. This is not the principle of institutional settlement from the legal process school of jurisprudence. That doctrine suggests that one institution ought to accept with finality the findings of another. The vision here is of collaboration and combines the ideas of one body giving weight and deference to the views of another, but also of oversight and the power to challenge, set aside, and revisit the findings of other institutions within an overall framework of comity and collaboration.

in Canada, Australia, New Zealand, and possibly South Africa, as well as much of Continental Europe (apart from condition one). I do not, however, believe these conditions prevail in the United States, because conditions two, five, and arguably three and eight, and possibly even seven (due to the political appointment and change of bureau chiefs) do not apply in any reliable sense.[17] It is common also to hear lawyers from India question whether conditions three and five apply there. As for Latin America and Africa, the situations are too complex and varied to comment.

Notably, it is not necessary that a country be particularly wealthy for these conditions to apply. However, conditions two through five and especially seven have proved harder to stabilise in less wealthy states.

B   When the conditions do not apply

Although the prescriptions in this book are aimed centrally at states manifesting the background political conditions set out above, that fact does not mean that they are irrelevant to other states. The principles and theme of incrementalism may or may not apply. It may be the case, as with the United States, that several of the background political conditions do not apply. In that case, I would think that the suggestions do not apply in two different senses. On the one hand, the theory in this book would not support introducing constitutional social rights of the sort I discuss, at least not without further discussion of the peculiarities of local institutions. Something more or less might be needed. On the other hand, it might not be appropriate for the courts to adopt a default position of judicial incrementalism. It is no surprise, for instance, that there is quite radical structural reform litigation for social rights litigation at the state level in America and India, when due note is taken of the clarity of the constitutional provisions and the radical underfunding or other problems encountered in some of those cases.[18] It may, on the contrary, simply be that because of the way adjudication functions, it would be too risky to introduce such rights. Having said this, it remains the case that in most countries courts will face substantial epistemic limitations that make incrementalism an attractive strategy for decision-making. Even if the non-judicial institutions are 'not working' and the case for democratic

---

[17] Despite this, I address a range of American law and legal theory throughout this book. The experience there teaches important lessons, and the scholarship is too brilliant to ignore.
[18] See Chapter 9, section III.A.3; Chapter 10, section IV.B.

restraint is weak, those epistemic limitations and the potential for the negative consequences detailed in Part II of this book remain. As noted in Chapter 3, the experience in Latin America thus far would appear to confirm that.

A more interesting question is what ought to occur when such conditions ordinarily apply, but do not apply in respect of a particular issue. It may be that on a particular social issue there is a breakdown in the presumption of inter-institutional collaboration, for example a patent legislative failure, a breakdown in agency government, or an ethnic or cultural division that prevents some institution from carrying out its task. That was the case, for example, with race relations in post-Second World War America, and with Aids denialism in the South African government at the end of the twentieth century. Or judges may divide along party, regional, or ethnic lines. If the conditions fail to apply, there may well be a case for departing from the core suggestions set out in this book. In some cases it may counsel a more active judicial role. I argue in Chapter 9 that where inter-institutional collaboration breaks down, there can be a case for more intrusive remedies. In other cases, perhaps where judges are likely to disagree ideologically, it may counsel a more restrictive role. Any determination in this regard is wholly contextual and little more in the abstract can usefully be said on the matter.

VI   Conclusion

This book ranges over legal and political theory, legal doctrine and judicial decisions, and social science and in particular socio-legal studies. This is not out of any methodological ambition. It is rather that the case for constitutional social rights is a complex one. It depends in part on normative political arguments about which institutions of the state should have interpretive authority over defining our human rights. It also requires information about how judicial and other institutions will respond to the demands of constitutional social rights adjudication, and about whether they can and will conform to the expectations of the theory put forward. That information is frequently doctrinal, empirical, and predictive all at once. It requires looking at comparative law, socio-legal studies, and organisation theory. And since some involve a level of speculation about the nature of judicial decision-making, legal theory will also bear on how these questions are answered.

Notwithstanding the wide-ranging nature of the material examined, it all drives clearly towards two key arguments. The first is that there is a good case that constitutionalising social rights in countries having the background political conditions set out in this chapter will be a worthwhile and important endeavour. The second is that the ideal role for courts, and the one that makes the case for social rights succeed, is structured by four key principles of judicial restraint whose chief theme is judicial incrementalism. Notwithstanding the accent on incrementalism, it is hoped that, by the end of the book, the reader can see that it is in fact an ambitious strategy for providing greater justice in the welfare state.

PART I

The case for constitutional social rights

The case for social rights

I Introduction

This book on the whole aims to present an argument for why we should constitutionalise social rights, and how judges could go about interpreting them in a way that keeps with that rationale. The present chapter is concerned with the first of these tasks. Making the case for social rights requires showing why items like health care, social security, housing, and education can rank alongside fair trials and freedom from torture in our list of fundamental rights. Showing that means making a moral and political argument. Yet once that argument is made out, it is then necessary to explore the different institutional mechanisms that the state can use to secure such entitlements. Anyone familiar with the history of the welfare state knows that courts of law are not the first port of call for social justice. In awareness of that fact, this chapter presents the case for constitutional social rights in a way that situates their role within a broader multi-institutional setting. This not only helps us to understand the role of the constitution in context, but it also clarifies why talk of judicial restraint in Part II of this book can be understood not as timidity or inertia, but as bona fide concern to strike the right institutional balance for taking social rights seriously.

Presenting this case requires refining the very idea of social rights, for, as I show in section II, there are at least five different moral and legal senses in which the expression is used. In section III I explore the use of human rights language and in particular the normative arguments in favour of calling social rights human rights. Not content to rest after pairing social rights with abstract ideas such as autonomy or well-being alone, I argue that we have a right to a social minimum, which is the bundle of resources that would secure a minimally decent life. I propose three thresholds that such a bundle must satisfy, and defend the idea that the social participation and agency thresholds are both meaningful and necessary aspects of the social minimum. I then explore a set of basic state duties that would arise in respect of the social minimum, and which impose both progressive obligations of conduct and immediate obligations of result.

Having identified the substance of social human rights obligations in this manner, I proceed in section IV to explore the basic institutional modes of protection, namely, legislative, administrative, adjudicative, and constitutional. After an examination of the extensive protection and accountability mechanisms already present at the legislative, executive, and (non-constitutional) adjudicative level, the chapter squarely confronts the challenge of showing what adding enforceable social rights to the constitution will do to help secure the social minimum. I argue that justiciable constitutional social rights offer real advantages over non-justiciable ones. They may channel and sometimes generate state and civil society action. They can provide a state shield for social programmes against litigants seeking to disable them. And they can provide a claimant with enforceable public law remedies that ensure their social rights are taken seriously in both legislation and administration. The constitution, on this view, plays a subsidiary, but important supporting role in the multi-institutional scheme of protecting social rights.

II   Different senses of 'social rights'

For the purposes of this book, I am chiefly concerned with a (large) subset of social rights: the rights to health care, housing, education, and social security.[1] Even so focused, the expression 'social rights' can be used in at least five different senses, and I will use the following labels for greater clarity:

Moral senses
1. *Social human rights*: These are the human rights the philosophers speak about, rights we enjoy as a matter of political morality and whose existence is not dependent on any legal recognition. Because they are *human* rights, they are considered global baseline standards, and they therefore have a minimalist character.[2]

---

[1] Notably, I am not focused on labour rights. The main concern for the thesis in this book is the manner in which public law courts judicially review state action that implicates the allocation of public resources. The field of labour relations often involves none of the above, and for that reason has developed into a complex and distinct field of social rights regulation.
[2] See below, section III.A.

2. *Social citizenship rights*: These are the social rights generated by some account of distributive justice but which may be limited to particular communities, and which thus typically go beyond the minimalism of social human rights. They specify the requirements of a more egalitarian vision of social citizenship. These rights can be quite specific and seem generous when specified in legal form, and may include entitlements such as four-week annual holidays with pay, extensive protections for collective bargaining, paid maternity and paternity leave, and legal protections against unjustified dismissal.[3]

Legal senses

3. *International social rights*: These are the social rights recognised in international law, which are chiefly designed to mirror our social human rights but which may extend beyond or fall short of them in elements of detail. They may also include social citizenship rights, as do the Revised European Social Charter and elements of the EU Charter of Fundamental Rights, and the bulk of the International Labour Organisation's many labour and social security conventions.

4. *Legislative social rights*: These are the rights embedded in legislation and enforceable in ordinary public law before the courts and tribunals. The expression is used this way by sociologists such as T. H. Marshall and Gøsta Esping-Anderson.[4]

5. *Constitutional social rights*: These rights are enacted in constitutions and may be justiciable or non-justiciable, and may include social human rights, social citizenship rights, and references to relevant international social rights. Henceforth, when I write about constitutional social rights, I mean to refer to justiciable ones.

This catalogue helps prevent people from talking past each other, such as when one replies with a legalistic argument to a moral objection (or vice versa). It also clarifies how some human rights conventions or constitutions can seem to go beyond the minimalist character of social human rights. Our legal social rights may reflect both social human rights and social citizenship rights, or only some: it is not a category mistake to

---

[3] Art. 2(3) European Social Charter 1996, ETS 163 (paid holidays); Art. *(1) (14 weeks paid maternity leave); Arts. 30 and 34(2), Charter of Fundamental Rights of the European Union, OJ [2007] C303/1 (protection against unjustified dismissal and right to social security for those residing legally in the European Union).

[4] T. H. Marshall, 'Citizenship and Social Class', in T. H. Marshall and T. Bottomore, *Citizenship and Social Class* (London: Pluto Press, 1992), pp. 3, 27ff.; G. Esping-Anderson, *The Three Worlds of Welfare Capitalism* (Cambridge: Polity Press, 1990), pp. 21ff.

include both in one document. Finally, some may advocate any or all of the first four types of social rights, but object to constitutional social rights. Such critics should not be mistaken with those who reject the very idea of moral and legal social rights. I endorse the existence and value of all five senses of social rights, and the idea that they ought to work in concert, and this is the view also generally prevailing in the United Nations (UN) system of human rights protection.

Nonetheless, this book is for the most part concerned with presenting and defending a case for constitutional social rights and especially in setting out a theory of adjudication in respect of them. These other forms of social rights, however, are crucial for understanding the normative and legal background that informs the interpretation of constitutional social rights.

III   Social rights, human rights, and the welfare state

In my view, constitutional social rights are an institutional mode for protecting our social human rights and those social citizenship rights that a community may include among its constitutional commitments. Before considering the question of implementation, more must be said about the actual rights that courts are supposed to implement. I focus in this section on social human rights.

International law provides one legalistic answer to the question of what human rights we have, and includes a quite long list of social rights provisions at the United Nations and regional levels.[5] But it is important to press beyond an index of our international social rights. We want to know the normative reasons we seek to call social rights human rights in the first place.

A   Social rights as human rights: form and justification

We must first start with an account of the idea of human rights. I take James Nickel's definition of the contemporary idea of human rights to be the most accurate account of how the idea is understood in both theory and practice.[6] Nickel's explanation can be summarised (omitting some

---

[5] See Appendix 1 to this book.

[6] J. W. Nickel, *Making Sense of Human Rights* (2nd edn, Oxford: Blackwell Press, 2007), pp. 9–10. For other contemporary philosophical accounts see H. Shue, *Basic Rights: Subsistence, Affluence, and US Foreign Policy* (2nd edn, Princeton University Press, 1980), Chapter 1; R. Martin, *A System of Rights* (Oxford University Press, 1997); A. Sen, 'Elements

detail) as follows: rights are claims by right-holders against addressees, who are usually, though not only, states, that are held by all persons (i.e. are universal), are high priority or urgent norms, are numerous and specific claims (e.g. rights to fair trial, social security) instead of few and highly abstract claims (e.g. dignity and equality), are normative claims whose truth is not dependent on legal recognition, and are meant to be minimum standards instead of a complete statement of what is just (i.e. to say our human rights are satisfied is *not* to say that some situation is just, any more than that a minimum wage is a just wage). This minimalism is an important distinguishing feature of human rights in practice and theory.[7] The theory and practice of human rights implies that rights claims have a degree of priority over other political claims and procedures, such as the satisfaction of majority preferences, the desirability of economic growth, the use of ordinary modes of authority for dispute resolution (e.g. prison and school governors, managerial discretion etc.). Otherwise, we might have to recognise human rights to publicly funded opera and football stadiums.

There has been a traditional resistance among philosophers to consider social rights real human rights, as though the analytical nature of rights-talk would necessarily exclude the idea. So Maurice Cranston heaped scorn on the right to paid holidays; Onora O'Neill wrote about what she called the feasibility problem and drew on Kant's distinction between perfect obligations that have correlative rights and imperfect obligations (like charity) that do not; and Joel Feinberg wrote about social rights having an aspirational or 'manifesto' character.[8] These objections have now

of a Theory of Human Rights' (2004) 32 *Philosophy & Public Affairs* 315 (and now, *The Idea of Justice* (London: Penguin, 2009), Chapter 17); J. Griffin, *On Human Rights* (Oxford University Press, 2008); C. R. Beitz, *The Idea of Human Rights* (Oxford University Press, 2009); C. Wellman, *The Moral Dimensions of Human Rights* (Oxford University Press, 2010). See also L. W. Sumner's *The Moral Foundations of Rights* (Oxford University Press, 1986).

[7] Nickel, *Making Sense of Human Rights*, pp. 10, 36–7; Griffin, *On Human Rights*, p. 33, and on welfare rights in particular pp. 182–4. Beitz, *The Idea of Human Rights*, pp. 141–4 for a discussion. This should not be confused with the minimalism inherent in so-called political approaches to defining human rights, which view them as triggers for international intervention. For a rejection of this view (which is or was shared by John Rawls, Ronald Dworkin, Charles Beitz, and Joseph Raz), see the discussion in J. Tasioulas, 'Are Human Rights Essentially Triggers for Intervention?' (2009) 4 *Philosophy Compass* 938 and Griffin, *On Human Rights*, pp. 22–7.

[8] M. Cranston, *What Are Human Rights?* (London: Bodley Head, 1969); O. O'Neill 'The Dark Side of Human Rights' (2005) 81(2) *International Affairs* 427. J. Feinberg, *Social Philosophy* (Englewood-Cliffs: Prentice-Hall, 1973), pp. 67, 95.

been dispatched convincingly by what is emerging as a near consensus view among philosophers of human rights that social rights are very much a species of human rights, largely for similar reasons accepted by international lawyers and the UN system much earlier.[9] The question that is more interesting than the compatibility of rights-talk with social rights claims is what type of normative theory supports the claims of urgency and priority that we associate with human rights discourse. There are a few different candidates.

One is dignity, or natural rights or natural law. Dignity is offered as a key normative justification in the very first article of the Universal Declaration on Human Rights: 'All human beings are born free and equal in dignity and rights. They are endowed with reason and conscience and should act towards one another in a spirit of brotherhood.' This article – meant to provide the normative plateau on which representatives from various cultures could agree to the list of rights that follows that article – also reflects a clear debt to the natural rights tradition, and its religious antecedents.[10] One might also connect the idea of dignity to the idea of well-being, because, though different, both are attributes of the human condition that are affirmed by some philosophers as good in themselves and which may be conceptualised in a non-consequentialist manner.[11] The link between human dignity and adequate housing, health, social security, and education is too obvious to warrant any discussion – most of these items rank higher on any hierarchy of human needs than many cherished civil rights. One pertinent question, however, is why social

---

[9] See Shue, *Basic Rights, passim*; Sen, 'Elements of a Theory of Human Rights', pp. 345–8; Martin, *A System of Rights,* pp. 41–2; Nickel, *Making Sense of Human Rights*, Chapter 9; Griffin, *On Human Rights*, Chapter 10; Beitz, *The Idea of Human Rights*, pp. 161–74 (see also pp. 117–22, where he defends the idea of 'manifesto rights' as generating real obligations); Wellman, *The Moral Dimensions of Human Rights*, pp. 12–13. See also the distinguished volume of essays in T. Pogge (ed.), *Freedom from Poverty as a Human Right* (Oxford University Press/UNESCO, 2007), and especially, for a rebuttal of O'Neill and similar objections, Chapter 3 (J. Tasioulas' 'The Moral Reality of Human Rights').

[10] See T. Lindholm, 'Article 1: A New Beginning', in A. Eide *et al.* (eds.), *The Universal Declaration of Human Rights: A Commentary* (Oslo: Scandinavian University Press, 1992), p. 51 (thin normative consensus); J. Morsink, *The Universal Declaration on Human Rights: Origin, Drafting, Intent* (Philadelphia: University of Pennsylvania Press, 2000), Chapter 8, and now *Inherent Human Rights: The Philosophical Roots of the Universal Declaration* (Philadelphia: University of Pennsylvania Press, 2009), Chapter 1. In philosophy, see J. Donelly, 'Natural Rights as Human Rights' (1982) 4 *Human Rights Quarterly* 391; R. Dworkin, *Justice for Hedgehogs* (Cambridge, MA: Belknap Press, 2010), pp. 332–9.

[11] J. Griffin, *Well-being* (Oxford: Clarendon Press, 1986); J. Raz, *The Morality of Freedom* (Oxford University Press, 1986), Chapter 12.

rights were recognised historically after civil and political rights (i.e. are called 'second generation' rights instead of 'first generation' rights), if they are so crucial to human dignity in the way I consider obvious. This is a complex historical question, but one does not have to be a Marxist to notice that the chief audible mouthpiece for human rights claims prior to the twentieth century were the property-owning middle and upper professional classes in Britain, France, and the United States.[12] Social rights *qua* rights did make a brief appearance in the very short-lived French 'Montagnard' constitution of 1793,[13] the most egalitarian of the various early French attempts at constitutionalism and which introduced social rights and universal male suffrage side-by-side. Yet, it was alongside true universal suffrage in modern Western states that a state-level discourse of treating social rights as human rights began to emerge. This was evident in a series of speeches given by Franklin Delano Roosevelt and culminating in his 'four freedoms' speech to the US Congress in 1941, in an early statement of essential human rights adopted by scholars claiming to represent different cultures around the world (1944), and in the Universal Declaration of Human Rights itself (1948).[14] In other words, social rights began to be generally recognised as human rights around the same time democratic equality emerged in the West.

Another leading justification for social rights as human rights is found in the idea of freedom. This is sometimes called normative agency, or autonomy, or capabilities, or non-domination.[15] The idea here is that

---

[12] M. R. Ishay, *The History of Human Rights: From Ancient Times to the Globalization Era* (Berkeley: University of California Press, 2008), pp. 135ff.

[13] See L. Duguit, *Manuel de Droit Constitutionnel: Théorie générale de l'État* (3rd edn, Paris: Boccard, 1918), pp. 221–3 for a comparison in this regard.

[14] For Roosevelt's speech and its precursors, see C. R. Sunstein, *The Second Bill of Rights* (New York: Basic Books, 2004), Chapters 1 and 3; J. P. Frank, 'Statement of Essential Rights', in *American Law Institute, Seventy-Fifth Anniversary 1923–1998* (American Law Institute, 1998), p. 272.

[15] On autonomy, see Raz, *The Morality of Freedom*, Chapters 14 and 15 (on the positive state duties implied by personal autonomy); see also his *Ethics in the Public Domain: Essays in the Morality of Law and Politics* (Oxford University Press, 1994), Chapter 1; C. Fabre, *Social Rights Under the Constitution: Government and the Decent Life* (Oxford University Press, 2001); see also D. Bilchitz, *Poverty and Fundamental Rights: The Justification and Enforcement of SocioEconomic Rights* (Oxford University Press, 2007), esp. pp. 26–7. On capabilities, see Sen, 'Elements of a Theory of Human Rights', generally and esp. at pp. 345–8 (applying theories developed earlier in A. Sen, *Inequality Reexamined* (Oxford: Clarendon Press, 1992), Chapters 2–4; and A. Sen and M. Nussbaum (eds.), *The Quality of Life* (Oxford: Clarendon Press, 1993), and M. Nussbaum, *Women and Human Development* (Cambridge University Press, 2000)). On normative agency, see Griffin, *On Human Rights*, Chapters 2 and 10. On the idea of an economic guarantee against

freedom lies in being able to make meaningful choices about the lives we want to lead, of not being subject to another person's arbitrary control, about having the capacity to understand political complexities and run for office, and about having the health and income security that allows one to frame and act out a life plan. The most important thinker in this type of tradition is John Rawls.[16] In his later work Rawls believed that a social minimum, though less egalitarian than his difference principle, ought to be guaranteed and legally enforceable as a constitutional essential.[17]

A third justification might lie in utilitarianism or some similar form of consequentialism: theories that say actions are right to the extent they promote greater happiness, or satisfy more preferences, or improve welfare. On this view, we could argue that a system recognising legally protected social rights would promote greater aggregate utility than one that did not.[18] True, the utilitarian argument in general faces considerable difficulties in recognising moral rights.[19] With respect to social rights, the key problem is that utilitarianism appears to allow (theoretically) for extreme inequality, provided aggregate utility would be higher than any alternative. Some important economists advocate laissez-faire on essentially utilitarian grounds. But money alone is an extremely crude proxy for welfare or utility, and the view that a strong welfare state compromises efficiency is a weak one.[20] The better view is that, due to diminishing marginal utility, and the idea that each person counts for one, it is hard to imagine a real economic system that could deny any person a basic

---

domination by others, see P. Pettit, *Republicanism: A Theory of Freedom and Government* (Oxford University Press, 1997), Chapter 1 and pp. 158–63; see also J. Waldron, 'Homelessness and the Issue of Freedom', in J. Waldron (ed.), *Liberal Rights: Collected Papers 1981–1991* (Cambridge University Press, 1993), Chapter 13.

[16] J. Rawls, *A Theory of Justice* (Cambridge, MA: Harvard University Press, 1971; and rev. edn 1999); *Political Liberalism* (New York: Columbia University Press, 1996); *Justice as Fairness: A Restatement* (Cambridge, MA: Harvard University Press, 2001). Rawls' theory is best described as liberal egalitarian. Despite Rawls' importance to philosophy, it may be that Amartya Sen's impact on global public policy has been greater.

[17] Rawls, *Political Liberalism*, pp. 227–8; Rawls, *Justice as Fairness*, pp. 47–8, 161–2 (endorsing the idea and that they can be justiciable rights, adopting the view of Frank Michelman in 'The Supreme Court, 1968 Term – Foreword: On Protecting the Poor through the Fourteenth Amendment' (1969) 83 *Harvard Law Review* 7).

[18] See Sumner, *The Moral Foundations of Rights*, Chapter 6 and p. 212.

[19] D. Lyons, 'Between Utility and Rights', in J. Waldron (ed.), *Theories of Rights* (Oxford University Press, 1985).

[20] On both points, see R. E. Goodin, *Reasons for Welfare* (Princeton University Press, 1988), Chapter 8. On wealth as a false proxy for utility, see R. Dworkin, *A Matter of Principle* (Cambridge, MA: Harvard University Press, 1985), Chapters 12 and 13.

social minimum as a trade-off for improving someone else's welfare.[21] One would need to dream up the unlikely scenario in which the labour or resources of one meets the equally stringent needs of more numerous others to the exclusion of any other possible arrangement. In actual fact, there is a wealth of evidence supporting a causal relationship between legislative social rights and aggregate happiness, preferences, and well-being.[22] Nonetheless, a utilitarian or consequentialist justification for any moral human rights is perilous. A less difficult strategy is to use it to justify legal social rights (international, legislative, or constitutional),[23] a more flexible paradigm that permits limitations of rights and which is thus less bedevilled by highly unlikely counter-examples.

A fourth strategy for defending social human rights is found in the related ideas of social citizenship, civic republicanism, and deliberative democracy. These justifications consider social rights as instrumental in support of meaningful participation in political decision-making. It is crucial because on these approaches it is the process of decision-making itself that legitimates political outcomes. The civic republican branch of this theory has a literally ancient pedigree.[24] It proposes a conception of liberty as a form of self-mastery through self-government in politics, and it is contrasted with the Enlightenment idea of freedom as non-interference.

---

[21] R. E. Goodin, *Utilitarianism as a Public Philosophy* (Cambridge University Press, 1995), p. 23; R. M. Hare, *Freedom and Reason* (Oxford University Press, 1963); Dworkin, *A Matter of Principle*, pp. 247, 260, 274.

[22] See A. Pacek and B. Radcliff, 'Assessing the Welfare State' (2008) 6 *Perspectives on Politics* 267; R. E. Goodin, B. Headey, R. Muffels, and H.-J. Dirven, *The Real Worlds of Welfare Capitalism* (Cambridge University Press, 1999); R. Wilkinson and K. Pickett, *The Spirit Level: Why Equality is Better for Everyone* (London: Penguin, 2010). More hedged, though still supportive conclusions are reported in Á. Álvarez-Díaz, L. González, and B. Radcliff, 'The Politics of Happiness: On the Political Determinants of Quality of Life in the American States' (2010) 72 *The Journal of Politics* 894. Contrary conclusions are reported in R. Veenhoven, 'Well-Being in the Welfare State: Level Not Higher, Distribution Not More Equitable' (2003) 2 *Journal of Comparative Policy Analysis* 91.

[23] R. Hardin, *Morality within the Limits of Reason* (University of Chicago Press, 1988), Chapter 3.

[24] For an introduction, see K. Haakonssen, 'Republicanism', in R. Goodin. P. Pettit, and T. W. J. Pogge, *A Companion to Contemporary Political Philosophy* (2nd edn, Oxford: Blackwell, 2007), Chapter 43, and W. Kymlicka, *Contemporary Political Philosophy: An Introduction* (Oxford University Press, 2002), Chapter 7. For a contrast of civic republicanism with (republican) freedom as non-domination, see Pettit, *Republicanism*, Chapter 1. In legal theory, see F. Michelman, 'Law's Republic' (1988) 97 *Yale Law Journal* 1493; C. R. Sunstein, 'Beyond the Republican Revival' (1988) 97 *Yale Law Journal* 1539; M. Tushnet, *Red, White, and Blue: A Critical Analysis of Constitutional Law* (Cambridge, MA: Harvard University Press, 1988); and J. Habermas, *Between Facts and Norms*, trans. W. Rehg (Cambridge: Polity Press, 1996), pp. 267–79.

This participation in self-government is viewed either as an end in itself, or as instrumental towards securing greater freedom and equality. Civic republicans generally hold the view that meaningful participation in the political process, whether by running for office, influencing outcomes through debate, or simply comprehending the range of options, requires a guaranteed social minimum.[25]

Social citizenship theory traces a line upwards through the British 'new liberal' philosophers, directly through T. H. Marshall, and into more contemporary terrain.[26] One notable value of citizenship theory is that it accounts for a particular sociological phenomenon that is relevant to the public perception about 'rights' in the welfare state – namely, the fact that in wealthier liberal democracies we all contribute substantially over the course of our lives to the funding of the system, which generates a 'new property' type claim that the state 'owes' us a reciprocal obligation to provide promised or implied benefits.[27] Reciprocity is a key theme in Stuart White's discussion of social rights and economic citizenship.

The deliberative democrats affirm the importance of political processes for different reasons. They react to the problems faced by other political theories such as utilitarianism, comprehensive liberalism, religious worldviews, communitarianism, or Marxism. Such theories, on this view, cannot account for the problems of aggregating preferences that would change if confronted with new information, or social and public choice problems with the voting procedure, or of relying on controversial metaphysical propositions at a time when the entire philosophical support structure for such arguments is in substantial doubt.[28] But perhaps the

---

[25] See W. Forbath, 'Not so Simple Justice: Frank Michelman on Social Rights, 1969–Present' (2004) 39 *Tulsa Law Review* 597, esp. 630: 'Republican maxims hold that a measure of material independence is a necessary basis for political competence. That is Michelman's normative baseline.' See also F. I. Michelman, 'Welfare Rights in a Constitutional Democracy' (1979) *Washington University Law Quarterly* 659; Sunstein, 'Beyond the Republican Revival', 1571 (minimum welfare entitlements), 1580 (poverty). For the extensive philosophical literature, see citations in Fabre, *Social Rights Under the Constitution*, pp. 121–4.

[26] S. White, *The Civic Minimum: On the Rights and Obligations of Economic Citizenship* (Oxford University Press, 2003) is a particularly distinguished work in this vein. On the Victorian roots of the new liberalism, see A. Simhony and D. Weinstein (eds.), *The New Liberalism: Reconciling Liberty and Community* (Cambridge University Press, 2001).

[27] See C. Reich, 'The New Property' (1964) 73 *Yale Law Journal* 732.

[28] C. R. Sunstein, 'Preferences and Politics' (1991) 10 *Philosophy & Public Affairs* 3; J. Elster, *Sour Grapes: Studies in the Subversion of Rationality* (Cambridge University Press, 1985); J. Dryzek, *Deliberative Democracy and Beyond: Liberals, Critics and Contestations* (Oxford University Press, 2000), Chapters 1 and 2 (on the relevance of social choice); Habermas,

most significant problem motivating deliberative democrats is with what John Rawls and Joshua Cohen call the 'fact of reasonable pluralism', what Amy Gutman and Robert Thompson call 'persistent moral disagreement': the idea that there is good faith, enduring disagreement between members of the community on questions of justice, and a corresponding need for a political decision-making procedure that accounts fairly for it.[29] The core idea of the theory is that to get past this impediment, political decisions should be taken through a deliberative process in which those affected by political outcomes participate freely and equally in the decision-making process, being listened to respectfully, and all in the effort of striving for a solution that aims for the common good (rather than an aggregation of narrow self-interests) and thus seeks consensus.[30] Similar to the civic republicans, deliberative democrats tend to recognise social rights, or a social minimum, as preconditions for proper deliberation.[31]

All of these different justifications for social human rights are insightful, and an overlapping consensus between them about the need for social rights (or a social minimum) of some sort is politically significant. Each also has its weaknesses: dignity is vague and malleable; autonomy presupposes the capacity for agency; utilitarianism abhors constraints; and citizenship theory seems both dreamy and incomplete. But there is no need to

Between Facts and Norms, Chapter 1 and see also xii–xxiv of Rehg's introduction (on the need to get 'post-metaphysical').

[29] J. Rawls, *Political Liberalism*, Chapter 1, esp. pp. 35–40 ('the fact of reasonable pluralism'); J. Cohen, 'Procedure and Substance in Deliberative Democracy', reprinted in J. Bohman and W. Rehg, *Deliberative Democracy: Essays on Reason and Politics* (Cambridge, MA: MIT Press, 1997), pp. 407, 414; A. Gutman and D. Thompson, *Democracy and Disagreement* (Cambridge, MA: Harvard University Press, 1996), Chapter 1; see also Habermas, *Between Facts and Norms*, Chapter 1 (see also xii–xxiv of Rehg's introduction for deeper epistemological reasons for focusing on communication as a source of validity).

[30] J. Bohman and W. Rehg, *Deliberative Democracy: Essays on Reason and Politics* (Cambridge, MA: MIT Press, 1987) and Dryzek, *Deliberative Democracy and Beyond*, provide good introductions to the vast literature.

[31] Cohen, 'Procedure and Substance in Deliberative Democracy', p. 422; see also J. Cohen, 'The Economic Basis of Deliberative Democracy' (1989) 6 *Social Philosophy and Policy* 25, esp. 33; Gutman and Thompson, *Democracy and Disagreement*, Chapters 8 and 9; Habermas, *Between Facts and Norms*, pp. 417–18; J. Bohman, 'Deliberative Democracy and Effective Social Freedom: Capabilities, Resources, and Opportunities', in J. Bohman and W. Rehg, *Deliberative Democracy: Essays on Reason and Politics* (Cambridge, MA: MIT Press, 1987), p. 337, and J. Knight and J. Johnson, 'What Sort of Equality does Deliberative Democracy Require?', in J. Bohman and W. Rehg, *Deliberative Democracy: Essays on Reason and Politics* (Cambridge, MA: MIT Press, 1987), p. 279. For the application of this idea in the law of social rights, see S. Fredman, *Human Rights Transformed: Positive Rights and Positive Duties* (Oxford University Press, 2008).

take sides here, because one can be, for the present enterprise, ecumenical about the philosophical foundations of a moral theory of human rights.[32] The point is that no commonly accepted existing theory of human rights can reasonably exclude social rights, and the better theories against recognising them – that is communitarianism and Benthamite utilitarianism – would both probably go a lot further in the direction of supporting the kind of robust welfare state that social rights demand.[33]

So we can move on from the normative foundations of social human rights safe in the knowledge that plenty of philosophical wind fills our sails. We can now, therefore, concentrate on defining the abstract content of social rights, before pressing on to the question of their implementation.

B   The basic content of social human rights

According to Joseph Raz's interest-theory of rights, a person has a right if, other things being equal, an aspect of that person's well-being (her interest), is a sufficient reason for holding some person(s) under a duty.[34] Raz's account highlights the profound importance of the person's interest as a ground for another's duties, but his general account of rights must be refined to deal with human rights in particular.[35] I would, in this vein, propose that any subset of human rights ought to identify the following: (a) the nature of the human interest; (b) the urgency or fundamental character of that interest; (c) some indication of the state of affairs that would satisfy those interests; (d) the nature of the duties owed in respect of such

---

[32] My own view is in agreement with Cécile Fabre's arguments, in *Social Rights Under the Constitution*, Chapter 1, which derives an account of social rights from the values of autonomy and well-being. My aim in the present chapter is to indicate an emerging overlapping consensus rather than defend one theory against the others.

[33] I leave aside Edmund Burke's conservative critique of rights, and so-called political conceptions, which in my view erroneously view human rights as triggers for foreign military or diplomatic intervention: see Tasioulas, 'Are Human Rights Essentially Triggers for Intervention?'; Griffin, *On Human Rights*, pp. 22–7. On responses to right-libertarian objections to social rights, see R. Nozick, *Anarchy, State and Utopia* (Oxford: Basic Books, 1974); G. A. Cohen, *Self-Ownership, Freedom and Equality* (Cambridge University Press, 1995), and the left-libertarian theories that use self-ownership arguments to support redistribution: P. van Parijs, *Real Freedom for All* (Oxford University Press, 1995); M. Otsuka, *Libertarianism without Inequality* (Oxford University Press, 2003).

[34] Raz, *The Morality of Freedom*, p. 166.

[35] Notably, in 'Human Rights Without Foundations', in S. Besson and J. Tasioulas (eds.), *The Philosophy of International Law* (Oxford University Press, 2010), Raz himself advocates a political conception of human rights, which, as noted above, I reject for widely shared reasons.

interests; and (e) the identity of the duty-bearers. I identify the first four of these in the next two subsections, and the fifth in the section that follows them.

1 The social minimum

The justifications for human rights examined above all converge upon the three following core human interests: *well-being* (absence of physical suffering, basis of self-respect), *autonomy* ('a vision of people controlling, to some degree, their own destiny, fashioning it through successive decisions throughout their lives'[36]), and *social participation* (the meaningful potential for participation in social and communal life). If these interests are to ground social human rights claims and duties, then they must give rise to claims for resources required for a *minimally* decent life. Otherwise they could be far-reaching and lack urgency, which is incompatible with human rights discourse. Cécile Fabre speaks of this as respecting the 'prospects for a minimally decent life'[37] and Stuart White refers to 'a bundle of resources that a person needs in order to lead a minimally decent life in their society'.[38] This urgency or minimal character is reflected in the specification given below.

The substance of a social minimum would refer to a bundle of resources,[39] which could consist of cash benefits (including tax credits), services, or benefits-in-kind (e.g. housing, medical equipment, school facilities). The most important question relates to the quantum of such resources. Clearly, the quantum will vary with environmental and social circumstances, both between communities and in some cases within regions of a large community. I would nonetheless argue that minimal respect for the values of autonomy, well-being, and social participation would demand provision of a bundle of resources satisfying the following, in the order of their importance:

1. a *healthy subsistence threshold* meeting basic physical needs for shelter, nutrition, childhood development, health, and psychological integrity;

---

[36] Raz, *The Morality of Freedom*, p. 369; see also Rawls, *Political Liberalism*, pp. 19, 30, 310ff.

[37] Fabre, *Social Rights under the Constitution*, pp. 22–3.

[38] Stuart White, 'Social Minimum' (Stanford Encyclopedia of Philosophy, 2004), available at: http://plato.stanford.edu/entries/social-minimum (accessed 1 July 2011).

[39] I use the expression 'resources' in a broad sense, I believe compatibly with the view of Amartya Sen and Martha Nussbaum that resources are merely instrumental for achieving human capabilities.

2. a *social participation threshold*, which would guarantee an education sufficient for basic economic and social participation, insurance
against economic shocks, and the resources required for minimal
social engagement with family and peers; and

3. an *agency threshold*, which would require the education and economic stability required, in a given society, to engage in basic life-
planning, including the capacity to frame and achieve long-term
goals.[40]

The definition of poverty and minimum essential needs is a very much-
studied issue, in both the subsistence and participation elements, and
there are various baskets of resources and basic needs that have been identified.[41] The Copenhagen Declaration adopted at the World Summit for
Social Development and signed by 117 countries, defined absolute poverty
as 'a condition characterised by severe deprivation of basic human needs,
including food, safe drinking water, sanitation facilities, health, shelter,
education and information. It depends not only on income but also on
access to social services.'[42] The United Nations Committee on Economic,
Social and Cultural Rights has also identified what it calls the 'normative content' of the various social rights in a series of General Comments,
drawing on the expertise of UN agencies and non-governmental organisations.[43] These Comments are relevant as global baseline standards,
though they are on the one hand too broad to specify the content with
sufficient precision for specific communities, and on the other they have

---

[40] Fabre, *Social Rights Under the Constitution*, pp. 9–12 (defining autonomy in reference to
the work of John Rawls as 'able to frame, revise and pursue a conception of the good, and
to deliberate in accordance with it').

[41] For introductory surveys see R. Lister, *Poverty* (Cambridge: Polity Press, 2004) and
P. Alcock, *Understanding Poverty* (3rd edn, London: Palgrave-Macmillan, 2006), and
for the United States, see C. Citro and R. Michael, *Measuring Poverty: A New Approach*
(Washington DC: National Academies Press, 1995). The landmark study confirming the
importance of social participation is: P. Townsend, *Poverty in the United Kingdom: A
Survey of Household Resources and Standards of Living* (London: Penguin Books, 1979).
See also A. Sen, 'Poor, Relatively Speaking' (1983) 35 *Oxford Economic Papers* 135. See
further, C. Pantazis, D. Gordon, and R. Levitas (eds.), *Poverty and Social Exclusion in
Britain: The Millennium Survey* (Bristol: Policy Press, 2006), Part I and esp., Chapters 2
('The Concept and Measurement of Poverty') and 4 ('The Necessities of Life').

[42] The Copenhagen Declaration and Programme of Action: World Summit for Social
Development, UN Doc., A/CONF.166/9 (1995).

[43] All the General Comments referred to in this chapter may be found in United Nations
Secretariat, *Compilation of General Comments and General Recommendations Adopted
by Human Rights Treaty Bodies*, UN Doc. HRI/GEN/1/Rev.7 (12 May 2004).

been criticised for having gone beyond what the idea of social human rights can reasonably support.[44]

The idea of a healthy subsistence threshold should not give rise to much controversy, if we bracket the notably vexed issue of funding life-saving drugs and rationing medical services for persons nearing the end of their lives.[45] It is the social participation and agency thresholds that might be challenged as insufficiently minimalist to be considered suitable for social human rights. In fact our international social rights and typically legislative social rights go well beyond these thresholds. Those who study poverty acknowledge a near consensus that a modicum of social participation is an essential for a minimally decent life.[46] But we can focus for the moment on the philosophical objection. A weak version of this objection would be that the social minimum need provide for no social participation at all – only subsistence. It is a weak objection because even the barest notions of autonomy and well-being require more than mere survival. Joseph Raz clarified this best with the example of a man trapped in a pit but who had lowered down to him all the necessities of life – such a life is in no conceivable way an autonomous one.[47] The example was not far-fetched: life in the Victorian poor house was on some views not much better, and almost certainly more humiliating. The notion of well-being also clearly supports the idea. The human needs for friendship, family, a degree of social acceptance, a feeling of contribution and worth within the community, are nearly as basic as the physiological ones.[48]

We thus encounter the stronger philosophical objection, which is that the particular thresholds I have identified are not minimal or fundamental. The question is, therefore, how much social participation and agency is enough? It will be difficult to say exactly where the line will be drawn, and as noted it will vary between and within communities. One option is to ask people – to use subjective surveys and deem those items necessary that have been identified as such by the overwhelming majority of

---

[44] Griffin, *On Human Rights*, pp. 182–4; Nickel, *Making Sense of Human Rights*, p. 139; M. Langford and J. King, 'The Committee on Economic, Social and Cultural Rights', in M. Langford (ed.), *Social Rights Jurisprudence: Emerging Trends in Comparative and International Law* (Cambridge University Press, 2009), pp. 492–3.

[45] On which see N. Daniels, *Just Health Care* (Cambridge University Press, 1985) and G. Calabresi and P. Bobbit, *Tragic Choices* (New York: W. W. Norton & Co, 1978).

[46] Townsend, *Poverty in the United Kingdom*, Chapter 1 (the most brilliant explanation of the notion of relativity); Lister, *Poverty*, Chapter 1 (explaining the merging of absolute and relative definitions in the literature).

[47] Raz, *The Morality of Freedom*, pp. 373ff.

[48] Townsend, *Poverty in the United Kingdom*, pp. 50–3.

respondents.[49] On that measure, the threshold offered here is by no means ambitious, at least for the United Kingdom and countries like it, and the thresholds are framed abstractly enough to suit countries having different levels of resources.

If we seek a more abstract statement, however, it may be found in the idea of self-respect.[50] Self-respect is plausibly viewed as a component of well-being, and a pre-condition of autonomy. Self-respect is typically contingent on one's experience within one's community. That provides the link to social participation. It might be that the conditions for full self-respect could vary considerably between people and across time, and the resources required for full self-respect might be very demanding. But it must also be the case that at least a material foundation for self-respect, one that makes self-respect a *real possibility*, is an aspect of *minimal* well-being and autonomy. A real possibility means being able to attain self-respect by effort alone, even though extraordinary effort may be required. The precise quantum of resources required for that will depend entirely on context, but some generalisations are possible.

I have listed an education necessary for basic economic and social participation because one cannot engage with any sense of self-respect with peers and make one's way in society without this capacity. This ordinarily requires functional literacy and numeracy to participate in the workforce, but depending on the society's degree of economic advancement, it may require more or less. Security against economic shocks is included because of the fundamental impact that unemployment and other economic dislocation can have on social participation (e.g. eviction, arrangements for schooling, banking, social services, loss of social capital). There must be at least some basic cushion against such shocks (e.g. jobseeker's allowance, a widow's benefit, child benefit) if one is to have a minimally decent life.

It is common for philosophers (especially citizenship theorists) to emphasise political participation and underrate the all-important notion of engagement with peers, but social surveys reveal that in fact most people have it the other way around. A 1999 survey of poverty and social exclusion in Britain was revealing in this regard. Over 80 per cent of people surveyed identified as necessary (instead of desirable) items like attending

---

[49] Pantazis *et al.* (eds.), *Poverty and Social Exclusion in Britain*, Chapter 4.
[50] Rawls, *A Theory of Justice*, rev. edn, pp. 386–91. See also the essays in R. S. Dillon (ed.), *Dignity, Character, and Self-Respect* (New York: Routledge, 1995). I am especially grateful to Adam Swift for clarifications on this point. It may be that the concept of dignity plays the same role as self-respect for the purposes of this argument.

weddings and funerals, visits to school on sports days, visits to family and friends in hospitals, with collecting the children from school following closely behind.[51] By comparison, items ranked much lower included washing machines, telephones, and pocket money, and only 30 per cent identified having a daily newspaper, and 6 per cent access to the Internet, as necessaries.[52] For most people, social participation of the purely social (as opposed to political) variety is a core aspect of human dignity, well-being, and ability to function autonomously. Thus the social participation threshold must at least include a minimum supplement that enables one to engage, with some dignity, socially with family and peers.

An agency threshold exists because there is an undeniable core of liberty in the very idea of social human rights, and it would be possible to meet both the healthy subsistence and social participation thresholds under conditions that would deny it. A well-run prison could meet it, for example. Poverty provides its own prisons. Many working poor have jobs and live in a community (including slums) that offers the basics of social participation. But they only manage to earn a subsistence salary and live in perpetual fear of unemployment, inflation, and insecurity of housing tenure. Under such conditions, only a lucky few can engage in basic life planning, such as forming and realising long-term goals, 'controlling, to some extent, their destiny'.[53] Here too, therefore, some income supplement and a basic level of education (including technical or vocational training) must provide for a real possibility for navigating society's opportunities and pitfalls.

A bundle of resources satisfying these three thresholds would in my view meet the social minimum. The quantum of resources required to meet these abstract thresholds will depend entirely on the nature of the community and prevailing economic trends. There are two perhaps surprising omissions from this social minimum. The first is the role for higher education. Can it be said that a university education is required for a minimally decent life around the world? International human rights law is equivocal on this point. The International Covenant on Economic, Social and Cultural Rights (ICESCR) sets out the right to post-secondary education: Art. 13(2)(c) 'Higher education shall be made equally accessible to

---

[51] Pantazis *et al.* (eds.), *Poverty and Social Exclusion in Britain*, p. 95.

[52] *Ibid.* I do not mean socialising per se. The PSE Survey, *ibid.*, shows that new clothes were viewed as necessary by 48 per cent; an evening out once a fortnight by 37 per cent; and a trip to the pub in that time by 20 per cent. No doubt internet access would rank much higher were the survey carried out today.

[53] Raz, *The Morality of Freedom*, p. 369.

all, on the basis of capacity, by every appropriate means, and in particular by the progressive introduction of free education.'[54] This is in direct contrast to the right to a secondary education, which is to be made '*generally available* and accessible to all'.[55] European human rights law is more equivocal still on the point.[56]

It cannot at present be said that a higher university education is required to satisfy any of the thresholds of the social minimum given above. This is a stark conclusion, but the contrary view would be a disingenuous interpretation of the social minimum. It is only with great difficulty that something can be considered essential to the social minimum when we restrict access to it on the basis of academic capacity, and which great numbers of people even in wealthy countries choose to forego and go on to lead happy lives. Nonetheless, it does make sense to speak about a fundamental social right to higher education as a social citizenship right in particular polities, something that will go beyond the social minimum. Particularly in wealthier countries and liberal democracies, it is plausibly viewed as a right of equal citizenship. First, it makes possible effective social mobility, which may well be regarded as being a pre-condition for political equality. And second, it is now a nearly de facto prerequisite in the more wealthy countries for holding public office, and it is central tenet of a liberal democracy that such offices should be open to all in a meaningful way.[57] So a wealthy liberal state committed to social rights could, and in my view should, constitutionalise a right of fair access to higher education on the basis of academic capacity as well.

The other surprising omission is the idea of a political participation threshold. Instinctively, one feels that in any just society the bundle of resources ought to be aimed in large part at facilitating effective political participation. I agree that political participation is supremely important,

---

[54] GA res. 2200A (XXI), 21 UN GAOR Supp. (No. 16) at 49, UN Doc. A/6316 (1966); 993 UNTS 3; 6 ILM 368 (1967).

[55] Art. 13(2)(b). See also the UN Committee on Economic, Social and Cultural Rights (CESCR), *General Comment No. 13: The Right to Education (Art. 13 of the Covenant)*, 8 December 1999, E/C.12/1999/10, 17–20, available at: www.unhcr.org/refworld/docid/4538838c22.html (accessed 8 July 2011).

[56] It is notably absent from the EU Charter of Fundamental Rights, Art. 14. It has been gradually read in to the European Social Charter, 529 UNTS 89; ETS 35, Art. 10(1), which was initially focused on the role of higher education for vocational training. See European Committee on Social Rights, *European Social Charter (Revised): Conclusions: France* (2003) p. 35.

[57] See Rawls, *Political Liberalism*, p. 327 (see generally pp. 318, 324–31) on the 'fair value of the political liberties'; see also Rawls, *Justice as Fairness*, pp. 148–50; Rawls, *A Theory of Justice*, p. 179 (on poverty and the 'worth of liberty').

but feel that claims to political equality are best addressed through the concept of social citizenship rights (and through civil and political human rights), rather than through the idea of a social minimum. Otherwise, the idea of a social minimum risks becoming a Trojan horse for a complete theory of justice. It also would risk losing touch with the idea of human rights, and the way in which the concepts of poverty and basic needs operate in actual discourse, as well as the opinions of citizens polled on the subject. The language of social citizenship rights gives adequate recognition to the value of political participation without risking the more tenuous claim that failing to distribute resources in a way that secures political equality violates global social rights standards.

2   The basic duties in respect of the social minimum

The nature of state duties will vary, and it is by now commonly understood in both international law and in philosophy that there will be duties to respect (show restraint), protect (regulate against third-party invasion or denial) and fulfil (directly provide) social rights.[58] Yet it will help to focus here on the third of these, to deal with the issue in its most acute form. The following account builds in part on the scheme presented in the ICESCR, but in a manner connected to the discussion of the social minimum above. I believe that respect for social human rights entails at a minimum the following basic duties:

1. A duty to take expeditious steps, to the maximum of available resources, and subject to reasonable conditions of eligibility (e.g. residency, personal responsibility, conditionality),[59] to secure the social minimum to all; and
2. To give immediate effect to the following obligations:
   (a) To define and regularly update the healthy subsistence, social participation, and agency thresholds;
   (b) To establish framework legislation and executive institutions for securing the social minimum to all; and

---

[58] Shue, *Basic Rights*; a similar typology was developed contemporaneously by Asbjorn Eide, ultimately adopted by the United Nations in A. Eide (UN Special Rapporteur on the Right to Food), *The Right to Food* (Final Report) UN.Doc. E/CN.4/Sub.2/1987/23 (1987), paras. 66–69. See Fabre, *Social Rights Under the Constitution*, Chapter 2.

[59] On personal responsibility see R. Dworkin, *Sovereign Virtue: The Theory and Practice of Equality* (Cambridge, MA: Harvard University Press, 2000), Chapter 2; Dworkin, *Justice for Hedgehogs*, Chapters 9 and 10; on conditionality and social rights, see White, *The Civic Minimum*. I do not endorse this notion but accept it as potentially relevant.

> (c) To hear and respond to complaints, in an official and public cap-
> acity, about alleged deprivations of the social minimum.

The first duty, which can be called a progressive obligation, requires some explanation, because it admittedly looks at first sight more like a promise to try than a real guarantee. The expression 'to the maximum of available resources' is borrowed from Art. 2(1) of the ICESCR, and in one sense represents something of a compromise given its global coverage.[60] But it is also similar to the Constitution of South Africa, which requires the state, in several provisions, to take reasonable steps, 'within available resources', to guarantee the various rights.[61] The UN Committee on Economic, Social and Cultural Rights has confirmed that the obligation imposed by Art. 2(1) is an obligation of conduct and of result, meaning that states-parties may be obligated to take steps in a certain fashion, without achieving any particular result, or be obligated to achieve a result with discretion as to means.[62] Obligations of conduct are common in law. There are labour law duties to negotiate in good faith, there is the duty to act with due diligence in US securities law and in international law, to behave reasonably in tort, administrative law, and criminal procedure, to use due care, or act with 'all deliberate speed', or ensure that trials be conducted in a reasonable time in human rights law.[63] In some senses, the pervasive obligation that limitations of human rights or the execution of military activities be proportionate is in a sense an obligation of conduct. So it would be false to say that a duty to implement rights expeditiously or reasonably to the maximum of available resources is incompatible with it being a real and even justiciable standard. The standard becomes meaningful when it is applied in particular contexts, typically by comparing particular decisions with other decisions or behaviour in similar situations, or by addressing problems particular to the process of decision-making or reasoning in a particular case.

The question of what constitutes 'available resources' or 'expeditious steps'[64] will depend on context, and there will be much room for

---

[60] See M. Craven, *The International Covenant on Economic, Social and Cultural Rights: A Perspective on its Development* (Oxford University Press, 1995); and Langford and King, 'The Committee on Economic, Social and Cultural Rights'.

[61] Constitution of the Republic of South Africa, Arts. 25–27.

[62] For a relevant analysis, see Langford and King, 'The Committee on Economic, Social and Cultural Rights', pp. 482–3.

[63] See Chapter 4, section II.C.

[64] On 'available resources' in the ICESCR see Craven, *The International Covenant on Economic, Social and Cultural Rights*, pp.136–43; and the UN Committee on Economic,

disagreement on how these standards are applied in practice. It will naturally be the case that a number of highly impoverished countries will be unable always to meet the social minimum. That does not make rights-language inapplicable, any more than the fact that equality for women is at least a generation away in most countries would make women's rights a category mistake. But if we accept that the social minimum is indeed a minimal standard, then the working assumption in wealthy countries like the United Kingdom must be that the resources exist to provide it. Does this mean, though, that courts should therefore just order governments to guarantee the social minimum at the behest of whoever steps up to the legal plate? The answer is no, and the reason is simple. We cannot presently be sure that the judicial order to provide resources will not (i) take them away from some other needy recipient, and/or (ii) corrupt the overall mode of distribution in a way that is negative on the whole. That institutional reality is why the role of courts in enforcing *constitutional* social rights requires a more careful theory of adjudication as provided in this book. (On the subject of enforcing legislative rights, there is a working though at times contested presumption that the funding arrangements are such as to properly fund the statutory duties.[65]) With due note taken of the institutional limitations of courts, however, it is quite different for a citizen, parliamentarian, or international body to declare unequivocally that a country like the United Kingdom can in no way excuse a systematic failure to guarantee the social minimum.

Another important caveat applies. Many real disputes in such countries will be not about the truth of these abstract thresholds and duties, but how they are to be defined and implemented in respect of particular issues. It is possible for persons to share in this conception of social human rights, but to disagree strongly about how to define and satisfy the concrete thresholds, and which policies give proper effect to the minimum so-defined.[66]

The second subset of duties also requires elaboration. I list them as immediate obligations, because a state claiming to respect social human

---

Social and Cultural Rights, 'An evaluation of the obligation to take steps to the "maximum of available resources" under an Optional Protocol', Statement, U/N. Doc. E/C.12/2007/1 (2007). For an argument that the Covenant should be read to require 'expeditious steps', see Langford and King, 'The Committee on Economic, Social and Cultural Rights', pp. 499–500.

[65] However, at times the courts will reject this principle as well. See *Holmes-Moorhouse* v. *Richmond upon Thames LBC* [2009] UKHL 7 (judgment of Lord Hoffmann).

[66] C. R. Sunstein, *Legal Reasoning and Political Conflict* (New York: Oxford University Press, 1996), Chapter 2 (on 'incompletely theorized agreements').

rights would have an urgent duty, in my view, to establish these three items without delay.[67] It is necessary to define the social minimum thresholds, for without such a definition it will be impossible to judge the adequate level of resources required to fully discharge the primary duty. It is necessary to update it regularly because of inflation and other economic trends. This is familiar territory for poverty experts. However, and in my view, a very important practical consequence of the analysis here is that these thresholds *must be established by independent expert opinion* and not through ordinary political channels. The determination of the three thresholds is a matter of professional expertise and is conceptually independent of the question of scarcity. Macro-level resource allocation can be a radically polycentric issue, the resolution of which requires the diverse inputs and compromises afforded by legislatures and experimentation by the executive. But setting the three thresholds does not. It is defined socially and scientifically, requiring a different set of tools and for which the expected degree of disagreement will be radically smaller. It is a matter for individual and collective professional expertise, as defined in Chapter 8, and the risk of non-expert bias must be avoided. This more or less calls, therefore, for the establishment of an administrative body or agency that is independent and non-partisan, and that would determine and revise the thresholds on an ongoing basis, with due attention to regional and other relevant variations such as gender, age, and ethnicity.[68]

The duty to establish framework legislation will become clear in section III.C and section IV below. I argue there that the primary duty-bearer is the state, and that framework legislation is the key instrument for giving effect to social rights – the *sine qua non* of real social rights.

The duty to establish a complaints system follows, in my view, quite clearly from the very idea of human *rights*. The legal principle *ubi jus, ibi remedium* ('where there are rights, there are remedies') is not only a maxim of equity, but a fundamental principle of human rights law.[69] It plays a conceptual role as well. The idea of human rights is the identification of fundamental, minimal standards that must be respected as a matter of priority. It is a corollary, in my view, of the very idea of this

---

[67] On immediate obligations under the ICESCR, including on the obligation to adopt legislation, see Langford and King, 'The Committee on Economic, Social and Cultural Rights', pp. 486–9.

[68] For an example of such a non-partisan independent agency, see UK National Statistics, www.statistics.gov.uk.

[69] General Comment No. 9; D. Shelton, *Remedies in International Human Rights Law* (2nd edn, New York: Oxford University Press, 2006).

quality of being fundamental and high priority that some mechanism be designed to identify lapses and remedy them as a matter of urgency. Our interest in the social minimum is a sufficient reason for holding the state to be under a duty to provide a remedial mechanism. Although courts immediately come to mind for such a remedy, this need not be the only (or even principal) mechanism. Yet whatever the mechanism is, however, the adjudicator should adopt an attitude of independence and procedures that allow the transparent consideration of allegations. Examples of such procedures would include those relating to ombudspersons, inquiries by independent experts, former politicians, or judges, commissions, quasi-adjudicative panels, or tribunals and courts. The mere possibility of writing a letter to a Member of Parliament will not do.

C   State responsibility and the welfare state

On this conception, the state is responsible for securing our social rights, from the cradle to the grave. Just as with prisons or the court service, the state cannot withdraw from the business: it has a duty to provide or to regulate for the provision. That the state (as opposed to family, social networks, or church) is responsible in this way is implied in the contemporary philosophical idea of human rights.[70] The state is the institution through which the community acts collectively to secure important public and even some private goods (e.g. marriage, funerals). And of course states are the primary if not only duty-bearers in respect of social rights recognised in international human rights law. I leave to one side the burning questions about the extent to which the state can contract out its functions to private providers, and the question of which legal human rights obligations can bind non-state actors.

One might ask whether respecting social human rights commits one to a particular variant of the welfare state.[71] Richard Titmuss, in an early study, distinguished between residual and institutional welfare states.[72] The former focused on means-tested assistance that would be provided

---

[70] Nickel, *Making Sense of Human Rights*, p. 10; Griffen, *On Human Rights,* pp. 101–4; Beitz, *The Idea of Human Rights,* pp. 122–5.

[71] The UN Committee on Economic, Social and Cultural Rights' answer is a clear 'no': see UN Committee on Economic, Social and Cultural Rights (CESCR), *General Comment No. 3: The Nature of States Parties' Obligations (Art. 2, Para. 1, of the Covenant),* 14 December 1990, E/1991/23, para. 8, available at: www.unhcr.org/refworld/docid/4538838e10.html (accessed 25 July 2011).

[72] R. Titmuss, *Essays on the Welfare State* (London: Allen and Unwin, 1958).

when markets or families failed (and one might add religious groups to this list). The latter was universal and available to all residents regardless of means (e.g. like the National Health Service in the United Kingdom), an option that would promote social solidarity and cohesiveness. In his classic comparative study of welfare states, Gøsta Esping-Anderson built on Titmuss and others in identifying three models of the welfare state that are used in the richer capitalist countries.[73] The first was a residual liberal model, which prioritises economic growth and which focuses on means-tested, typically modest benefits with strict entitlement rules that may be and often are associated with stigma for claimants. The United States, Canada, and Australia were considered archetypical examples, and the UK model was viewed then (1980) as now to hover around its edges. The second is a conservative, corporatist model that aims to preserve status differences in society and in families. It prefers social stability and is less concerned with growth and efficiencies. The state provides generous benefits for families and regulates the labour market quite heavily, but in ways that tend to preserve existing status and roles. The provision of legislative social rights was never controversial for these countries. Germany, Austria, and France are considered leading examples, and the Elizabethan Poor Law of 1601 (so-called 43rd of Elizabeth) might also be considered an early example of a benefits system whose chief aim was social stability.[74] The third type is the social democratic model, which combines strong universalism in access to benefits with a commitment to reduce inequalities aggressively by aiming for nearly full employment. The Scandinavian countries were leading examples. Esping-Anderson's study is rich, and has stood the test of time and comparative analysis and retesting rather well, notwithstanding a plethora of studies that refine and extend this framework, as well as critique it.[75]

Does the acceptance of the idea of social human rights commit a state to any of these models? Robert Goodin and his co-authors have shown through sophisticated panel data (i.e. data tracking the relevant phenomenon continuously over an extended period of time in different countries)

[73] Esping-Anderson, *The Three Worlds of Welfare Capitalism*, Chapter 1.
[74] An Act for the Relief of the Poor 1601. Its stabilising, but paternalistic harshness is described in D. Fraser, *The Evolution of the British Welfare State* (3rd edn, London: Palgrave, 2003), pp. 34–40; see also D. Roberts, *Victorian Origins of the British Welfare State* (New Haven: Yale University Press, 1960), p. 59 (discussing paternalistic Tory backlash against factory abuse and harshness of the new poor law).
[75] W. A. Arts and J. Gelissen, 'Models of the Welfare State', in F. G. Castles *et al.* (eds.), *The Oxford Handbook of the Welfare State* (Oxford University Press, 2010), Chapter 39.

that the social democratic model was equal to or superior to the other two models on each of the three so-called competing main goals: economic growth, social stability, and poverty reduction.[76] Let us assume the upshot of that study is correct. Even so, I would argue that recognising social human rights does not commit us to a particular type of welfare state, any more than recognising civil human rights commits us to a particular model of democracy or voting system,[77] even if over time one emerges as the superior model. This is a corollary of the minimalism of social human rights discourse. Neither should it be forgotten that each model may fail in elements of detail: benefit levels may be too low, conditions for entitlement too harsh, opportunities for appeal too remote, or the revision of the scheme too careless or destructive in a given case.

IV   Multi-institutional protection of social rights

How might a state fulfil its basic responsibility to guarantee our social rights? Subsumed within any of the three main models just mentioned is a vast range of potential strategies. It is nonetheless possible to shed light on the principal modes of protection by concentrating on the role of the key branches of government and the constitution itself. A brief exploration – drawing on the British experience in particular – will help to show the complexity of the project, the interdependence and collaboration between various branches of government, as well as between legal, administrative and political forms of action. Above all, it is a lesson about how adjudication and in particular constitutional adjudication fits into the crucially important larger picture.

A   Legislative

The main engine for protecting social rights is and always will be primary legislation adopted by a representative legislature, and so any good-faith commitment begins here. Framework legislation allocates duties and rights, establishes the basic scheme, and specifies the various elements of the system of protection in the level of detail required to address the broad subject-matter. The key statutes in the United Kingdom that comprise this framework for social rights (apart from labour rights) include a series of acts now known as, conveniently enough, the Education

---

[76] Goodin *et al.*, *The Real Worlds of Welfare Capitalism*, Part III.
[77] D. Held, *Models of Democracy* (3rd edn, Cambridge: Polity Press, 2006).

Acts, Social Security Acts, National Assistance Acts (covering residential care for the sick, elderly or disabled), National Health Service Acts, and Housing Acts. To these classic pillars we can join two more modern ones – the Children Act 1989 and the Mental Health Acts, both of which impose extensive state duties, and could perhaps include the Legal Aid and Advice Act 1949 which made access to civil justice in courts of law a social right as well. Each statute is immensely complex, often due to an intricate regime that combines state provision with regulation of private providers.

Housing provides a typical example. The key statute in this area is now the Housing Act 1996, which consolidates over a century of statutory developments. It addresses a large array of topics: the recognition and management of registered social landlords; the regulation of landlord and tenants' rights (which merely modify the common law); the payment of housing benefit, a means-tested cash benefit; the scheme for repossessing housing and dealing with anti-social behaviour; the allocation of social housing to people on queues for public housing; the provision of housing to the homeless (this being a different part of the Act than social housing allocation); and various miscellaneous provisions as well. All in all – and leaving aside the hugely relevant subject of planning legislation – the Act presently consists of 232 sections, 12 typically detailed schedules/ appendices, and is subject, as of the date of writing, to over 500 subsequent legislative amendments or other consequent changes. The 1996 Act alone amounts to 311 typed pages.[78]

Social security is probably more complicated.[79] The range of benefits is mind-boggling: it presently ranges from carers' allowances, to child benefit, to council tax benefit, to income support, jobseeker's allowance, incapacity (disability) benefit, to pensions credit, discretionary social fund, statutory sick pay, to many others – at the time of writing there were forty-seven different social security benefits and tax credits.[80] The volume of primary legislation itself is vast – the Department for Work and Pensions' guide book *The Law of Social Security* (the 'Blue Volumes') presently lists some fifty-seven pieces of relevant primary legislation adopted since 1965

---

[78] Unless stated otherwise, all quoted statistics are available on and were obtained from www.legislation.gov.uk.

[79] The main consolidating act is presently the Social Security Contributions and Benefits Act 1992.

[80] See HMRC, *Employment Income Manual*, at EIM76100 and EIM76101, available at: www. hmrc.gov.uk.

and still applicable,[81] as well as over 1,000 statutory instruments giving effect to and sometimes varying the terms of such primary legislation.[82]

This same exercise could be continued with health care and education, both of which are arguably more complicated than either of the above,[83] but the message is clear. These acts provide the basic enabling framework of the welfare state. Their scope, intricate subject-matter, the political compromises they embody, the frequency and necessity of their revision, and the input and participation required to make them workable, make it clear that only a body with the structure and methods of Parliament, administratively supported by government, could provide the basic framework of a good model.[84]

For these very reasons, the UK, German, French, American, and most other legislatures have committees to help them with bill scrutiny and scrutiny of the government. In the UK these committees have cross-bench (i.e. multi-party) representation, and take oral and written evidence from ministers, experts, and the public.[85] There are select committees for all departments, including on health, work and pensions, communities and local government (covering housing), and education, as well as a Lords Constitution Committee and a Joint Committee (of the House of Commons and Lords) on Human Rights. The select committees' key role is oversight of their respective Department, focusing on policy, spending, administration, and assisting parliamentary debate.[86]

---

[81] See the DWP, 'The Law of Social Security – The Blue Volumes', Supplement No. 93 (10 December 2011) 'List of Statutes – All Volumes', available at www.dwp.gov.uk/publications/specialist-guides/law-volumes/.

[82] Ibid., 'Alphabetical List of Statutory Instruments – All Volumes.' The (somewhat dated) bible is N. Wikeley, *The Law of Social Security* (5th edn, London: Butterworths, 2002).

[83] See the consolidating acts for the National Health Service Act 2006, consisting of 278 sections and 22 schedules, and the Education Act 1996, consisting of 583 sections, 40 schedules, and which has been amended or otherwise affected by subsequent legislation 810 times, to date.

[84] The British model is probably needlessly complex and overwrought, partly due to an obtuse system of legislative drafting (on which see the critical survey in M. Zander, *The Law-Making Process* (6th edn, Cambridge University Press, 2004), pp. 25–52) and due to the schizophrenic compromises between Beveridge's universalism and Thatcherite neo-liberal retrenchment (on which see Fraser, *The Evolution of the British Welfare State*, Chapter 10; R. Lowe, *The Welfare State in Britain Since 1945* (Basingstoke: Palgrave Macmillan, 2005), Chapters 12–15). Those facts do not diminish the point made here.

[85] For details see R. Blackburn and A. Kenyon, *Griffith & Ryle on Parliament: Functions, Practice and Procedures* (2nd edn, London: Sweet & Maxwell, 2003), Chapter 11. The up-to-date list of committees together with documentation is available on Parliament's website, www.parliament.uk.

[86] Annual Report of the Liaison Committee for 2004, HC 419 of 2004–05.

They are productive too. For example, in the 2009–2010 annual session of Parliament, the Health Committee alone published 14 reports and transcripts of hearings, exceeding 1,600 typed pages in total.[87] And it cannot be forgotten that these committees are more than a group of working experts or civil servants: they enjoy the democratic legitimacy of elected or appointed parliamentarians, as well as their flaws.

But there is an even simpler reason why the legislature's role is crucial: the power of the purse. The annual Appropriations Acts are the legislation through which the UK Parliament exercises its constitutional right to control the spending process.[88] They may be short and straightforward – usually five or six sections long – but their importance is paramount because they endorse the government's budget and fund its statutory obligations. Among the many important lessons drawn from the French and American revolutions – as well as from English constitutional history – perhaps the greatest is that, to preserve social peace and stability, those who pay into the public purse should generally be represented in the key decisions about spending. Since, as I showed in the first chapter, spending on social rights accounts for around 70 per cent of the national budget, the lesson is rather apposite.

B   Executive/administrative

Notwithstanding its complexity, the framework legislation and budget allocations are only the very beginning. The bulk of preparing the legislation above, and the running of extensive public consultations during the lead-up, is carried out before the first bill is introduced into Parliament for discussion. This is all run by the executive branch, often called the government in the United Kingdom, but of course the executive branch extends beyond the Departments or Ministries and includes the Civil Service, the various executive agencies and related public bodies at arms' length from government, as well as local or municipal government bodies.[89] Local

---

[87] The Reports of the Committee are available at www.parliament.uk/healthcom. On the effectiveness of committees, see Blackburn and Kenyon, *Griffith and Ryle on Parliament*, pp. 601–2.

[88] See Bill of Rights 1689, clause 4: 'That levying money for or to the use of the Crown by pretence of prerogative, without grant of Parliament, for longer time, or in other manner than the same is or shall be granted, is illegal.' The Appropriation Acts are only one part of a complex process: see M. Jack (ed.), *Erskine May's Treatise on the Law, Privileges, Proceedings and Usage of Parliament* (London: Lexis Nexis, 2011), Part V.

[89] See P. P. Craig, *Administrative Law* (6th edn, London: Sweet & Maxwell, 2008), Chapters 2–6 for a succinct discussion of the various units and the important role of contracting out public services.

government, to take one sub-branch, is enormously important in the education, community care, and housing fields in the United Kingdom. There are, at the time of writing, over 400 local authorities organised chiefly into councils and districts.[90] All the executive bodies' functions vary enormously, but we can take the right to housing, more specifically the obligations of local authorities to house the homeless under Part VII of the Housing Act 1996, as a relevant and *relatively* simple example to explore how these bodies play intricate and interdependent roles in implementing social rights.

Part VII defines how both the Secretary of State responsible for that matter (presently the Minister responsible for the Department for Communities and Local Government) and local housing authorities, which are run and funded through local government, are responsible for housing the homeless. The Act defines someone as homeless when he 'ha[s] no accommodation available for his occupation', and to count as 'available' the accommodation must be 'reasonable for him to continue to occupy'.[91] Some situations – such as domestic or other violence – are automatically deemed by s. 177(1) of the 1996 Act to make accommodation unavailable, and the Secretary of State also has a statutory power to expand (by Order, a statutory instrument) the list of situations where it would be 'not reasonable' for someone to occupy premises.[92]

The Act imposes a range of legally enforceable duties upon the local housing authority in respect of homeless persons, though the duties vary depending on whether they are homeless intentionally or not, and whether in priority need (statutorily defined). For the unintentionally homeless in priority need, there is an interim duty to accommodate, as well as a duty to secure permanent accommodation. Once the authority satisfies itself that these conditions are met, it must make a 'suitable' offer of accommodation before the duty may be considered discharged. For those unintentionally homeless but not in priority need, there is a duty to provide information and assistance, but not to house.

The framework requires the local authority to make statutory assessments about priority need, intentionality, interim obligations, and suitability of their offers. Further, when assessing whether an offer of accommodation is 'suitable', the authority may and frequently will take

---

[90] Here too the law is vast and in constant flux: see A. Arden *et al.*, *Local Government Constitutional and Administrative Law* (2nd edn, London: Sweet and Maxwell, 2008), Chapter 1 and esp., pp. 18–28.

[91] Section 175(1), (3) Housing Act 1996.

[92] Section 177(3) Housing Act 1996.

account of the general availability of housing in the area.[93] It is also common to place people who have been assessed as having an interim need for accommodation in a bed and breakfast hotel as temporary accommodation,[94] and so the council must also manage its relationships with such institutions to ensure quality and avoid problems and scandals. Moreover, the financing of the operation is intricate. The authorities draw their finance partly from their revenue from local taxes and various charges and levies, but mainly through a combination of various support grants given by central government.[95] The level of such grants can not only vary drastically with the prevailing political winds, but can also be used by central government to control local government policy through conditionality arrangements.[96]

Since this process is run locally but within a consistent national statutory framework, there is a need to balance national coherence with local needs and resources. One such technique is through the availability of judicial review (discussed below). Another is through the Secretary of State's statutory power to issue guidance to the local housing authorities to help them understand and give effect to their statutory obligations. The homelessness codes of guidance – which are not binding but must be considered[97] and which have important practical impact – usually number a few hundred pages.[98] They are compiled about every four to six years by a ministry of central government (presently the Department for Communities and Local Government), and aim to reflect both the

[93] *Begum v. Tower Hamlets* [2003] 2 AC 430; *Ali v. Birmingham City Council* [2010] UKSC 8.

[94] See Department for Communities and Local Government, *Homelessness Code of Guidance for Local Authorities* (London: TSO, 2006), Annex 17 ('Recommended Minimum Standards for Bed and Breakfast Accommodation').

[95] See Arden *et al.*, *Local Government Constitutional and Administrative Law*, Chapter 6, p. 891 for a ninety-page 'outline' of the subject.

[96] M. Loughlin, *Legality and Locality: The Role of Law in Central–Local Government Relations* (Oxford University Press, 1996).

[97] The statutes usually state that authorities must have regard to the guidance. See e.g. s.182 Housing Act 1996, s.118 (2D) Mental Health Act 1983.

[98] Department for Communities and Local Government, *Homelessness Code of Guidance*. See also Office of the Deputy Prime Minister, *Allocation of Accommodation: Code of Guidance for Local Housing Authorities* (London: TSO, 2002). See also Department of Health, *Code of Practice: Mental Health Act 1983* (London: TSO, 2008). Some are shorter: Department for Communities and Local Government, *Allocation of Accommodation: Choice Based Lettings Code of Guidance for Local Housing Authorities* (London: TSO, 2008).

legal and statutory developments in the intervening periods, as well as the Department's overall policy objectives. They are meant to guide the assessments of front-line workers and managers alike in the various local authorities. Civil society and professional organisations are consulted on the form and content of the codes of guidance. In one sense, they embody the wisdom of many.[99]

This schema – provided it is reasonably well funded – is one good example of how a state committed to protecting the right to housing could do so for its homeless (or at least those in priority need). It shows how enforceable rights and duties woven throughout the enabling legislation are supplemented, amplified, and implemented through various forms of administrative action. Assessments require close interactions with service-users and reference to local circumstances, both in a context of fluctuating resources. And despite the intricacy of the homelessness part of the Act, it is merely one small part of the local authority's overall legal duties that could be described as giving effect to the right to housing. All authorities spend vastly more time and money on allocating social housing under Part VI of the Housing Act 1996, and on various other housing benefits. In a recent year, homelessness accounted for a mere 11 per cent of nationwide local government spending from the pot they reserve for housing services alone.[100]

All this activity generates a need for oversight, and lawyers instinctively assume judicial review can provide it. But it would be irresponsible administration – and probably a violation of our social human rights – to let that be even the main quality control device. Bureaucratic systems tend to develop their own internal oversight mechanisms. So, quality control commissions, external and internal auditors, inspectors, internal review panels, as well as good old-fashioned hierarchical managerial control, are all ways that the welfare and regulatory state seek and ought to seek to maintain robust standards.[101]

---

[99] These observations are based on interviews with officials responsible for drafting or redrafting the codes of guidance for homelessness, and the guidance for housing allocation, in the Department for Communities and Local Government. Frances Walker, DCLG (9 September 2009); Alan Edwards, DCLG (25 September 2009).

[100] See e.g. Department for Communities and Local Government, 'Local authority revenue expenditure and financing England: 2010–11 Budget (Revised)', Statistical Release (17 February 2011) available at: www.communities.gov.uk/documents/statistics/pdf/1846276.pdf.

[101] The masterpiece on the comparative merits of bureaucratic oversight is: J. L. Mashaw, *Bureaucratic Justice* (New Haven: Yale University Press, 1985).

National systems will vary in their modes of protecting the poor, but in all countries there is bound to be, where it is good, some similar combination of statutory assessments, some form of local government involvement, central government guidance, multivariate funding formulas, and non-adjudicative oversight and quality control.

C   Adjudicative

The very idea of social 'rights' implies the recognition of *entitlements* that one can *claim* against the state. Sometimes the statutory framework is framed explicitly in terms of rights and duties, such as the British homelessness, child protection, social security, and community care frameworks.[102] At other times, the regime confers on public authorities a range of discretionary powers that allow but do not oblige them to distribute public goods. This is found more in the fields of health care and social housing allocation. But even where statutes empower rather than compel public authorities to protect our social rights, general public law provides an extensive framework for controlling such discretionary power, including ensuring that it was used for the purposes for which it was conferred.[103] That framework itself generates rights, which, though different from legislative and constitutional rights, are public law rights nonetheless. In fact, much of administrative law is in fact really about protecting people's social and immigration rights in the modern administrative state, and the advocate of constitutional social rights ought to look there first for lessons about judicial control of welfare allocation. If some advocates of constitutional social rights have not seen far, it is because they stood on the shoulders of the wrong giants.

T. H. Marshall was right in his sociological observation and prediction about the growth of legally protected social rights in the welfare state.[104] The legislative pillars I outlined above provide the locus for a lot of legal activity.[105] Such activity is visible in the existence of specialist areas of law, and their respective reports. The two leading treatises on homelessness and housing allocation law alone (forget landlord and tenant

---

[102] See e.g. s. 193 Housing Act 1996; s. 20 Children Act 1989; s. 21 National Assistance Act 1948.

[103] *Padfield* v. *Minister of Agriculture, Fisheries and Food* [1968] AC 997.

[104] Marshall, 'Citizenship and Social Class', pp. 27–43.

[105] It is for this reason that critics such as Titmuss (see Chapter 3, section III.C) and Goodin, *Reasons for Welfare*, Chapter 7, opposed legislative social rights to some extent.

law) are more daunting than any treatise on constitutional and human rights law.[106] But homelessness law is hardly exceptional in this respect. So, in the UK there are the Housing Law Reports, Community Care Law Reports, Butterworths Medico-Legal Reports, the Medical Law Reports, Education Law Reports, and Mental Health Law Reports. Much of the legal activity in these reports is the application of the regular principles of public law and statutory interpretation, and most are complemented often by door-stopper textbooks that synthesise law, guidance, and practice for practitioners and lawyers.[107]

Notable for their absence in that list are social security law reports.[108] That is all the more interesting because it is the most litigated area of the domestic law of social rights. One reason is that the main avenue for social security disputes (as with employment law disputes) has been through specialist tribunals, whose decisions have traditionally not been reported. The tribunal system in the UK was largely developed for dealing with disputes over statutory entitlements in the social security and taxation fields, and the volume of decision-making is enormous by comparison to the role of the High Court in judicial review cases. In the area of social security and child support alone, for example, in a recent year the tribunal service disposed of nearly 279,000 cases, with over 70 per cent of these having been disposed of by formal hearing and ruling.[109] In the same year, the Administrative Court disposed of 495 substantive judicial review applications, covering all topics.[110]

---

[106] J. Luba and L. Davies, *Housing Allocation and Homelessness: Law and Practice* (2nd edn, Bristol: Jordan Publishing Limited, 2010); A. Arden, C. Hunter, and L. Johnson, *Homelessness and Allocations* (7th edn, London: Legal Action Group, 2006).

[107] L. Clements and P. Thompson, *Community Care and the Law* (4th edn, London: Legal Action Group, 2007); R. Jones, *Mental Health Act Manual* (London: Sweet & Maxwell, 2010); Wikeley, *The Law of Social Security*.

[108] But see the *Journal for Social Security Law*, which does report some cases and tribunal decisions, as well as legislative updates. Tribunal reform is expected to usher in a new role for precedent: T. Buck, 'Precedent in Tribunals and the Development of Principles' (2006) 25(4) *Civil Justice Quarterly* 458–84.

[109] *Quarterly Statistics for the Tribunal Service*, 3rd Quarter, 2010–2011, 1 October 2010– 31 December 2010, 'Table 1.2d SSCS Outcomes by Benefit Type' (Ministry of Justice, 31 March 2011) p. 34 provides statistics for that Quarter (comparing with overall disposal rate in Table 1.2c). The same exercise with the 1st and 2nd Quarter reports shows that on average 73 per cent of disposed cases were cleared after hearing, with about a 38 per cent success rate for claimants overall.

[110] Ministry of Justice, *Judicial and Court Statistics 2009*, p. 158, available at www.justice. gov.uk/publications/docs/jcs-stats-2009-211010.pdf.

Ombudsmen[111] also play a very important role in preventing and remedying maladministration in the welfare state in England and Wales. In 2009–2010 the Local Government Ombudsman disposed of 10,309 complaints, with just under a third being in favour of a settlement or a report in the complainant's favour.[112] Housing, education, adult social care, and other welfare support services added up to roughly half of the subject-matter of the complaints that year. The Parliamentary and Health Service Ombudsman, addressing complaints against central government departments and the National Health Service, was just as busy. Her office 'resolved' 24,240 enquiries,[113] though it accepted, from this overall number, only 308 for investigation. But some 170 of these concerned parliamentary bodies, and the remaining 138 the Health Service. Of the parliamentary bodies, the Department for Work and Pensions (responsible for social security) continued its tradition of being subject to the largest number of ombudsman investigations of any single department (thirty-one in total). Here too, therefore, we see that roughly half the work of this busy institution is concerned with complaints relating to social rights.

The lesson taken from Chapter 3 is that these modes may well be *superior* forms of adjudication to judicial review proceedings for the day-to-day protection of social rights.[114] Both were designed to promote better access to justice, be cheaper, fairer, more accessible, more managerial (or enabling) than passive, and less daunting. This potential was not lost (though perhaps underemphasised) on the UN Committee on Economic, Social and Cultural Rights either, which singled out ombudsmen and administrative remedies as offering important potential as modes of implementing social rights and remedying their violation.[115] But the other conclusion from Chapter 3 is that they are (a) not really best viewed as alternatives to

---

[111] I feel compelled to use the expression 'ombudsman' over 'ombudsperson' because it is the official name of the institution in the United Kingdom. I prefer the latter expression because it rightly removes any question about sexist usage.

[112] See Local Government Ombudsman, 'Annual Report 2009–2010: Delivering Public Value' (Commission for Local Administration in England), pp. 15–18, available at www.lgo.org.uk/publications/annual-report/.

[113] Though the bulk of these were resolved by turning the complainant away for prematurity, complaint being improperly made, and other matters.

[114] Chapter 3, section IV.

[115] *General Comment No. 9: The domestic application of the Covenant*, [9] (administrative remedies); *General Comment No. 10: The role of national human rights institutions in the protection of economic, social and cultural rights*, [2] (human rights ombudsman offices).

adjudication, but rather forms of adjudication, and (b) there are tasks well suited for courts that lie beyond their ordinary aptitudes.

So, on the one hand, we can see that any charge that welfare rights are non-justiciable looks pretty silly in light of the heavy legalisation of our welfare entitlements already. But on the other, we come squarely to the tough question that advocates of constitutional social rights face, at roughly the point at which they face it, namely: what is constitutionalising social rights going to add to all this?

D   *Constitutional*

Constitutions have many purposes, but I will take it as uncontroversial that they include at least the following: (a) the legal establishment or recognition of the basic institutions and departments of the state, including federal or other subnational units within it; (b) the division and allocation of responsibilities between the institutions or departments of state; and (c) the articulation of a set of foundational political principles to which the institutions of the state are meant to give effect, and, typically, which include a list of human or citizens' rights or related state duties. An examination of the written constitutions of the countries of the world clarifies that at the present time these are among the key common denominators.[116]

The third function is particularly relevant to the question about the role of constitutionalisation as a mode of implementation. What is the point of setting out such core principles? It no doubt plays an *expressive* function of constitutive political principles either agreed at the time of formation or which were instantiated in practice or even conventions when constitutional reform was undertaken. But surely the framers wanted more than preamble-type rhetoric. They must also have hoped that the principles would *channel* or *guide* the state's public institutions and provide an agreed normative standard for public criticism. Such principles can serve as political beacons that both direct institutions and demarcate certain topics as fundamental and important, signalling that adverse tampering requires the utmost care and public scrutiny. It would be naïve to think this is the everyday role for such principles, but foolish to deny

---

[116] See R. Wolfrum and R. Groter (eds.), *Constitutions of the Countries of the World*, Loose Leaf (New York: Oxford University Press, 1971 (with updates)). All references to constitutions are in reference to those in force and printed in this compilation (also available with online subscription) at the time of writing.

that role altogether. Finally, such core political principles serve an *enforcement* or *remedial* function by founding or supplementing claims in the courts or other institutions such as constitutional councils or parliamentary committees. While this remedial function might seem obvious, in fact many constitutions contain standards that aim to guide but are rarely expected to found legal actions. Constitutional conventions are an obvious and quite important example of such norms in the UK constitution, but written constitutions also abound with such clauses, such as Canada's clause on regional disparity, and the French provisions on republican government.[117]

So, should such principles include a commitment to the view that social rights are constitutional or human rights, as one mode of implementation? The answer in respect of the guiding and expressive functions seems an unequivocal 'yes'. If one includes other basic principles and rights-based commitments, then excluding social rights would (a) allow for an incomplete statement of basic rights, (b) deprive the polity of any guiding role that might have emerged in respect of social rights, and (c) amount to potential harm by prioritising rights that emphasise state restraint instead of those requiring state action for protecting social rights (especially tax and regulation). For sceptics of the constitution, this is much like Pascal's wager – whether one thinks the guiding role makes a difference or not, the safe bet is to include them.

However, this guiding function does not obviously entail any role for courts. Some constitutions contain abstract principled commitments to social rights or social solidarity, such as Germany's social state principle,[118] and Sweden's commitment (outside its fundamental rights chapter) to secure social rights.[119] Other constitutions contain sections commonly referred to as directive principles of state policy, which embody the principled commitment to social rights but with the ordinary implication that they do not found claims in the courts.[120] Such non-justiciable principles

---

[117] For an extended discussion of this view, see also J. A. King, 'Constitutions as Mission Statements', in D. J. Galligan and M. Versteeg, *The Social and Political Foundations of Constitutions* (Cambridge University Press, 2012) (where I also argue that statements of core principles in constitutions also play a legitimation role).

[118] The Basic Law of the Federal Republic of Germany, 1949 (as amended to 2009), Art. 20(1).

[119] Instrument of Government, 1974 (as amended), Chapter 1, Art. 2.

[120] The Constitutions of Ireland and India are early examples of this model, but at present Eritrea, Gambia, Ghana, Nepal, Nigeria, Papua New Guinea, Sri Lanka, Sudan, Swaziland, Thailand, Uganda, and Zambia also include them. See Wolfrum and Groter, *Constitutions of the Countries of the World*.

could have important legal consequences: the *Lochner*[121] era in the United States may well have been much more difficult had the American constitution included textual constitutional duties to protect social rights. But should the commitment go beyond this type?

In my view it should, and the resort to directive principles fails to meet the positive *guiding* potential for constitutions. First of all, the division of the rights into justiciable and non-justiciable sections can imply for some that the non-justiciable ones are subordinate. This was regarded to be the case in India for a while,[122] until it was corrected in the concurring opinion of Justice Bhagwati in *Minerva Mills* v. *Union of India* (and not so overtly by the majority opinion in that case).[123] And one interpretation of the European Court of Justice's *Viking* and *Laval* cases is that the less explicitly justiciable social rights principles were of a lower rank than the right to free movement of services, being treated as a mere legitimate aim to be implemented by proportionate means, rather than as a competing right – a contest among equals.[124] And it is common for judges to take the view that civil rights are matters of principle, social rights mere policy, and that the state's latitude regarding the latter is not to be questioned. One might say this is just confused practice, but in my view the division encourages and justifies it.

A second and more important argument is that justiciability enhances the guiding role of the constitution's political commitments. The existence of real judicial remedies can drive political actors and bureaucracy alike to take the rights more seriously in their planning. Justiciability can actually invigorate the political and administrative process, and send a message of seriousness. Where's the proof for this bold claim? For one, I take it to be the main message of one of the most rigorous and sustained empirical studies on the question of courts and social rights.[125] I also show

---

[121] *Lochner* v. *New York*, 198 US 45 (1905). For analysis, see Chapter 4, section III.A; Chapter 8, section II.A.

[122] *State of Madras* v. *Champakam Dorairajan* (1951) AIR 226 (SC).

[123] *Minerva Mills* v. *Union of India* (1981) 1 SCR 206, 259 (Chandrachud CJ). However, in his concurring judgment, Bhagwati J held, at 323, precisely the opposite – that non-justiciability did not imply normative inferiority. This is now the prevailing view. I would thank Dr Tarunabh Khaitan for assistance with this point.

[124] Case C-438/05 *International Transport Workers' Federation* v. *Viking Line ABP* [2007] ECR I-000; Case C–341/05 *Laval un Partneri Ltd* v. *Svenska Byggnads-arbetareförbundet and others* [2007] ECR I-000.

[125] V. Gauri and D. Brinks (eds.), *Courting Social Justice: Judicial Enforcement of Social and Economic Rights in the Developing World* (Cambridge University Press, 2008). See the discussion of this and a more ambivalent collection in Chapter 3, section III.D.

in the next chapter that there is burgeoning literature, drawing upon the earlier work in this vein by Stuart Scheingold, which shows that judicial decisions that declare rights essentially are the beginning of a political process that unfolds thereafter. Apart from these studies, it can be hard to show in a reasonably social scientific way that justiciability makes a worthwhile difference. One would need an example in which a state is committed to the rights values in non-justiciable form at one time, and then the same values in justiciable form at a later time, and compare general respect for them. Quite conveniently, however, exactly this situation did prevail in the United Kingdom (our central case in this study) before and after the adoption of the Human Rights Act 1998 (HRA). A rigorous and elaborate empirical study shows that the adoption of the Act, which only gave a remedy in UK courts for violations of Convention rights, in fact led to some worthwhile bureaucratic engagement with the rights values in the Convention by public bodies.[126] Some bodies mainstreamed the standards into day-to-day practice, and a number of officials were on the whole quite positive about the bureaucratic influence the new culture of rights had created. And that study did not even address the crucial role of the Joint Committee on Human Rights (JCHR), which is formally separate from the HRA but was part of the same process of 'Bringing Rights Home.' (The JCHR was for its first ten years more enthusiastic about human rights, and about social rights in particular, than the courts were, by a considerable margin.[127]) So *justiciable* rights can spur better political and administrative action – the institutions can move in concert in this way. Litigation (in addition to the possibility or threat of litigation)[128] can serve as a gadfly to further development in many subtle ways, some of which are explored in the next chapter.

Of course, including justiciable social rights can provide enforceable remedies: the remedial or enforcement function of constitutionalism. In the next chapter I offer an abbreviated account of what I take to be the prima facie benefits of legal accountability, and they serve as my most basic statement of the instrumental advantages of giving a dispute

---

[126] Equality and Human Rights Commission, *Human Rights Inquiry: Report of the EHRC* (London: EHRC, 2009).

[127] Joint Committee on Human Rights, 'The International Covenant on Economic, Social and Cultural Rights' (Twenty-First Report of Session 2003–2004), 10 October 2004; Joint Committee on Human Rights, 'A Bill of Rights for the UK?' (Twenty-Ninth Report of Session 2007–2008), 10 August 2008.

[128] V. Bondy and M. Sunkin, 'Settlement in Judicial Review Proceedings' [2009] *Public Law* 237.

resolution role concerning rights to courts. These benefits include issue-focus, principled reasoning, constitutional authority, independence and impartiality, rule interpretation competence, procedural fairness competence, participation and voice, expressiveness, and inter-institutional collaboration. It is obvious that these benefits are prima facie only, and even that modest claim must be defended against threshold objections.[129] Even when it is made out, the benefits remain rather abstract.

More concretely, then, constitutional social rights can also serve either as a state shield or claimant sword for the protection of social rights. In the defensive role, they can protect state social policies from attacks by litigants that are themselves founded on commercial or civil rights claims. Civil and political rights to property, to liberty, or to trade freely cannot reasonably claim superior status to a social policy that gives effect to or protects people's social rights. In *Kyalami Ridge*, the Constitutional Court of South Africa accepted the argument that the source of a government's power to build temporary accommodation for flood victims could be derived directly from the constitutional duty to implement the right to housing.[130] Nearby residents had objected to the emergency measure as being *ultra vires* and taken without proper consultation. In similar fashion, social rights have helped soften the terms of evictions both in South Africa, and through progressive interpretations of the European Convention on Human Rights, especially in cases against Britain.[131] In *Viking* and *Laval*, even if it is interpreted as having given unequal status to social rights principles, it very much did make clear that the protection of the social rights in Chapter IV of the EU Charter of Fundamental Rights provided a legitimate ground for limiting the commercial freedoms in EU law, and that balancing between the freedoms and social rights provisions was necessary. In *Chaoulli*, it may well have been the absence of social rights from the Canadian constitution that allowed the Canadian court to prioritise the right to life of the prospective insurance buyer who suffered from wait times, over the right to health of poorer Canadians who benefited from the state-led one-tier system of rationing.[132]

---

[129] See Chapter 3, section II.

[130] *Minister of Public Works & Ors.* v. *Kyalami Ridge Environmental Association & Ors.* [2002] 1 LRC 139; (2002) 3 CHRLD 313.

[131] *Jaftha* v. *Schoeman and others, Van Rooyen* v. *Stoltz and others,* 2005 (2) SA 140 (CC); *Connors* v. *United Kingdom* (2005) 40 EHRR 9; *McCann* v. *United Kingdom* (1995) 21 EHRR 97.

[132] *Chaoulli* v. *Quebec (Attorney General)* [2005] 1 SCR 791. See the critical discussion in Chapter 4, section III.A; Chapter 10, section III.A.1.

Finally, the use of social rights as a sword by claimants (i.e. to claim benefits from the state) can be in the eyes of advocates among its greatest virtues. This type of use could be to get an authority to revisit a policy; to support a particular strained reading of a statute; to impose greater procedural fairness in the benefits determination process; to require greater participation rights where there is radical overhaul of welfare institutions; to prevent an authority from manifestly ignoring its statutory or constitutional obligations; to require an authority to structure its own administrative discretion on a particular matter. These types of cases form the subject-matter of much of this book. These are real benefits to many, but to detractors from social rights, these effects can be among the idea's greatest vices. For them, such a constitutional power invites the judiciary to engage in broad review of the issues not exhausted by the statutory framework and which may thus be of a high policy nature, and offer remedies that will simply shift around money within the respective department rather than increase overall funding. And at its worst, as evidenced by the well-documented problem case of Brazil, this can be done at the behest of the wealthy at the expense of the poor.[133] At this stage of the book, it can only be observed that the court requiring the state to provide services to someone is ordinarily a prima facie benefit, and I know of no critic who objects when this is the outcome of adjudication in the highly legalised areas of welfare law (or tax or regulation) and ombudsperson compensation that I described above. That of course does not mean that enforceable remedies are an unqualified good. One must offer a theory of adjudication that gives us good reason to believe that when paying Paul, we are not always robbing Peter to do it. More dryly, such a theory must be sensitive to the distortive effects of constitutional adjudication and ensure to a reasonable extent that constitutional remedies offer a net gain over and above these disruptions to the achievement of social rights and related goals.[134] I think the approach offered in Parts II and III of this book is a sound proposal for doing just that. It would allow learning by doing and would overtly respect and support the legislative, administrative, adjudicative, and constitutional functions identified above. It emphasises respect for the complex, interlocking web of statutes and administrative regulations, as well as soft-law guidance, that typically regulate social services in the

---

[133] O. L. M. Ferraz, 'The Right to Health in the Courts of Brazil: Worsening Health Inequities?' (2009) 11 *Health and Human Rights: An International Journal* 33.

[134] Answering this question is no doubt difficult, but no more so than the meaningful ones about whether to adopt a written constitution, engage in devolution or federalism, adopt a national health service, or create a new oversight agency.

contemporary state, as well as the role of specialised adjudication for providing accountability within it. If I am right, then the judicial enforcement of social rights at the constitutional level can serve to give claimants
remedies in the incremental fashion already familiar to us under bills of
rights throughout the world, under a style of litigation that does involve
trade-offs and uncertainty, and problem areas or countries, but which
most observers and practitioners agree have led to steady though at times
ineffable improvements in public administration.

V   Conclusion

This chapter has presented a holistic account of the case for social rights.
It sought to make clear why it makes good sense to conceptualise social
rights within the rubric of fundamental human rights, but also why the
minimalism inherent in that discourse does not prevent a constitution
from being more ambitious. The separation of the various senses of the
term social rights allows us to better understand the variable nature of the
connections between them.

While most of this book is concerned with how judges should apply
vague constitutional rights principles and provisions, and the role of judicial restraint within such a process, it is important not to disregard the
foundational question of what substantive content our social rights can
be said to have. This is important first because such content may in specific cases guide the tasks of adjudicators, legislators, and the executive,
but also because it provides a much needed conceptual completeness to
our thinking about constitutional social rights. The discussion of the
social minimum sought to provide the normative bedrock for precisely
what is meant by talk of social human rights. I argued that the substantive
content of our social rights entitlements can be understood as an entitlement to a bundle of resources that satisfies three minimal thresholds: the
healthy subsistence, social participation, and agency thresholds. I further
explained the nature of the duties in respect of these thresholds, and that
the state is the primary duty-bearer. This account is consistent with the
interpretation of our social rights in international law.

The state is multifaceted, and a state that takes social rights seriously
must give effect to its duties at the legislative, executive, (non-constitutional) adjudicative, and constitutional levels. In a good system these
institutions will view themselves as collaborating on a joint enterprise.
I present the more focused case for constitutional social rights at the
end of a long discussion of the role of other institutions. This was quite

intentional. It is intended to emphasise the role of other institutions and the foundations upon which a sensible social rights jurisprudence must base itself, and also to add a tenor of sobriety to the calls for constitutional social justice. Yet once the role of these institutions is duly accounted for, it remains the case that justiciable constitutional social rights offer real advantages towards helping secure a just recognition of the social minimum.

3

The value of courts in light of the alternatives

I   Introduction

In the last chapter, I argued that constitutional legal accountability could be a valuable tool for protecting social human rights. The purpose of this chapter is to defend that modest claim and elaborate more precisely upon what value courts offer both in themselves, and when seen in light of the accountability benefits that alternatives to courts can offer. I first outline my understanding of the prima facie benefits of legal accountability – the institutional advantages or assets of legal institutions as a dispute resolution mechanism for social rights claims. The abstract nature of those benefits, however, makes them liable to some familiar challenges. The main one is that courts offer a hollow hope for social change. That claim smarts when social rights are at issue, because if securing privacy, criminal justice, or formal equality through courts is hard, then securing substantive economic equality or the social minimum will seem quite a bit harder. A related challenge, drawing on studies of administrative justice, is that the courts even in routine public law cases have relatively little impact on the functioning of welfare bureaucracies – or make them worse. My answers to these two challenges still leave untouched a third, which is that courts are a hollow hope for poor people in particular. It is here that it is necessary to examine that claim in general, and by considering some empirical studies on constitutional social rights in particular.

The exploration of this literature is chastening for those who look to the courts for significant social reform. But it also provides encouraging evidence that legal mobilisation can and has been a valued strategy in successful multifaceted approaches to advocacy. In particular, this chapter combines the insights from literature concerning legal mobilisation on the one hand, and studies of impact in the field of administrative justice on the other. In both cases I am at pains to recall and reinforce the importance of individual redress, namely, about the importance to individuals of claiming rights before recognised adjudicative institutions. Though too much is at times made of that point by lawyers, critical legal scholars return the favour by ignoring it in their wide-ranging search for whether courts create nationwide policy change.

Yet supporting the claim that social rights can and do provide a valuable tool also means showing that constitutional legal accountability offers something that some obvious alternatives do not. I explore the idea that alternative mechanisms of individual redress, such as specialised adjudication, ombudsmen, and alternative dispute resolution, meet that need. I conclude that they do not eclipse a role for courts. However, a careful examination of their role shows that some of them are ideal forms of accountability for day-to-day welfare disputes, and there is a need to give special weight to some of their general findings.

II   The prima facie benefits of legal accountability

Constitutionalising social rights does involve risks. So at the table of constitutional design, statespersons will want to know in some detail what the potential benefits are as well. A satisfying answer will no doubt involve a close look at the empirical and comparative record, something I undertake in section III of this chapter and elsewhere in this book. But there is a more general sense in which the answer must be abstract, just as the answer to the question about what the good is of free information, or expression, or public inquiries, or administrative law.

The good that might be expected from constitutional social rights is connected to the good provided by legal accountability in general. One can rightly say that legal accountability is essentially required in order to uphold the rule of law and to prevent the abuse of power. But that answer fails to say what institutional features courts and other adjudicative institutions have that make them good for doing just these types of things. My reply to that concern is that there are what I consider to be ten prima facie benefits to legal accountability. These benefits provide an instrumentalist reason for why legal accountability, and constitutional legal accountability, can provide a good dispute resolution mechanism for some classes of disputes. The benefits, stated without a number of important qualifications that I will turn to shortly, are as follows:

1. *Focus*: Adjudication situates an issue within particular social circumstances and compels the state to address the issue instead of ignoring it or deferring consideration.

2. *Principled reasoning*: Adjudicators are required to give decisions that are an interpretation of a pre-existing standard, they must give reasons for their decision, they must observe consistency of treatment (fairness), and decide matters in a transparent way that is ordinarily subject to appeal, and which is always subject to scrutiny for its rationality and consistency by judicial peers, the legal profession, the public, and the academy in particular. Judges tend to be very intelligent, which is an asset in the management and analysis of complex information.

3. *Constitutional authority*: Courts have a particular constitutional authority owing to their historical constitutional role, their role in protecting the rule of law, and as a forum for asserting individual rights. They play an extensive role in shaping and creating many of the rules governing private and public relations, most of them intentionally informed by moral considerations. This unique constitutional authority comprises four distinct benefits: political responsiveness to judgments; judicial confidence in respect of broader policy matters; general rather than balkanised jurisdiction over executive and legislative action; and remedial flexibility.

4. *Independence and impartiality*: While judicial decision-making is not value-free, it remains the case that, in the countries having the background political conditions set out in Chapter 1, judges are not party-political and in general they tend to remain reasonably impartial as between the state and the individual.

5. *Rule interpretation competence*: Judges draw upon a body of doctrine and practice in the interpretation of rules, and the consistent coordination between different bodies of rules and principles. This is a distinct asset in welfare rights adjudication, because constitutional social rights disputes are nearly always situated within complex schemes of rules and standards.

6. *Procedural fairness competence*: Public law has developed a distinct body of principles and practices relating to fairness, concerned with allowing individuals to hear the case against them and for them to have an impartial adjudicator review their claim. In the constitutional setting, this capacity has special relevance because there is a heightened demand, where positive rights are concerned, for procedural remedies.

7. *Participation*: The courts can be a forum for claimants to turn to, either as part of a broader campaign, or when all other options dry up. Expanded rules of standing and possibilities for third-party intervention provide supporting mechanisms for such participation.

8. *Expressiveness*: Courts play an expressive and at times educative role in adding symbolism and giving expressive meaning to some of our most basic constitutional commitments. They at times help to create and sustain what has been called the 'myth of rights', a myth that can have powerful indirect effects, even if the direct remedies provided by courts fail to create change.

9. *Publicity*: Constitutional litigation, given its overtly normative and expressive character, provides a series of occasions to rally political support and draw media attention to particular issues. Activists exploit these avenues and view them as a direct part of their overall strategy. Even lost cases may be and often are victories by providing salience to the issue.

10. *Inter-institutional collaboration*: General jurisdiction and flexible remedies allow judges to fashion an approach to adjudication that can adjust to the strengths and weaknesses of other institutions, by showing deference when they are working well, and using remedies of various intrusiveness when they perform poorly.

These benefits can be used as instruments to promote more transparent and more flexible decision-making, provide individual redress, ensure a modicum of formal rationality and consistency in decision-making, control the abuse of power at the executive and legislative stages of decision-making, and give enforceable substantive entitlements to the resources required to secure the social minimum.

These are, nonetheless, prima facie benefits because there are various objections to all these claims, some of which are good. They thus amount to potential benefits. Elsewhere, I have defended the claim that these are prima facie benefits, and answered the more obvious objections.[1] My conclusion is that those objections qualify the importance of each benefit but do not refute any of the claims made above. The qualifications, some of which are very important, ought to condition the interpretive approach taken by judges. And it is in Part II of this book that most of those important qualifications are chiefly accounted for. Nonetheless, there are two more fundamental challenges to the value of legal accountability that require immediate attention: that it has little positive impact or generates little political responsiveness, and that its benefits are adequately

---

[1] J. A. King, 'The Value of Legal Accountability', in N. Bamforth and P. Leyland, *Accountability in the Contemporary Constitution* (Oxford University Press [forthcoming]).

provided for by other alternatives. These two claims are the subject of the rest of this chapter.

III   The courts and social change

The claimant in the very important *Grootboom* case in South Africa died homeless and penniless, in her forties, some eight years after she won the most widely known South African social rights case concerning her right to housing.[2] Does that fact prove that constitutional social rights are marginal or even useless? For some, that type of story does, and it connects quite well with an argument that emerges from some influential sceptical American studies of legal impact. In this section I defend the idea that courts can provide a worthwhile avenue for social change in respect of social rights. I do so by examining a range of studies of impact, legal mobilisation, and some empirical studies directly concerned with welfare rights and social rights. The conclusion is that constitutional legal accountability can provide worthwhile benefits in general, and for social rights in particular.

A   Significant social change

In *The Hollow Hope*, Gerald Rosenberg argued that the salutary effects of litigation, even under the sweeping mandate of the US Bill of Rights, have been vastly overrated.[3] He found, for instance, that *Brown* v. *Board of Education*[4] (finding racial segregation in educational facilities to be unconstitutional) and *Roe* v. *Wade*[5] (finding limitations to the right to abortion in the first trimester to be unconstitutional) were mostly unhelpful and in some cases outright harmful for the social movements for racial equality and women's right to choose.

Rosenberg critically examines two competing views of how courts work. The first is the 'dynamic court view', which views courts as 'powerful, vigorous, and potent proponents of change'.[6] He contrasts this with

---

[2] *Grootboom and Others* v. *Oostenberg and Others*, 2000 (11) BCLR 1169 (CC). P. Joubert, 'Grootboom Dies Homeless and Penniless', *Mail and Guardian*, 14 August 2008, p. 35.

[3] G. Rosenberg, *The Hollow Hope: Can Courts Bring About Social Change?* (University of Chicago Press, 1991); see also the second edition (2008), though citations are to the first edition unless otherwise stated. In an equally superb vein, see D. L. Horowitz, *The Courts and Social Policy* (Washington DC: Brookings Institution, 1977), esp. pp. 34–51.

[4] 347 US 483 (1954).   [5] 410 US 113 (1973).   [6] *Ibid.*, 2; see esp. 21–7.

the 'constrained court view', which portrays courts as 'weak, ineffective, and powerless.'[7] While neither is perfectly accurate, he says, the mass of data he presents shows the constrained court view to prevail in the areas concerning racial desegregation, abortion, environmental law, reapportionment, criminal justice, and in the second edition, same-sex marriage. He argues that three general constraints account for constrained court view: (1) the bounded nature of constitutional rights claims exclude more creative and normatively ambitious forms of social activism; (2) the judiciary lacks needed independence; and (3) it lacks the proactive tools required to order significant reform.[8] The chief claim in the book is that courts cannot or at any rate do not, in America, produce *significant social reform*, which is defined as 'policy change with nationwide impact'.[9]

Rosenberg's thesis, so stated, is in fact compatible with the incrementalist approach advocated here. The incrementalist approach maintains legal accountability provides *worthwhile* benefits, and there is nothing in Rosenberg's central argument that rebuts this claim (though he does speak to that point as well, as I will shortly discuss). That courts can present worthwhile benefits is evident in numerous parts of Rosenberg's book, particularly in his discussion of abortion,[10] but it can also be demonstrated by considering the *Brown* case a bit more carefully.

Brown is hardly a central case of rights adjudication. Churches were bombed, lawyers lynched, judges threatened, Ku Klux Klan membership soared, and radical institutional reform was required to carry out the judgment. But neither can one hide behind these atypical features, given its importance and the reliance placed on the case by supporters of constitutional judicial review. The pre-eminent analysis of *Brown* has now been carried out by Michael Klarman.[11] His investigation is consistent with Rosenberg in some ways but is more in-depth and nuanced.[12] He

---

[7] *Ibid.*, 3.   [8] Rosenberg, *The Hollow Hope*, pp. 10–21.

[9] *Ibid.*, pp. 4–5.

[10] On this issue, others have presented quite significant contrary evidence. See B. C. Canon and C. A. Johnson, *Judicial Policies: Implementation and Impact* (2nd edn, Washington DC: Congressional Quarterly Inc., 1999), Chapter 1 and pp. 213–14, and esp. p. 215.

[11] M. Klarman, *From Jim Crow to Civil Rights: The Supreme Court and the Struggle for Racial Equality* (New York: Oxford University Press, 2004).

[12] Malcolm Feeley and Michael McCann both criticise Rosenberg for writing a one-sided account that disregards both contrary evidence and more balanced studies: see M. M. Feeley, 'Hollow Hopes, Flypaper, and Metaphors' (1993) 17 *Law and Social Inquiry* 745, 746 ('[H]e has written a brief rather than a theoretically informed social science study.') and M. McCann, 'Reform Litigation on Trial' (1992) 17 *Law and Social Inquiry*

agrees with Rosenberg that there was relatively little change in macro-level terms created by *Brown* v. *Board of Education*, but argues in favour of a 'backlash thesis' that roughly states that violent white resistance to *Brown*'s desegregation requirements was portrayed graphically in the media in a way that generated political support for the effective legislative changes that came in the 1960s, especially the Civil Rights Act 1964.[13] This is a revisionist account of *Brown*'s impact, one I am in no position to quarrel with.[14] But one does not need to work with Klarman's backlash thesis to point out that *Brown* led to important changes. A few representative examples of events caused by the *Brown* case as clarified in Klarman's study, confirms this:

- desegregation of border-state cities, including Baltimore (Maryland), Wilmington (Delaware), Kansas City, St Louis (Missouri), Louisville (Kentucky), Oklahoma;[15]
- even openly recalcitrant judges invalidated segregation laws out of fidelity to the Supreme Court's jurisdiction;[16]
- the judicial nullification of tokenistic compliance programmes, such as the grade-a-year plan in Tennessee and Virginia, and other programmes in North Carolina and Arkansas;[17]
- a direct cause of the passage of the Civil Rights Act of 1957 (not 1964), which, though ineffective in many respects, created the Commission on Civil Rights and the Civil Rights Division of the Attorney General's office;[18]

715, 722–4, 728ff. Rosenberg's response is printed at 761–76 of the same volume. For further critique, see P. R. Shuck, 'Public Law Litigation and Social Reform' (1993) 100 *Yale Law Journal* 1763.

[13] Klarman, *From Jim Crow to Civil Rights*, pp. 385–442.

[14] The earlier, more popular and more sanguine study is R. Kluger, *Simple Justice: The History of Brown* v. *Board of Education and Black America's Struggle for Equality* (New York: Vintage USA, 2004). For a substantial reply to Klarman by a legal historian, see P. Finkelman, 'Book Review: Civil Rights in Historical Context: In Defense of *Brown*' (2008) 118 *Harvard Law Review* 973. See also the collection of essays by a distinguished group of historians in B. J. Daugherity and C. C. Bolton (eds.), *With All Deliberate Speed: Implementing Brown v. Board of Education* (Fayetteville: University of Arkansas Press, 2008), p. xvi ('As the essays in this volume demonstrate, segregated schools were eventually destroyed through a combination of sustained black protest and litigation, and uneven federal support.')

[15] Klarman, *From Jim Crow to Civil Rights*, pp. 346–55.

[16] *Ibid.*, pp. 355–6.   [17] *Ibid.*, p. 361.

[18] The Civil Rights Act of 1957, Parts I and II (42 USC 1975); Klarman, *From Jim Crow to Civil Rights*, p. 366.

- it fostered the introduction of the civil rights injunction, which revolutionised the public law paradigm;[19]
- it prompted significant direct action, and was critical to desegregating Montgomery buses;[20]
- Martin Luther King, Jr. led a prayer pilgrimage to Washington DC, of between 15,000 and 25,000 people, on the third anniversary of the *Brown* judgment;[21]
- one black newspaper proclaimed it to be 'the greatest victory for the Negro people since the Emancipation Proclamation'.[22]

That seems like enough impact to say that the game was worth the candle.[23] Of course, it would not be if the consequent violence and other negative effects precipitated by the *Brown* case outweighed the benefits sampled above. Klarman's backlash thesis is not merely a causal explanation of the passage of the 1964 Civil Rights Act, but also a normatively loaded thesis about the negative potential of rights adjudication. Klarman shows that in the South, *Brown* radicalised politics, foregrounded desegregated education over other pressing civil liberties issues in the black community, caused conflict within the civil rights movement about whether to prioritise litigation or direct action, and led to significant increases in lynchings, bombings, and Ku Klux Klan membership.[24] Some authors read his analysis as concluding that *Brown* may well have done more harm than good,[25] though Klarman is more cautious in his

---

[19] A. Chayes, 'The Role of the Judge in Public Law Litigation' (1976) 89 *Harvard Law Review* 1281; O. Fiss, *The Civil Rights Injunction* (Bloomington: Indiana University Press, 1978). For a contemporary analysis, see C. F. Sabel and W. H. Simon, 'Destabilization Rights: How Public Law Litigation Succeeds' (2003–2004) 117 *Harvard Law Review* 1016.

[20] Klarman, *From Jim Crow to Civil Rights*, pp. 372, 467; however, cf. pp. 372–5 (the connection was 'indirect and convoluted'). Others argue that Brown was critical to the success of the Montgomery bus boycott: R. J. Glennon, 'The Role of Law in the Civil Movement: The Montgomery Bus Boycott, 1955–1957' (1991) 9 *Law and History Review* 59 and R. Kennedy, 'Martin Luther King's Constitution: A Legal History of the Montgomery Bus Boycott' (1989) 98 *Yale Law Journal* 999. See more generally, K. W. Mack, 'Rethinking Civil Rights Era Lawyering and Politics in the Era before Brown' (2005) 115 *Yale Law Journal* 256.

[21] Klarman, *From Jim Crow to Civil Rights*, pp. 372–3.

[22] *Ibid.*, p. 369.

[23] See also M. Minnow, *In Brown's Wake: Legacies of America's Educational Landmark* (New York: Oxford University Press, 2011).

[24] Klarman, *From Jim Crow to Civil Rights*, Chapter 7.

[25] Finkelman, 'Book Review: In Defense of Brown', 975–6; T. M. Keck, 'Beyond Backlash: Assessing the Impact of Judicial Decisions on LGBT Rights' (2009) 43 *Law and Society Review* 151, 152.

conclusions.[26] But both Klarman and Rosenberg imply or argue outright that this (potentially) negative phenomenon extends to the cases of abortion and same-sex marriage as well.[27]

The phenomenon of backlash is complex and its implications contestable. There is evidence of backlash in all these cases, but it is not clear on the one hand whether the status quo ante was any better, and on the other whether backlash would arise whenever conservative attitudes were ultimately confronted. In the *Brown* case itself, it is far from obvious that the price paid in backlash was not worth the change that Klarman himself confirms it (indirectly) produced. More importantly, other studies reject the normative backlash argument (i.e. that the bad often outweighs the good) in the area of same-sex marriage, abortion, and within social movements.[28] And if there is a significant measure of truth to Klarman and Rosenberg's arguments on this point – a big if for many – there would then also be a problem of American exceptionalism on this issue. Same-sex marriage decisions in Canada and South Africa were achieved with apparently little backlash, as was the implementation of the decision of the European Court of Human Rights requiring Britain to allow homosexuals to serve openly in its military, and affirmative action has been accepted around the world in forms that would likely astonish the American public.[29] Recall the applicable background political conditions in Chapter 1.

---

[26] Klarman, *From Jim Crow to Civil Rights*, p. 377 (saying that the view that litigation discouraged direct action is ultimately 'speculative', though there is evidence for it: see pp. 377–84 for the nuanced discussion of the issue).

[27] *Ibid.*, p. 465; Rosenberg, *The Hollow Hope*, 2nd edn, Chapters 12 and 13.

[28] Keck, 'Beyond Backlash', generally and at 155 (citing studies by Pinello, Eskridge Jr., and others); R. Post and R. Siegal, 'Roe Rage: Democratic Constitutionalism and Backlash' (2007) 42 *Harvard Civil Rights–Civil Liberties Law Review* 373; L. Vanhala, 'Social Movements Lashing Back: Law, Social Change, and Intra-Social Movement Backlash in Canada' (2011) 54 *Studies in Law, Politics and Society* 113. Vanhala qualifies the argument by showing how some of its dynamic effects can be positive, rather than rejecting it outright.

[29] On abortion, compare *R v. Morgentaler* [1988] 1 SCR 30 (SCC) (striking down an abortion restriction by 7–2). On same-sex marriage, see M. Smith, *Political Institutions and Lesbian and Gay Rights in the United States and Canada* (New York: Routledge, 2008) (finding that the legal movement in Canada was more successful); *Halpern* v. *Attorney General* (2003) 63 OR (3d) 161 (OCA) (requiring the immediate recognition of same-sex marriages in Ontario); *Reference re Same-Sex Marriage* [2004] 3 SCR 698 (SCC) (confirming federal authority to legislate for the recognition of same-sex marriage); *Minister of Home Affairs* v. *Fourie* (2003) (3) BCLR 355 (CC) (mandating recognition of same-sex marriage in South Africa); *Smith and Grady* v. *United Kingdom* (1999) 29 EHRR 493 (ECtHR) (gays and lesbians in the British military). On affirmative action, see the

What Rosenberg and Klarman have succeeded in doing is to show that there is compelling evidence to show that a quixotic vision of civil rights justice in courts can be misguided, naïve possibly – at least in the American context. They have shown that courts are a questionable engine for direct *significant social reform* (and a lot turns on what one counts as 'significant' here – one might rather say 'revolutionary').[30] Rosenberg's informed law and society critics not only agree with that conclusion, but also think that it was already clearly established in the literature and that to a large extent he chose a false target.[31]

Worthwhile social change does not have to be revolutionary. Other research has shown that judicial impact of a positive kind can and does arise in prison reform litigation,[32] disability rights,[33] and school finance reform,[34] and with Charter litigation in Canada,[35] as well as noteworthy

constitutional recognition in the Canadian Charter of Rights and Freedoms (s. 15(2)), the Constitution of South Africa, s. 9, Constitution of India, Art. 16(4); EC Treaty, Art. 141(4) (affirmative action in relation to gender equality); for judicial treatments, see *Belgian Linguistics* [1967] 1 EHHR 241 (ECtHR); *Re Parsons' Application for Judicial Review* [2002] NI 378 (QBD).

[30] Even this conclusion must contend with empirical counter-studies such as Canon and Johnson, *Judicial Policies* and C. Epp, *Making Rights Real: Activists, Bureaucrats, and the Creation of the Legalistic State* (University of Chicago Press, 2010).

[31] This is especially the case with Feeley's review, 'Hollow Hopes, Flypaper, and Metaphor', esp., 749ff., and confirming at 751 that it is not particularly new. See S. Scheingold, *The Politics of Rights: Lawyers, Public Policy and Political Change* (New Haven: Yale University Press, 1974), esp. Part I ('The Myth of Rights').

[32] M. Feeley and E. Rubin, *Judicial Policy Making in the Modern State: How the Courts Reformed America's Prisons* (Cambridge University Press, 2000).

[33] L. Vanhala, *Making Rights a Reality? Disability Rights Activists and Legal Mobilization* (Cambridge University Press, 2011); J. L. Erkulwater, *Disability Rights and the American Social Safety Net* (Ithaca: Cornell University Press, 2006). Erkulwater recognises the achievements through legal mobilisation, but is also critical of the courts (see esp. Chapter 5).

[34] M. Paris, *Framing Equal Opportunity: Law and Politics of School Finance Reform* (Stanford University Press, 2010); A. Lukemeyer, *Courts as Policymakers: School Finance Reform Litigation* (New York: LFB Scholarly Publishing, 2003); M. A. Rebell and A. R. Block, *Equality and Education: Federal Civil Rights Enforcement in the New York City School System* (Princeton University Press, 1985).

[35] Vanhala, *Making Rights a Reality?*, Chapters 3–4; T. Q. Ridell, 'The Impact of Legal Mobilization and Judicial Decisions: The Case of Official Minority-Language Education Policy in Canada for Francophones Outside Quebec' (2004) 38 *Law and Society Review* 584; L. Sossin 'How Judicial Decisions Influence Bureaucracy in Canada', in M. Hertogh and S. Halliday (eds.), *Judicial Review and Bureaucratic Impact: International and Interdisciplinary Perspectives* (Cambridge University Press, 2004), pp. 146–52.

though more subtle impact of human rights adjudication in the UK.[36] So it seems clear that courts can and often do offer worthwhile benefits. This would be enough to support incrementalism, but note must be taken of the coda to Rosenberg's book that argues that advocates may be distracted by legal action and thus divert resources away from more meaningful political action, a prospect captured colourfully with the metaphor of a 'fly-paper court'.[37] The evidence he marshals here is sparse, although there is good evidence elsewhere of resistance by the National Association for the Advancement of Colored People (NAACP) to direct action immediately after the *Brown* case.[38] In my view, Rosenberg misunderstands the nature of advocacy, which is normally multi-pronged, with litigation being one strategy run simultaneously with others.[39] The contrary view risks denigrating the views and experiences of activists and rights-constituencies. As Malcolm Feeley notes, '[w]e know why flies are attracted to fly-paper; flypaper is aromatic and flies are dumb. But the people Rosenberg identifies ... are not so dumb; they are prominent lawyers, journalists, and public officials. How can they be so misguided?'[40] One relevant non-dumb view, forged in the aftermath of *Brown* by the chief architect of direct action, was that of Martin Luther King Jr. He attacked the 'fallacious and dangerously divisive philosophy' that viewed law and protest as mutually exclusive:

> Direct action is not a substitute for work in the courts and halls of government. Bringing about passage of a new and broad law by a city council, state legislature or Congress, or pleading cases before the courts of the land, does not eliminate the necessity for bringing about the mass dramatization of injustice in front of a city hall. Indeed, direct action and legal action complement one another; when skilfully employed, each becomes

---

[36] Equality and Human Rights Commission, *Human Rights Inquiry: Report of the EHRC* (London: EHRC, 2009), esp. Appendix 4.

[37] Rosenberg, *The Hollow Hope*, Chapter 12.

[38] Klarman, *From Jim Crow to Civil Rights*, pp. 377–80. Mack, 'Rethinking Civil Rights Era Lawyering', presents evidence to suggest that this view, if true, was not representative of the civil rights movement as a whole, and A. Sarat and S. Scheingold suggest that cause lawyers today are less likely to fall into such a trap: 'Introduction', in A. Sarat and A. Scheingold (eds.), *Cause Lawyers and Social Movements* (Stanford University Press, 2010), p. 10.

[39] M. McCann and H. Silverstein, 'Rethinking Law's Allurements: A Relational Analysis of Social Movement Lawyers in the United States', in A. Sarat and S. Scheingold (eds.), *Cause Lawyering and the State in a Global Era* (New York: Oxford University Press, 1998), p. 261.

[40] Feeley, 'Hollow Hopes, Flypaper, and Metaphors', 757.

more effective. The chronology of the sit-ins confirms this observation ...
[B]y the creative use of the law, it was possible to prove that officials com-
bating the demonstrations were using the power of the police state to
deny the Negro equal protection of the law. This brought many of the
cases squarely under the jurisdiction of the Fourteenth Amendment. As
a consequence of combining direct and legal action, far-reaching precedents were established, which served, in turn, to extend the areas of
desegregation.[41]

King Jr's observations coincide entirely with a range of legal mobilisation
studies that show an iterative symbiosis between campaigning and litigation. This point is exemplified in the work of Michael McCann, but was the
main point of the second half of Stuart Scheingold's earlier classic on legal
mobilisation, and is confirmed in subsequent studies by Malcolm Feeley
and Edward Rubin on prison reform, Charles Epp, and many others.[42]

B   Impact and administrative justice

The fascination with macro-level significant reform is a peculiarly
American phenomenon. In Britain and elsewhere in the Commonwealth,
there has been a rich, empirically informed literature on the way in which
individuated decision-making in complex welfare bureaucracies can be
made more fair and responsive to user needs. This is the micro-level literature on impact that is broadly concerned with administrative justice.[43]

---

[41] Martin Luther King Jr., *Why We Can't Wait* (New York: Signet, 2000 [1964]), pp. 28–9.
For his other reflections on courts, see pp. 4–5, 20, 57–8. See also pp. 97–8. King was also
critical of the NAACP's hostility to direct action as well: see Klarman, *From Jim Crow to
Civil Rights*, pp. 379–80.

[42] Scheingold, *The Politics of Rights*; Feeley and Rubin, *Judicial Policy Making in the Modern
State*; M. McCann, *Rights at Work: Pay Equity Reform and the Politics of Legal Mobilization*
(University of Chicago Press, 1994); C. Epp, *The Rights Revolution: Lawyers, Activists
and Supreme Court in Comparative Perspective* (University of Chicago Press, 1998); Epp,
Making Rights Real; Vanhala, *Making Rights a Reality?* For surveys of the voluminous
literature, see M. McCann, 'Litigation and Legal Mobilization' and C. Epp, 'Law as an
Instrument of Social Reform', in K. E. Whittington, R. D. Kelemen, and G. A. Caldeira
(eds.) *The Oxford Handbook of Law and Politics* (New York: Oxford University Press,
2010), Chapters 30 and 34 respectively.

[43] In addition to others discussed below, see also H. Street, *Justice in the Welfare State*
(London: Steven & Sons, 1968); M. Adler and A. Bradley (eds.), *Justice, Discretion and
Poverty: Supplementary Benefit Appeal Tribunals in Britain* (London: Professional Books,
1975); M. Adler and S. Asquith (eds.), *Discretion and Welfare* (London: Heinemann
Educational, 1981); R. Sainsbury, 'Administrative Justice: Discretion and Procedure in
Social Security Decision-Making', in K. Hawkins (ed.), *The Uses of Discretion* (Oxford
University Press, 1992); J. Baldwin, N. Wikeley, and R. Young, *Judging Social Security: The
Adjudication of Claims for Benefit in Britain* (Oxford: Clarendon Press, 1992); T. Buck,

Much of the insightful academic research pertinent to social rights concerns the impact (or lack thereof) of judicial review on front-line decision-making in welfare bureaucracies. Much of it is critical of judicial control.

Simon Halliday and Ian Loveland have both completed careful examinations of homelessness decision-making in Britain, including extensive interviewing and participant observation of three local authorities.[44] Both concluded that there was widespread failure to comply with the letter and spirit of administrative law within such authorities.[45] Loveland concludes that 'optimism about judicial review's "ripple effect" in respect of homelessness decisions is largely unfounded – not just between authorities, but also within them'.[46] Halliday's conclusions are similar.[47] The studies both conclude, essentially, that (1) there are few applications for judicial review; (2) there is little absorption of legal standards identified on review; and (3) there is a problem of 'creative compliance', whereby authorities exploit their knowledge of the legal process to avoid legal control either through abuse of legal process or through 'bullet-proofing' decisions.[48] Overall, the picture is of local authorities acting largely in subtle evasion if not outright defiance of public law duties identified in court.

Both Genevra Richardson and Jill Peay observe a clash of bureaucratic, clinical, and legal cultures in their examinations of the decision-making of the Mental Health Review Tribunals.[49] Peay observes that there is a fundamental and possibly irresolvable tension between the legalism of the tribunal and the clinical imperatives and expertise of the bureaucracy. This leads to deliberate evasion and non-compliance with tribunal decision-making. Richardson and John Machin examined the phenomenon of judicial review of the Mental Health Review Tribunal's

---

Judicial Review and Social Welfare (London: Pinter, 1998); C. Harlow and R. Rawlings, *Law and Administration* (3rd edn, Cambridge University Press, 2009), esp. Chapter 11; T. Buck, D. Bonner and R. Sainsbury, *Making Social Security Law: The Role and Work of the Social Security and Child Support Commissioners* (Aldershot: Ashgate, 2005).

[44] S. Halliday, *Judicial Review and Compliance with Administrative Law* (Oxford: Hart Publishing, 2004); I. Loveland, *Housing Homeless Persons* (Oxford University Press, 1995).

[45] Loveland, *Housing Homeless Persons*, p. 302; Halliday, *Judicial Review and Compliance with Administrative Law*, Chapter 3.

[46] Loveland, *Housing Homeless Persons*, p. 281.

[47] Halliday, *Judicial Review and Compliance with Administrative Law*, Chapters 2–4.

[48] *Ibid.*, pp. 61–5; Loveland, *Housing Homeless Persons,* Chapter 11 generally.

[49] J. Peay, *Tribunals on Trial: A Study of Decision-Making under the Mental Health Act 1983* (Oxford: Clarendon Press, 1989); G. Richardson, 'Impact Studies in the UK', in M. Hertogh and S. Halliday, *Judicial Review and Bureaucratic Impact: International and Interdisciplinary Perspectives* (Cambridge University Press, 2004), p. 103.

decision-making.[50] It was expected that judicial review of a quasi-judicial tribunal would be relatively effective in securing compliance, due to the legal conscientiousness of both bodies. But the data surprisingly pointed in the other direction, including on core areas of judicial competence such as statutory interpretation and procedural fairness determinations.

At the outset of *Bureaucratic Justice*, Jerry Mashaw sets the tone of his book by claiming that, in America, 'in a study of hearings and judicial review in the Social Security disability program my colleagues and I found that the tens of thousands of judicial review proceedings that have been held since the disability program's inception have either had no perceptible impact on its functioning or have made it worse'.[51] Mashaw's chief preoccupation is with presenting and defending the ideal of bureaucratic rationality as the dominant and most effective way to secure administrative justice within the Social Security Administration.[52]

These studies and indeed a powerful trend in UK impact scholarship indicate a limited function for judicial review to influence bureaucratic behaviour. The studies are enlightening not least of all for their wealth of data. But they also raise troubling issues, and no strong conclusion that judicial review is irrelevant or marginal to bureaucratic behaviour can emerge from them. First, it can be noted that the UK literature discussed above might not be representative of the administrative justice field as a whole. Some of the studies mentioned concern groups who have a limited capacity for using the legal process: the homeless and the mentally incapacitated. These groups to some extent lack support structures that use legal mobilisation to attain goals. The research conducted by Loveland and Halliday was also within the legal shadow cast by the *ex parte Puhlhofer* case, which infamously directed High Court judges not to allow applications for review in homelessness cases.[53] Other forms of welfare rights adjudication have returned more positive results. In social security adjudication, for instance, and notably different from Mashaw's findings in the United States, Baldwin, Wikeley, and Young paint a rosier picture:

---

[50] Richardson, 'Impact Studies in the UK', pp. 115–26.

[51] J. Mashaw, *Bureaucratic Justice* (New Haven: Yale University Press, 1985), p. 7.

[52] For a critical review, see A. Ogus, 'Bureaucrats as Institutional Heroes' (1987) 7 *Oxford Journal of Legal Studies* 305.

[53] *R v. Hillingdon LBC, ex parte Puhlhofer* [1986] 1 AC 485 (HL) 518: 'Where the existence or non-existence of a fact is left to the judgment and discretion of a public body and that fact involves a broad spectrum ranging from the obvious to the debatable to the just conceivable, it is the duty of the court to leave the decision of that fact to the public body to whom Parliament has entrusted the decision making power save in a case where it is obvious that the public body ... are acting perversely.'

The measures aimed at improving social security tribunals have undoubtedly had a wider impact on the system as a whole. In particular, the internal review carried out by an adjudication officer on receiving an appeal can be much influenced by the prospect of the case being heard by an independent tribunal. Tribunals perform a useful educative function not only in this sense but also for those adjudication officers who appear as presenting officers at appeal hearings. To some extent at least, the lessons learnt in presenting cases are carried over into the routine business of adjudication and the carrying out of internal reviews … Social security appeal tribunals have opened up procedures to critical scrutiny, shed light on the work of adjudication officers, and blown fresh judicial air into the anonymous corridors of local offices.[54]

Trevor Buck's empirical work on the Discretionary Social Fund in Britain and social security law-making more generally is also much more upbeat,[55] as is Vanhala's study of disability rights mobilisation in Canada and the UK.[56] Hammond offered a similar view in the UK Treasury context.[57] And there is absolutely no doubt, notwithstanding the findings in Richardson's and Peay's studies, that the field of mental health law has been significantly restructured as a result of the European Convention on Human Rights, both legislatively and administratively.[58] Despite his critical themes, Mashaw does in fact, as his later work confirms, believe

---

[54] Baldwin *et al.*, *Judging Social Security*, pp. 208–9.

[55] T. Buck, 'Judicial Review and the Discretionary Social Fund: The Impact on a Respondent Organisation', in Buck, *Judicial Review and Social Welfare* (London: Pinter, 1998). See also more generally Buck *et al.*, *Making Social Security Law*. Cf. M. Sunkin and K. Pick, 'The Changing Impact of Judicial Review' [2001] *Public Law* 736 (noting a more uneven record of compliance).

[56] Vanhala, *Making Rights a Reality?*

[57] A. H. Hammond 'Judicial Review: The Continuing Interplay Between Law and Policy' [1998] *Public Law* 34. Richardson, 'Impact Studies in the UK', p. 110, views this as exceptionally optimistic.

[58] Thus far, two s. 4 declarations of incompatibility under the HRA concerned deficiencies with the Mental Health Act regime: see *R (on the application of H)* v. *Mental Health Review Tribunal for the North and East London Region & the Secretary of State for Health*; [2001] EWCA Civ 415 (remedied by Mental Health Act 1983 (Remedial) Order 2001 (SI 2001 No.3712)); *R (on the application of M)* v. *Secretary of State for Health Administrative Court* [2003] EWHC 1094 (Admin) (remedied by ss. 23–26 of the Mental Health Act 2007). However, the most sweeping reforms arose as a result of *HL* v. *United Kingdom* (2004) 40 EHRR 761 (ECtHR) (the *Bournewood* case), which led to a reform of the system and introduction of the Mental Capacity Act 2005. See also Department of Health, *Code of Practice: Mental Health Act 1983* (London: TSO, 2008), especially s. 1 ('statement of guiding principles' which have been framed according to human rights principles and which 'necessarily includes compliance with the Human Rights Act 1998'). Mental health non-legal practitioners also receive extensive human rights training and often know the *Bournewood* case by name.

that courts play an important if not crucial role in the overall account-ability landscape – his work is best read as emphasising that different models of accountability compete with one another and the role for legal accountability must be sensitive to that fact by not unduly disrupting other mechanisms.[59]

The second problem is that it is further doubtful whether these studies, notwithstanding their participant-observation character, take adequate note of how practitioners themselves view the role of law and human rights law in particular. The leading practitioner's manual in men-tal health law – used by front-line practitioners and tribunal members alike – shows the pervasive influence of judicial decisions, the Human Rights Act 1998 (HRA) and law and guidance.[60] The very first sentence of *Blackstone's Police Operational Handbook 2010* is '[s]ince its introduc-tion the HRA has greatly affected operational policing'.[61] A curious fact revealed in Vanhala's study of UK disability rights campaigning was that groups having greater management representation of the disabled constituency they represented were more likely to engage in litigation activity.[62]

Third, other countries also return more mixed results than the down-beat British studies. In Canada, as Sossin's study shows, there was dis-semination of soft-law memoranda and other materials, which seemed to have a concrete impact on bureaucratic practice.[63] Similar results were recorded in Australia,[64] and quite naturally in the USA, where

---

[59] See his 'Bureaucracy, Democracy and Judicial Review: The Uneasy Coexistence of Legal, Managerial and Political Accountability', in R. F. Durant (ed.), *The Oxford Handbook of American Bureaucracy* (New York: Oxford University Press, 2010), Chapter 24. The last pages in particular echo almost perfectly the approach this book takes.

[60] The 'bible' for legal and non-legal practitioners of mental health in Britain is R. Jones, *Mental Health Act Manual* (8th edn, London: Thomson Reuters, 2008). Practitioners report that this book is used in preference to the government's Code of Practice cited above.

[61] I. Bridges (ed.), *Blackstone's Police Operational Handbook 2010: Law* (Oxford University Press, 2010), p. 1. The editor was a police officer for thirty years and is senior legal adviser at the Police National Legal Database. See also Epp, *Making Rights Real*, Chapter 7 (on the important role of tort liability in the fight against institutional racism in the British police); see also Equality and Human Rights Commission, *Human Rights Inquiry*, pp. 51–2.

[62] Vanhala, *Making Rights a Reality?*, pp. 166–7.

[63] Sossin, 'How Judicial Decisions Influence Bureaucracy in Canada'.

[64] R. Creyke and J. McMillan, 'The Operation of Judicial Review in Australia', in M. Hertogh and S. Halliday (eds.), *Judicial Review and Bureaucratic Impact: International and Interdisciplinary Perspectives* (Cambridge University Press, 2004), p. 161.

there can be little doubt of the more micro-level influence of structural injunctions.[65] Much of the research reviewed in section II.1 also presented evidence of impact.

Fourth, the studies do not for the most part consider the value of individual redress. Many writers look for evidence of policy-level impact, and whether social movements have achieved their collective goals. But just as lawyers often overestimate policy impact, these writers underrate the importance of individual redress. Figures from the UK social security tribunals, for instance, show that, in a recent year, about 38 per cent of those taking their claims through to hearing were successful – which amounted in one representative year to over 77,000 successful claims before the social security tribunals, not counting those that were negotiated to their satisfaction.[66] The number of cases taken forward in judicial review is much smaller, but the figures concerning cases proceeding to substantive hearing do not tell the entire impact story. As Bondy and Sunkin have shown in recent research, 'for every ten threats of litigation more than six are resolved without proceedings being commenced' and that 'the majority of threats were resolved when the authorities accepted the claim'.[67] Legal activity can clothe people with rights, and possessing rights is a real form of individual empowerment. To say individual redress is unimportant is to ignore the importance of access to justice and legal needs. Practitioners recognise that it was no accident that the Legal Aid and Advice Act 1949 was introduced along with the other key pillars of the modern British welfare state.

Fifth, the research has tended to be very much on the qualitative end of things. There is certainly an important role for qualitative research, but absent more quantitative data it is difficult to draw any conclusions about whether judicial review and legal accountability are marginal.[68] A more

---

[65] M. M. Feeley, 'Implementing Court Orders in the United States: Judges as Executives', in M. Hertogh and S. Halliday (eds.), *Judicial Review and Bureaucratic Impact: International and Interdisciplinary Perspectives* (Cambridge University Press, 2004), p. 221. See also Chapter 9, section III.A.3, and Chapter 10, section IV.B.

[66] Quarterly Statistics for the Tribunal Service, 3rd Quarter, 2010–2011, 1 October 2010–31 December 2010, 'Table 1.2d SSCS Outcomes by Benefit Type' (Ministry of Justice, 31 March 2011, p. 34 (available at www.justice.gov.uk/publications/statistics-and-data/tribunals/quarterly.htm) provides statistics for that Quarter (comparing with overall disposal rate in Table 1.2c).

[67] V. Bondy and M. Sunkin, 'Settlement in Judicial Review Proceedings' [2009] *Public Law* 237, 244.

[68] Notably, much of the work by McCann and Epp is also qualitative, but it is usually combined with quantitative data, and I would argue that the views of activists themselves are crucial to assessing the value of law to mobilisation, whereas the opinions of

recent survey of impact by Sunkin and colleagues employs a quite sophisticated quantitative methodology.[69] Their research assessed the impact of
judicial review cases (administrative law review) on local authority performance in England. They examined multivariate data relating to about
150 authorities over a three-year period, comparing the extent of judicial
review cases and the impact it had on their rating by public sector auditors (while controlling for several variables).[70] They found strong support
for the view that judicial review not only did not worsen performance
(as some critics maintained), but in fact was correlated in a statistically
significant way to modest improvements in performance over time. The
Public Law Project's research into the impact of the HRA on the practice of judicial review in the early days of the Act is also illuminating.
The study employed a quantitative and qualitative methodology, not only
tracking the number of claims overall in which human rights arguments
were made at both the permission and substantive stages, but also sam-
pling a profile of thirty-nine cases and assessing qualitatively whether the
human rights arguments added any value to the claims that were in most
cases viable on ordinary public law principles.[71] The report found that the
HRA was cited in just under half of all judicial review claims analysed,
that it had not led to a substantial increase in overall claims, and that,
although the differences were not great in most cases and the Act had
been overused, it had added value, in the profile sample, to twenty-two
cases and in thirteen of these it added 20 per cent or more value in the
views of consultant assessors.[72] The impact was by no means great, but
neither was it negligible or marginal. Claimants were on the whole better
off with the HRA.

C   A pathology of legalism?

The 'pathology of legalism' is a phrase borrowed from Richard Titmuss'
important 1971 essay 'Welfare "Rights", Law and Discretion', in which

administrative decision-makers are not crucial to whether they actually are abiding by or
even internalising norms.

[69] L. Platt, M. Sunkin and K. Calvo, 'Judicial Review Litigation as an Incentive to Change
in Local Authority Public Services in England and Wales' (2010) 20 *Journal of Public
Administration Research and Theory*, 243–60.

[70] They used the Comprehensive Performance Assessment scores applied by the Audit
Commission.

[71] V. Bondy, *The Impact of the Human Rights Act on Judicial Review: An Empirical Study*
(London: Public Law Project, 2003).

[72] *Ibid.*, pp. 28–30, 32.

he criticised the tendency towards legalism and rights in the activist discourse of the 1960s and 1970s.[73] He defined legalism as 'insistence on legal rules based on precedent and responsive only very slowly to rapidly changing human needs and circumstances'.[74] One example given by Titmuss of an excessive form of rigidity is a definition of an entitlement in precise material and itemised terms which, by prohibiting flexibility, 'would mean that whatever the level of provision it would become the maximum which no official or tribunal could exceed.'[75] A similar phenomenon was examined by Mashaw, namely, the use of 'grid regulations' in social security decision-making. The 'grid regulations' present a series of data – age, exertion capability, type of occupation, transferability of skills – in a tabulated form that is used somewhat mechanically to designate the eligibility of a given person for assistance.[76] He notes the obvious potential for the constriction of beneficially exercised discretion.

The existence of administrative discretion has since the days of Albert Venn Dicey[77] been regarded by many lawyers as a form of tyranny, unhinged from the tight confines of the rule of law. This attitude was criticised by Kenneth Culp Davis as representing the 'extravagant version of the rule of law'.[78] Davis sought to demonstrate both why discretion was necessary and important, and how it could be structured to avoid the unsettling degree of power it appeared to confer on public officials.[79] But critics in the UK accused Davis of introducing too much rulish behaviour into discretion: 'The rule may not so much offer consistency as a way to "routinize" and rationalise decisions – its major result may be to limit the attention that is paid to the circumstances of a particular case.'[80] Others argue that certain legalistic reforms to social security adjudication have been little more than deflective posturing dressed up in rights language in order to conceal serious substantive retrenchment in the availability of benefits.[81]

---

[73] (1971) 42 Political Quarterly 113. For a similar but more theoretical argument, see R. Goodin, 'Welfare, Rights and Discretion' (1986) 6 Oxford Journal of Legal Studies 232.

[74] Titmuss, 'Welfare "Rights", Law and Discretion', 124–5.

[75] Ibid., 126.

[76] Mashaw, Bureaucratic Justice, pp. 116–23.

[77] A. V. Dicey, Introduction to the Law of the Constitution (8th edn, London: MacMillan, 1915) is widely regarded as the most historically important single text in English constitutional law.

[78] Davis, Discretionary Justice, pp. 28–33.

[79] Ibid., Chapter IV.

[80] R. Baldwin, Rules and Government (Oxford University Press, 1995), p. 14; see esp. R. Baldwin and K. Hawkins, 'Discretionary Justice: Davis Reconsidered' [1984] Public Law 570.

[81] T. Prosser, 'Poverty, Ideology and Legality: Supplementary Benefit Appeals Tribunals and their Predecessors' (1977) 4 British Journal of Law and Society 44. Concerning the

Some of these concerns are true but others are exaggerated. First, Titmuss offers a simplistic account of legalism and rules. He confuses the more determinate rules in contract and tort with the more flexible legal standards and remedies used in administrative law. Indeed, the undue fettering of discretion by decision-makers who have a choice of alternatives is itself illegal, and courts have often been used to battle against inflexible administration, as Chapter 9 of this book explains. Second, rules can be used as a floor and not a ceiling for the assessment of statutory benefits: '[it is] always open to the parties to go beyond their statutory obligations.'[82] On the other hand, there can be certain benefits to having a regulated, 'rulish' type system. Despite his awareness of the rigidity of the grid regulations, Mashaw nonetheless endorsed them, because the potential for inaccuracy (and presumably bias)[83] without the grid was extraordinary, and because the grids did in fact have exceptions and open-textured standards that reduced the potential for mechanical application.[84] Lack of legal (adjudicative) accountability can present the same problem, and its use of the same flexibility. Third, the problem with tight rules is in many cases a problem not with the law courts and tribunals, but with political decision-making about confining the powers of administration to exercise beneficial discretion. Rules can easily be framed to impose duties or rights of a claimant-friendly character, while also conferring discretions to go beyond these duties. Part VII of the Housing Act 1996 (concerning homelessness) does precisely this, and the existence of enforceable duties has been crucial in giving the homeless real rights to housing in the UK. Chapter 9 shows that constitutional legal accountability can be used as a tool for maintaining flexibility in social welfare policy.

By far the most damaging fact for Titmuss' thesis about pathological legalism is that it is wholly at odds with the no-impact literature. In fact, one can detect a common pattern of oscillation in the critical literature between two incompatible claims: either too much law, or so little influence as to make it irrelevant. A particular discussion in Simon Halliday's study demonstrates this phenomenon. He records that in the case of one local authority, the content of interview guidance used for homelessness decision-making had been developed largely in reference to experiences

---

similarly insidious nature of the Social Security Act 1998, see M. Adler, 'Substantive Justice and Procedural Fairness in Social Security, UK', in P. Robson and A. Kjønstad (eds.), *Poverty and the Law* (Oxford: Hart Publishing, 2001), p. 121.

[82] *Cowl* v. *Plymouth City Council* [2001] EWCA Civ 193 [26].

[83] S. Halliday, 'Institutional Racism in Bureaucratic Decision-Making: A Case Study in the Administration of Homelessness Law' (2000) 27 *Journal of Law and Society* 449.

[84] Mashaw, *Bureaucratic Justice*, pp. 120–3.

of judicial review.[85] But despite this apparent evidence of legal impact, Halliday highlights what he regards as excessive formalism and constriction of discretion.[86] However, one cannot have it both ways. If the no-impact claim is one extreme of the spectrum, then the pathology of legalism is the other. And while both claims are sometimes true, surely wisdom is the mean that lies between them. At the present time that mean is a familiar one: some impact, occasionally too much, more often too little.

D   A hollow hope for the poor?

Many accept as a virtual truism that courts provide little solace for the poor. There are studies in the United States showing how the poor have had trouble using law to achieve their goals.[87] In a now somewhat dated study, *Test Cases for the Poor,* Tony Prosser reports that welfare rights advocates in Britain and in some US cases were frustrated and in many cases their victories were legislatively reversed.[88] His conclusions are ominous:

> [I]n the field of social welfare the courts alone are most unlikely to be a useful vehicle for achieving social change … [W]hile the courts cannot be ignored, they cannot be relied upon to be friends of the poor … [T]he role of courts is overall marginal.[89]

But if we are to look more closely at the figures concerning legal needs and access to justice in public law in Britain, these claims are either false or require significant qualification. For one thing, the Child Poverty Action Group (CPAG), which published Prosser's study, itself continues to run a quite active 'test case' programme.[90] More empirically rigorous evidence is evident in Hazel Genn's important *Paths to Justice* study, an extensive qualitative and quantitative survey of legal needs in England and Wales.[91] According to that study, over a quarter of those respondents

---

[85] *Ibid.*, p. 77.   [86] *Ibid.*, pp. 77–8.

[87] See McCann, 'Litigation and Legal Mobilization', 528–9 (and studies cited therein); Epp, 'Law as an Instrument of Social Reform', 608–9 (and the studies cited therein).

[88] T. Prosser, *Test Cases for the Poor: Legal Techniques in the Politics of Social Welfare* (London: Child Poverty Action Group, 1983). See also C. Harlow and R. Rawlings, *Pressure through Law* (London: Routledge, 1992).

[89] Prosser, *Test Cases for the Poor*, pp. 83, 85, 86.

[90] At the time of writing, CPAG lists ten test cases involving welfare rights claims, and even has a section for 'test cases needed' on its website: see www.cpag.org.uk/.

[91] H. Genn *et al.*, *Paths to Justice: What People Do and Think About Going to Law* (Oxford: Hart Publishing, 1999).

who incurred legal costs were legally aided.[92] Other recent studies have found that judicial review is actually higher in London boroughs that are more marginalised and poorer.[93] Indeed, the poor in Britain are actually *more likely* to consult a lawyer in a grievance against the government than are the wealthy or middle classes.[94] While it is no doubt relevant, it is not only the UK's relatively generous legal aid system that is significant here. Herbert Kritzer consolidated comparative studies on legal needs covering eight countries.[95] He found that the findings were 'remarkably consistent', in showing that 'income has relatively little impact on decisions to seek the assistance or advice of a lawyer'.[96] While this conclusion may be too rosy,[97] it shows that the received wisdom on the issue requires revisitation. The data on this topic is in flux, and is dependent to some extent on legal aid provision, which fluctuates within and between countries. Yet a recent snapshot can shed further light on the matter. Dr Nigel Balmer (University College London) and I analysed the data from the 2006-2009 English and Welsh Civil and Social Justice Survey, a legal needs survey based on face-to-face interviews with 10,537 respondents, and which involved in-depth analysis of what respondents did about 6,112 justiciable problems.[98] We determined the following: that in a subset of all justiciable problems relating chiefly to social welfare (i.e. homelessness, children, welfare benefits, rented social housing, and immigration, which

---

[92] *Ibid.*, p. 166. The figures that follow were taken from pp. 215–26. Earlier research that gives different results – focusing more negatively than the following figures – is distinguished and criticised in *ibid.*, pp. 5–9. See also H. M. Kritzer, 'To Lawyer or Not to Lawyer? Is that the question?' (2008) 5 *Journal of Empirical Legal Studies* 875 for further explanation of the incompatibility of earlier studies.

[93] Platt *et al.*, 'Judicial Review Litigation as an Incentive to Change in Local Authority Public Services', 243–60.

[94] Kritzer, 'To lawyer or not to lawyer', Figure 12, citing the data of P. Pleasence, N. Balmer, and A. Buck, *Causes of Action: Civil Law and Social Justice* (2nd edn, London: Legal Services Research Centre, 2006).

[95] Kritzer, 'To Lawyer or Not to Lawyer? (The countries included the United States, England and Wales, Canada, Australia, New Zealand, the Netherlands, and Japan).

[96] *Ibid.*, at 875.

[97] See the critique in P. Pleasence and N. J. Balmer, 'Caught in the Middle: Income, Justiciable Problems and Use of Lawyers' in M. Trebilcock, A. Duggan, and L. Sossin (eds.), *Middle Income Access to Justice* (University of Toronto Press, 2012).

[98] P. Pleasence, N. Balmer, A. Patel, and C. Denvir, *Civil Justice in England and Wales 2009: Report of the 2006–2009 English and Welsh Civil and Social Justice Survey* (London: Legal Services Commission, 2010). 'Justiciable problems' are those that could ultimately be subject to legal proceedings, and are non-trivial. Cutbacks to legal aid, which will take effect as this book goes to press, will presumably reduce access to courts and tribunals in a way material to this snapshot.

amounted to 772 justiciable problems), 9.8 per cent of such problems were ultimately subject to the commencement of legal proceedings in a court or tribunal (with this figure remaining at 9 per cent when considering only problems initiated by the individual and not the state). Further, roughly half of the persons involved in such proceedings belonged in the bottom third income bracket (which corresponds roughly to legal aid eligibility). More telling, this rate for the commencement of legal proceedings was almost identical to that applicable to all other justiciable problems in the survey (9.9 per cent). The courts and tribunals, in this snapshot (which omits law-driven settlements), are just as relevant to the resolution of welfare rights problems as they are for the other justiciable problems. And their role is not marginal in respect of either.

What about constitutional welfare rights in particular? If we begin with America – no paragon of social rights but which looked at one time like it might be on the cusp of a judicial step in that direction[99] – one can find in the work of Susan Lawrence and Martha Davis that quite substantial gains were made by welfare rights claimants through the Legal Services Program in the United States during the 1960s and 1970s, and advocates and some commentators believed that considerable advances were made in right to education litigation at the state constitution level.[100] Even the less enthusiastic findings by Jennifer Erkulwater, Shep Melnick, and Elizabeth Bussiere show that statutory and constitutional rights litigation provided notable gains for claimants asserting welfare rights.[101] Few apart from Mashaw have suggested that constitutional welfare rights claims may have done more harm than good.[102] The more common lamentation is that they failed to live up to their potential.

Outside America, there has not been a large amount of empirical research on the new generation of constitutional social rights litigation in

---

[99] F. I. Michelman, 'Foreword: On Protecting the Poor through the Fourteenth Amendment' (1968) 83 *Harvard Law Review* 7.

[100] S. E. Lawrence, *The Poor in Court: The Legal Services Program and Supreme Court Decision Making* (Princeton University Press, 1990); Davis, *Brutal Need*; Rebell and Block, *Equality and Education*; Lukemeyer, *Courts as Policymakers*. But see below, Chapter 9, section III.A.3 and Chapter 10, section VI.B for misgivings about this approach.

[101] Erkulwater, *Disability Rights*; R. S. Melnick, *Between the Lines: Interpreting Welfare Rights* (Washington DC: Brookings Institution Press, 1994); E. Brussiere, *(Dis)entitling the Poor: The Warren Court, Welfare Rights, and the American Political Tradition* (University Park, PA: Pennsylvania State University Press, 1997), pp. 158ff.

[102] In addition to *Bureaucratic Justice*, see also his *Due Process in the Administrative State* (New Haven: Yale University Press, 1985), and my commentary on these two works in Chapters 8 and 9.

particular. Another few studies from South Africa show that a constitutional right to health care was relied upon by campaigners both to defend government laws on licensing the generic production of antiretroviral drugs, and for quite significant gains against the government in respect of treatment of HIV and responding to the problem of Aids denialism in official quarters.[103] To the extent Canada's positive constitutional commitment to provide minority (French) language education where numbers warrant this is viewed as a constitutional social right, there is also evidence of positive impact.[104] These studies agree with the general claims made about legal mobilisation canvassed above.

Book-length empirical studies of constitutional social rights are a very recent phenomenon. One study of the impact of social rights litigation and social movements in South Africa, Brazil, India, and Nigeria found that on the whole '[u]nder certain conditions, legalization can bring some measure of dignity to those in our world who continue to live in conditions of extreme poverty and deprivation'.[105] The study borrowed significantly from Rosenberg's methodology and assumptions, and tested some of his theses. Notwithstanding this general finding, they also found that such litigation tended at present to favour the middle or lower middle classes more than the wholly marginalised.[106] Its conclusions wholly support the vision set out in this book, though the emphasis here on vulnerable groups would, I believe, correct some of the more questionable tendencies noted in that study. A contemporaneous study that examined the question in both empirical and theoretical terms found that newer democracies tended to provide for rights-rich constitutions, and that an increase in democracy coincided with an increase in social rights

---

[103] See M. Pieterse, 'Health, Social Movements, and Rights-based Litigation in South Africa' (2008) 35 *Journal of Law and Society,* 364, and especially M. Heywood, 'Preventing Mother-to-Child HIV Transmission in South Africa; Background, Strategies and Outcomes of the Treatment Action Campaign Case against the Minister of Health' (2003) 19 *South African Journal On Human Rights* 278; and Heywood, 'Debunking Conglomo-talk: A Case Study of the Amicus Curiae as an Instrument for Advocacy, Investigation and Mobilisation' (2001) 5 *Law, Democracy & Development* 133.

[104] Ridell, 'The Case of Official Minority-Language Education Policy in Canada'.

[105] V. Gauri and D. M. Brinks, 'Introduction: The Elements of Legalization and the Triangular Shape of Social and Economic Rights', in V. Gauri and D. M. Brinks (eds.), *Courting Social Justice: Judicial Enforcement of Social and Economic Rights in the Developing World* (Cambridge University Press, 2008), p. 35. Neither author is a lawyer.

[106] V. Gauri and D. M. Brinks, 'A New Policy Landscape: Legalizing Social and Economic Rights in the Developing World', in Gauri and Brinks (eds.), *Courting Social Justice: Judicial Enforcement of Social and Economic Rights in the Developing World*, Chapter 8, and esp. pp. 336–8.

litigation.[107] Although the findings were varied, it also found that the courts did provide an institutional voice for the poor in Hungary, South Africa, India, and in Latin America.

The most recent study of constitutional health rights litigation presents a more divided empirical record.[108] Its overall findings are nuanced, suggesting that in India and South Africa some important advances were made in health equity. Although the situation in India is described in more equivocal terms than in the studies presented above, the authors found that there is evidence of positive influence but that the impact of the indirect political effects is difficult to gauge. However, a superb set of more critical studies emerge in that book, building on earlier studies, that show alarming trends in Brazil and other Latin American countries.[109] Using an impeccably rigorous quantitative methodology, these authors have confirmed in independent studies that due to the Brazilian judges' willingness to enforce health claims while disregarding resource implications, they have ordered the provision of drugs to enormous numbers of claimants – up to 40,000 a year in recent years – consuming up to 4 per cent of the federal Ministry of Health's medicines budget, alongside a startling rate of growth.[110] That degree of allocative impact alone would itself be cause for great alarm (as Parts II and III of this book will make clear), but the point of the studies was even gloomier. They showed that those who gained more were the better-off and that the evidence suggests that the litigation actually worsened health equity by diverting health resources from cost-effective treatment for the poor towards

[107] R. Gargarella, P. Domingo, and T. Roux, *Courts and Social Transformation: A New Institutional Voice for the Poor?* (Aldershot: Ashgate, 2009).

[108] A. E. Yamin and S. Gloppen (eds.), *Litigation Health Rights: Can Courts Bring More Justice to Health?* (Cambridge, MA: Harvard University Press, 2011).

[109] See esp. O. Mæstad, L. Rakner, and O. L. A. Ferraz, 'Assessing the Impact of Health Rights Litigation: A Comparative Study of Argentina, Colombia, Costa Rica, India and South Africa', in Yamin and Gloppen (eds.), *Litigating Health Rights: Can Courts Bring More Justice to Health?*, Chapter 11. On Brazil in particular, see esp. V. Afonso da Silva and F. Vargas Terrazas, 'Claiming the Right to Health in Brazilian Courts: The Exclusion of the Already Excluded?' (2011) 36 *Law & Social Inquiry* 825; O. Ferraz, 'The Right to Health in the Courts of Brazil: Worsening Health Inequities?' (2009) 11 *Health and Human Rights: An International Journal* 33, and see now especially Ferraz, 'Brazil: Health Inequalities, Rights and Courts: The Social Impact of Judicialization of Health', in Yamin and Gloppen (eds.), *Litigating Health Rights: Can Courts Bring More Justice to Health?*, Chapter 4.

[110] See Mæstad *et al.*, 'Assessing the Impact of Health Rights Litigation', pp. 282, 290. Ferraz, 'Brazil: Health Inequalities, Rights and Courts', pp. 81–2 reports that between 2003 and 2009 there was a five-fold increase in cases and a twenty-fold increase in associated costs.

more expensive treatment for the wealthy (and in fewer numbers). The researchers judged the income of those using the courts by matching their residency to known data on average incomes, as well as by matching the number of cases involving doctors from private medical practices or hospitals instead of those coming from the state sector.

This is damning evidence of the way the system has worked in Brazil, Argentina, and Colombia. But it represents, as Octavio Ferraz calls it, 'the Brazilian model of the right to health litigation',[111] though it might rather be dubbed the 'Latin American model' given the broader findings in the book. The general problem in the Latin American cases is evident upon closer examination of the situation of Brazil. It was built doctrinally on a case that essentially found that resource constraints are irrelevant and that the state must respect the right to life.[112] That is a doctrinal error of colossal proportions, one rejected outright in this book, and rejected wholeheartedly in one of the earliest South African social rights cases,[113] and now also by the Colombian Supreme Court in its recognition of the problem these authors highlight. No writer – and certainly not the UN Committee on Economic, Social and Cultural Rights[114] – has to my knowledge ever proposed that judges disregard allocative impact entirely. And neither has anyone proposed that judges disregard the systemic implications of the individual remedies they give. One would not think such a principle needs formalisation, but I do so anyway in Chapter 10 under the idea of particularisation. It is implausible to think that the outcome in Latin America, on that point, is likely in the countries having the background political conditions outlined in Chapter 1. Therefore, in my view the problem lies with the approach of some of the Latin American judges and the legal doctrine used there, not with the very idea of constitutional

---

[111] Ferraz, 'The Right to Health in the Courts of Brazil', 35ff.

[112] *Ibid.*, 35 (quoting the judgment RE 271.286 AgR- RS (2000), *Relator Min. Celso de Mello*). A further problem, as Ferraz notes at 42 (n. 12), is that technically the courts have not been bound by any doctrine of precedent, which has meant that the courts need not formally consider the influence of their decision on other cases. This is incompatible with the first background social condition I identify in Chapter 1, namely, of common law adjudication that includes a doctrine of precedent.

[113] *Soobramoney* v. *Minister of Health (KwaZulu-Natal)*, 1997 (12) BCLR 1696 (CC); P. Alston and C. M. Scott 'Adjudicating Constitutional Priorities in a Transnational Context: A Comment on Soobramoney's Legacy and Grootboom's Promise' (2000) 16 *South African Journal of Human Rights* 206–68 (where the authors accept the outcome of the case as right but not its reasoning).

[114] Neither the minimum core obligations doctrine set out in General Comment No. 3, nor its elaboration by good writers such as David Bilchitz or Katherine Young, suggest anything to the contrary. See Chapter 4, section III.B.

social rights. The experience in India, South Africa, and Canada has been notably different, and it is only the basic outline of the South African model that this book endorses.

So, with due note taken of the important Latin American hiccup, the evidence on the whole suggests that constitutional welfare rights can provide an avenue for worthwhile social change, though we should expect it neither to revolutionise welfare provision nor secure the social minimum to all. This is an empirical question and it requires revisitation over time. At the moment, the record is positive enough to support constitutional adjudication, if caution is not thrown to the wind. I can thus return to the question of Irene Grootboom's death and what implications can be drawn from it. One outcome of the *Grootboom*[115] case of the South African Constitutional Court was that it led to two new chapters of the Housing Code,[116] new legislation that will channel state action into the foreseeable future. So Irene Grootboom may have died prematurely and penniless, but she left an important legacy in the fight for real social rights.

IV   Alternatives to courts: partner or substitute?

Even if constitutional legal accountability can provide for worthwhile change, only a fool would disregard the substantial remaining barriers in access to justice faced by impecunious claimants in their quest for justice in the welfare state. The courts can be daunting, affordable lawyers unavailable, political support for legal aid erratic, and social rights claims too numerous to be accommodated within the traditional court structure. And nor can it be forgotten that legal accountability can compete with and disrupt other avenues for providing administrative justice. Reflection on the topic of alternatives to courts is thus necessary. As the issue is peculiarly dependent on the legal context of particular jurisdictions, the discussion will concentrate on the United Kingdom. However, the institutions discussed find counterparts in many countries.

In discussing this matter, some authors distinguish helpfully between external and internal mechanisms of accountability.[117] Examples of internal mechanisms would consist of managerial control, internal review, audit, qualitative assessments, and so on. They play an important role in

[115] *Republic of South Africa* v. *Grootboom*, 2000 (11) BCLR 1169 (CC).

[116] K. McLean, 'Housing', in S. Woolman and others (eds.), *The Constitutional Law of South Africa* (2nd edn, Cape Town: Juta & Co., 2007), pp. 55–1, 55–144ff.

[117] M. Adler, 'A Socio-Legal Approach to Administrative Justice' (2003) 25 *Law and Policy* 323.

attaining justice in the welfare state. Yet no one suggests that they are any substitute for external oversight that allows individuals to lodge claims by right (individual redress). The best analyses of internal mechanisms suggest that legal accountability can compete with and upset the model of bureaucratic efficiency, and so the role for legal accountability must be framed in awareness of that fact. There is a need for some principle of coordination between adjudication and what Jerry Mashaw calls 'bureaucratic rationality' in his magisterial book *Bureaucratic Justice*. I outline my view of the appropriate degree of coordination in Part II of this book, and in particular in Chapters 7–9. Whether external mechanisms of accountability ought to be substitutes for courts is a more important consideration, because they can meet what appear to be legal needs in what at times looks to be a superior manner.

A   Specialised adjudication – tribunals

Tribunals were first established in the United Kingdom in 1911 to assess claims for unemployment benefits.[118] The reasons for forming the tribunals included interests of speed, cheapness, and efficiency.[119] There were also concerns that courts were biased in favour of employers or taxpayers, and used overly literal construction of statutes to frustrate the social aims of the legislation.[120] The tribunals offered a cheaper alternative to courts, and would have lay representation on the panel of adjudicators, which served a variety of functions, from offsetting concerns of bias, to being more accessible, to bringing subject-matter expertise to bear. Though these features have led commentators to emphasise the differences between courts and tribunals, there was always a functional similarity between them.[121] They grew in number and character,

---

[118] Street, *Justice in the Welfare State*, pp. 2–3. See generally: Donoughmore Committee, Report of the Committee on Ministers' Powers, Cmnd: 4060 (1932); Franks Committee, Report of the Committee on Tribunals and Inquiries, Cmnd 218 (1957) (the 'Franks Report'); P. Cane, *Administrative Tribunals and Adjudication* (Oxford: Hart Publishing, 2009).

[119] Franks Report, p. 9; P. P. Craig, *Administrative Law* (6th edn, London: Sweet & Maxwell, 2008), pp. 65–8; Street, *Justice in the Welfare State*, pp. 5–10.

[120] Craig, *Administrative Law*, 6th edn, pp. 55–6; Street, *Justice in the Welfare State*, pp. 5–6.

[121] Franks Report, [40]; All Souls/Justice, *Administrative Justice: Some Necessary Reforms* (Oxford University Press, 1988), Chapter 9, esp. 213–14; Craig, *Administrative Law*, 6th edn, pp. 68–9; Buck *et al.*, *Making Social Security Law*, p. 52, saying the Commissioners have evolved into the 'equivalent of a specialised branch of the High Court'.

in piecemeal fashion, and led to concerns over their unclear mandate and lack of transparency in procedures. The Franks Commission on Tribunals and Inquiries met and reported on the situation in 1957, its key findings being that the 'tribunals should properly be regarded as machinery provided by Parliament of adjudication rather than as part of the machinery of administration',[122] and that there should be a formal duty to give reasons to claimants, and that proceedings had to respect the principles of openness, fairness, and impartiality.[123] Even after the proposed reforms were largely adopted in 1958, the tribunals continued to grow in piecemeal fashion, and remained part of the administrative body they reviewed.

This was all changed by the Tribunals, Courts and Enforcement Act 2007, which rationalised the system by creating an Upper Tribunal to hear appeals and to exercise a judicial review function, consolidating the legal nature of this role both through the Upper Tribunal, and by creating a role of tribunal 'judges' that received a guarantee of judicial independence.[124] Tribunals are now composed of legally trained 'judges', and non-legally trained 'members', though both are appointed by the Judicial Appointments Commission. The Act also provided for the creation of a variety of First Tier Tribunal chambers, noteworthy among them being the Health, Education and Social Care (the 'HESC') Chamber and the Social Entitlement Chamber.[125]

Tribunals were and are quite similar to courts. Although they were not historically concerned with precedent in any strict sense, there is now an established practice of publishing precedent cases, and it is expected that they will be followed.[126] Nonetheless, some very important differences between courts and tribunals remain. The most important is lay representation and subject-matter expertise. For example, the Social Entitlement Chamber, when hearing disability allowance claims, will be composed of one legally trained chair, a registered medical practitioner, and a member having a recognised disability qualification as set out in other secondary legislation. For special educational needs, for example, the panel

---

[122] Franks Report, [9].   [123] Franks Report, [42].
[124] Sections 15–21 of the Tribunals, Courts and Enforcement Act 2007.
[125] S. 7(1) Tribunals, Courts and Enforcement Act 2007 empowers the Lord Chancellor to appoint chambers of the First Tier Tribunal and Upper Tribunal, which was given effect in The First-tier Tribunal and Upper Tribunal (Chambers) Order 2008.
[126] Street, *Justice in the Welfare State*, pp. 27–8; T. Buck, 'Precedent in Tribunals and the Development of Principles' (2006) 25 *Civil Justice Quarterly* 458.

must include one judge and two members having 'substantial experience of educational, child care, health, or social care matters'.[127] Similarly, it is noteworthy here that in addition to this subject-matter expertise, a claimant may benefit from a multi-member panel at first instance – something extremely rare in most courts of law. The tribunal also uses an 'enabling' or managerial procedure to help the claimant develop her case.[128]

Anyone concerned with social rights must welcome these institutional features. The reason one can be so optimistic about tribunals, however, is that they have taken the good of legal accountability and combined it with accessibility features and subject-matter expertise of professional social welfare experts. They are thus (notwithstanding their chequered development in Britain) an evolution of legal accountability, what I call specialised adjudicative expertise in Chapter 8. Though they are sometimes apparently viewed as home-grown non-legal forms of accountability, ever at risk of being judicialised into courts of law, they are in fact quite similar to analogous social and labour tribunals and courts in France and Germany.[129] In all cases, they manifest a balance between expertise and independent accountability. Despite this, claimants are also permitted to appeal to the Court of Appeal on any question of law with the leave of the Upper Tribunal or with that of the Court of Appeal,[130] and there is a quite steady flow of appeals from the various tribunals to the Court of

---

[127] *Practice Statement: Composition of Tribunals in relation to matters that fall to be decided by the Health, Education and Social Care Chamber on or after 18/1/10* (Lord Justice Carnwath, Senior President of Tribunals, 16 December 2009), adopted under First Tier Tribunal and Upper Tribunal (Composition of Tribunal) Order 2008.

[128] *CE/841/2010* [2010] UKUT 430 (AAC), [10] (Judge Lane) (the Upper Tribunal can override a claimant's request not to have an oral hearing where it is in the interests of justice (and that claimant) to do so). It is well known that the emphasis placed on this procedure by reformers has been used to dismiss calls for legal aid and legal representation (see *Transforming Public Services: Complaints, Redress and Tribunals*, Cm 6243 (2004), [2.10], [8.5], [10.14]), which is a mistake: see H. Genn and Y. Genn, *The Effectiveness of Representation at Tribunals* (London: Lord Chancellor's Department, 1989).

[129] For France, the body is the Tribunal des affaires de sécurité sociale, but the labour courts and incapacity benefits courts, which have non-legal labour and business representation, are similar. See *Code de la Securite Sociale*, Art. L-142–4. In Germany the Social Courts and two appellate bodies (Sozialgerichte, Landessozialgerichte, Bundessozialgericht) have legally trained and lay members right up to the highest appellate levels: see Sozialgerichtsgezetz, §§7–27, 29, 33, 39. There is a similar arrangement with its Labour Courts, with employer and employee representation: see Arbeitsgerichtsgesetz, §§ 2–3, 8, 14–31, 10–11, 33–39, 64.

[130] Section 13 of the Tribunals, Courts and Enforcement Act 2007. This right applies in respect of questions that are not 'excluded' (s. 13(1)) and the right to judicial review of other questions is now established in *R (Cart)* v. *The Upper Tribunal* [2011] UKSC 28.

Appeal and from there on to the Supreme Court.[131] Are these mistakes? Should the tribunals be seen as accountability substitutes for courts and thus immune from judicial oversight?

This raises a complex question about the relationship between courts and tribunals in the United Kingdom, and this is not the place to state a view on that broad but parochial doctrinal issue. Insofar as the question of constitutional accountability is concerned, however, there are distinct advantages offered by court structures that are not presently available in the tribunal system. Tribunals presently lack general jurisdiction, both as to remedies and topical coverage, though this has expanded some-what with the Upper Tribunal, which is effectively a court of law staffed by judges applying common law principles. They ordinarily lack the capacity to apply legal principles that are coordinated with other bodies of law, to ensure system-wide consistency. There is less use of participatory features such as interventions (though these are now allowed in the Upper Tribunal), and flexible rules of standing. The publicity function is greatly reduced, and the expressive role of articulating standards of right and fairness compares unfavourably with courts of law. Further, it is impossible to imagine the tribunals in the UK having the constitutional authority that courts have, nor the institutional position that could command the same kind of resources, including the number and quality of top barristers and interveners preparing the cases, the number and quality of judges giving judgment, and subsequent academic and professional scrutiny of the judgments. It is presumably for this reason that, although tribunals are empowered to apply the HRA in interpretation of legislation, the power to declare legislation incompatible with the Convention rights is expressly reserved for courts alone.[132] These institutional features and resources provide an asset for testing factual and principled claims through the adversarial process, comparing with foreign experiences, and so on. Where the legal issue has significant policy content or raises an issue of broad application, there is a distinct advantage to a ruling from an apex court of law[133] having the full constitutional authority and other prima facie benefits of legal accountability set out in section II of this chapter.

---

[131] Buck *et al.*, *Making Social Security Law*, pp. 94–96, 178.
[132] See ss. 3, 4, 6, 7(1) of the HRA.
[133] Specialised apex courts, such as labour, social security, or constitutional courts, are in my view a good idea provided they have the features described here.

What is rather needed is a principle of coordination as between courts and specialised tribunals. The appropriate principle is a doctrine of judicial restraint in respect of tribunal or other specialised adjudicative decisions, in view of their combination of subject-matter expertise with a good range of the benefits of legal accountability. There is currently a substantial measure of judicial deference to the expertise of tribunals for precisely these reasons.[134] In Canada the Supreme Court has found that deference on matters of human rights would be inappropriate.[135] Yet if constitutional social rights were at issue, this conclusion is questionable and the issue of how much weight to give to the tribunal's finding will depend heavily on the extent to which the narrow issue on appeal falls squarely within its subject-matter expertise. The analysis both here and in Chapter 8 supports that position.

B   Ombudsmen

Like tribunals, ombudsmen are highly important for providing redress for abuse of power in the resource allocation context.[136] In the UK they are statutorily empowered to investigate 'maladministration', and the main public service ombudsmen include a Parliamentary and Health Service Ombudsman and (presently) three Local Government Ombudsmen.[137] Richard Crossman MP described 'maladministration' during the passage of what became the Parliamentary Commissioner Act 1967 as consisting of 'bias, neglect, inattention, delay, incompetence, ineptitude, perversity, turpitude and arbitrariness and so on'.[138] Ombudsmen have flexible

---

[134] *Cooke* v. *Secretary of State for Social Security* [2002] 2 All ER 279 (Hale LJ, as she then was); *Hinchy* v. *Secretary of State for Work and Pensions* [2005] UKHL 16; *AH (Sudan)* v. *Secretary of State for the Home Department* [2007] UKHL 49.

[135] *Canada (Attorney-General)* v. *Mossop* [1993] 1 SCR 554; *Gould* v. *Yukon Order of Pioneers* [1996] 1 SCR 571 (notably, the Court highlighted the absence of an applicable ouster clause as part of its finding that a correctness standard of review should apply).

[136] M. Seneviratne, *Ombudsmen: Public Services and Administrative Justice* (London: Butterworths, 2002); All Souls/Justice, *Administrative Justice*, Chapter 5; see also L. Clements *Community Care and the Law* (3rd edn, London: Legal Action Group, 2004), p. 529. See more generally P. R. Verkuil, 'The Ombudsman and the Limits of the Adversary System' (1975) 75 *Columbia Law Review* 845. I have adopted the expression 'ombudsman' instead of 'ombudsperson' for reasons given in Chapter 1, n. 111.

[137] Parliamentary Commissioner Act 1967; Health Services Commissioners Act 1993; The Local Government Act 1974; The Local Government and Public Involvement in Health Act 2007; Regulatory Reform (Collaboration etc between Ombudsmen) Order 2007.

[138] Hansard, HC, vol. 734, col. 51, 18 October 1966 (Mr Crossman). See also Parliamentary Commissioner for Administration, Annual Report for 1993, HC 290 (1993/4) [7] for an

investigative powers, the power to recommend that compensation be awarded, and they can issue policy recommendations. The investigative nature and flexible approach of the ombudsman has led Marc Hertogh to contrast the *cooperative* approach of Dutch ombudsmen with the *coercive* approach of the Dutch administrative courts.[139] He finds that the coercive model of courts is less effective than the cooperative style of ombudsmen services for three principal reasons: the latter produces fewer ambivalent decisions (i.e. unclear ones); it produces less policy tension; it produces fewer defensive reactions.[140] Further, they are more accessible to welfare rights claimants than courts are. Ombudsmen can and do advise on policy matters,[141] and the central thrust of Hertogh's study is that their policy impact is greater. Ombudsmen may even have some of the administrative expertise associated with managers. And a not insignificant consideration is the fact that they often recommend compensation – always a blessing to a welfare rights claimant though rarely available in public law.

As widely recognised, resource allocation disputes are often polycentric, so the ombudsman's investigative powers could be a particular asset, allowing her to investigate the dynamic implications of a proposed course of action. For just these reasons, Lon Fuller pointed out the option of an ombudsman as a superior form to adjudication for the resolution of disputes over resource allocation.[142] The Parliamentary Ombudsman herself and other commentators have recently drawn attention to the potential for the ombudsman's role in human rights matters and social rights disputes in particular.[143]

As with tribunals, ombudsmen ought to be regarded as a highly effective and cost-effective avenue for ensuring day-to-day justice in the welfare state. However, they are no substitute for constitutional legal accountability. First, maladministration and legality are different, and the former is mostly operational whereas the latter can concern the

---

expanded list of grounds, and now Parliamentary Commissioner for Administration, *Principles of Good Administration* (London: TSO, 2007).

[139] M. Hertogh, 'Coercion, Cooperation, and Control: Understanding the Policy Impact of Administrative Courts and the Ombudsman in the Netherlands' (2001) 23 *Law and Policy* 54.

[140] *Ibid.*, 55–63.

[141] R. Kirkham 'Auditing by Stealth? Special Reports and the Ombudsman' [2004] *Public Law* 740, 747–8; Seneviratne, *Ombudsmen*, pp. 16–21.

[142] L. Fuller, *The Morality of Law* (rev. edn, New Haven: Yale University Press, 1969), pp. 176–7.

[143] A. Abraham, 'The Ombudsman and Individual Rights' (2009) 61 *Parliamentary Affairs* 370–9; N. O'Brien, 'Social Rights Adjudication and the Ombudsman' [2009] *Public Law* 466.

substantive rationale for some behaviour or policy, or the plausibility of interpretations of legislative or constitutional mandates. Second, the ombudsman is largely in control of the investigation and fact-finding process, thus diminishing the client's agency in building the case. As the All Souls/Justice Committee noted in connection with the idea of integrating the jurisdiction of the civil courts and Parliamentary Commissioner of Administration: 'Many lawyers would want to preserve [the] traditional weapons [of discovery and interrogatories] for establishing the facts and would be sceptical of the court's ability to carry out equally rigorous research.'[144] Third, there is the possibility of ombudsman pre-judgment, or lack of client control created inconspicuously by the combination of fact-determination and deciding.[145] There is not, to my knowledge, any grievance about ombudsman independence. But the procedures may at one point become suspect or require reforms that might render it more judicial if courts were not an alternative option. In Hertogh's study, for example, one policy-maker reported: '[i]f our first reaction indicates great practical difficulties, the ombudsman will sometimes reconsider his recommendation. This is regular practice, not official procedure. It is often just a matter of a mere telephone call.'[146] Another reported that '[w]e communicate [with the ombudsman's office] on a daily basis. We give each other the room to explain things.'[147] No doubt this gives the ombudsman insight, but transparency problems may be compounded as the stakes are raised.

Fourth, the resources are a problem for ombudsmen too. Luke Clements notes that the main drawbacks of the local authority ombudsmen are the apparent reluctance of the local ombudsman to accept many complaints, the fact that less than 5 per cent of all complaints lead to a report, and the substantial length of time taken to complete investigations.[148] That is a problem that can be remedied, but it might be easier for a government to underfund ombudsman services (as it typically does with various inspectors and regulators) than to do so with courts, given their constitutional authority and independence. Fifth, with notable exceptions,[149] ombudsmen presently have much less constitutional authority, little

---

[144] All Souls/Justice, *Administrative Justice*, p. 98.
[145] L. Fuller and J. D. Randall, 'Professional Responsibility: Report of the Joint Conference' (1958) 44 *American Bar Association Journal* 1159, 1160.
[146] Hertogh, 'Coercion, Cooperation and Control', p. 57.
[147] *Ibid.*, p. 56.
[148] Clements, *Community Care and the Law*, p. 529.
[149] R. Kirkham, 'Challenging the Authority of the Ombudsman: The Parliamentary Ombudsman's Special report on Wartime Detainees' (2006) 69 *Modern Law Review* 792.

by way of an expressive function, and even less of a publicity function, though this might change. Sixth, there remains an important role for law in constitutional questions. Important legal questions implicating rights in the welfare allocation context do arise, and may require authoritative legal ruling alongside the questions of fairness, reasonableness, proportionality and so on.[150] And of course, the compliance of legislation itself with social rights is something beyond the existing or foreseeable remit of the ombudsman. The decisions of courts in theory and often in practice are available to other citizens, unlike decisions of the ombudsman. One rarely bargains in the shadow of an ombudsman report.

As with tribunals, therefore, there is a need for a principle of coordination. Yet here, too, the present position in law and policy already reflects this need. Notably, the ombudsman herself sees a basic complementarity between her role and the role of the courts in judicial review, a view also shared by the Law Commission and most commentators.[151] The need for improved coordination is itself also now a trite observation, supported by both the ombudsmen and the Law Commission in proposals to further integrate and coordinate their respective functions.[152] If constitutional social rights were adopted, it is clear that the expertise of the ombudsman could be used as an alternative complaints venue at the first instance, but also as a partner where the respective competency of the ombudsman is relevant. The possibilities for cooperation will depend much on context and institutional culture. In the UK the ombudsmen enjoy a strong measure of independence and professionalism, and therefore they might be used to investigate disputes of a factual nature or to resolve complex questions of administrative workability, or to work out suitable settlement arrangements between claimants and respondent bureaucracies or ministers. Coordination would complement constitutional social rights.

C Alternative dispute resolution (ADR)

'Alternative dispute resolution' can mean many things, but I intend it here to refer to arbitration, conciliation, negotiation, and especially

---

[150] All Souls/Justice, *Administrative Justice*, p. 99.

[151] A. Abraham, 'The Ombudsman and "Paths to Justice": A Just Alternative or Just an Alternative?" [2008] *Public Law* 1; All Souls/Justice, *Administrative Justice*, pp. 98–9; Seneviratne, *Ombudsmen*, p. 63.

[152] Law Commission, 'Public Services Ombudsmen', Law Com No. 329, 13 July 2011. Recommendations 4 (judicial stay and referral) and 7 (reference to courts on point of law) (see [3.61] and [4.78] for the support of the public services ombudsmen).

mediation. In Britain Lord Woolf MR, in both judicial and extra-judicial capacity, strongly encouraged (to put it mildly) parties to public law disputes to consider the option of ADR (and particularly mediation).[153] The idea of mediation sounds attractive, and the confrontational aspect of litigation or 'adversarial legalism' is well known.[154] We can therefore cut to the chase: does mediation constitute an attractive compulsory alternative to adjudication? Unlike my more sanguine view of tribunals and ombudsmen, I argue here that the answer ought to be an emphatic 'no'.

There are a range of problems with the idea of pushing ADR too strongly, some concerned with substance, others with process, and others still with practicality. As to substance, since settlements are individualised and private, there is no public scrutiny of the decision-maker's behaviour. There is thus only minute incentive for authorities to change their behaviour, with no possibility of impact or system-wide application of precedent or absorption into guidance. Widespread use of mediation might actually undermine the development of the substantive law.[155]

The process-based concerns are greater still. First, there is Owen Fiss' well-known argument that due to the inequality of arms in many negotiations, there is great potential for injustice.[156] This has been shown to be the case also in the UK,[157] and is a particular problem in disputes between the state and the individual, especially the poor. Another is that given the nature of public law entitlements, it is hard to see how mediation is to contribute to negotiation. It cannot work without the framework of rules and sanctions provided by litigation as an incentive for parties to negotiate: '[i]t is the coercive, menacing character of the court process that is valued – it is the anvil against which the hammer of negotiation strikes; it is the second hand clapping.'[158] The problems of adversarial legalism can also at times be exaggerated. It is true that claimants found, in Genn's study, that courts and tribunals were more stressful and more alienating

---

[153] R (Cowl) v. Plymouth City Council [2001] EWCA Civ 1935 (per Lord Woolf). This reflects his influential proposals in his report, Access to Justice: The Final Report (London: TSO, 1996).

[154] R. A. Kagan, Adversarial Legalism: The American Way of Law (Cambridge, MA: Harvard University Press, 2003).

[155] H. Genn, Hard Bargaining: Out of Court Settlement in Personal Injury Actions (Oxford: Clarendon Press, 1987), p. 264.

[156] O. Fiss, 'Against Settlement' (1984) 93 Yale Law Journal 1073.

[157] Genn, Hard Bargaining, Chapters 6 and 9.

[158] Genn, Hard Bargaining, p. 11, quoting M. Galanter, 'Words and Deals: Using Negotiation to Teach about Legal Process' (1984) 12 Journal of Legal Education 268.

than mediation.[159] Yet, ironically perhaps, more tribunal and court users said they would definitely or probably repeat the process again, by comparison with those who used mediation: 85 per cent versus 67 per cent.[160] And further, the most common response of disappointed claimants was that they had not pursued sufficiently *formal* means to resolve their disputes.[161]

Lastly, it would seem the option presently has limited effectiveness outside commercial cases. By 2005 John Peysner and Mary Seneviratne had demonstrated that after the Woolf reforms, although there was a very substantial increase in out-of-court settlement, there was only a marginal uptake in the use of ADR.[162] The Public Law Project has reported similar findings in respect of public law claims in particular.[163] Though it was more positive about the potential for mediation, it showed that, contrary to widespread belief, it was not less expensive than adjudication, because lawyers are still needed (as all consultees agreed), and could not function as a substitute for recourse to courts.[164]

All told, there is presently no compelling evidence that ADR would be cheaper, fairer, or substantially more congenial to claimant interests. It may be, and some experimentation is no doubt a good idea. Yet one can say clearly that ADR is no substitute for legal accountability, and that any coordination between the two must be cautious.

V   Conclusion: the role of law in an incrementalist approach

After articulating perhaps the most renown and somewhat devastating critique of the various developments in post-war American administrative law, Richard Stewart concludes that 'reliance on judges and public interest litigants to rectify the failings of the administrative system may be indispensable if unorganized interests are to enjoy an acceptable measure of recognition'.[165] Mashaw, similarly, concluded even in his original tour de

---

[159] Genn *et al.*, *Paths to Justice*, pp. 194–5.
[160] *Ibid.*, 218, 222.
[161] *Ibid.*, 205. There was no suggestion that ADR itself was not sufficiently formal.
[162] J. Peysner and M. Seneviratne, *The Management of Civil Cases: The Courts and Post-Woolf Landscape* (DCA Research Series 9/05, 2005), pp. 35–46.
[163] V. Bondy, L. Mulcahy *et al.*, *Mediation and Judicial Review: An Empirical Research Study* (London: Public Law Project, 2009). See also M. Supperstone *et al.*, 'ADR and Public Law' [2006] *Public Law* 299.
[164] Bondy *et al.*, *Mediation and Judicial Review*, sections 6 and 7.
[165] R. B. Stewart, 'The Reformation of American Administrative Law' (1975) 88 *Harvard Law Review* 1669, 1809.

force that 'some mixture of justice models and decisional techniques may be necessary to deal with the predictable failures of the systems engineers to fully rationalize bureaucratic implementation'.[166] This sometimes grudging acceptance of the role of legal accountability is common among critics of judicial review, as well as those people who hold ambivalent to positive attitudes to it.[167] The lessons learned from the wide-ranging critical studies on judicial review is that the positive impact of legal accountability can often be overrated, that it would be naïve to expect it to usher in revolutionary social change, and that alternatives to traditional court-based adjudication can often deliver some of the core prima facie benefits of legal accountability with fewer accessibility and expertise deficits. The *cri-de-coeur* is heard. What does it say about what we should do?

The incrementalist approach in Parts II and III of this book gives adequate recognition to all these lessons, and suggests a proactive programme for constitutional adjudication. It emphasises learning by doing, and is therefore sensitive to changes in social conditions. It affirms the role of the executive and legislative branches in the overall project of protecting social rights, while recognising that inter-institutional collaboration does not eclipse a sometimes powerful role for the courts. The accent on principles of restraint seeks to discriminate between those instances where the conditions commend judicial restraint, and those instances where the case for restraint is weak and that for oversight strong. And the theme of incrementalism both complements and in some ways indicates reasons to be happy about the pace of change. The case for constitutional social rights remains strong.

---

[166] Mashaw, *Bureaucratic Justice*, p. 77.

[167] See also Richardson, 'Impact Studies in the UK', 121 (law part of the 'administrative soup' of influences); D. J. Galligan, *Due Process and Fair Procedures: A Study of Administrative Procedures* (Oxford: Clarendon Press, 1996), p. 214 (need for diverse techniques); Adler, 'A Socio-Legal Approach to Administrative Justice', 340–2.

4

A basic interpretive approach

I   Introduction

When one thinks of a right to health, education, or social security, one typically thinks of a right to certain resources, as I showed in Chapter 2. We often think that a substantive core of an entitlement exists, and that a judge's job is to define it and require the state to implement it. On that view, surely a theory of social rights adjudication cannot be all about judicial restraint! It must also be about the substantive legal content of the right and the interests it protects.

I made clear in Chapter 2 that there is, in my view, a substantive content to *social human rights* in the sense that we have a human right to a social minimum, and one can form a reasonably clear picture of the thresholds that a bundle of resources would need to meet that minimum. But I also argued there that it will not ordinarily be the role of the judge to define this social minimum in all its aspects, nor even to state what constitutes full compliance with a state's human rights obligation in respect of it. Part of the role of this chapter is to explain why that is so, and to clarify how judging, in most contemporary rights adjudication as well as in social rights adjudication, focuses on the application of fairly vague terms that in practice invite judges to evaluate the process of decision-making taken in respect of certain interests. I argue that the main role for the judge in applying such vague standards is to focus on the acceptability of the justifications put forward for interferences with or denials of the interests in question. This process, in my view, generates a distinct need for an approach to judicial restraint. So in section III of this chapter, I show both why that is by reference to some important cases, and why some of the best existing proposals for constitutional social rights adjudication do not give adequate recognition to this need.

II   Constitutional social rights: a basic interpretive approach

Upon close examination of the practice of judicial review of rights, or indeed any public law review, it emerges that the role of the court typically involves adjudicating competing arguments about the satisfaction of a vague legal norm that relates more to the state's obligation than to the scope of the individual interest in receiving some resource. This section clarifies the role of constitutional text, and of judicial interpretation of the text, in a manner that highlights the inescapable vagueness of the legal standards that are applied.

A   The structure of rights: scope of interest and nature of obligation

It is common in contemporary rights adjudication, and with social rights adjudication, to see two distinct structural features of the rights, typically presented in the text itself. This structure can be made evident in a hypothetical example of a social rights provision:

The right to X

1. Everyone has the right to adequate x.
2. The state shall take reasonable measures, within available resources, to implement the right to x.

In this formula, x specifies the range of interests that constitute the substantive content of the individual interest(s) protected by the right, and which serve as the object of the state's obligation that is set out in the second subsection. So, if x were 'health', then it would signify some combination of the individual's needs and a range of services required to meet those needs. If x were 'social security', then it would refer to benefits aimed at satisfying basic needs for social security. And so on with education, housing, and other potential social rights. This is the common form for more recently adopted constitutional social rights provisions, such as those of South Africa and Kenya.[1] It borrows its form from the International Covenant on Economic, Social and Cultural Rights (ICESCR).[2] Article 2(1) of that Covenant sets out a general progressive, positive obligation to implement the rights 'recognised' in Part III of the Covenant, where the various rights are listed. This also accords with my observations on the conceptual structure of social human rights in Chapter 2.

---

[1] See R. Wolfrum and R. Groter (eds.), *Constitutions of the Countries of the World*, Loose Leaf (New York: Oxford University Press, 1971 (with updates)). All references to constitutions in this chapter, including to the Canadian Charter, are to the provisions in force at the time of writing and as listed in these volumes.

[2] GA res. 2200A (XXI), 21 UN GAOR Supp. (No. 16) at 49, UN Doc. A/6316 (1966); 993 UNTS 3; 6 ILM 368 (1967).

This is similar in form (though not identical in terminology) to the widely used approach to constitutional rights adjudication in which rights are set forth in one part of a given bill of rights, and the permissible limitations of such rights or interests are set out in another provision.[3] This is the model pursued under the Canadian Charter of Rights and Freedoms, which states in s. 1 that the Charter 'guarantees the rights and freedoms set out in it subject only to such reasonable limits prescribed by law as can be demonstrably justified in a free and democratic society'.[4] This has been interpreted as requiring that limitations to rights are for a pressing social need and are a proportionate means for achieving it.[5] It borrowed explicitly from the European Convention on Human Rights (ECHR) in this respect. The ECHR sets out certain rights that have explicit qualifications in various subsections.[6] In the adjudication of a range of rights under the ECHR and the Canadian Charter, the most important issue is typically whether limitations of the right, or infringement of the interest, are proportionate and thus justified.[7]

Therefore, one can see a distinction in practice between the scope of the interest or right, and the nature of the obligation in respect of such an interest (or the nature of the state's power to limit or infringe such interests/rights). A few points may be made in reference to this distinction. The first is that, in my view, the most important interpretive role of the court will, in the overwhelming majority of cases, concern the assessment of the obligation, not the scope of the interest. Often the claim may plainly engage the interest, or the task of setting a precedent on the question will be too cumbersome (or ill-advised) for the court and the defendant state, and so both will proceed on the assumption that it is engaged. Second, and nonetheless, the scope of the interest

---

[3] See M. Kumm, 'The Idea of Socratic Contestation and the Right to Justification: The Point of Rights-Based Proportionality Review' (2010) 4 *Law and Ethics of Human Rights* 141, 144ff.

[4] This is becoming a more common provision: see also s. 36, Constitution of the Republic of South Africa 1996.

[5] *R* v. *Oakes* [1984] 2 SCR 145.

[6] See ECHR Arts. 2(2), 5(1)(a)–(f), and esp. 8–11.

[7] There is an analytical question about whether it is sensible to speak of limitations of *rights*, or whether we ought rather to speak of infringed *interests*, or *prima facie* rights, which only become *violated rights* after it is shown the infringement is not justified. The text of the Canadian Charter, the ICESCR, and the ECHR, all use the language of limited/progressively implemented *rights*. I take no strong view on this issue but adopt the terminology of 'interests' in order to avoid the problem. On the issue of using the language of 'infringements' in connection with positive rights, see my discussion of proportionality in section III.2 below.

is still a question that matters. Sometimes the text of the constitution will indicate a certain applicable scope. The provision might specify a particular dimension of the right, such as a right to water, or it might specify a particular service, such as emergency medical care, or special treatment of children. It might also matter where a claimant asserts an interest that is too remote from the idea of social rights, such as that a right to housing applies to a luxury yacht or holiday home, or a right to health comprises a right to non-medically indicated cosmetic surgery. Such claims ought to be stopped at the scope of interest stage, because constitutional review costs valuable time and resources, and because it is important to maintain the conceptual integrity of the bill of rights. Third, and finally, as I mentioned in Chapter 2, the determination of the scope of the interest – what might be considered similar to the social minimum and its thresholds – is largely a task for professional expert opinion on human needs. Ironically, therefore, though scope matters less in adjudication, it is an aspect of interpretation that may be more amenable to the judicial process (provided judges are using rather than contradicting expert opinion on the matter) than the assessment of some aspects of the obligation.

There may be arguments for and against setting out the scope of the interest with great specificity. My own view is that a general right or interest should be stated in the abstract, together with any further specification that might assist to highlight a jurisdiction's important institutional mechanisms or hard commitments, or to delimit the scope of the interest and thus limit the range of cases that could be brought under it. This approach will afford interpretive flexibility, which, as I show in Chapter 9, is crucial.

B Constitutional text: absolute and qualified obligations

While the scope of the interest can vary quite widely in constitutional texts, it is possible to identify a pattern in the ways that they set out the state's obligations. Sometimes the provision will expressly or impliedly declare that the state has an *absolute obligation* in respect of the interest or right.[8] An example can be found in the Constitution of Finland:

---

[8] One might link this idea with the notion of immediate obligations under the ICESCR, or the idea of obligations of result in international law. See Chapter 2 for a discussion and references. I use this terminology to highlight the similarity of structure between social rights and civil and political rights.

Section 19 – The right to social security

Those who cannot obtain the means necessary for a life of dignity have the right to receive indispensable subsistence and care.

Everyone shall be guaranteed by an Act the right to basic subsistence in the event of unemployment, illness, and disability and during old age as well as at the birth of a child or the loss of a provider.

The public authorities shall guarantee for everyone, as provided in more detail by an Act, adequate social, health and medical services and promote the health of the population.

The scope of the interests specified by this provision include 'indispensable subsistence and care', and 'basic subsistence', and 'adequate social, health and medical services.' The provision itself appears on its face to create an absolute obligation to secure these items.[9] This is found in the absence of qualification (e.g. 'right to receive') and the expressions 'shall guarantee' and 'shall be guaranteed'. Once it is established that the claimant's interest is not satisfied, the state has (textually) an absolute obligation to provide it.

Similar examples can be found in other constitutions. In the Constitution of the State of New York, for example, one finds:

Article IX (1)

[t]he legislature shall provide for the maintenance and support of a system of free common schools, wherein all the children of this state may be educated.

The Court of Appeals of New York has interpreted this provision, reasonably, as requiring a 'sound, basic education'.[10] In litigation, the New York courts have assessed non-compliance with this obligation and ordered the provision of very substantial resources to the schools concerned.[11] The constitutions of various Latin American countries also at times set out the rights in this way, as does the Constitution of Hungary.[12]

This type of constitutional text is open to a reasonable interpretation that a court is not to give weight to resource scarcity when it interprets

---

[9] It appears that this is the interpretation also given to these provisions by the Finnish courts: see M. Scheinin, 'Protection of Economic, Social and Cultural Rights in Finland – A Rights-Based Variant of the Welfare State', in M. Scheinin (ed.), *The Welfare State and Nordic Constitutionalism in the Nordic Countries* (Copenhagen: Nordic Council of Ministers, 2001), esp. pp. 251–60.

[10] *Campaign for Fiscal Equity* v. *State of New York*, 86 NY2d 307, 316 (1995).

[11] *Campaign for Fiscal Equity* v. *State of New York*, 8 N.Y.3d 14 (2006). This case was the final case in a thirteen-year saga of litigation.

[12] See Constitution of the Republic of Hungary, Arts. 70/D, 70/E, and 70/f in particular.

the right. It is possible for a court to read in an implied limitation, or 'underenforce' the constitutional norm.[13] However, the text not only does not require it, but affirmatively invites judges to disregard scarcity and other related factors. In my view, it would ordinarily be a serious mistake to do so, wherever it cannot be assumed with confidence that the existing legislative and administrative system nearly guarantees the right to all already. If that assumption holds, then any deviation from that norm would constitute an aberration, and the judicial enforcement of the obligation would by its nature be an incremental adjustment, a matter of correction, and so would conform to the approach set out in Parts II and III of this book. However, it will only rarely be the case that these conditions obtain for the full sweep of social rights. It may be the case in Finland, and perhaps other Scandinavian and northern European countries, but it is not in New York, or Hungary, and certainly not in Latin America – nor, it may be added, in the United Kingdom and other wealthy Commonwealth nations. Absent that condition, to disregard resource scarcity is to be blind to the dynamic implications of ordering the provision of resources, blind to where the resources will come from and what its impact on others will be. And it could supplant a more rational (even if imperfect) legislatively and administratively led scheme of resource allocation as set out in Chapter 2, with a system that responds to whomever gets to court first to demonstrate the non-satisfaction of the interest. Several aspects of the discussion in Chapter 3 show why this would be a mistake.

Having said this, it remains that sometimes absolute obligations are appropriate when they pertain to a narrow class of interests or rights (e.g. emergency medical care, children's rights, minority language rights),[14] or where there is some particular broad class of service where the state can be confident that the political support is in place and can thus be guaranteed (e.g. free, state-paid medical treatment in the United Kingdom or Canada, free primary and secondary education for all).

---

[13] See e.g. The *Belgian Linguistics Case (No 2)* (1968) 1 EHRR 252; L. G. Sager, 'Fair Measure: The Underenforcement of Constitutional Norms' (1978) 91 *Harvard Law Review* 1212. I believe this type of interpretation, or underenforcement, would ordinarily be appropriate unless the structure of the text suggests, perhaps by intra-text comparison, that an absolute obligation really was meant to apply: compare Art. 3 ECHR with Art. 6 ECHR; and ss. 26(1) and (2) with s. 26(3) of the Constitution of the Republic of South Africa.

[14] See e.g. Constitution of the Republic of South Africa, Art. 26 (eviction), s. 27(3) (emergency medical treatment); Constitution of Canada, s. 23 (minority language rights).

More commonly, the constitutional text will support the view that the state has a *qualified obligation*. By this, it is meant that the obligation is variable in that the interest may be limited in some way or left partially unfulfilled provided the state has met the obligation specified.[15] A constitutional text can state qualified obligations in two different ways. First, it can qualify it *implicitly* through the use of vague legal terms that give a margin of interpretive latitude in relation to the character of the state's obligation.[16] For example, Art. 6 of the European Convention on Human Rights guarantees a right to a 'fair' trial, within a 'reasonable' time. Much of the litigation over this article concerns what the requirements of fairness are, just as the question of what process is 'due' is an issue in cases concerning the due process clause of the fourteenth amendment of the US Bill of Rights.[17] For constitutional social rights, similar techniques are at times deployed. For example, the EU Charter of Fundamental Rights[18] states the right to health care as follows:

Article 35 – health care

Everyone has the right of access to preventive health care and the right to benefit from medical treatment under the conditions established by national laws and practices.

Were this provision to become the object of litigation, presumably much of the argument would concentrate on what 'access' entails (e.g. wait times for treatment?), and what the 'right to benefit' entails (e.g. funding of expensive experimental treatments?). Similarly, the EU Charter sets out the right to fair and just working conditions in the following form:

Article 31 – fair and just working conditions

Every worker has the right to working conditions which respect his or her health, safety and dignity.

Here as well, litigation would likely focus on whether certain treatment amounts to 'respect' for the worker's interests in health, safety, and dignity.

---

[15] One might liken this to progressive obligations under the ICESCR, or to obligations of conduct. I prefer 'qualified' in order to highlight the similarities with other rights adjudication that do not involve positive obligations.

[16] One might question the use of the expression 'qualified' in respect of rights formulated in this way. One might argue that there is an absolute right to a 'fair' trial.

[17] *Tsfayo* v. *United Kingdom* [2006] All ER (D) 177; (2006) 48 EHRR 18; *Mathews* v. *Eldridge* 424 US 319 (1976).

[18] European Union, Charter of Fundamental Rights of the European Union, OJ [2007] C303/1.

Presumably, resource scarcity and other considerations will become relevant at this stage.

The second way that social rights can be qualified is when the qualification is stated *explicitly*, that is, directly in such terms in the constitutional text. This is the model of the limitations provisions of the Canadian Charter and some provisions of the ECHR discussed above. It is also the main model used for social rights in South Africa's constitution. This is evident in the following sample provisions from the South African constitution, though it can be noted that the following provisions in fact combine elements of absolute obligations, explicit qualified obligations, and implicitly qualified obligations.

Section 26. Housing

1. Everyone has the right to have access to adequate housing.
2. The state must take reasonable legislative and other measures, within its available resources, to achieve the progressive realisation of this right.
3. No one may be evicted from their home, or have their home demolished, without an order of court made after considering all the relevant circumstances. No legislation may permit arbitrary evictions.

Section 27. Health care, food, water, and social security

1. Everyone has the right to have access to
   a. health care services, including reproductive health care;
   b. sufficient food and water; and
   c. social security, including, if they are unable to support themselves and their dependants, appropriate social assistance.
2. The state must take reasonable legislative and other measures, within its available resources, to achieve the progressive realisation of each of these rights.
3. No one may be refused emergency medical treatment.

These provisions show how the various forms of state obligations can be mixed within one text. The term 'access' is used (signifying an implicit qualification), and subsections 3 of both provisions state absolute obligations in respect of a restricted class of interests. Nonetheless, the main substance of sections 26 and 27, and the aspect on which most leading cases have focused, is the state's obligation to take reasonable legislative and other measures to achieve the realisation of these rights (or what we might call interests).

In sum, in a given constitutional text, the nature of the obligation in respect of the interest or right may be stated as absolute or qualified. It may be qualified implicitly or explicitly. My view is that the appropriate model for the text of a constitutional bill of social rights is to specify *explicit qualified obligations* in respect of *general or broadly stated interests or rights*. Doing this is an appropriate way to direct the courts that resource implications remain relevant to interpretation. However, if there is a class of interests where it can reasonably be assumed that the political support structure either is present or can be expected to be present, then it can be appropriate to state these as absolute obligations and for the courts to enforce them as such. It also remains open for the court to declare through interpretation, presumably after some experience, that some particular isolated interest or service now attracts an absolute obligation. There is nothing in the qualified obligation that prevents that,[19] and it is inherent in the concept of progressive obligations that the state ought to move progressively over time towards the complete protection of the interest. In a nutshell, I believe the South African model is the exemplar to work from, with country-specific adaptations where political conditions make it appropriate.

C   Judicial interpretation: the inescapability of vagueness

So the adjudication of constitutional social rights will require the state to assess qualified obligations, and resource scarcity will become a relevant consideration during the interpretation. The main question in constitutional social rights adjudication in South Africa is whether the state's conduct has been 'reasonable'.[20] Sometimes, during interpretation, the courts may recognise other relevant standards as a subcategory. For example, in *Occupiers of 51 Olivia Rd*,[21] the issue for the Constitutional Court was the compliance with the s. 26 right to housing of a procedure used to evict illegal occupiers of apartment buildings on grounds of health and safety. The Court found the procedure to be constitutionally defective, and

---

[19] See *Minister of Health and others* v. *Treatment Action Campaign and Others* (*TAC* case) 2002 (10) BCLR 1033 (CC); and *Mazibuko and Others* v. *City of Johannesburg and Others* (CCT 39/09) 2010 (4) SA 1 (CC) for an acknowledgement of this possibility in connection with the doctrine of minimum core obligations.

[20] *Grootboom and Others* v. *Oostenberg and Others*, 2000 (11) BCLR 1169 (CC); *TAC* case; *Khosa and others* v. *Minister of Social Development and others* 2004 (6) BCLR 569 (CC); *Mazibuko and Others* v. *City of Johannesburg and Others* (CCT 39/09) 2010 (4) SA 1 (CC), [48]–[68] (O'Regan J, reviewing the jurisprudence of the Court).

[21] *Occupiers of 51 Olivia Rd* v. *City of Johannesburg* 2008 (3) SA 208 (CC).

ordered that in such cases the state must observe a requirement of 'meaningful engagement'.[22] That is now the new standard applied in adjudication in that class of dispute. The same is found in the *Brown v. Board of Education (Brown II)* case, in which the Supreme Court of the United States found that there was a duty to desegregate educational facilities with 'all deliberate speed'.[23] These judicially created standards, like the textual ones of 'reasonable', 'necessary', 'fair' and so on, will all be vague standards, and necessarily so. This fact is not only inescapable, but, in the context of constitutional adjudication, can be desirable for the reasons I set out in Chapter 10.

One might object to the adjudication of vague norms by reason of their vagueness alone. I hinted at why this objection is weak in Chapter 1, but we can consider the objection more carefully in light of the pervasive nature of vague norms:

- the duty in administrative law that decisions not be unreasonable, and that procedures followed are fair;[24]
- that police are generally empowered to stop and search only on grounds of 'reasonable suspicion';[25]
- the human rights obligation that limitations of rights be 'necessary in a democratic society' and strike a 'fair balance';[26]
- the duty to take reasonable care in the law of negligence;
- the employment law right to not to be 'unfairly dismissed';[27]
- health, safety, financial, environmental, and other forms of regulation;
- the inclusion and adjudication of contractual clauses undertaking to make 'reasonable endeavours' to secure some end;[28]
- the duty to negotiate in good faith in labour law;[29]

---

[22] *Ibid.*, [14].

[23] *Brown v. Board of Education (Brown II)*, 349 US 294 (1955).

[24] *Council of Civil Service Unions v. Minister for the Civil Service (GCHQ)* [1985] 1 AC 374.

[25] Section 1 of the Police and Criminal Evidence Act 1984; section 47 of the Firearms Act 1968; section 23 of the Misuse of Drugs Act 1971.

[26] *Smith and Grady v. United Kingdom* (1999) 29 EHRR 493.

[27] Section 94 of the Employment Rights Act 1996.

[28] *Brauer v. James Clark* [1952] 2 All ER 497 (CA); *IBM United Kingdom Ltd v. Rockware Glass Ltd* [1980] FSR 335 (CA); *Rhodia International Holdings Ltd and another v. Huntsman International LLC* [2007] EWHC 292 (Comm).

[29] See e.g. *Canadian Union of Public Employees v. Labour Relations Board (N.S.) et al.* [1983] 2 SCR 31 (SCC); A. Bogg, *Democratic Aspects of Trade Union Membership* (Oxford: Hart, 2009) Chapters IV–VI.

- a duty to act with due diligence in many areas of domestic and international law;[30]
- a general anti-avoidance principle in the law of taxation.[31]

This is not a random collection of peripheral norms in law – a number of them are central to day-to-day adjudication, while others are fully justiciable. It is therefore absurd to suggest that, due to vagueness alone, the system of constitutional rights obligations is inoperable. The vagueness objection must be coupled with something stronger.

Before I proceed to stating that stronger argument, it is important to highlight the general implications of the basic interpretive approach stated here. The special role of the court foreseen in contemporary constitutional adjudication and especially social rights adjudication is that it focuses on the process of decision-making in respect of the asserted human rights interest, rather than on the state's achievement of some particular state of affairs. It seeks to test the adequacy of the justification or reasoning underlying the public action or omission, the plausibility of its premises, and validity of its inferences, and at times the scope of participation afforded during that process, the availability of effective policy alternatives, and (where applicable) the compatibility of the resulting decision with the conceptual core of the asserted right. To prove that a right has been violated, it is not enough to show that someone has been incarcerated without a hearing, or evicted from a home despite substantial need, or was prevented from speaking at a political rally. We know only after assessing the state's justification, unless (in rare cases) the constitution states an absolute obligation that triggers an irresistible duty upon some conditions having been met. Similarly, it is pointless to believe

---

[30] See Section 11 of the Securities Act of 1933, 15 USC § 77k, as interpreted in *Herman & Maclean* v. *Huddleston et al.*, 459 US 375, 382 (1982); *Johnson* v. *United States*, 544 US 295 (2005) (criminal procedure); *Nissan Fire & Marine Ins. Co.* v. *M/V Hyundai Explorer*, 93 F.3d 641 (9th Cir. 1996) (maritime law). In Canada, see *R* v. *Sault Ste Marie* [1978] 2 SCR 1299 (introducing due diligence as a defence for strict liability regulatory offences). Similar regulatory defences abound in the UK: see s. 21 Food Safety Act 1990 (food hygiene); s. 141A(4) of the Criminal Justice Act 1988 (sale of knives to minors); s. 14A(b) of the Video Recordings Act 1984 (sale of video without certificate). In international law, see R. P. Barnidge, 'The Due Diligence Principle under International Law' (2006) 8 *International Community Law Review* 81.

[31] See, in Canada, s. 245 of the Income Tax Act 1985 (RSC 1985, c. 1 (5th Supp.)) and its interpretation in *Canada Trustco Mortgage Co.* v. *Canada* [2005] 2 SCR 601 (SCC); J. Freedman, 'Defining Taxpayer Responsibility: In Support of a General Anti-Avoidance Principle' [2004] *British Tax Review* 332.

that demonstrating an unfulfilled social minimum (even where resources exist to provide it) will conclude the question of whether social rights have been violated.

The implications of this view are crucial to the theory set out in this book. It is relevant to the question of democratic legitimacy, because the same policy might stand or fall depending on how it was enacted. It is relevant to how remedies are framed, and to how much restraint to show in respect of expert opinion: a policy devised on the fly might be struck down, whereas the same one backed by good evidence might be upheld. And it is relevant to recognising the importance and constitutional acceptability of the principle of flexibility, because the evidence for policy can change over time. It is relevant above all because, though the relevant interests may remain relatively steady over time, the nature of the justification for any state action in relation to them may change, and fall to be assessed under different circumstances.

III   The need for an approach to judicial restraint

The stronger objection that builds upon the sheer fact of vagueness is that there is something particularly problematic about using vague norms for constitutional review of the welfare state in particular. There is enough to this objection, in my view, to justify a need for a distinct approach to judicial restraint.[32] This section illustrates that need by reference to a few important cases, and then shows why the current plausible approaches to adjudicating social rights do not meet the current need.

A   Social rights in the shadow of Lochner and Dicey

In *Lochner* v. *New York*[33] the Supreme Court of the United States declared unconstitutional a New York law that limited a baker's working time to sixty hours per week, with no more than ten hours per day. Joseph Lochner's argument was that this type of regulation interfered impermissibly with the employer and employee's freedom of contract. The Court was bitterly divided, but all agreed that the freedom to contract was given basic protection under the Fourteenth Amendment, and also, notably,

---

[32]   My view is that contemporary public law adjudication in general requires a doctrine of restraint, as set out in J. A. King, 'Institutional Approaches to Judicial Restraint' (2008) 28 *Oxford Journal of Legal Studies* 409.

[33]   198 US 45 (1905).

that restrictions on that right were acceptable on grounds of health and safety. Beyond this, the Brethren parted ways. The majority emphasised repeatedly that the restrictions, even on health grounds, must be limited in some way. Otherwise, the substantive right itself would be meaningless. The question was whether the restriction was 'unreasonable, unnecessary and arbitrary interference with the right and liberty of the individual to contract'.[34] The Court found that the evidence presented did not justify the limitation, for it could not reasonably be said that a baker's profession was considerably more dangerous than those of other employees. It is crucial, therefore, to note that the Court is in fact, in the *Lochner* case, applying a constitutional test of *reasonableness* of the limitation of the right. It is not a standard 'rights as trumps' scenario, or a straightforward case of legal formalism in which a court declares the right to be breached without further ado. Rather, the Court analysed and rejected the State of New York's studies showing that bakers were subject to unusual health risks and needed protection. The dissenting judges showed in their judgment, in fact, that there were a large number of uncontested studies that proved that the health of these bakers was severely – even shockingly – poor by comparison to other workers in New York and beyond.

The *Lochner* case (on the conventional account) opened a period of aggressive judicial interventionism, from 1905 to 1937, that led, on one estimate, to the nullification of approximately 170 labour statutes alone,[35] including the very possibility of a minimum wage in the case of *Adkins* v. *Children's Hospital* (1923).[36] The total damage went considerably beyond labour regulation, however, and included a number of laws regulating broader areas of the economy, as I show in Chapter 8. In this respect, it substantially interfered with the entire New Deal programme, which was essentially a national plan of action to protect social human rights.

In *Chaoulli* v. *Quebec (AG)*, the claimants attacked the constitutionality of the Canadian health care regime, which banned private medical insurance in the effort to create a robust and egalitarian one-tier public health care service. The majority of the Supreme Court of Canada found that the ban was not a proportionate limitation of the right to the security of the person, and three judges even found it to be 'arbitrary' on the basis of the social science evidence they reviewed.[37] In that case, a patient, who

---

[34] *Ibid.*, 56.   [35] See Chapter 8, section II.A for discussion.
[36] 261 US 525 (1923).
[37] *Chaoulli* v. *Quebec (Attorney General)* [2005] 1 SCR 791; see S. Choudry, 'Worse than Lochner?', in C. Flood, K. Roach, and L. Sossin (eds.), *Access to Care, Access to Justice* (University of Toronto Press, 2005), p. 75; J. A. King, 'Constitutional Rights and Social

had been placed on waiting lists for a variety of treatments, joined forces with a doctor (Jacques Chaoulli) who wanted to open a private hospital for apparently commercial reasons. The two argued that the ban interfered with the patient's security of the person by putting his life in jeopardy as a result of requiring him to wait for treatment. Three judges of the Court, who were in the majority, accepted that the state either had to 'provide public health care of a reasonable standard within a reasonable time',[38] that is, make the queues for public treatment reasonable, or lift the ban on private insurance. Here again, the Court applied open-textured concepts of 'arbitrary' and 'proportionate', and the need to observe 'reasonable' wait times. The effect of the case could have been to cause stark and irreversible changes to the health care rights of less well-off Canadians. It is unclear what implications it may ultimately have.

Of course, the UK never faced quite the same constitutional impediments, but, as is explained in Chapter 8, there was also a noticeable if sometimes academically exaggerated measure of judicial hostility to the welfare state in administrative law.[39] Albert Venn Dicey was notorious in his opposition to the expansion of administrative discretion, which he viewed as a threat to the constitutional principle of the rule of law. The essence of the functionalist and political constitutionalist legal schools of thought in Britain are that the judiciary has essentially played a corrosive role in the contemporary British welfare state.[40]

One might argue that the failure to include social rights in a constitution is more likely to lead to the type of outcome found in *Lochner* and *Chaoulli*. That may well be so. But one may equally ask whether *Lochner* might have been decided similarly on the grounds of the employee's right to work, and *Chaoulli* on the individual's right to health care. The structure of judicial discretion in those scenarios could have been largely the same (depending on precedent and constitutional text of course). The inescapability of vagueness could leave that door open.

Welfare: A Comment on the Canadian *Chaoulli* Health Care Decision' (2006) 69 *Modern Law Review* 631–43.

[38] *Chaoulli*, [105] (McLachlin CJ, Major and Bastarache JJ).

[39] I suggest some exaggeration because perhaps the two most significant leading cases in administrative law prior to the Second World War are *Local Government Board* v. *Arlidge* [1915] AC 120 and *Associated Provincial Picture Houses* v. *Wednesbury Corporation* [1948] 1 KB 223, both hallmarks of judicial deference to the administrative exigencies of the modern regulatory state.

[40] C. Harlow and R. Rawlings, *Law and Administration* (3rd edn, Cambridge University Press, 2009), Chapter 1; M. Loughlin, *Public Law and Political Theory* (Oxford University Press, 1992).

John Hart Ely famously said that much of US constitutional theory was preoccupied with giving a theory that justifies *Brown* v. *Board of Education* and rejects *Lochner*.[41] My goal in this book is to construct a theory that would clearly and reliably prevent Lochnerism, and promote multi-institutionalism in the context of social rights adjudication. This theory would neither compel the adoption of a sweeping set of determinate social policies, nor permit that statutes governing substantial elements of national welfare policy be struck down in wholesale and irreversible fashion.

B   *The allure and limits of existing interpretive approaches*

There are a variety of approaches to the judicial review of social rights that have been offered or are obvious candidates. I review some of these here and argue that though they have merit, they are incomplete. There are other candidates for an interpretive approach that are closer to the incrementalist approach set out in this book, and I defer consideration of their differences until Chapter 10, section IV.

1   Interpretivism

According to Ronald Dworkin, the law follows from the set of principles that provide the best constructive interpretation of a community's legal practice, namely, those principles which best fit the existing legal practice and provide the best political justification of it.[42] I agree with much of Dworkin's general characterisation of adjudication subject to some important caveats about the role of principle and policy arguments in adjudication, and about whether the choice exercised by judges in hard cases is best described as 'judgment' about what constitutes the 'right answer' to legal problems, or is better characterised as an exercise of discretion and thus constitutes a form of interstitial law-making as his positivist critics assert.[43] In particular, I agree about the role of principles in legal interpretation, that the dimensions of fit and justification

---

[41] J. H. Ely, *Democracy and Distrust: A Theory of Judicial Review* (Cambridge, MA: Harvard University Press, 1980), p. 65.

[42] See R. Dworkin, *Law's Empire* (Cambridge, MA: Harvard University Press, 1986), esp. Chapter 7.

[43] On these questions, see R. Dworkin, *Taking Rights Seriously* (2nd edn, London: Duckworth, 1996), Chapter 4; *A Matter of Principle* (Cambridge, MA: Harvard University Press, 1985), Chapter 5; and the essays in Parts 2 and 3 of M. Cohen (ed.), *Ronald Dworkin and Contemporary Jurisprudence* (London: Duckworth, 1984).

are crucial to the exercise of legal interpretation, and that the question of justification involves considerations of political morality. From the present point of view, Dworkin's theory is not so much wrong in any crucial way, but is rather radically incomplete so far as social rights adjudication is concerned. While it is a good abstract description of judging, it is a poor programme for averting the risks to which I have drawn attention. The requirement of integrity suggests a principled consistency between the case at issue and past legal decisions, statutes, and policies, which might appear at first to be a conservative and inertial constraint, possibly incrementalist. But no: '[i]ntegrity is a more dynamic and radical standard than it first seemed, because it encourages the judge to be wide-ranging and imaginative in his search for coherence with fundamental principle.'[44] So Dworkin's theory is not only incomplete, but without some theory of restraint it might encourage the judicial hubris that is linked to some good arguments against social rights.[45] Nonetheless, I do think on the one hand that Dworkin recognises that some sort of restraint on institutional grounds is appropriate at times,[46] and on the other that the principles detailed in Part II of this book are in fact legal principles that judges would ordinarily find in the legal practice of most communities.[47]

2   Principles, balancing, and proportionality

Robert Alexy's monumental *Theory of Constitutional Rights* presents a sophisticated theory of the structure of constitutional rights norms and legal argumentation, focusing on the idea of rights as principles that must be optimised against competing considerations. Alexy devotes a chapter to the topic of constitutional social rights. He finds that social rights are not greatly different from civil rights in most respects, and he dispatches a number of weak arguments against them.[48] The principle that justifies them is the principle of factual freedom, which is that social rights must exist to facilitate, in instrumental fashion, the right to autonomy.

---

[44] *Ibid.*, p. 220.

[45] See e.g. Dworkin, *Taking Rights Seriously*, 2nd edn, Chapter 5.

[46] Though such statements are rare, a representative one can be seen in Dworkin, *A Matter of Principle*, p. 101. ('[T]he Court may defer, on grounds of expert knowledge, to the agency's judgment on the consequentialist components of the question.')

[47] The exception here, from the Dworkinian point of view, would be Chapter 6 (Democratic Legitimacy), which departs quite substantially from Dworkin's 'constitutional conception of democracy' as set out in 'Introduction: The Moral Reading and the Majoritarian Premise', in his *Freedom's Law: The Moral Reading of the American Institution* (Cambridge, MA: Harvard University Press, 1996).

[48] R. Alexy, *A Theory of Constitutional Rights*, trans. J. Rivers (Oxford University Press, 2002), pp. 340–3.

However, they are by their nature quite costly.[49] He finds that the solution is to view such rights as principles,[50] and that an individual has a definitive entitlement whenever the principle of factual freedom outweighs, in his model of balancing, the competing formal and substantive principles of the separation of powers and democracy.[51] This helps to acknowledge the similarities between constitutional social rights and other constitutional rights, but it falls well short of what is needed. It proposes an impossible arithmetic with radically contestable variables. It encapsulates the dilemma instead of providing a solution. Alexy also offers no discussion of the problems of institutional competence in this part of his book.

The same can be said about the principle of proportionality, which is central in Alexy's theory and can thus be addressed here. It is a very useful scheme for evaluating the competing interests in the structure of constitutional rights litigation. But there are a few problems with relying on it to rescue the enterprise. For one, social rights adjudication has an uneasy relationship with the doctrine, and its focus on *limitations*, and courts have been hesitant to use it to assess state inaction on grounds of scarcity.[52] The more difficult problem with it is that it underdetermines the outcomes of the process. It must not be forgotten that *Lochner* could have been decided through the doctrinal sieve of proportionality (in fact it asked the more deferential question of whether the limitation was *reasonable*), and in fact *Chaoulli* was decided that way. We therefore need something more robust.

3 Deliberative democracy

Some sophisticated arguments suggest that the role for courts can be to promote deliberative democracy, a basic outline of which I presented in Chapter 2. Some important legal scholars and philosophers have advocated the view that courts can provide a forum for the participation of vulnerable and excluded groups in public decision-making, giving them an institutional voice that they have been denied in electoral politics.[53] I agree with the general sentiment. The approach I set out in Chapter 6

---

49 *Ibid.*, p. 342.   50 *Ibid.*, p. 344.   51 *Ibid.*, p. 347.
52 *Khosa and Others* v. *Minister of Social Development and Others*, 2004 (6) BCLR 569 (CC) [83]–[84]; *Jaftha* v. *Schoeman and others, Van Rooyen* v. *Stoltz and others*, 2005 (2) SA 140 (CC) [34]–[35]ff. Article 4 of the International Covenant on Economic, Social and Cultural Rights is a general limitations clause, but it was understood by the drafters as being for the purpose of dealing with limitations of rights on grounds other than resource scarcity: see P. Alston and G. Quinn, 'Nature and Scope of States parties Obligations' (1987) 9 *Human Rights Quarterly* 156, 192–203.
53 J. Habermas, *Between Facts and Norms*, trans. W. Rehg (Cambridge: Polity Press, 1996); S. Fredman, *Human Rights Transformed: Positive Rights and Positive Duties*

goes some distance to respecting and formalising it. But the problem with banking so much on a concept such as deliberative democracy is that the idea does not straightforwardly support a strong judicial role, it is at times blind to institutional limitations, and it can, in its undeveloped form, encourage judicial outcomes that can upset participation patterns that are in fact more egalitarian and deliberative. For example, its advocates typically fail to acknowledge the problems engendered by extending robust procedural rights in systems of mass decision-making (as I discuss in Chapter 9). There is also rarely any explicit recognition that, on the deliberative view, it is hard to justify that middle-class or wealthy citizens should be able to claim strong remedies from the courts, given their ample representation in politics already. Further, there is no attention paid to the problem that strong judicial review might, if not carefully circumscribed, actually worsen participation overall. If one patient can upset a statutory scheme enacted by a government after a hard-fought election on account of inadequate representation, an unanswered question remains – what about the representation of all those millions whose decision (embodied in the statute) is effectively overturned? Further, why should a theory like deliberative democracy support hard remedies (like striking down statutes) instead of stronger participation rights at the legislative and administrative stages? And on that point, the mechanisms provided in those stages on some views compare quite favourably with judicial procedures. I think that deliberative democracy can answer some or perhaps all of these questions, but, if so, it would need to be expanded into a theory that approximates something like the principles presented in this book. My own attempt brandishes Ockham's razor to cut straight to directly reconciling social rights with the idea of legislative failure as detailed in Chapter 6, and with limitations on competency and in the area of participation rights in Chapters 7 through 9.

4   The minimum-core approach

The minimum core approach to social rights adjudication is one that proposes the augmentation of judicial scrutiny of decisions that affect the substantial, minimum existential needs of rights claimants. For example, the minimum core of a right to housing might guarantee someone a structurally sound building protecting its occupant from threats to health, but

---

(Oxford University Press, 2008). Notably, A. Gutman and R. Thompson, *Democracy and Disagreement* (Cambridge, MA: Harvard University Press, 1996), pp. 34, 46–48, overtly reject the idea that deliberative democracy entails a role for judges.

not anything beyond it. David Bilchitz has published a sophisticated elaboration of this approach.[54] There is doubtless a basic kernel of truth to this idea of a minimum core: surely there must be a special urgency to act against threats to people's basic existential needs, and surely too priority should be given to interests that are more urgent than those that are not. But the approach of the South African Constitutional Court has explicitly endorsed this use of the idea while rejecting the more robust type advocated by Bilchitz,[55] and in this respect I am in agreement. There are a few difficulties with the idea. The first is doctrinal. It can be difficult to say what constitutes the minimum core,[56] but more importantly it is more difficult to say just how much more intense the degree of scrutiny ought to be (in both cases giving ample account to the UN Committee on Economic, Social and Cultural Rights' work on this topic). The South African Constitutional Court, for instance, thought that a minimum core approach would require immediate provision of basic entitlements, something which is a doctrinal error, but a quite understandable one. What else is it supposed to mean? The answer is rather subtle: increased (quasi) judicial scrutiny, but not an absolute obligation because ultimately scarcity can justify non-fulfilment. The larger problem here is that cases involving the minimum core may well become quite central, rather than exceptional, to social rights adjudication. Cases in health, housing, and social security may often be tied to the minimum core in ways that judges in many cases are simply likely to accept for the sake of argument. All the leading cases in South Africa fit this pattern, as do the life-saving drugs cases in Brazil, Colombia, and Argentina. But the key question in most cases is how the state's conduct can be justified, and the minimum core approach offers thin guidance here. And if increased judicial scrutiny is regressive (as it seems to have been in Brazil), then it might even make things worse.

---

[54] D. Bilchitz, *Poverty and Fundamental Rights: The Justification and Enforcement of SocioEconmoic Rights* (Oxford University Press, 2007). See my book review, 'Poverty and Fundamental Rights, by D. Bilchitz (Oxford University Press 2007)' [2008] PL 820–824. See also K. Young, 'The Minimum Core of Economic and Social Rights: A Concept in Search of Content' (2008) 33 *Yale Journal of International Law* 113. See also, in respect of the UN Covenant, M. Langford and J. King, 'The United Nations Committee on Economic, Social and Cultural Rights', in M. Langford (ed.), *Social Rights Jurisprudence: Comparative and International Trends* (Cambridge University Press, 2009), pp. 492–5.

[55] *TAC* case, [34] (Yacoob J); see also *Mazibuko and Others* v. *City of Johannesburg and Others* (CCT 39/09) 2010 (4) SA 1 (CC).

[56] *Ibid.*, [37].

5   Institutional reform approach

Some argue that the institutional limitations of courts may be overcome by considering the reform of the common law adversarial legal process. We might follow the Indian or the American experience[57] by using a combination of supervisory jurisdiction (structural injunctions) and/or the appointment of administrative officials who are accountable to the judge, who may compensate for lacunae in expertise and investigatory powers. I assumed among the background political conditions set out in Chapter 1 that the familiar mode of common law (and where similar, civil law) adjudication would not change, and I can now suggest why. First, the common law system is unlikely to change greatly, and so making the case for social rights contingent on that modification would render it less politically viable. Second, the procedural techniques employed in the USA and India raise their own particular problems, some of which are addressed in Chapter 9. I argue there that structural injunctions are in light of these problems best viewed as a last-resort option to be used only when the presumption of inter-institutional collaboration breaks down. Third, these procedural techniques, where most justified, were borne of the extraordinary intransigence and patently unconstitutional behaviour of certain executive officials, or glaring failure to carry out basic state functions. There were real and undeniable rule of law problems in those cases. Such conditions – especially the clarity of the constitutional breach – are not the norm in the countries towards which this book is primarily directed. They therefore do not provide a general model for the standard case, even if radical structural overhaul could be achieved.

6   South African reasonableness

The South African Constitutional Court has focused on the requirement of reasonableness, which is a more robust standard than that found in administrative law.[58] Some may feel that this experience can be relied on to say that courts will find their way, and bring greater protection, judging with caution and integrity. I agree that it is working. Indeed, I believe the approach set out in this book fits the correctly decided cases of the South African court and helps to explain why they were rightly decided. However, it is not a good idea to rely on this precedent alone. For one,

---

[57] See Chapter 9, section III.A.3.
[58] See M. Wesson, 'Grootboom and Beyond: Assessing the Socio-Economic Jurisprudence of the South African Constitutional Court' (2004) 20 *South African Journal of Human Rights* 284.

it is not the only way courts have gone, as Chapter 3 made clear. But for another, the Constitutional Court has thus far been staffed largely with outstanding lawyers and academics, many of whom were notable civil rights campaigners or rights activists. As time moves on and the post-Apartheid idealism wears off, and new elites congeal, we may become more worried about both the judicial appointments and the judgments. Furthermore, it is not satisfactory to bank on a record of judicial wisdom alone. Certain decision – such as the *Khosa* case,[59] which mandated the provision of social security to all permanent residents – may be criticised for failing to understand the dynamic risks associated with significant budgetary impact. Above all, we ought to press on to say why the experience is working, what features of the jurisprudence stand out as appropriate, and what guidance is to be found in it for future and foreign cases. I suspect the judges of the Constitutional Court would themselves happily admit that further doctrinal elaboration would be welcome.

IV   Conclusion

This chapter has explained in what, in my view, the basic interpretive approach to constitutional social rights would consist. The surprising result is that the scope of the interest in receiving the social minimum is not the crucial aspect of what judges would be called upon to specify. In this respect, social rights are no different from most civil and political rights. Rather, when judges adjudicate qualified obligations – and I have argued that constitutional texts should frame social rights in this way – the crucial question for them is whether the state has satisfied a general obligation. Such obligations are ordinarily vague, and inescapably so in adjudication. And again, that type of vagueness is not at all unique to social rights. More constructively, however, what emerges from the recognition of this is that when adjudicating qualified obligations, the role of the court is essentially concerned with identifying the acceptability of justifications in support of proposed policies, and not with the categorical acceptability of those policies themselves. In short, courts are concerned with justifications, and not, in the ordinary run of things, with the scope of interests.

It is not enough, however, to show that the legal standards applied in both social and civil rights adjudication are fundamentally similar in this respect. There is a particular concern over the use of vague legal standards

---

[59] See Chapter 10, section VI.B for criticism.

to meddle in the welfare state in particular. That is the acute concern of many scholars and judges who are great friends of economic equality. In my view, that legitimate concern gives rise to a need for a doctrine of judicial restraint. Further, the important and insightful doctrines presented by a range of scholars and courts – some concerning adjudication in general, and others social rights in particular – do not in my view give adequate recognition to this need. There is a need for a distinct theory of judicial restraint.

PART II

A theory of judicial restraint

Institutional approaches to judicial restraint

I   Introduction

Part I of this book has made clear that there is a good case for social rights, and for constitutional social rights in particular. Yet it also concluded that there was a distinct need for an approach to judicial restraint. Part II of the book presents a theory of judicial restraint for constitutional social rights. Any such theory must begin with an account of judicial restraint itself, for there are several competing ideas and models that are relevant to the question.

This chapter seeks to explain, justify, and elaborate what I call institutional approaches to judicial restraint. Institutional approaches focus on the comparative merits and drawbacks of the judicial process as an institutional mechanism for solving problems. On my account, institutional approaches to restraint put emphasis on the problem of uncertainty and judicial fallibility, on the systemic impact of court rulings, and on rights as prima facie entitlements subject to balancing rather than as trumps over collective welfare. For precisely these reasons, institutional approaches tend to advocate a somewhat modest, case-by-case and incrementalist role for courts in public law adjudication. To understand the reasons why institutional approaches have these features, however, it is necessary to see the faults of their two principal alternatives: non-doctrinal approaches and formalist approaches. Non-doctrinal approaches suggest that we ought to trust judges to use their good sense of restraint on a case-by-case basis rather than employ any conceptual framework. We have already seen in Chapters 3 and 4 why this is not an adequate approach for constitutional social rights adjudication, and I argue elsewhere that it is not an adequate approach for public law adjudication in general.[1]

---

[1] See J. A. King, 'Institutional Approaches to Judicial Restraint' (2008) 28 *Oxford Journal of Legal Studies* 409, 411–14. The present chapter for the most part reproduces that article, though I have omitted the discussion of non-doctrinal approaches to restraint, and there are minor stylistic and substantive changes made to better suit the topic of this book.

Formalists believe that judges should apply abstract categories such as 'law', 'politics', 'policy', and 'non-justiciable' that they believe properly allocate decision-making functions between different branches of government. This is a more serious challenge, because precisely these types of distinctions are used to rebuff any talk of legally enforceable social rights. Institutional approaches largely grew out of a reaction to the problems with non-doctrinal and formalist approaches, and can only be properly understood in that light. Therefore, section II of the chapter will critique the formalist approaches, before I elaborate the general features of the institutional approaches in section III.

I refer to institutional 'approaches' because the general features of institutionalism actually lend support to two sharply conflicting views of the judge's role. Restrictive institutionalists believe judges should act wherever possible with great restraint, rejecting a role for balancing, and preferring adherence to bright-line rules and containing the expansion of precedent. Contextual institutionalists, on the other hand, believe more in the promise of the judicial process and advocate a particular tool to address the problems of broad judicial discretion under conditions of limited institutional competency – principles of restraint. If the principles of restraint embody the institutional considerations and can be workably incorporated into adjudication, they believe, the concerns can be met without rejecting the role of the courts foreseen in much contemporary public law adjudication.

The contextual institutional approach is the general approach to judicial restraint that I advocate for the adjudication of constitutional social rights. Chapters 6–9 of this book set out in detail the four key principles of restraint that I believe can be given weight in adjudication. However, there are a number of prior questions about how such principles may be used in day-to-day adjudication, what should happen when they conflict, and how, practically speaking, they may be made a part of judging. These considerations need to be attended to before the analysis of the principles themselves can be carried out.

II   Formalist approaches

There are three somewhat distinct models of judicial restraint, commonly or traditionally employed in English public law, that are premised on a formalist separation of powers between legislatures, the executive, and the courts: the distinctions between law and politics, principle and policy, and justiciability and non-justiciability. These models are marked by what H. L. A. Hart called 'the vice known to legal theory as formalism or conceptualism'.[2] By formalist, I mean conceptual formalism, a belief in the capacity of judges to deduce objective and apolitical legal answers from abstract legal rules, principles, or categories, without recourse to policy considerations.[3]

Conceptual formalism is prone to familiar problems. The obvious one is a false pretence to objectivity. As Hart observed, the belief in objective deduction, so-called 'mechanical jurisprudence',[4] tended to 'disguise' and 'minimise' the role actually played by policy beliefs and personal preferences.[5] As Justice Oliver Wendell Holmes Jr famously wrote, '[g]eneral propositions do not decide concrete cases.'[6] Another problem is that conceptual formalism is rigid and resists revision on the basis of any adverse consequences it produces. The belief in rational objectivity promotes the view that, if a view is logically correct, its consequences are of minor importance. This leads judges and scholars to ignore, lament, or gloss over anomalous or unfair cases.[7] This led to another of Holmes' great aphorisms: '[t]he life of the law has not been logic; it has been experience.'[8] The belief in rational objectivity, especially when coupled with the doctrine of *stare decisis*, tends to create conservative inertia in the law. Once lines have been drawn, erasing them becomes difficult. Both of these problems are evident in the models reviewed below.

A   The distinction between law and politics

In several cases British judges have invoked a distinction between law and politics, implying of course that one is for judges and the other for Parliament and the executive.[9] This approach finds some pedigree in

---

[2] H. L. A. Hart, *The Concept of Law* (2nd edn, Oxford University Press, 1994), p. 129.

[3] See also N. Duxbury, *Patterns of American Jurisprudence* (Oxford University Press, 1992), Chapter 1: 'The Challenge of Formalism', esp. p. 10; Hart, *The Concept of Law*; D. Kennedy, *A Critique of Adjudication: Fin de Siècle* (Cambridge, MA: Harvard University Press, 1997), p. 105.

[4] R. Pound, 'Mechanical Jurisprudence' (1908) 8 *Columbia Law Review* 605.

[5] Hart, *The Concept of Law*, p. 129.

[6] *Lochner* v. *New York* 198 US 45 (1905) at 76.

[7] W. Twining, *Karl Llewellyn and the Realist Movement* (London: Weidenfeld and Nicolson, 1973), p. 8.

[8] O. W. Holmes Jr, *The Common Law* (Boston: Little Brown, 1881), p. 1.

[9] *A and Others; X and Others* v. *Secretary of State for the Home Department* [2004] UKHL 56 [93] (Lord Bingham); *R (Hooper)* v. *Secretary of State for Work and Pensions* [2005] UKHL 29 [32]; see also *R* v. *Secretary of State for the Home Department, ex parte Fire Brigades Union* [1995] 2 AC 513 (HL) 544 (Lord Keith, dissenting).

the American doctrine of 'political questions' as developed in *Baker v. Carr.*[10] Some functionalist legal scholars also at times appear to advocate this type of bright-line approach, with their strong notion of separate and autonomous functions for the different branches of government.[11]

The problem with this approach is that it is mostly a matter of judicial intuition where this line will be drawn. The conclusion that an issue is 'political' and thus inappropriate to determine in a court of law *might* be acceptable as a conclusory label, but it does not obviate the need for a method of analysis. This criticism is entirely consistent with the 'political questions' approach under *Baker v. Carr*, in which the United States Supreme Court found that the question should be analysed by determining whether there is, among other factors, 'a textually demonstrable constitutional commitment of the issue to a coordinate political department; or a lack of judicially discoverable and manageable standards for resolving it'.[12]

Absent grounding in any particular theory, such a distinction is liable to be applied in an inconsistent and unfair manner. This occurred with the recommendation of the Donoughmore Committee in 1932 that judges identify issues as 'judicial', 'quasi-judicial', or 'administrative', a framework that Stanley de Smith later observed to have been used 'loosely and without deliberation' and 'as a contrivance to support a conclusion reached on non-conceptual grounds'.[13] The same problem has rendered all but obsolete the doctrine of *actes de gouvernement* in French administrative law.[14] Many other well-worn examples, such as the rights/privileges and jurisdictional/non-jurisdictional error distinctions, make the point equally well.

---

[10] 369 US 186 (1962).

[11] M. Loughlin, *The Idea of Public Law* (Oxford University Press, 2003) (on the morality/politics distinction); cf. N. Barber 'Professor Loughlin's Idea of Public Law' (2005) 25 *Oxford Journal of Legal Studies* 157, 158–65.

[12] *Baker v. Carr* 369 US 186 (1962) at 217.

[13] Donoughmore Committee, Report of the Committee on Ministers' Powers, Cmnd 4060 (1932). S. A. de Smith, *Judicial Review of Administrative Action* (4th edn, London: Stevens, 1980), pp. 58–9. See also C. Harlow and R. Rawlings, *Law and Administration* (2nd edn, London: Butterworths, 1997), pp. 31–4.

[14] M. Virally, 'L'introuvable acte de gouvernement' (1952) *Revue de Droit Publique* 317; R. Chapus, *Droit administratif général* (12th edn, Paris: Editions Monchrestien, 1998), pp. 871–8; G. Peiser, *Droit administratif général* (23rd edn, Paris: Dalloz, 2006), pp. 190–2; L. N. Brown and J. S. Bell, *French Administrative Law* (5th edn, Oxford University Press, 1998), pp. 161–5.

B *The principle/policy distinction*

A number of judges, and in particular Lord Hoffmann, have also sought to structure judicial restraint by reference to a distinction between principle and policy.[15] The implication is that courts are the forum of principle and that policy is to be decided by democratically accountable bodies. Such judicial uses of the distinction are often thought to have their pedigree in Ronald Dworkin's articulation and defence of the idea, the original statement being as follows:

> [A] 'policy' [is] that kind of standard that sets out a goal to be reached, generally an improvement in some economic, political or social feature of the community ... [A] 'principle' [is] a standard that is to be observed, not because it will advance ... an economic, political, or social situation deemed desirable, but because it is a requirement of justice or fairness or some other dimension of morality.[16]

Dworkin advanced this thesis as a complement to his 'rights as trumps' model, in part to help illustrate the intuition that majoritarian preferences cannot override rights. The familiar upshot of the analysis is that courts should decide cases on principle, and that policy matters are for accountable bodies and not courts. The distinction is thus formalist because it proposes a rigid, conceptual allocation of decision-making functions between courts and legislatures, and it is not in principle revisable by reference to the negative consequences it produces.

The criticism of this idea is so deep and trenchant that one could be forgiven for thinking another round is unnecessary.[17] But as the decided

---

[15] *R (on the application of Pro Life Alliance)* v. *BBC* [2003] UKHL 23 [76] (Lord Hoffmann); *R (Alconbury)* v. *Secretary of State for the Environment, Transport and the Regions* [2001] UKHL 23 [76] (Lord Hoffmann); *Huang* v. *Secretary of State for the Home Department* [2005] EWCA Civ 105 [53]. See also *Bushell* v. *Secretary of State for the Environment* [1981] AC 75 (HL) 98 (Lord Diplock) and 105–6, 115 (Viscount Dilhorne); Franks Committee, Report of the Committee on Administrative Tribunals and Inquiries, Cmnd 218 (1957) at [288]; C. Gearty, *Principles of Human Rights Adjudication* (Oxford University Press, 2004), pp. 121–2.

[16] *Taking Rights Seriously* (Cambridge, MA: Harvard University Press, 1978), p. 22, and see also pp. 84–5, 90–100, and especially his 'Reply to Critics', pp. 294–330 (reply to Kent Greenawalt), as well as his reply to Greenawalt in M. Cohen (ed.), *Ronald Dworkin and Contemporary Jurisprudence* (London: Duckworth, 1984), pp. 263–8; Dworkin, *A Matter of Principle* (Cambridge, MA: Harvard University Press, 1985), Chapter 3; *Law's Empire* (Cambridge, MA: Harvard University Press, 1986), pp. 221–4, 243–4, 310–2, 338–9.

[17] K. Greenawalt, 'Discretion and Judicial Decision: The Elusive Quest for the Fetters that Bind Judges' (1975) 75 *Columbia Law Review* 359; Greenawalt, 'Dworkin's Rights

cases show, it still is. And, furthermore, the problems with this distinction illuminate what is promising in the institutional approaches, on which I will elaborate shortly.

Dworkin's distinction appears to suffer from three general problems: conceptual difficulties, descriptive inaccuracy, and negative consequences. As to the first, one conceptual difficulty is the role played by consequences in his theory. Many have understood him to be saying that judges will determine questions on principle, as matters of fairness and justice, and not yield to arguments about consequences or utility. He accuses his critics of misunderstanding him on this point: judges are allowed fully to consider consequences in defining the requirements of principle.[18] Yet his supporters also miss this nuance.[19] He ultimately claims that the difference is 'between two kinds of questions that a political institution might put to itself, not a difference in the kinds of facts that can figure in an answer' and that an argument of principle may be 'thoroughly consequentialist in detail'.[20] But, if so, then rights look increasingly less like trumps.[21] This lack of clarity on the role of consequences has led legal theorists to argue that Dworkin's definition is highly stipulative and thus liable to confuse the reader, 'if not the author himself'.[22]

Another conceptual problem is the rigid allocation of decision-making functions and methods he proposes between courts and other institutions.[23] It is neither descriptively accurate nor politically desirable. The

---

Thesis' (1976) 74 *Michigan Law Review* 1167; Greenawalt, 'Policy, Rights, and Judicial Decision' 11 *Georgia Law Review* 991 (1977); N. MacCormick, *Legal Reasoning and Legal Theory* (Oxford University Press, 1978), pp. 259–64; J. Bell, *Policy Arguments in Judicial Decisions* (Oxford University Press, 1983), pp. 207–13; M. Weaver, 'Is a General Theory of Adjudication Possible? The Example of the Principle/Policy Distinction' (1985) 48 *Modern Law Review* 613, esp. 642–3; E. W. Thomas, *The Judicial Process* (Cambridge University Press, 2005), pp. 195–201; D. Kyritsis, 'Principles, Policies and the Powers of Courts' (2007) 20 *Canadian Journal of Law and Jurisprudence* 1; A. Kavanagh, 'Deference or Defiance? The Limits of the Judicial Role in Constitutional Adjudication', in G. Huscroft (ed.) *Expounding the Constitution: Essays in Constitutional Theory* (New York: Cambridge University Press, 2008), pp. 184, 194–200.

[18] Dwokin, *Taking Rights Seriously*, p. 294.

[19] S. Guest, *Ronald Dworkin* (2nd edn, Edinburgh University Press, 1997), pp. 50–1.

[20] Dworkin, *Taking Rights Seriously*, p. 297.

[21] See e.g. *ibid.*, p. 309.

[22] MacCormick, *Legal Reasoning and Legal Theory*, p. 259; see also Greenawalt, 'Dworkin's Rights Thesis', 1179 (accusing the author of 'conceptual gerrymandering').

[23] Dworkin, *Taking Rights Seriously*, pp. 315–17; Cohen (ed.), *Ronald Dworkin and Contemporary Jurisprudence*, pp. 265, 267; Dworkin, *A Matter of Principle*, Chapter 3 generally, but esp. p. 77; Dworkin, *Law's Empire*, pp. 221–4, 243–4.

truth is that judges consider both types of reasons (as illustrated further below), and so for that matter do legislatures.[24] And, further, we want each of them to consider both. Any view to the contrary will ultimately lead to tedious and strained interpretations of what 'principle' and 'policy' actually are. Dworkin's view of what constitutes a matter of principle is very expansive (one I and many liberal egalitarians would agree with), but others will take a much more restrictive view. The debates between such camps will be intractable.

The second general problem with the distinction is that it is not descriptively accurate. This weakens it conceptually, as already noted. But it is also a matter of justice. It is unfair for judges to employ the distinction selectively. The problem of descriptive inaccuracy can be seen in the uneasy way Dworkin manages the many counter-examples presented by authors such as Greenawalt.[25] Dworkin's replies, to borrow his own (unimpeachable) prose from another context, have 'the artificiality and strain of theories that defenders of a sacred faith construct in the face of embarrassing evidence'.[26] In a number of cases he rejects the reasoning of the courts.[27] In others he offers what appears like tedious and counter-intuitive reinterpretations of the judges' reasoning to render it consistent with his own theory.[28]

The problem of counter-examples has only strengthened since these early critiques were published. It is now becoming increasingly common for there to be an explicit limitation of rights claims. The most obvious example is the proportionate limitations of human rights.[29] Another is the recognition of substantive legitimate expectations in English law, where the court will weigh 'the requirements of fairness against any overriding

---

[24] The best elaboration of this argument is in Kyritsis, 'Principles, Policies and the Powers of Courts', 9.

[25] See generally 'Discretion and Judicial Decision', 'Dworkin's Rights Thesis', 'Policy, Rights, and Judicial Decision', and also the many examples provided by Bell and Weaver.

[26] *Justice in Robes* (Cambridge, MA: Harvard University Press, 2006), p. 212.

[27] Dworkin, *Taking Rights Seriously*, p. 309; Dworkin, *A Matter of Principle*, pp. 76, 100 (saying that if Jerry Mashaw's claim that the US Supreme Court's *Mathews* v. *Eldridge*, 424 US 319 (1976) brought a utilitarian balancing test into certain due process claims, which it certainly did, then 'the court was wrong').

[28] Dworkin, *Taking Rights Seriously*, pp. 296, 299, 306–7, 308–10; Dworkin, *A Matter of Principle*, p. 94. On the relevance of third-party interests, compare Restatement (Third) of Torts, §942.

[29] T. R. S. Allan, 'Human Rights and Judicial Review: A Critique of "Due Deference"' [2006] *Cambridge Law Journal* 671–95; J. Jowell, 'Judicial Deference: Servility, Civility or Institutional Capacity?' [2003] *Public Law* 592–601, 593–4.

interest relied upon for the change of policy'.[30] The question of whether the recognition of a common law duty to give reasons for administrative decisions would lead to undue ossification of bureaucratic discretion provides yet another example.[31] And yet another concerns the negligence liability of public authorities, where it is patently clear that policy concerns can negate any prima facie duty of care.[32]

Some might argue the principle/policy distinction is meant to *prescribe* rather than *describe* judicial conduct. This would be notably different from what Dworkin claimed. But, furthermore, there is little to think that the cases constituting counter-examples above *should* be decided differently. Suggesting that principle alone resolves such issues would be a gross oversimplification of how to respond to the complex constellation of interests in such cases. Such a proposal would exemplify the vice of formalism.

The third general problem with the principle/policy distinction is that it produces negative consequences. One such consequence can be called the *polarizing effect*. The distinction encourages the judicial view that a matter is either fully within the province of courts, the 'forum of principle', or wholly outside it. The distinction does not tolerate degrees as a concept (though some have tried, in my view unpersuasively, to use it this way).[33] An issue in the Dworkinian scheme is either a matter of principle, or of policy, with no twilight admitted between them. This raises the problem of judicial hubris on some issues, and judicial passivity on others.

The other negative consequence is unworkability and inconsistency.[34] The distinction has been applied differently by the House of Lords and Dworkin even to the same disputes or types of dispute. For instance, Dworkin says that the division of responsibilities he outlines is fully consistent with the decision in the House of Lords in *Bushell* v. *Secretary of State for the Environment*.[35] The case involved a challenge in a planning inquiry to the Minister's refusal to disclose for cross-examination the contents of a statistical survey it used to plan a motorway. While Dworkin found it uncontroversial that the decision of 'whether to build a highway

---

[30] *R* v. *North and East Devon Health Authority, ex parte Coughlan* [2001] QB 213 (CA) [57], [83]–[89].

[31] See P. P. Craig, *Administrative Law* (5th edn, London: Sweet & Maxwell, 2004), pp. 436–44; Harlow and Rawlings, *Law and Administration*, 2nd edn, pp. 522–8.

[32] C. Booth and D. Squires, *The Negligence Liability of Public Authorities* (Oxford University Press, 2006), pp. 165–228.

[33] See Gearty, *Principles of Human Rights Adjudication*, pp. 221–2.

[34] This is the central point in Weaver, 'Is a General Theory of Adjudication Possible?', 642–3; see also Bell, *Policy Arguments in Judicial Decisions*.

[35] [1981] AC 75.

in a particular direction is … a matter of policy',[36] the House of Lords, by contrast, distinguished between 'general policy', which they held unreviewable in that context, with questions more reviewable, such as 'what exact line the road should follow'.[37] Furthermore, the House of Lords found that, even in cases of general policy, there was a duty to be fair to all concerned and that the content of this duty varied depending on various contextual factors.[38] Another example is presented by Lord Hoffmann's finding in *Begum (Runa)* v. *Tower Hamlets*[39] that the rule of law requires that adjudications of private rights be decided by judges, and that this '*basic principle* does not yield to *utilitarian arguments* that it would be cheaper or more efficient to have these matters decided by administrators'.[40] This is clearly rooted in the Dworkinian idea of principle and its resistance to collective welfare and efficiency arguments. He went on: '[b]ut utilitarian considerations have their place when it comes to setting up, for example, schemes of regulation or social welfare.'[41] This dichotomy directly conflicts with Dworkin's own view on the same question. While Dworkin criticised the US Supreme Court's finding in *Mathews* v. *Eldridge*[42] on a very similar issue, Lord Hoffmann cited the majority opinion with approval.[43] In that case the Supreme Court found that the due process clause did not guarantee someone a right to an evidentiary hearing before the termination of his disability benefits. Dworkin found that the question in *Mathews* was a question of principle, and that it would be a 'serious mistake' if the court allowed a 'utilitarian analysis'.[44] If Lord Hoffmann and Ronald Dworkin do not have the combined brilliance to agree on the application of such a distinction, the conclusion that it is unworkable in practice looks rather safe.

C   Justiciability

The idea of justiciability is a commonly employed concept for demarcating judicial restraint. In his important essay on the topic, Geoffrey

---

[36] Dworkin, *A Matter of Principle*, p. 78.
[37] *Bushell* v. *Secretary of State for the Environment* [1981] AC 75 (HL) 98, 97–8, 108–9, 121–3.
[38] *Ibid.*, 95 (Lord Diplock).
[39] [2003] UKHL 5.   [40] *Ibid.*, [42] (emphasis added).
[41] *Ibid.*, [43]. For a critique, see Craig, *Administrative Law*, 5th edn, pp. 768–9.
[42] 424 US 319 (1976).
[43] Dworkin, *A Matter of Principle*, pp. 100–1; *Begum* v. *Tower Hamlets* [2003] UKHL 5 [45].
[44] Dworkin, *A Matter of Principle*, p. 100.

Marshall explains that the term 'justiciability' has a fact-stating sense and a prescriptive sense.[45] The idea of a 'fact-stating' sense is that a claim may be procedurally unenforceable, regardless of the inherent amenability of the issue to judicial review. Questioning proceedings of Parliament is a good example, as was the non-reviewability of prerogative powers prior to the *GCHQ* case.[46]

The prescriptive sense of justiciability refers to 'the aptness of a question for judicial solution'.[47] Various authors have further broken down this prescriptive sense of justiciability into two categories, best captured by Lorne Sossin's terminology of institutional capacity and institutional legitimacy.[48] Institutional capacity concerns whether there are judicially discoverable and manageable standards for resolving the issue.[49] Polycentric issues, and issues whose resolution requires significant expertise, are commonly regarded as unsuitable for judicial resolution in precisely this way. Institutional legitimacy, by contrast, refers to the normative political legitimacy of the judiciary as an institution for resolving the question. Many issues are said to be best left to politically accountable branches of government, regardless of judicial capacity considerations.

The concept thus has dimensions of procedure, capacity, and legitimacy, any one of which may colour an issue as non-justiciable. Thus conceived, it appears that the justiciability question asks, or could be regarded as asking, essentially the same or very similar question to the institutional approaches discussed in section 3 below. If so, why is Murray Hunt so critical?

One source of confusion may be the ambiguous usage of the term. Justiciability has variously been described as a property of disputes,[50]

---

[45] G. Marshall, 'Justiciability', in A. G. Guest (ed.), *Oxford Essays in Jurisprudence* (Oxford University Press, 1961), pp. 265, 267–8.

[46] Bill of Rights 1689; s. 3 Parliament Act 1911; *Council of Civil Service Unions* v. *Minister for the Civil Service* [1985] AC 374 (HL).

[47] Marshall, 'Justiciability', p. 269.

[48] L. Sossin, *Boundaries of Judicial Review: The Law of Justiciability in Canada* (Toronto: Carswell, 1999), p. 233; see also D. J. Galligan, *Discretionary Powers: A Study of Official Discretion* (Oxford University Press, 1986), p. 241; Booth and Squires, *The Negligence Liability of Public Authorities*, pp. 33–41.

[49] *Baker* v. *Carr*, 369 US 186 (1962), 217 (Brennan J); *Buttes Gas and Oil Co* v. *Hammer (No 3)* [1982] AC 888 (HL) 938 (Lord Wilberforce); *Kuwait Airways Corpn* v. *Iraqi Airways Co (Nos 4 and 5)* [2002] UKHL 22 [24]–[26] (Lord Nicholls).

[50] Marshall, 'Justiciability', p. 56 (citing Lord McDermott's usage); R. Summers, 'Justiciability' (1963) 26 *Modern Law Review* 530–8, 531.

areas,[51] decisions,[52] claims,[53] acts,[54] and rights.[55] All these uses are unduly broad. Marshall correctly observed that '"[c]learing a slum", "Implementing a social policy", "Extinguishing private rights", "Resolving a dispute between parties" are … all possible descriptions from different standpoints of what may be the same process'.[56] In this sense, Hunt's critique of what he calls the 'spatial approach' – the tendency to hive off areas of decision-making such as national security or resource allocation – is justified, and in this T. R. S. Allan agrees.[57] Both authors call for a more nuanced, contextual approach. However, the idea could be, and in fact often is, applied differently. One could argue that the idea should properly apply only to discrete legal issues or questions, understood in their narrow context. In fact, many judges use the term in precisely this careful way,[58] as do scholars such as Lorne Sossin and Robert Summers.[59]

I nonetheless agree that justiciability provides an inappropriate model of judicial restraint because it presents three significant practical problems. The first is that, regardless of whether it is *necessarily* tied to the spatial approach, it is highly vulnerable to such an interpretation. Recasting the doctrine would be to swim against the tide. It *is* viewed as different

---

[51] R (Douglas) v. (1) North Tyneside Metropolitan Borough Council and (2) Secretary of State for Education and Skills [2003] EWCA Civ 1847 [62] (warning that 'the discretionary area of resource allocation … is not justiciable'); R (on the application of Pro Life Alliance) v. BBC [2003] UKHL 23 [44]. See also the judgments of Lord Hoffmann in Marcic v. Thames Water Utilities Ltd [2003] UKHL 66 [70] (priorities in water management) and Secretary of State for the Home Department v. Rehman [2001] UKHL 47 [57] (national security) and R v. Jones and another [2006] UKHL 16 [67] (power to make war).

[52] Carty v. Croydon LBC [2005] EWCA Civ 19 [21] (Dyson LJ); see also P. Cane, Administrative Law (4th edn, Oxford University Press, 2004), p. 54; H. Woolf, J. Jowell, A. P. Le Sueur, and S. A. de Smith, Principles of Judicial Review (London: Sweet & Maxwell, 1999), p. 169.

[53] Booth and Squires, The Negligence Liability of Public Authorities, p. 29.

[54] Cane, Administrative Law, p. 54.

[55] In re Certification of the Constitution of the Republic of South Africa, 1996 (4) SA 744 (CC) [78].

[56] Marshall, 'Justiciability', p. 269.

[57] M. Hunt, 'Sovereignty's Blight: Why Contemporary Public Law Needs the Concept of "Due Deference"', in N. Bamforth and P. Leyland (eds.), Public Law in a Multi-Layered Constitution (Oxford: Hart Publishing, 2003), pp. 339, 346–8; Allan, 'Human Rights and Judicial Review', 671, 672–3.

[58] Jackson and Others v. Attorney General [2005] UKHL 56 [110] (Lord Hope); Kuwait Airways Corpn v. Iraqi Airways Co (Nos. 4 and 5) [2002] UKHL 22 [26] (Lord Nicholls); Barrett v. Enfield LBC [1999] UKHL 25, [2001] 2 AC 550 at 571 (Lord Slynn); Canada (Auditor General) v. Canada Minister of Energy, Mines & Resources [1989] 2 SCR 49 (SCC) 90–1 (Dickson CJ); Buttes Gas and Oil Co v. Hammer (No 3) 938 [1982] AC 888 (HL) (Lord Wilberforce).

[59] Sossin, Boundaries of Judicial Review, pp. 236–8; Summers, 'Justiciability', 535–7.

from the idea of deference or judicial restraint by several commentators[60] and judges.[61] Using it thus constitutes an ongoing risk.

The second concern is the categorical nature of a finding of non-justiciability.[62] The precedential force of a non-justiciability finding can be extremely strong and potentially sweeping. It is a rather nuclear option. When taken, the fact-stating and prescriptive senses of justiciability combine in an insidious way, for once a judge declares something non-justiciable on prescriptive grounds, a decision-making power can become so in the procedural or fact-stating sense. This creates zones of legal unaccountability that can only be altered slowly over time or at the behest of a new legal instrument. In fact, this is a problem common to most types of conceptual formalism.

The third and related problem is that the concept has the polarizing effect already discussed above in connection with the principle/policy distinction. On the one hand it creates zones of legal unaccountability and, on the other, it has nothing to say about the appropriate degree of judicial restraint when a matter clearly is justiciable. It rather commends judicial hubris. If an issue is justiciable, is it not the province of the judiciary to adjudicate it? The common answer here is that some restraint may still be needed when adjudicating justiciable issues, and this very answer further confirms the poverty of the approach for the task at hand.

III   Institutional approaches

Non-doctrinalism looked particularly troubling after both the *Lochner*[63] era in the United States and Diceyan inspired English judicial hostility to the alleged new despotism of the welfare state. Formalism too lost favour both because its pretensions to truth were philosophically unsound and it gave a veneer of objectivity to a number of inarticulate major premises.

---

[60] In addition to Hunt, 'Sovereignty's Blight'; see D. Dyzenhaus, 'The Politics of Judicial Deference: Judicial Review and Democracy', in M. Taggart (ed.), *The Province of Administrative Law* (Oxford: Hart Publishing, 1997), p. 286; Cane, *Administrative Law*, p. 58; Dworkin, *A Matter of Principle*, p. 101.

[61] See generally Lord Steyn, 'Deference: A Tangled Story' [2005] *Public Law* 346–59; *R v. Ministry of Defence, ex parte Smith* [1996] QB 517 (CA) 556 (Bingham MR); see also *Operation Dismantle v. The Queen* [1985] 1 SCR 441 (SCC) [51]–[54] (Wilson J).

[62] C. Scott and P. Macklem, 'Constitutional Ropes of Sand or Justiciable Guarantees? Social Rights in a New South African Constitution' (1992) 141 *University of Pennsylvania Law Review* 1, 27.

[63] *Lochner v. New York* 198 US 45 (1905).

Institutional approaches arose out of the awareness of these two problems. In this section I seek to explain part of its background before turning to defining and refining its general features. I will then discuss how institutionalism has led scholars down two different paths, one taking a restrictive view of the judge's role, and the other a more expansive one that would see judges take a wide view of what is justiciable but employ factors or principles of restraint in the process.

A   The rising tide of institutionalism

The terminology of 'institutional competence' can be traced directly to the legal process school of jurisprudence, a post-war American school of thought based at Harvard Law School. It was guided chiefly by Henry Hart, Albert Sacks, and Lon Fuller. In the materials for their legal process course, Hart and Sacks elaborated three general themes: the belief in courts as a forum of reason, rational argumentation, and neutral principles; the centrality of process in ensuring the integrity of reasoned elaboration, which was the key to 'sound' decision-making; and the principle of 'institutional settlement', namely, that citizens have a duty to follow decisions 'duly arrived at' by the state.[64] For his part, Lon Fuller developed a theory of the role of adjudication in his posthumously published 'Forms and Limits of Adjudication', in which he sought to identify the distinguishing features of adjudication (chiefly, the participation by affected parties in adjudication by way of presenting proofs and reasons for a decision in one's favour).[65] He thereby also identified subject-matter that is unsuited for courts, most notably polycentric tasks.

The concept of relative institutional competence was most clearly imported into English law through the influential writings of Jeffrey Jowell, who had himself conducted advanced research in Boston working in part with Hart and Fuller.[66] Jowell has revived interest in the concept of

---

[64] See H. M. Hart Jr and A. M. Sacks, *The Legal Process: Basic Problems in the Making and Application of Law* (Westbury, NY: Foundation Press, 1994), p. 102. See generally Duxbury, *Patterns of American Jurisprudence*, Chapter 4. On 'institutional settlement', see Hart and Sacks, *The Legal Process*, pp. 1–9, and the introductory essay by Eskridge Jr and Frickey, p. xcvi.

[65] L. Fuller, 'The Forms and Limits of Adjudication,' (1978–1979) 92 *Harvard Law Review* 353.

[66] See J. L. Jowell, *Law and Bureaucracy: Administrative Discretion and the Limits of Legal Action* (New York: Dunellen Pub Co, 1975); Jowell, 'The Legal Control of Administrative Discretion' [1973] *Public Law* 178–220; Jowell, 'Judicial Deference and Human Rights: A Question of Competence', in P. Craig and R. Rawlings (eds.), *Law and Administration in*

relative institutional competence in more recent work, largely to address the question of deference under the Human Rights Act 1998. This work was cited with approval by Lord Bingham in his leading speech in the *A and Others* case.[67]

Although the allure of legal process faded during the Warren Court-era optimism, there has been an American revival in the idea of institutional competence. A notable instance is found in the work of Neil Komesar.[68] He argues that there is a pervasive vice in legal scholarship of viewing the merits of courts in 'single-institutional' terms: one of focusing on the need for courts in a certain area, or by contrast the deficits of courts in a certain area. In his view, such approaches fail to give adequate attention to the comparative merits of courts and their alternatives by understanding the dynamic relationships between the institutions and how they handle particular problems. In *Law's Limits*, he captures this in two pithy claims: that institutions move together and that, as numbers and complexity increase, shifting tasks from courts to other institutions becomes both more necessary and more problematic. A similar set of concerns is evident in the work of Cass Sunstein on legal reasoning and later on judicial minimalism, in both of which he argued in favour of case-by-case, casuistic reasoning instead of grand theorising.[69] In a co-authored piece, Sunstein and Adrian Vermeule proclaim an 'institutional turn' in legal interpretation.[70]

In many ways, institutional competence is merely a way of describing what courts are good and (more often) bad at doing. This type of analysis has existed in Britain since the early advent of functionalism in public law. Functionalism itself built upon legal realist and philosophical pragmatist trends in American jurisprudence and philosophy. Thus while the terminology of 'institutional competence' and much useful analysis has

---

Europe: Essays in Honour of Carol Harlow (Oxford University Press, 2003), p. 67; see also Jowell, 'Judicial Deference'.

[67] *A and Others; X and Others* v. *Secretary of State for the Home Department* [2004] UKHL 56.

[68] N. Komesar, *Imperfect Alternatives: Choosing Institutions in Law, Economics and Public Policy* (University of Chicago Press, 1994); Komesar, *Law's Limits: The Rule of Law and the Supply and Demand of Rights* (Cambridge University Press, 2001).

[69] C. R. Sunstein, *Legal Reasoning and Political Conflict* (New York: Oxford University Press, 1996); Sunstein, *One Case at a Time: Judicial Minimalism on the Supreme Court* (Cambridge, MA: Harvard University Press, 2001).

[70] C. R. Sunstein and A. Vermeule, 'Institutions and Interpretation' (2003) 101 *Michigan Law Review* 885.

developed across the Atlantic, there is no reason to think the underlying concerns are in any way foreign.[71]

The increasing Anglo-Canadian attention devoted to the idea of judicial deference stems from a quite similar set of concerns. Commentators such as Richard Clayton, Guy Davidov, David Dyzenhaus, Richard Edwards, Murray Hunt, Aileen Kavanagh, Julian Rivers, and Lord Steyn see the refined concept as providing an alternative to outdated forms of justiciability and other instances of conceptual formalism.[72] One finds within this same family of ideas the notion of a discretionary area of judgment developed by Anthony Lester and David Pannick.[73] Under the various deference approaches, the authors suggest essentially three key features. The first is that judges should take an expansive view of what is reviewable and justiciable, encapsulated by Etienne Mureinik's idea of a 'culture of justification'.[74] The second is that judges should assign significant *weight* to the views of other decision-makers. The third, though not universal, feature is that the analysis of deference should be structured somehow by reference to principles or factors. These three features are the essence of the contextual institutional approach that I advocate.

Along the same path broken by Murray Hunt's important essay, Aileen Kavanagh has now provided the most sophisticated analysis. She links the judicial concern for deference to a concern 'about the limits of their institutional role in the constitutional framework'.[75] For Kavanagh, deference 'is a matter of assigning weight to the judgment of another, either where it is at variance with one's own assessment, or where one is uncertain of what the correct assessment should be'.[76] A court ultimately may

---

[71] Harlow and Rawlings, *Law and Administration*, 2nd edn; see also M. Loughlin, *Public Law and Political Theory* (Oxford: Clarendon Press, 1992), Chapters 6–8.

[72] Dyzenhaus, 'The Politics of Judicial Deference'; G. Davidov, 'The Paradox of Judicial Deference' (2001) 12 *National Journal of Constitutional Law* 133; R. Edwards, 'Judicial Deference under the Human Rights Act' (2002) 65 *Modern Law Review* 859–82; Hunt, 'Sovereignty's Blight'; Lord Steyn, 'Deference: A Tangled Story'; R. Clayton, 'Principles for Judicial Deference' [2006] *Judicial Review* 109; J. Rivers, 'Proportionality and the Variable Standard of Review' [2006] *Cambridge Law Journal* 174; Kavanagh, 'Deference or Defiance?'. See esp. T. Hickman, *Public Law after the Human Rights Act* (Oxford: Hart Publishing, 2010), Chapter 5.

[73] A. Lester and D. Pannick (eds.), *Human Rights: Law and Practice* (2nd edn, London: Lexis-Nexis, 2004) [3.19].

[74] See D. Dyzenhaus, 'Law as Justification: Etienne Mureinik's Conception of Legal Culture' (1998) 14 *South African Journal of Human Rights* 11.

[75] Kavanagh, 'Deference or Defiance?', p. 190. See also Part II of her *Constitutional Review under the UK Human Rights Act* (Cambridge University Press, 2009).

[76] *Ibid.*, p. 185.

wish to defer for *epistemic reasons* or for *reasons of authority*. She differs between minimal deference, which is always owed, and substantial deference, which is to be earned by the decision-maker and only when the judge recognises her 'institutional shortcomings' in respect of an issue. The three main situations where this occurs are when there is a deficit of (a) institutional competence, (b) expertise, or (c) institutional or democratic legitimacy.[77] She also identifies situations in which, although there may be no deficit in any of these areas, there may be *prudential* reasons to defer. Kavanagh's analysis is entirely apt and much richer than this brief statement, and the contextual institutional approach I develop below travels in precisely the same direction.

B   General features of institutional approaches

The following account is in large part reconstructive. Many of its features can be found in the works discussed in the preceding section. However, it may and does depart from the views of the particular authors and, to the extent it does, it is my own elaboration and refinement of the approach.

Acceptance of uncertainty and judicial fallibility. Institutional theories accept that in many forms of litigation judges will need to make choices that will be based on assumptions that might turn out not to be true. They may be unsure of the reliability of evidence, expert witness credibility, or the likely effect of the judgment on patterns of behaviour. The concern over the judicial capacity to adjudicate 'social' or 'legislative' facts – namely those recurrent patterns of social behaviour upon which policy is to be based – is a case in point.[78] Other familiar examples would include judgments about whether a ruling will generate floods of new claims or create market instability; whether a new common law rule – such as a duty to give reasons – might render administration unworkably difficult; whether imposing a duty of care on a public authority will adversely affect service provision; or whether a given period of pre-trial detention is required to carry out effective counter-terrorism operations. Uncertainty is compounded when the impact of the judgment might or

---

[77] *Ibid.*, p. 192.
[78] K. C. Davis, *Administrative Law Treatise* (St Paul, MN: West Publishing Co, 1958), vol. II, p. 353 [15.03]; see also *A and Others; X and Others* v. *Secretary of State for the Home Department* [2004] UKHL 56 [29].

will be widespread. Thus, when the validity or Convention compatibility of legislation is in question, the concerns become even more acute as the legislation often may (though might not) affect many persons. Institutional approaches emphasise that judges have certain *epistemic* deficits in evaluating such effects, and that they should be aware of them when deciding cases.

The preoccupation with uncertainty is not limited solely to impact. One of the most significant issues in contemporary political philosophy, especially liberalism, is how to account for disagreement about justice. John Rawls calls this type of problem the 'fact of reasonable pluralism', whereas Jeremy Waldron calls it 'reasonable disagreement'.[79] Some acceptance of this idea leads (some) institutionalists to be wary of both highly abstract theorising about rights and with judges handing down sweeping judgments because it is 'simply the right thing to do'. Yet this scepticism can lead to different conclusions, and those who give weight to institutional considerations may disagree quite radically on the extent to which reasonable disagreement should affect the judicial role.[80] While for many writers reasonable disagreement does not imply that courts must abstain from answering the question, for all those who accept it, it does clearly imply some measure both of judicial humility and respect for the moral authority of representative institutions.

Concern with consequences and systemic effect. Due to the problem of uncertainty and disagreement, the consequences of a judgment are of direct concern to institutionalists. The number of people adversely or beneficially affected in concrete terms (e.g. hearings, prison releases, halted deportations, compensation) speaks volumes. The vindication of principle alone is worth something less, though it is not irrelevant. Consequences are not important because institutionalists are necessarily consequentialists. It is rather that in the face of uncertainty over institutional capacity and systemic impact, reports of positive or

---

[79] J. Waldron, *Law and Disagreement* (Oxford: Clarendon Press, 1999); J. Rawls, *Political Liberalism* (New York: Columbia University Press, 1996); J. Habermas, *Between Facts and Norms*, trans. W. Rehg (Cambridge: Polity Press, 1996); A. Gutman and D. Thompson, *Democracy and Disagreement* (Cambridge, MA: Belknap Press, 1996).

[80] J. Raz, 'Disagreement in Politics,' (1998) 43 *American Journal of Jurisprudence* 25, 45; A. Kavanagh, 'Participation and Judicial Review: A Reply to Jeremy Waldron' (2003) 22 *Law and Philosophy* 451, 466; Rawls, *Political Liberalism*, pp. 231ff.; Sunstein, *Legal Reasoning and Political Conflict*; Sunstein, *One Case at a Time* (both works address this theme). I respond to Sunstein's role for pluralism in Chapter 10, section IV.A.

negative consequences tend to appeal neutrally to *either* deontological or consequentialist moral theories. They therefore provide a helpful and often uncontroversial metric by which we can evaluate the success of the judicial role. This is the essence of Sunstein's argument for incompletely theorised agreements: '[t]he distinctly legal solution to the problem of pluralism is to produce agreement on particulars, with the thought that often people who are puzzled by general principles, or who disagree on them, can agree on individual cases.'[81] For this reason, institutional approaches ought to be concerned with the empirical study of law familiar to the law and society and socio-legal studies fields of scholarship.

Rights as prima facie claims subject to balancing. Given uncertainty, the weight given to consequences, and the rejection of formalism, values such as fairness, the rule of law, and rights tend to become principles or factors that are given considerable weight but are ultimately subject to balancing against competing concerns. Thus institutionalists tend to reject the idea that rights are trumps, or side-constraints, or no-go zones for public action. Institutional approaches to restraint are sceptical about the promise of a priori judicial theorising about the essence of rights. They rather see the process of rights adjudication as a form of accountability in which a challenged decision is filtered through a judicial process of reasoned, public justification according to a set of legal and moral standards. Judging may be one kind of politics, on this view, but one with its own institutional features that provide particular benefits in terms of how arguments are advanced and responded to.

This approach to rights adjudication tends to take an expansive view of what interests are to be protected under the rubric of a constitutional right. So there is little hand-wringing over what liberty or free expression 'really' are, in their essential nature. Rather, under this approach it is uncontroversial whether feeding pigeons in a square is an exercise of liberty and pornography is an exercise of expression. The balancing stage allows the court to acknowledge that the interest is engaged but that regulation of it is permissible. For similar reasons, institutionalists are less absolutist about rights and this makes them less uneasy about positive rights.[82]

---

[81] Sunstein, *Legal Reasoning and Political Conflict*, p. 47.

[82] R. Alexy, *A Theory of Constitutional Rights*, trans. J. Rivers (Oxford University Press, 2002), Chapter 9. While Alexy's theory is largely unconcerned with the institutional issues identified here, it does exemplify an approach that takes an expansive view of justiciability and assigns a strong role to judicial balancing under the doctrine of proportionality.

Inter-institutional comity and collaboration. Recognising the limitations and legitimacy of the judicial process leads quite naturally to courts viewing their merits in a comparative light. Kavanagh captures this in the idea of *inter-institutional comity*.[83] I would suggest that to this idea we must join that of collaboration (or complementarity). Comity can exist between two wholly separate institutions – such as the respect accorded by one national court to the judgment of another. But the institutional approach also takes the view that the three primary branches of government essentially collaborate in the general promotion of commonly accepted public values such as fairness, autonomy, welfare, transparency, efficiency, and so on. Parliament, the executive, and courts are on this vision part of a joint enterprise for the betterment of society. Conflicts between them are subsumed within one vision of governance. Tension and disagreement between institutions is not regarded as a cacophonous power struggle, but rather as part of the dynamic process of give and take that the public chooses as part of the complete package of modern democratic government. This may just be a different way of reiterating old observations about the value of checks and balances. And clearly one could pay lip service to this idea while advocating a highly interventionist judicial role. But the idea ought to have, and in the hands of institutionalists normally does have, certain practical implications. Judges are more humble on this vision than under non-doctrinal approaches, and the vision of the distribution of decision-making functions is less compartmentalised and is rather more fluid than formalist ones. Tasks may be addressed in a multi-institutional rather than in the single-institutional fashion envisaged by the more rigid functionalist and formalist approaches. A useful but by no means uncontroversial metaphor capturing this idea is that of a dialogue between courts and legislatures.[84] Whether the judicial review of constitutional rights actually meets the lofty aspirations of this label is a hotly debated question, but that such aspirations are reflected in the institutional approaches is beyond doubt.

The extent to which democratic legitimacy ought to be regarded as a relevant factor is a divisive issue even among those who accept the legitimacy of judicial review of constitutional rights. Jowell, on the one hand,

---

[83] Kavanagh, 'Deference or Defiance?', p. 188.

[84] See (2007) 45 *Osgoode Hall Law Journal* 1–201 in its entirety for a critical retrospective on the use of this metaphor in Canadian constitutional theory. See also T. R. Hickman 'Constitutional Dialogue, Constitutional Theories and the Human Rights Act 1998' [2005] *Public Law* 306.

emphasises that the Human Rights Act 1998 secured the 'constitutional competence' of the courts in respect of rights and that strong deference to Parliament on legitimacy grounds would be misplaced.[85] Kavanagh, Hunt, and Rivers believe that the views of Parliament remain important and relevant.[86] In one sense, there is less distance between these thinkers than one might initially think. I believe they would all agree, as I would, on the following passage from *R* v. *Lichniak* by Lord Bingham:

> [T]he fact that [the statute] represents the settled will of a democratic assembly is not a conclusive reason for upholding it, but a degree of deference is due to the judgment of a democratic assembly on how a social problem is best tackled.[87]

However, their reasons for agreement with this claim may differ. Whereas some would agree on grounds of both institutional capacity and legitimacy, Jowell would do so for reasons of institutional capacity alone. Indeed, he claims that the decision about 'whether the overall benefit of limiting the relevant right is necessary to democracy … is for the courts alone'.[88] In agreement with Kavanagh and Hunt, I feel that this statement goes too far. It does seem true to say that the courts do have the last word on this issue under the Human Rights Act 1998. But that is not quite the same as saying that democratic legitimacy is *irrelevant,* and the tenor of Jowell's piece approximates this latter claim. I think that this would fall foul of the institutional approach. If we accept judicial fallibility in respect of consequences and impact, as Jowell does, can we assume their infallibility with respect to reasoning on moral and political matters? And, if not, is not *some* reliance on the comparative *legitimacy* of representative self-government, warts and all, not a logical response to such judicial uncertainty?

Incrementalism. One strategy for judges to deal with all the above is to decide cases in incremental steps. Reasoning by analogy, following precedent, and deciding cases on narrow grounds are all familiar tools of the common law judge. In Chapter 10 I review the different techniques of incrementalism and how they fit the general pattern of judicial decision-making in cases of both welfare rights jurisdiction and more generally.

---

[85] Jowell, 'Judicial Deference and Human Rights'.
[86] Kavanagh, 'Deference or Defiance?'; Hunt, 'Sovereignty's Blight'; Rivers, 'Proportionality and the Variable Standard of Review'.
[87] *R* v. *Lichniak* [2002] UKHL 47. This is cited by Jowell, 'Judicial Deference', 598.
[88] Jowell, 'Judicial Deference and Human Rights', p. 81.

C   Two paths diverge: restrictive vs. contextual institutionalism

People can agree on much of the above while disagreeing about the role of courts in public law adjudication. In fact, there is an almost radical disagreement on precisely this point from *within* the institutional approaches.

Contextual institutionalism. Contextual institutionalists are those who believe judges should bear in mind the foregoing considerations during the course of adjudication. They should contextualise each issue and consider institutional factors when attributing weight to the views of other officials or the threat of uncertainty. They believe that judicial discretion can be structured by the use of principles of judicial restraint and that judges can be trusted to balance these occasionally under-represented considerations in the course of adjudication. Contextual institutionalists also believe more in the power of ideas, that there is some intersubjectively stable normative content to the idea of human rights and other public values, and that they express something important and that is worth protecting. There is weight given to the role of rational argumentation in courts, and some credence given to the capacity of courts to deliver predictable results under those terms. I believe this description fits the theories of a number of those public law scholars and judges who advocate a doctrine of judicial deference at the present time.

Restrictive institutionalism. Others would propose, on the same grounds of institutional competency, retaining bright-line rules that lessen the use of judicial discretion, either in certain pre-designated 'areas' (e.g. resource allocation, immigration, national security) or simply as a more general posture of judicial restraint (e.g. political constitutionalism).[89] The stronger form's advocates are so thoroughly convinced of judicial fallibility and the prominence of uncertainty that they would restrict the role of courts whenever possible. They would put less emphasis on the idea of inter-institutional collaboration, preferring the absolute supremacy of legislatures, which they find more legitimate. They might find the contextual institutionalists naïve for thinking that the process of balancing under expansive notions of justiciability will not lead to an unsustainable proliferation of the institutional competency problems that

---

[89] J. A. G. Griffith, 'The Political Constitution' (1979) 42 *Modern Law Review* 1; A. Tomkins, *Our Republican Constitution* (Oxford: Hart Publishing, 2004); R. Bellamy, *Political Constitutionalism: A Republican Defence of the Constitutionality of Democracy* (Cambridge University Press, 2007).

they have themselves identified. The net social consequences of employing bright-line rules (even if occasionally arbitrary) may be superior to allowing multi-factoral judicial weighing to take place on a case-by-case basis. This argument is made well in the American context in a book by Adrian Vermeule.[90] It appears that the work of political constitutionalists such as Adam Tomkins and Richard Bellamy, and possibly functionalists such as Carol Harlow and Richard Rawlings, would also lend strong support to this view.

These two categories in fact represent points at the opposite ends of a spectrum. There is a significant grey area. Some restrictive institutionalists might reject some models of constitutional rights while accepting others, while others might reject them all. They may also take different views on the value of the rule of law. And some contextual institutionalists may advocate contextualism on some issues (e.g. civil rights) while being more restrictive on others (e.g. social rights or national security). None of this should be surprising, if they all accept the basics of institutionalism. It is to be expected that they have different appraisals of acceptable levels of impact and uncertainty.

D   Measuring the success of institutional approaches

Because institutional approaches focus on so many variables and are overtly concerned with instrumentality and impact, estimating the value of institutional approaches must be a *dynamic process*. Doctrines (e.g. restrictive or contextual) must be tried, and their results analysed and open to revisitation as circumstances change. Whether courts are a good choice for implementing specific objectives is both geographically and temporally specific. Any approach must remain open to review – including the one for social rights set out in this book.

This also means that the value of a given institutional approach to judicial restraint depends on its *potential* to bring about desirable or undesirable outcomes. The question is not 'does it work?' but rather 'can it be made to work?' This is true because all the relevant variables can and do change over time. In my view, potential must be assessed by reference to (a) the history and empirical record of judging, both in terms of the decisions as between parties as well as their systemic effects; (b) the analytical coherence and instrumental value of any newly proposed legal doctrines

---

[90] A. Vermeule, *Judging under Uncertainty: An Institutional Theory of Legal Interpretation* (Cambridge, MA: Harvard University Press, 2006).

(e.g. a theory of deference, the abandonment of a distinction, adoption of civil procedure rules), by which I mean their ability to improve outcomes; (c) the prevailing public culture and its likely impact on judging; and (d) judicial attitudes, both actual and likely. Notably, items (b)–(d) can be changed. Scholars and judges invent new doctrines when old ones appear obsolete. Public awareness campaigns and new institutions (e.g. ombudspersons and parliamentary committees) or instruments (e.g. the Human Rights Act 1998) can change public views on values and the need for accountability, just as judicial training and diversity can improve judging. The evaluation process would have to be dynamic and experimental. If history demonstrates failure, we can tinker with items (b)–(d), then try again, in a perhaps more chastened manner.

If the two types of institutionalists are to stay true to the underlying approach, they must meet one another halfway. The restrictive institutionalists must be willing to recognise that history is but one, admittedly important (and equivocal), part of the equation, and be willing to experiment further. They have tended to underemphasise the importance of changing circumstances and principled idealism, of the possibility of fixing what they regard as hopelessly broken. They may be unduly fatalistic. And the contextual institutionalists must in turn not take a Panglossian attitude in the light of persistent failure. They must give weight to the equivocal record of judicial success. They – even as institutionalists – have often not done this.

IV Developing the contextual institutional approach

The leading problem with this approach is that it gives judges expansive jurisdiction over important questions of the public interest. One often finds a particular tool offered in response to this problem: principles of restraint. These principles would structure the exercise of judicial discretion (or judgment), and that is the key difference from the non-doctrinal approaches. Using such principles or factors nonetheless raises a number of concerns and questions. I will address these in an attempt to refine the approach and to indicate what work remains to be done.

A The nature of legal reasoning under a 'principled approach'

Reasoning with principles and factors. Institutional considerations such as expertise and democratic legitimacy can be stated as principles or factors. Principles will likely have more profound significance and be stated at a higher level of generality, whereas factors may be more mundane and specific. So a statutory indication to consider the jurisprudence of the European Court of Human Rights may be a factor, and the view that respect ought to be accorded to the views of Parliament may be encapsulated in a principle of democratic legitimacy. But both principles and factors have the same key quality – weight. Since they have weight, they exert a pull on outcomes, but are not decisive. They can both give way to other considerations. They can therefore be contrasted with rules and can conflict with one another in the circumstances of a given case. Judicial reasoning with both principles and factors is a well-established and much studied part of judging.[91] As used within this approach to restraint, they are perhaps most usefully described as 'guiding standards'. Their purpose is to structure and confine the exercise of judicial discretion where institutional considerations are relevant.

Choosing principles. There have been a number of principles of restraint or deference offered by various judges and scholars, as alluded to in section III above: relative expertise, availability of alternatives for accountability, polycentricity and complexity, nature of the interest or right, democratic legitimacy, whether there has been legislative protection of a vulnerable group, consideration of social science evidence, and risk of judicial error. One example from the UK can be found in the set of principles provided by Laws LJ in his minority judgment in *International Transport Roth GmbH and others* v. *Secretary of State for the Home Department*, which he intended to assist in interpretation of the ECHR:[92]

(a) 'greater deference is to be paid to an Act of Parliament than to a decision of the executive or subordinate measure';
(b) 'there is more scope for deference where the "Convention itself requires a balance to be struck, much less so where the right is stated in terms which are unqualified"';
(c) 'greater deference will be due to the democratic powers where the subject-matter in hand is peculiarly within their constitutional responsibility, and less when it lies more particularly within the constitutional responsibility of the courts'; and

[91] Dworkin, *Taking Rights Seriously*, pp. 22–8; MacCormick, *Legal Reasoning and Legal Theory*, Chapter VII; Alexy, *A Theory of Constitutional Rights*, Chapter 3; see also T. Eckhoff, 'Guiding Standards in Legal Reasoning' (1976) 29 *Current Legal Problems* 205; Sunstein, *Legal Reasoning and Political Conflict*, pp. 28–31.
[92] [2002] EWCA Civ 158 [81]–[87].

(d) 'greater or less deference will be due according to whether the subject matter lies more readily within the actual or potential expertise of the democratic powers or the courts.'[93]

This list comprises both principles and factors. It is not free from problems. The first principle is not always warranted – an antiquated or arcane part of an Act may be entitled to less deference than the unequivocal and highly publicised decision of a minister on a matter of national importance. The second factor seems rather uncontroversial, whereas the third is both vague and reminiscent of formalism. In any case, the potential for variation from this list is clear and some years after the judgment the proposal has still to be applied in any consistent fashion.

Other courts have used principled or factoral approaches to judicial restraint in public law adjudication. For over a decade the Supreme Court of Canada has replaced the formalistic collateral fact doctrine in administrative law with what it until recently has called the 'pragmatic and functional approach' to determining the correct standard of review of tribunals, and later to administrative discretion. It is a well-known four-part analysis focusing on (a) the existence of an ouster clause, (b) expertise, (c) the purpose of the Act, and (d) the nature of the problem, specifically, whether it is a question of law or fact.[94] This test is quite evidently oriented towards the needs of administrative law. So far as human rights cases are concerned, Justice Bastarache proposed in the *M* v. *H*[95] case another set of factors for assisting in evaluating judicial deference within the proportionality enquiry under s. 1 of the Charter of Rights. The principles included asking (a) whether the interest is fundamental, (b) whether the groups concerned are particularly vulnerable, (c) whether the scheme is highly complex and/or expertise is required, (d) what is the source or democratic origins of the rule, and (e) whether there is a strong role for moral judgments in setting policy.[96] While each of these factors do appear to be relevant to restraint in Canadian case law, Bastarache J wrote alone and such principles have not caught on as a freestanding deference test.

One interesting feature of these approaches is that they have tended to vary between different subject-matter. This is natural, as the role of the

---

[93] *Ibid.*, [82]–[87].

[94] *Pushpanathan* v. *Minister of Citizenship and Immigration* [1998] 1 SCR 982 [26]; *Baker* v. *Minister of Citizenship and Immigration* [1999] 2 SCR 817; *Dunsmuir* v. *New Brunswick* [2008] 1 SCR 190 (revisiting the analysis).

[95] [1999] 2 SCR 3.

[96] *Ibid.*, [302].

court and the needs of administration and claimants will indeed vary between areas of law. It may even vary between rights or types of rights. This variation is likely to be achieved through combinations of subject-specific factors as well as general principles. This variety, as well as general prudence, also suggests that any list of factors should remain open to review and be non-exhaustive.

The primary focus in this book is social rights adjudication. In my view, a sound approach to social rights adjudication, and indeed a sound approach to much of public law adjudication beyond it, would commend the consideration of at least four general principles of restraint: democratic legitimacy, polycentricity, expertise, and flexibility. Each of them is complex and highly nuanced. The greatest need in any theory of restraint is to expound the role of each of these principles by showing how they may be given weight in adjudication. That is the task of the subsequent four chapters. Before embarking on it, it is necessary to consider a number of potential problems with the very nature of the contextual institutional approach that must first be addressed.

Conflict, incommensurability, and equilibrium. In some cases all the factors will point one way. However, where they do not, the degree of conflict will increase the element of legal uncertainty. Both conflict and incommensurability are common to both moral reasoning and in any form of adjudication and indeed practical reasoning.[97] But this uncertainty can impede access to justice for claimants seeking advice. I will shortly turn to how practically this might be dealt with, but it is necessary to consider further how this process of balancing might take place. First, it can be hoped that greater refinement of the principles themselves will help settle their application to concrete instances. It ought to be a goal of such refinement that workability and specificity are achieved. Yet where they remain unclear or conflict with one another in a given case, we will be thrown back to the judge's sense of judgment, informed by the submissions of the parties. Thus, second, the judge must try to balance and adjust the application of the various principles and factors, together with an intuitive sense of the justice of their application to the concrete case, all in the attempt to achieve coherence and equilibrium between them. It must be acknowledged that, even though the principles leave room for

---

[97] J. Raz, *Engaging Reason: On the Theory of Value and Action* (Oxford University Press, 1999), Chapter 6; Raz, *The Morality of Freedom* (Oxford University Press, 1986), Chapter 13.

discretion, the scope of that discretion is still significantly structured by the elaborated principles and factors. While the remaining scope for judgment may still be unsatisfactory for restrictive institutionalists, we have doubtless travelled a considerable distance from the expansive non-doctrinal options.

Complexity and workability. Institutional approaches ought always to be concerned with systemic impact. It should be clear that the process just laid out can lead to highly complex determinations.[98] If there is to be this form of multi-factoral balancing, what are the 'transaction costs' of this process? Does the degree of discretion shot through the entire process make each trial or appeal like a throw of the dice? As I will explain below, the principles would not be uniformly applicable in public law – they would likely arise in some but not all cases. Nonetheless, the problem remains.

My main answer to this problem in this book is that where it is the case that several principles discussed in Chapters 6–9 apply, and the result appears cacophonous, the appropriate approach is to have recourse to the techniques of incrementalism set out in Chapter 10. Those techniques provide a rough heuristic for approximating the result that would respect those principles.

Trust and judicial fallibility. Trusting judges to carry out this balancing exercise appropriately is the major article of faith in the contextual institutional approach. It is the one the restrictive institutionalists reject. Sunstein and Vermeule place much emphasis on judicial fallibility.[99] They claim that too many theorists adopt theories on the assumption that judges should decide cases like academic specialists, and that such theorists disregard the generalist persuasion of such judges. This comment contains some truth. Indeed, they may have added that judges also need to decide under far more severe time constraints as well. But I do not think the proposals contained in this part of the book stray far from the ordinary business of judging. The use of factors and contextual tests rather than bright-line rules has not posed insurmountable problems for judges thus far. Indeed, it appears that public law judging in Britain has in fact moved more in that direction.

---

[98] See *Dunsmuir* v. *New Brunswick* [2008] 1 SCR 190), esp. [192], where Binnie J noted that '[t]here is afoot in the legal profession a desire for clearer guidance than is provided by lists of principles, factors and spectrums'.

[99] Sunstein and Vermeule, 'Institutions and Interpretation'.

B   Pragmatics: how should judges apply an institutional approach?

When the principles are relevant. The principles of restraint are relevant whenever existing legal standards leave significant judicial discretion, and either (a) there is potential for significant impact beyond the parties to the dispute, or (b) there is a significant measure of uncertainty as to a relevant fact or moral principle. Few institutionalists would accept the Dworkinian idea that there is very little judicial discretion in adjudication. However, if one were inclined to take that view, I would argue that institutional considerations are ordinarily relevant to the best constructive interpretation of a community's legal practice, for surely the best interpretation commends judges not answering questions that both reach beyond their epistemic capacity and that could adversely affect a large number of people.

When the principles are not relevant. In many run-of-the-mill cases the parties will accept that the development or application of a given standard is part of the judge's ordinary function and any reference to institutional competence will appear out of place. The parties will play a crucial role in determining this. A useful heuristic device that accounts for the concerns of institutionalism is the application of precedent or the analogical extension of precedent.[100] In both cases, the relevant institutions have typically adjusted to earlier findings, and the systemic distortions one expects from an analogical extension of precedent are both modest and conducted in a context in which earlier cases have put the public on notice of the direction of the law. There is, however, one case where this presumption should not apply. Where there is evidence that an earlier precedent or approach has created problems – such as regulatory ossification in the United States – courts ought to have regard for this and be hesitant to extend its application in the light of the new evidence. This is captured in the idea that evaluation of institutional approaches to restraint must remain dynamic, and in the technique of incrementalism that I call revisitation in Chapter 10.

Where in the judgment should the principles be addressed? Allan argues against the idea that there should be a freestanding 'doctrine' of deference, one that operates as a stand-alone test or checklist that judges must address in their judgments. He worries this would short-circuit a

---

[100]   Sunstein, *Legal Reasoning and Political Conflict*, Chapter 3.

contextual inquiry. I think he is correct in worrying about this, and he is not alone. It was precisely the view of Iacobucci J, when he responded for the majority of the Supreme Court of Canada to Bastarache J's approach to applying principles of deference in the context of section 1 of the Canadian Charter (the general proportionality limitations clause):

> Courts must be cautious not to overstep the bounds of their institutional competence … The question of deference … is intimately tied up with the nature of the particular claim or evidence at issue and not in the general application of the s. 1 [proportionality] test; it can only be discussed in relation to such specific claims or evidence and not at the outset of the analysis.
>
> I am concerned that Bastarache J. implies that the question of deference in a general sense should also be determined at the outset of the inquiry … The question of deference to the role of the legislature certainly enters into any discussion of remedy, … and can enter into the discussion of whether the legislature has discharged its burden under any of the steps of the s. 1 test. However, the question of deference is not an issue that can be determined prior to engaging in any of these specific inquiries. Nor should it be determined at the outset of the inquiry, given the court's important role in applying s. 1 of the Charter to determine whether the infringement of a guaranteed right can be justified in a free and democratic society.[101]

I believe that Iacobucci J's comments meet both Allan's criticism and the essence of the contextual institutional approach. The key is that any reference to principles of restraint should remain contextual. This means, likely, that a structured test of the sort advocated by Laws LJ in the *Roth* case may be inadvisable. What can be the alternative? It is surely right to identify a list of principles, but that is different from showing how they might be applied. In my view, the principles should 'float' in the legal analysis, rather than be fixed as a test to be met at an early schematic point in the judgment. The courts can adjudicate the claims by reference to the ordinarily applicable legal standards, contextualise the narrow legal issues, and then consider the principles of restraint if and when they become 'relevant' in the sense identified above. Some will be relevant in some cases and others obviously inapplicable. Invariably the parties will play a significant role in showing where they are relevant. This approach would deflect both of Allan's valid criticisms: the concern to preserve

---

[101] *M* v. *H* [1999] 2 SCR 3 [79]–[80].

contextual application, and the concern about double-counting deference at multiple points in the legal analysis.

V   Conclusion

The question of how judges ought to exercise judicial restraint is a crucially important constitutional issue, one that goes to the heart of the role of courts in social rights adjudication. In an earlier chapter I showed why non-doctrinal approaches to judicial restraint are insufficiently attentive to judicial errors, and in this chapter that formalist approaches are too rigid and are liable to be applied erratically. Institutional approaches build on these lessons by suggesting that uncertainty and judicial fallibility remain important issues and should stay in the foreground, that approaches dependent entirely on the sound exercise of judicial discretion or judgment are to be suspect. And further, they suggest that the judicial role is not a privileged form of higher law, situated above common politics. It is rather one institutional method of problem-solving acting in concert with other institutions, one that will vary across time and context.

Restrictive institutionalists largely agree with all the above and suggest that it may provide a good reason for rejecting constitutional rights (and if so, most certainly constitutional social rights). The next four chapters constitute my rebuttal of that view. I believe that the weaknesses in democratic and administrative oversight generate a need for legal accountability, and that judges do not lack the institutional competence to fill that need in the manner specified there. And further, the resulting proposal does not equate to an exotic theory that is foreign to judges and unlikely to be applied, but rather culminates, where the principles are not clear, in a theme of judicial incrementalism that is as workable as it is justified.

That approach, a contextual institutional approach, expresses confidence in the idea that judges can take a wide view of what ought to be justiciable, provided they are prepared to show restraint in the appropriate circumstances. That is the irony of all the talk of judicial restraint – it emerges as a discourse that liberates social rights (and similarly contentious public law rights) from the fetters of the non-justiciability doctrine. Judges can identify the appropriate circumstances for restraint by giving *weight* to principles of restraint in adjudication. I said nothing about the content of such principles in this chapter. I rather discussed the way in which judges might reason with them and, notably, the problems of conflicting principles and incommensurability, and whether to use the principles as a stand-alone 'test' in the judgment, or to bear them in mind as background principles and apply them when an issue calls for it. The crucially important remaining work is to expound the detail of the principles of restraint themselves, principles that bear in particular on the adjudication of constitutional social rights. That is the task of the next four chapters.

Democratic legitimacy

I   Introduction

Respect for basic social rights is a necessary feature of a just democracy, if we believe that political equality is what legitimises democracy. Yet that does not mean that we have a case for the judicial review of legislation. That case must overcome some powerful objections. Spending on health, housing, education, and assistance for the needy makes up nearly 70 per cent of the national budget in the United Kingdom.[1] Should control over its substance and minutiae be given to a bare majority of the Supreme Court? Or should it rather go to Parliament, its respective constituencies, and the broader culture of political accountability that has grown up around it?

While this may be an overstated way of putting the issue, it has a grain of truth. It is overstated because few advocates of social rights call for courts to take control of significant portions of the welfare budget, and judges in the countries this book addresses are nearly certain to reject any such role. But the concern does have a grain of truth to it, because in some cases the courts have travelled in that direction. In Hungary the Constitutional Court interfered substantially in controversial welfare reform.[2] And as Robert Dahl has noted by reference to the *Lochner* era in the United States, '[t]he Supreme Court effectively delayed an apparently intense law-making majority for as much as a quarter of a century.'[3] So the argument above is not always an overstated way of putting the issue.

For most judges, the question of democratic legitimacy will arise in a different way than it does for political theorists or those engaged in constitutional design. For judges, the question is for the most part already

---

[1] See Chapter 1, section III.C.
[2] See A. Sajo, 'How the Rule of Law Killed Hungarian Welfare Reform' (1996) 5 *East European Constitutional Review* 31.
[3] R. A. Dahl, *A Preface to Democratic Theory* (expanded edn, University of Chicago Press, 1956), p. 111.

answered – it would *not* be democratically legitimate for judges to *refuse* a job thrust upon them in a bill of rights adopted by the legislature or the people. That is why much of the critical commentary about the counter-majoritarian problem in judicial review will be of dubious relevance for them. I will nonetheless show below how the arguments pertaining to constitutional design in fact have important implications for how judges should adjudicate specific cases. This would be true of a new constitution that endorses an incrementalist approach, but also of any constitution where the principle of democratic legitimacy is a relevant legal principle.

This chapter sets out two main arguments. The first is that legislation adopted in a democracy manifesting the background political conditions set out in Chapter 1 is entitled, on grounds of political equality, to great and in some cases nearly final weight in political decision-making about rights. However, there are two main conditions in which the argument from equality no longer supports that presumption: where there has been an absence of legislative focus on a rights issue, and where the legislation addresses the right of someone belonging to a politically marginalised group. Poverty, I show, is a source of political marginalisation.

The second argument is that constitutional judicial review can provide a workable and proportionate response to these two problems. It can be used to ensure legislative focus, and to extend protection to groups that are particularly vulnerable to majoritarian bias or neglect. I illustrate how these two aims can be achieved through a principle of democratic legitimacy that can be given weight in adjudication. While at the theoretical and doctrinal level this approach departs at times from the practice of specific courts, in fact the outcomes counselled by this approach fit and to some extent justify as democratically legitimate the legal outcomes seen in both the United Kingdom and in the social rights jurisprudence of the Constitutional Court of South Africa.

II   The dignity of legislation

Why should legislation be viewed as so hallowed in the first place? Human rights advocates often say that if our conception of democracy either includes or is subject to human rights, then any law that violates our rights is entitled to no deference. Surely that is right to a quite significant extent, but it misses the point. The issue for some sceptics of judicial review is whether a given law does in fact breach a human rights principle. Their argument is concerned with which institution ought to have the authority for resolving that disputed question. It is an important argument with a significant core of truth, one that requires close examination.

A   The argument from political equality

The best argument in favour of the presumptive legitimacy of legislation in a democratic society is based on the concept of political equality.[4] Legislation produced by a democratic representative legislature is adopted under a procedure that seeks to give equal weight to every adult person's view, and, thereby, it gives effect to our notion that we ought to rule ourselves, rather than be ruled or 'dominated' by others. It must at once be recognised that both the notion of what constitutes equal treatment, and of non-domination or self-government, are themselves subject to considerable disagreement. There may be a range of institutional combinations that might satisfy it. In particular, many of those political theorists who advocate an equality-based theory of democracy support are open to judicial review in some form (usually in a representation reinforcing form).[5] And of course Ronald Dworkin's influential argument reconciling democracy with judicial review is itself based, as with

---

[4] R. A. Dahl, *On Democracy* (New Haven: Yale University Press, 1998), Chapters 5 and 6 for a readable introduction, and *Democracy and its Critics* (New Haven: Yale University Press, 1989), Chapter 6; C. R. Beitz, *On Political Equality: An Essay in Democratic Theory* (Princeton University Press, 1990); T. Christiano, *The Constitution of Equality: Democratic Authority and Its Limits* (Oxford University Press, 2008); A. Gutman and D. Thompson, *Democracy and Disagreement* (Cambridge, MA: Belknap Press, 1996), p. 26 ('Democracy ... is a conception of government that accords equal respect to the moral claims of each citizen').

[5] Dahl, *Democracy and its Critics*, pp. 187–91, and *How Democratic is the American Constitution?* (2nd edn, New Haven: Yale University Press, 2003), pp. 152–4; Beitz, *On Political Equality*, pp. 110–11, 228; Christiano, *The Constitution of Equality*, Chapter 7; I. Shapiro, *The State of Democratic Theory* (Princeton University Press, 2003), Chapter 3. Gutmann and Thompson, *Democracy and Disagreement*, pp. 45–8, have a very nuanced view, finding that it depends on empirical facts, a claim that reflects my own position. Some other democratic theorists have different theories of democracy (i.e. not derived chiefly from political equality), under which constitutional judicial review nonetheless plays an important role: J. Rawls, *Political Liberalism* (New York: Columbia University Press, 1996); J. Habermas, *Between Facts and Norms*, trans. W. Rehg (Cambridge: Polity Press, 1996), p. 280 ('[A] rather bold constitutional adjudication is even required in cases that concern the implementation of democratic procedure and the deliberative form of political opinion and will-formation'); P. Pettit, *Republicanism: A Theory of Freedom and Government* (Oxford University Press, 1997), pp. 180–3; D. Held, *Models of Democracy* (3rd edn, Cambridge: Polity Press, 2006), pp. 264–5, 282 (Held's notion of democratic autonomy).

his theory of rights and distributive justice, on the idea of showing equal respect and concern to all citizens.[6]

Nevertheless, some important thinkers argue that respecting the ideal of political equality means, essentially, observing a commitment to formal voting equality as the decision procedure for resolving reasonable disagreement between members of the political community over the meaning of our rights. Jeremy Waldron's book *Law and Disagreement* is very important.[7] Parsing his argument into premises and conclusion will facilitate the careful attention it deserves:

1. A liberal theory of rights-based morality is plausible, and any well–functioning democracy ought to protect liberal rights (Chapters 10 and 13).
2. There is good-faith reasonable disagreement between persons about the meaning of rights, and therefore a need to allocate to some institution the authority for resolving such disagreement. This disagreement, and the need for public action-in-concert in the face of it, are the two 'circumstances of politics' (Chapter 5).
3. Both legislatures and courts resolve disagreement about rights by majority voting after reasoned debate (Chapter 5).
4. Moral objectivity is 'irrelevant' because neither institution enjoys privileged access to any such truth (Chapter 8).
5. Legislatures are a sophisticated deliberative forum having many institutional advantages that facilitate equal treatment, and their conclusions are entitled to great respect (Chapters 5 and 6).
6. Legislatures are generally superior to courts because they attach 'positive decisional weight' and 'equal potential decisiveness' to the views of citizens in the process of decision-making (Chapter 5). They thereby respect the indisputable right of rights: participation in self-government (Chapter 11). Courts do neither of these.
7. Rights instrumentalism (defined as the idea that people may choose courts as a *means* of getting to right answers about rights) is implausible because one cannot rely on rights achievement as a metric of success when we disagree about their meaning.

---

[6] *Freedom's Law: The Moral Reading of the American Institution* (Cambridge, MA: Harvard University Press, 1996), 'Introduction', and *A Matter of Principle* (Cambridge, MA: Harvard University Press, 1985), Chapter 2.

[7] *Law and Disagreement* (Oxford: Clarendon Press, 1999). For an important supplement, see J. Waldron, 'The Core of the Case Against Judicial Review' (2006) 115 *Yale Law Journal* 1347.

Therefore:

8. In conflicts of authority between courts and legislatures over the meaning of rights, legislatures should prevail.

To be clear about my own view, I agree with premises one to five of Waldron's argument, but disagree with the rest for reasons I will shortly make clear. What is important in Waldron's argument is his focus on the issue of interpretive authority. He accepts that majority preferences can be wrong about what human rights and other political principles require. His point is that legislatures are morally superior to courts for defining such rights, for the same egalitarian reasons that support the legitimacy of democratic legislation.

In his later essay,[8] Waldron (1) makes clear that this argument applies under certain political conditions, which include general respect for human rights and well-functioning democratic institutions; and (2) he abandons premise seven and accepts that instrumentalism, or outcome-based arguments, *may* justify judicial review. His revised argument in that essay is that the outcome-based arguments are in fact equivocal at best, whereas the process arguments identified in premise six above all support legislatures over courts. This argument is weaker because of the role it opens up for outcome-based arguments in favour of judicial review, an uncertain variable that is highly contextual. His arguments in that essay do not begin to engage with the impact literature that I myself only began to engage with in Chapter 3. But my present concern is to show why the process-related arguments are problematic and require us to qualify his conclusion in a way that makes space for the possibility of judicial review.

B   Limits

Generally speaking, Waldron's argument for what might be called formal voting equality is liable to two general weaknesses.

1   The gap between preferences and outcomes

The first weakness is that legislatures very often do not, in fact, give equal weight to each voter's preferences except in a very nominal way. Waldron admits to presenting an ideal view of the legislative process, a 'rosy picture', that matches the 'naïvety' and 'idealism' of the picture of courts

---

[8] Waldron, 'The Core of the Case Against Judicial Review'.

presented by some legal philosophers.[9] Does that quip mean he agrees that his presentation is problematic on that point?[10] An account of each institution must strive for accuracy, rather than what Vermeule calls the 'nirvana fallacy': 'a pseudo institutional analysis that compares a worst-case picture of one institution to a best-case picture of another.'[11]

In the Westminster system, we all know that party whips discourage departures from central party policy, the executive in some cases dominates the legislature, and in a first-past-the-post electoral system the governing party rarely enjoys majority support. Issues are lumped together at election time such that one feels obliged, as a distant second best, to support a party in spite of many of its policies. So quite often legislative policy-making is more driven by the priorities of the few at the top of a party which enjoy less than majority support, than by free votes taken after a good-faith parliamentary debate between persons of open minds. Of course, the most obvious problem is the influence of lobbying and interest groups, or of parliamentarians selling their influence 'like a cab for hire'.[12] As noted long ago in America, 'there have been a number of exhaustive studies of lobbying, all of which, to one degree or another, have concluded that the interests of business and other well-financed and well-organized groups carry disproportionate weight in the legislature.'[13] That kind of rent-seeking behaviour remains a strong concern everywhere in the context of social rights. A strong welfare state – which comprises regulation of commerce as well as redistributive tax and spending – is, unlike most civil and political rights, *diametrically opposed* to the interests of the wealthy and is therefore precisely the target of the well-resourced lobbying interests. This is in line with Ian Shapiro's glum observation that 'there are numerous features of democratic systems that limit downward distribution and, indeed, even facilitate upward redistribution'.[14]

Even putting the facts aside, though, the *theory* of equal influence in the legislature does not fare much better. This much is made evident in

---

[9] Waldron, *Law and Disagreement*, pp. 32 and 90.

[10] As noted by R. A. Posner, 'Review of Jeremy Waldron, Law and Disagreement' (2000) 100 *Columbia Law Review* 582, 590–1; A. Vermeule, *Judging under Uncertainty: An Institutional Theory of Legal Interpretation* (Cambridge, MA: Harvard University Press, 2006), p. 17.

[11] Vermeule, *Judging under Uncertainty*, p. 17.

[12] C. Newell, J. Calvert, and S. Krause, 'Insight: "I'm like a cab for hire, at £5,000 pounds a day"' *The Sunday Times*, 21 March 2010, pp. 6–7 (exposing more than one MP).

[13] D. C. Freeman, 'Note: The Poor and the Political Process: Equal Access to Lobbying' (1969) 6 *Harvard Journal on Legislation* 369, 370 (citing numerous studies). See also J. Rawls, *A Theory of Justice* (Cambridge, MA: Belknap Press, 1971), p. 199.

[14] Shapiro, *The State of Democratic Theory*, p. 139, and see Chapter 5 more generally.

social and public choice theory, which have demonstrated severe problems with viewing electoral voting as a legitimate product of any sort of 'general will'.[15] Arrow's impossibility theorem purports to demonstrate that majority voting cannot meet minimum rationality requirements, due to problems such as preference-cycling, where the outcome of voting depends crucially on the order in which voting options are presented, rather than actual voter preferences, which gives great power to those who control the agenda.[16] Of this theory, Waldron is strikingly dismissive for one presenting a theory of legislation. Both theories are enormously influential in both economics and in law. His main ground for dismissal is that since judges vote by majority as well, any preference-cycling problems presented in social choice theory for legislatures are perforce faced by judges too.[17] This is an odd way out of the problem, however, because it is a concession that would undermine the legitimacy of both legislatures and courts. Also, it is doubtful that social choice problems (such as preference-cycling and agenda control) do in fact plague judicial decision-making in the same way as they might affect legislative decision-making. Judges deliberate (orally and through exchanging drafts) and vote differently. Arrow's impossibility theorem applied to voters selecting from more than two options and voting with a 'yes' or a 'no'. Judges in fact vote for either claimant or respondent, that is, it is a choice between two options in one respect. But they do not say 'yes' or 'no' except on that narrow issue. The rest of the judgment is a body of reasoned material that corresponds closely to their considered judgments, and that is the important part of the actual decision from the legal policy point of view. Further, while appellate judges do not deliberate nearly as much as many suppose, it is still true that judges deliberate in a responsive forum and try to decide by consensus.[18] Some writers see deliberation as the way out of the problems of social choice.[19]

---

[15] For a relevant introduction to the influential views of Kenneth Arrow, Gordon Tullock, James Buchanan, and William Riker, see D. A. Farber and P. J. Frickey, *Law and Public Choice: A Critical Introduction* (University of Chicago Press, 1991).

[16] *Ibid.*, Chapter 2.

[17] Waldron, *Law and Disagreement*, p.91; see also R. Bellamy, *Political Constitutionalism: A Republican Defence of the Constitutionality of Democracy* (Cambridge University Press, 2007), pp. 38–9; Dahl, *Democracy and its Critics*, p. 155.

[18] R. A. Posner, *How Judges Think* (Cambridge, MA: Harvard University Press, 2008), p. 34 (limited deliberation) and pp. 31–5 (on the 'sociological' theory of judicial behaviour which seeks to explain collegiate effects on decision-making).

[19] J. Dryzek, *Deliberative Democracy and Beyond: Liberals, Critics and Contestations* (Oxford University Press, 2000), Chapter 2.

I will not pretend to have a valuable opinion on whether social and public choice theory is fatal to the argument for the dignity of legislation. Even if the far-reaching claims in such theories were all true, legislation may well be defended as the best of the available alternatives. What does appear to be the case, however, is that those legal scholars who have studied public and social choice theory carefully believe at the very least that it deals the *legitimacy* case in favour of majority voting a quite serious blow. Farber and Frickey, upon whom Waldron relies to dismiss this argument, agree with that conclusion, and devote a chapter to showing how public choice theory can be used to improve public law.[20] Jerry Mashaw, a scholar who is quite critical of both courts and of public choice theory, believes that the theory at least shows that much of the scholarship concerned with the 'countermajoritarian difficulty' is misguided.[21] If, ultimately, the argument in favour of legislatures in the face of public and social choice theory is that it is the best we can do, then this attenuated conclusion is a far stretch from the crisp argument for formal equality, and is not at all obviously better than some combination of legislation and limited judicial review.

2 Equality or outcome-based departures from formal voting equality

A more serious weakness for the argument is that in fact we depart from the norm of strict voting equality all the time, and for all sorts of reasons. A brief survey will make the point more graphically.

- *Representative democracy*: The most obvious major departure from formal equality of participation is representative instead of direct democracy, a point raised against Waldron by a few critics.[22] We obviously need a representative system in a large modern state. But the idea of direct democracy remains a potent political force. For example, as of 2008 there had been at least twenty-one ballot initiatives (direct democracy on single issues) to ban gay marriage in various US states,[23] which

[20] Farber and Frickey, *Law and Public Choice*, Chapter 5. See also p. 57.
[21] J. L. Mashaw, *Greed, Chaos and Governance: Using Public Choice to Improve Public Law* (New Haven: Yale University Press, 1997), pp. 201–2; see also p. 15.
[22] D. Kyritsis, 'Representation and Waldron's Objection to Judicial Review' (2006) 26 *Oxford Journal of Legal Studies* 733; Posner, 'Review of Jeremy Waldon, Law and Disagreement'; D. Robertson, *The Judge as Political Theorist* (Princeton University Press, 2010), pp. 371–2.
[23] See R. C. Archibold and A. Goodnough, 'California Voters Ban Gay Marriage', *New York Times*, 5 November 2008, available at www.nytimes.com/2008/11/06/us/politics/06ballot. html.

is only one of many such issues.[24] In Ireland, the Eighth Amendment of the Constitution entrenched a right to life for the unborn, a response to what were perceived to be liberal court decisions.[25] In Switzerland, a referendum called for the banning of minarets on mosques and deportation of foreigners and refugees for petty crimes.[26] Waldron and Richard Bellamy both reject direct democracy because legislators, unlike populists, 'listen to one another and to settle on a common policy in a way that takes everyone's opinion into account'.[27] So the legislative forum is better at treating people as equals, of giving them equal voice. As a matter of empirical fact, this may be doubtful, and not only because many groups are marginalised in the legislature.[28] Most of the direct democracy issues listed above were very high profile and covered amply in the media and in many cases at churches as well. And surely Waldron and Bellamy would support referenda on big questions like joining the European Union or adopting a new constitution. At any rate, if we can depart from formal equality of voting to benefit from superior deliberative outcomes, then this opens a similar avenue for the justification of judicial review.

- *Unelected office-holders*: Many public positions require officials to resolve what we might call 'reasonable disagreement issues' of great importance. And many of these officials could be elected. Judges resolve all sorts of such issues outside review of legislation. Most countries do not follow the practice of the majority of US states and elect their judges,[29] because few of them want judges campaigning on conviction rates. The argument applies to other officials too: heads of administrative agencies,[30] central bank governors, heads of the police and military even. These individuals

---

[24] S. H. Verhovek, 'The 2000 Campaign: The Ballot Questions; "Oregon Ballot Full of Voter Initiatives Becomes Issue in Itself"', *The New York Times*, 25 October 2000, p. 1 (noting that volume I of the voter guide contained 376 pages, 26 ballot measures, and 607 arguments for and against).

[25] For a discussion in context, see N. Klashtorny, 'Comment: Ireland's Abortion Law: An Abuse of International Law' (1996) 10 *Temple International & Comparative Law Journal* 419, 422–31.

[26] I. Traynor, 'Four and No More: Swiss Referendum Bans Muslims from Building Minarets', *The Guardian* (London), 30 November 2009, p. 3.

[27] Waldron, *Law and Disagreement*, p. 110.

[28] See W. Eskridge Jr, 'Book Review: The Circumstances of Politics and the Application of Statutes' (2000) 100 *Columbia Law Review* 558, 580–1 for some astonishing statistics on the lack of diversity in the US Congress.

[29] See the short discussion in Posner, *How Judges Think*, pp. 134–8.

[30] See R. B. Stewart, 'The Reformation of American Administrative Law' (1975) 88 *Harvard Law Review* 1669, 1791–3 (for a discussion and rejection of the idea of electing administrative agency officials).

set much more contestable policy than do judges, even judges acting under entrenched bills of rights. It is true that the legislature can reverse their decisions, or remove them from office. But the power of reversal is rarely exercised, and where it is, it may be considered an affront to the independence of the institution. If democratic legitimation is the crucial issue, then according to Waldron's argument these people ought to be elected and removable by election.

- *Consociationalism*: The legislative assemblies of Northern Ireland, Lebanon, Switzerland, Belgium, Nigeria, and several newer states such as Bosnia and Herzegovina, all have political structures that require some degree of consensus decision-making by particular designated ethnic or social groups.[31] Consociationalism is not without its critics,[32] and it is ordinarily reserved for particularly divided societies, where normal representative modes do not work due to deep social cleavages. Yet it is nonetheless a more or less accepted form of consensus democracy for some important political communities.

- *Federalism*: Federal governments often have bicameral legislatures with strong federal representation in one of the chambers, as well as a written and entrenched constitution together with constitutional judicial review powers.[33] A standard model is to give each federal unit (whether state, province, or *Land*) equal representation in one chamber, irrespective of population, and to require that chamber's assent for the adoption of new laws. This basic idea exists in Germany, South Africa, Australia, and similar or variant systems exist in Austria, Brazil, Mexico, and many other states, as well as in the European Union. The US Senate is a particularly extreme example of this practice, giving rise to inequalities that are difficult to justify.[34]

- *Gender and ethnic quotas and reservations*: More than fifty countries around the world have adopted quota laws to regulate the selection or election of women to political office,[35] and at least twenty-four nations

---

[31] A. Lipjhart, *Democracy in Plural Societies* (New Haven: Yale University Press, 1977), Chapter 2.

[32] See B. Barry, "Political Accommodation and Consociational Democracy" (1975) 5(4) *British Journal of Political Science* 477–505; D. L. Horowitz, *Ethnic Groups in Conflict* (Berkeley: University of California Press, 1985), pp. 568–76 (a critique of but not a rejection of the consociational model).

[33] A. Lipjhart, *Patterns of Democracy: Government Form and Performance in Thirty-Six Countries* (New Haven: Yale University Press, 1999), p. 187.

[34] Dahl, *How Democratic is the American Constitution?*, pp. 43–54 (also confirming American exceptionalism).

[35] M. L. Krook, 'Quota Laws for Women in Politics: Implications for Feminist Practice' (2008) 15 *Social Politics* 345.

use them for ethnic groups as well.[36] Of course the *point* of these quotas and reservations is to ensure equality of representation. But so is the point of at least some theories of judicial review (especially the representation reinforcement or deliberative democracy theories).

- *Restricted franchise*: We deny the franchise to children and sometimes to people who lack mental capacity, not because they are less entitled to equal respect and concern (indeed both enjoy comprehensive legal protection), but because they are presumed to lack the ability to comprehend the issues that affect them and others.

- *Criminal justice*: Juries typically vote by consensus or super-majority, in the effort to exclude any reasonable doubt as to guilt. Sentencing convicted criminals is often reserved for judges, and popular control such as using juries or even direct political control of sentencing have been limited in favour of increased judicial control. Yet both sentencing and conviction involve issues on which there could be substantial reasonable disagreement.[37] We reject majority voting on juries to secure certainty, and we reject popular control of sentencing to avoid imposing cruel punishments that are insensitive to extenuating circumstances.

- *Constitutions*: It would not be particularly fair to use entrenched constitutions with constitutional judicial review as a counter-example, given that it is precisely their democratic legitimacy (rather than prevalence) that is challenged by Waldron and Bellamy. It is nonetheless a striking fact that now about 87 per cent of the world's constitutions provide for constitutional judicial review,[38] and the vast majority of these constitutions cannot be amended except for by a supermajority procedure. Any argument that affirms the wisdom of the multitude can only fumble with this increasingly embarrassing fact.

What do all these examples (apart from the last) demonstrate? They show that in many democracies we depart from the norm of formal equality of participation in the electoral and administrative process in order to

---

[36] M. Htun, 'Is Gender like Ethnicity? The Political Representation of Identity Groups' (2004) 2 *Perspectives on Politics* 439, 441; D. Ruedin, 'Ethnic Group Representation in Cross National Comparison' (2009) 15 *Journal of Legislative Studies* 335.

[37] See Pettit, *Republicanism*, pp. 196–7, for a discussion of why legislative representatives should in such situations 'tie their hands and gag their mouths' in the name of democracy.

[38] D. S. Law and M. Versteeg, 'The Evolution and Ideology of Global Constitutionalism' (2011) 99 *California Law Review* 101, 137 (also showing the evolution of the constitutional judicial review).

achieve certain goals. If one replies by arguing that in some of these cases the legislature has ultimate control, then one would seemingly accept at least a 'weak-form' type of judicial review.[39] Those goals may include obtaining expert or independent decision-making, improving representation of marginalised groups in decision-making, ensuring fairness in some decision-making process, or preserving social peace or institutional continuity. None of these measures are plausibly viewed as 'undemocratic' unless we are willing to adopt a particularly crude conception of the concept.[40] In more philosophical terms, these departures from the formal equality of voting may be viewed either as (1) measures designed to achieve a richer, more substantive conception of political equality; or (2) as limitations to the norm of formal political equality in pursuit of some other social goal or political principle.

At the same time, however, each of these departures from formal equality is supported by *very clear and pressing political reasons*. As a prima facie affront to political equality, each of them stands in need of special justification. Joseph Raz and Aileen Kavanagh have argued quite convincingly that we may have good reasons – mostly outcome-based – for choosing judicial review as a way of resolving disagreement about rights.[41] To make their point analogous to the examples given above, any case for judicial review ought likewise to respond to equally pressing political problems, and be capable of delivering some sort of remedy that is *proportionate* to such problems, by which I mean that it addresses the problem without inflicting more damage than it cures.

III   Two pressing problems with the finality of legislation

The following two problems justify constitutional judicial review because they are pressing and it is possible to develop a proportionate role for the judiciary in response to them. This section will set out the problems and the next will articulate a judicial role that in my view is a proportionate response to them.

---

[39] See the discussion in M. Tushnet, *Weak Courts, Strong Rights: Judicial Review and Social Welfare Rights in Comparative Constitutional Law* (Princeton University Press, 2008).

[40] Dahl agrees: see *Democracy and its Critics*, Chapters 10 and 11, and pp. 160–2 (though on his critique of courts, contrast pp. 155, 187–91).

[41] See J. Raz, 'Disagreement in Politics' (1998) 43 *American Journal of Jurisprudence* 26; A. Kavanagh, 'Participation and Judicial Review: A Reply to Jeremy Waldron' (2003) *Law and Philosophy* 451.

A   Absence of legislative focus

Waldron's argument falls at the first hurdle if the legislature has not actually discussed and voted on the rights issue. So in *Bellinger* v. *Bellinger*, a post-operative male-to-female transsexual challenged s. 11(c) of the Matrimonial Causes Act 1973 for its failure to provide for the possibility of marriage by persons having undergone gender reassignment.[42] No doubt the issue was not considered seriously in 1973. In *McR's Application for Judicial Review*, Kerr J found that s. 62 of the Offences Against the Person Act 1861, which outlawed buggery (i.e. anal intercourse) between consenting adults, was incompatible with Article 8 of the European Convention on Human Rights (ECHR).[43] The legislature in 1861 may well have intended to criminalise homosexual behaviour at the time, but any such determination cannot benefit from Waldron's argument for the dignity of legislation – they had no concept of the right to equality that now governs the issue.

In addition to undercutting Waldron's argument against judicial review, an absence of legislative focus raises two other democratic concerns. First, without such focus the claimant is denied the benefits associated with a proper legislative treatment of the issue. In *Bellinger* v. *Bellinger*, when the issue was re-examined in Parliament in the aftermath of litigation, there was a lively good-faith debate on the issue and predominant and in many places eloquent sympathy expressed over the problem of gender dysphoria,[44] and the resulting Gender Recognition Act 2004 provided a comprehensive recognition scheme together with a recognition panel/tribunal. Second, there are benefits to the general political culture by prompting parliamentarians to grapple with fundamental issues of principle, thus invigorating the duty of civic engagement with rights.[45]

The absence of legislative focus, and a corrective judicial role, has been raised as an issue on numerous occasions by other scholars, famously by

---

[42] [2003] UKHL 21.   [43] [2003] NI 1.

[44] For one representative exchange in the Commons, where the bill was debated for approximately ten hours, see Hansard, HC, vol. 421, col. 1502–1518, 25 May 2004. All Labour Party and Liberal Democrat MPs supported the measure in the Commons, and the Conservative Party held a free vote on the matter with roughly one third supporting the measure. The vote is reported at Hansard, HC, vol. 421, col. 1537–1538, 25 May 2004.

[45] J. S. Mill, 'Considerations on Representative Government' in *On Liberty and Other Essays*, ed. J. Gray (Oxford University Press, 1991 [1861]).

Alexander Bickel.[46] In the social rights context, Rosalind Dixon summarises these problems well by reference to what she calls 'blind spots' and 'burdens of inertia'.[47] I think this line of argument is sound, although it would not clearly anchor the more far-reaching review this chapter advocates, which would, as set out in section IV.C below, justify declaring unconstitutional certain laws where there plainly has been legislative focus of a recent and relevant sort.

One possible reply here is that what the legislature does and does not formally consider is itself part of the circumstances of politics. The agenda ought to, on this view, be for Parliament to set. There may or may not be a consequentialist argument in support of that view, but Waldron's case for the dignity of legislation (much of which I accept) depends on focused deliberation in legislatures as the legitimating factor.

B   Marginalisation

Perhaps the most common response to the argument for the dignity of legislation is that legislatures fail to protect politically marginalised groups, the so-called tyranny of the majority. Failure to deal with the issue satisfactorily was a serious omission from *Law and Disagreement*.[48] There have been vigorous attempts to blunt the force of this problem for legislative finality, but judicial review critics such as Waldron and Bellamy usually concede that this issue is a real limitation to the argument for the legitimacy of legislation, and switch to a different argument, which is that constitutional judicial review provides no adequate remedy.[49]

There is also some fancy footwork offered up on this issue. For example, Waldron points out that 'topical minorities' (i.e. those adversely affected by a measure) may not always align with 'decisional minorities' (i.e. those who lost the vote on the measure).[50] So on the gendered issue of the right to abortion, for example, American women disagree with each other in

---

[46] A. Bickel, *The Least Dangerous Branch* (2nd edn, New Haven: Yale University Press, 1962), esp. pp. 143–83.

[47] R. Dixon, 'Creating Dialogue about Socioeconomic Rights: Strong-Form versus Weak-Form Judicial Review Revisited' (2007) 5 *International Journal of Constitutional Law* 391.

[48] As noted also by Eskridge Jr, 'Book Review: The Circumstances of Politics and the Application of Statutes', 578; Posner, 'Review of Jeremy Waldron, Law and Disagreement', 589.

[49] Bellamy, *Political Constitutionalism*, pp. 26–48; Waldron, 'The Core of the Case Against Judicial Review', 1404.

[50] Waldron, 'The Core of the Case Against Judicial Review', 1396–8.

roughly equal numbers, as do men. This makes for an interesting footnote for atypical cases, but the main problem remains more or less in identical form. Waldron ultimately admits that in a divided society his argument would not run through,[51] but that concession underestimates the way in which John Hart Ely's theory of representation-reinforcing judicial review was offered up as a new paradigm, not a theory for non-central cases.

What is truly a concern is the way in which the legislative process accounts for the interests of people who are, to use a phrase that I develop and defend in greater depth below, *particularly vulnerable to majoritarian bias or neglect*. This is an acute problem in the area of poverty and social rights. Those reliant on the welfare state are liable to bias for familiar reasons. It is true that Britain is not as welfare-phobic as the USA, but Polly Toynbee and David Walker, both journalists and social commentators, nonetheless describe the British national press as 'Europhobic, Thatcher-adoring, tax-allergic, crime-neurotic, welfare-mean, liberal-bating, moral-prurient, feminist-detesting, punishment-addicted, foreigner-reviling, multicultural-contemptuous, state-paranoid and generosity-averse'.[52] Whether true or not, the even larger concern in countries like Britain is the dimension of neglect. This is because representatives who may act in good faith may nonetheless fail to protect the interests of vulnerable persons. They may not understand their plight due to a lack experience or acquaintance. Sometimes the lack of understanding can be basic ignorance. In a survey of British social attitudes, 56 per cent of respondents said that a twenty-five-year-old unemployed woman would be 'really poor' or 'hard up' if she lived only on benefits. But when told what the benefit levels actually were, 68 per cent of them described her situation so.[53] This story reveals the difference that basic (and excusable) ignorance can make to people who harbour no bias at all. Social progress often results after some scandal or social event awakens the public's conscience to a situation that was only dimly understood previously.[54] Even

---

[51] *Ibid.*, pp. 1403–6.

[52] P. Toynbee and D. Walker, *The Verdict: Did Labour Change Britain?* (London: Granta, 2010), p. 8.

[53] J. Hills, *Inequality and the State* (Oxford University Press, 2004), p. 65. The reverse was the case with unemployed single mothers and pensioners.

[54] Such a moment came about in Britain with the screening of the Ken Loach film *Cathy Come Home* on the BBC in 1966, watched by a quarter of the British population at the time and which brought the issues of homelessness, unemployment, and child services to national attention. It caused a surge in the membership of the campaigning group Shelter: see www.shelter.org for further details.

when representatives come to know the facts, their failure to truly empathise – to know what it is like[55] – combined with the pressure to respond to voter preferences that are more pressing and punitive at the ballot box, will make elements of the political process effectively dysfunctional.

The legislative process will in theory work best when each person has a roughly equal interest in the outcome of an issue, by which I mean that he or she stands to gain or lose in roughly equal measure with everyone else, whether directly in that case, or by abstract implication in considering how the principle applied to that issue would affect their own interest or those of members of their immediate community.[56] The further some group's interests get away from this baseline, the more imperfectly will the legislative process protect its interests. Some minorities (e.g. the ultra-wealthy) are powerful and highly influential, which offsets such potentially distortive effects. Others, the *vulnerable* and *marginalised*, are not, and are thus repeat losers.

The focus on vulnerable and excluded groups is probably the main theme of much of the recent important writing on social rights.[57] The poor are a marginalised group. Numerous American studies have shown that they are effectively excluded from political channels, stigmatised with rhetoric such as 'welfare queens', and that their interests have in fact become *more* marginalised as average incomes in fact rose over the last forty years.[58] This problem is much worse in the United States than it is in other rich countries,[59] but, as noted above, it exists in Britain as well, and not just among sections of the press. While the majority of people in Britain show nominal commitment to the reduction of poverty and inequality, it remains one of the most unequal countries in

---

[55] Dahl, *On Democracy*, p. 77 (quoting Mill's discussion of the interests of working classes not being represented adequately in Parliament).

[56] So the issue of whether to license more taxis in some situations can be analogous to the interests of small business owners, farmers, and members of professions. Each of the people in these other groups, and those who are related to them, can relate the issue to their own situation.

[57] See Chapter I (the case for social rights) on 'participation'.

[58] See B. L. Ross II and T. Smith, 'Minimum Responsiveness and the Political Exclusion of the Poor' (2009) 72 *Law and Contemporary Problems* 197, 204–12 (for a review of the social science literature and comparison with the marginalisation of black Americans).

[59] Hills, *Inequality and the State*, p. 69 (quoting a survey asking respondents to indicate why people live in need, by choosing between 'laziness and lack of willpower' or because 'society treats them unfairly'. In the USA, 61 per cent of respondents chose the former, whereas in Europe, only 8 to 20 per cent of respondents did likewise).

the richer EU countries, and has nearly the worst relative poverty rate among them.[60] A survey of British social attitudes shows that those living comfortably or coping financially are more likely to blame poverty on laziness or lack of will-power than are those less financially well off, a view that gained strength between 1986 and 2000.[61] Between 1994 and 2000 the number of people who blamed 'injustice in our society' for poverty dropped from 30 to 21 per cent.[62] And for those thinking that such trends are explicable due to improvements in the welfare state, think again: there was a direct correlation, in a Europe-wide survey, between higher levels of relative poverty and higher numbers of persons blaming poverty on laziness.[63]

The evidence also shows that poverty and income levels are linked to declining levels of civic engagement, including voting and other forms of social participation.[64] So the poor are not, effectively, electing to exercise what Waldron calls their right-of-rights. The true and troubling irony, in fact, is that as society grows wealthier, the very poor can become increasingly vulnerable, fractured, disorganised, and disengaged – a phenomenon captured by the expression 'social exclusion'.[65] Given that attending to the needs of such groups is not only a matter of overcoming stigma, indifference, and lack of empathy (as it is for most other minorities), but constitutes an actual monetary threat to wealthier taxpayers, the majority of voters and the highly wealthy in particular have reason to suppress their interests in redistribution.[66] All the political tools are withering, too. Corporate power has grown, unionisation has receded, top-rate taxation has lowered, inequality has grown, and political participation has dropped dramatically – all against a backdrop of traditional left-wing party policies moving, in 'third way' fashion,[67] towards the interests of middle-class voters. It would be silly, especially after considering the

---

[60] Hills, *Inequality and the State*, pp. 57, 66–71.

[61] *Ibid.*, pp. 66–7. Notably, however, not more than 25 per cent of either income group in Britain attributed poverty to laziness.

[62] *Ibid.*   [63] *Ibid.*, p. 68.

[64] R. Levitas, 'The Concept and Measurement of Social Exclusion', in C. Pantazis, D. Gordon and R. Levitas (eds.) *Poverty and Social Exclusion in Britain: The Millennium Survey* (Bristol: Policy Press, 2006), p. 146.

[65] *Ibid.*; see also E. Marlier *et al.*, *The EU and Social Inclusion: Facing the Challenges* (Policy Press, Bristol 2006).

[66] Shapiro, *The State of Democratic Theory*, Chapter 5.

[67] A. Giddens, *The Third Way: The Renewal of Social Democracy* (Cambridge: Polity Press, 1998).

studies examined in Chapter 3, to think that courts could reverse this trend. But can they do anything about it? I think they can do a little, and even a little can mean a lot.

IV   Giving weight to democratic legitimacy

The task of this section is to set out an approach to social rights adjudication that constitutes a proportionate response to the two problems with the finality of legislation. It will be apparent to some readers that the approach set out here will not accord in all elements of detail with the approach taken by some courts. My objective is not, however, to create a role that fits entirely the approach taken. It is to set out an approach that is suitable for application in countries like the UK, but which fits well with the rationale I have presented for it in sections II and III above.

A   Executive action: not pre-empting legislative focus

We tend to think of democratic legitimacy in connection only with statutes, but in fact many human rights cases involve the review of discretionary executive conduct. It is easy to think that no issue of democratic restraint exists in such cases. After all, we think it is a primary role of Parliament, as the democratic institution par excellence, to oversee executive conduct.[68] Neither Waldron nor Bellamy direct their arguments against judicial review of administrative action on grounds of rights. Yet the position is curious. *Governments* are elected, and in the Westminster system people tend to vote for parties that they fully expect to carry out detailed administrative agendas. Therefore, the actions of the executive in fact do in some cases have a distinctly democratic pedigree and legitimacy, one reaffirmed to some extent (perhaps weakly) by the doctrine of individual ministerial responsibility.[69]

A yet more significant democratic issue is that in reviewing executive action for compliance with rights, courts can make findings which

---

[68]   This theme is best brought out in the work of Adam Tomkins. See P. Craig and A. Tomkins (eds.) *The Executive in Public Law* (Oxford University Press, 2006), Chapter 1.

[69]   D. Woodhouse, 'Ministerial Responsibility', in V. Bogdanor (ed.), *The British Constitution in the Twentieth Century* (Oxford University Press, 2003), p. 281; Craig and Tomkins, *The Executive in Public Law*, pp. 140–59, places great emphasis on it. Others believe it has waned to the point of not deserving prominence in the accountability landscape: J. Jowell and D. Oliver, *The Changing Constitution* (4th edn, Oxford University Press, 2000), p. viii.

formally leave statutes alone but which can have distortive legislative effects. For example, in *Bellinger* v. *Bellinger* the Matrimonial Causes Act 1973 could linguistically have been read to allow a post-operative transgender female the right to marry.[70] Yet the court found that to do so would have been to effectively require a substantial change in administrative practice without any direct legislative focus on the issue, a focus they felt would be both appropriate democratically and which would have consequential benefits. Another example is where a ruling on its face concerns only the exercise of administrative discretion, but the issue is one that might well come before Parliament at some later time. For example, in *Begum* v. *Denbigh High School* the House of Lords held that a school did not infringe a student's freedom of religion by requiring her to wear the school uniform instead of her preferred body-covering called a jilbab.[71] However, had the House of Lords found her right infringed, and depending on how sweeping the ruling had been, then Parliament would have had a hard time coming to a different view, or even of justifying a debate on the issue. The court might have foreclosed a legislative investigation and debate over the issue, in reliance on a set of facts pertaining to one school's experience. Mark Tushnet has described a variant of this problem as policy distortion.[72]

At the same time, human rights standards are substantive legal standards that are in the ordinary course of public law adjudication applied to administration alongside other public law standards such as fairness and reasonableness. Further, just as there are cases that might come before Parliament, there are many others that involve low- or mid-level administrative decision-making where it would be perverse to think that the matter is one Parliament is likely to weigh in on in the future.

A court can give weight to the idea of democratic legitimacy in such situations in a few different ways. The first is that judges ought to be aware of when an issue is one that could potentially come before Parliament. One indication is where a legal issue is effectively a matter of high policy.[73]

---

[70] *Bellinger* v. *Bellinger* [2003] UKHL 21. I follow Kavanagh's analysis, *Constitutional Review under the UK Human Rights Act* (Cambridge University Press, 2009), pp. 137–42.

[71] *R (Begum)* v. *Governors of Denbigh High School* [2006] UKHL 15. A jilbab is a long coat-like garment worn by some Muslim women.

[72] See Chapter 9, section II.A.1 (on agenda control).

[73] On the legal idea of 'high policy', see H. Woolf, J. Jowell, A. Le Sueur, and S. A. De Smith, *Principles of Judicial Review* (London: Sweet & Maxwell, 1999), paras. 5–030, 5–032; Lord Irvine, 'Judges and Decision-Makers: The Theory and Practice of *Wednesbury* Review' [1996] *Public Law* 65, 67; E. C. Page, *Governing by Numbers: Delegated Legislation and Everyday Policy-Making* (Oxford: Hart Publishing, 2001), esp. pp. 177ff. and 186ff.

One way we can say an issue is a matter of high policy is when it reflects a policy either directly set or actively supported by a minister. Such support is ordinarily clear from the facts, but it could also be shown definitively through a ministerial statement filed as an affidavit. Second, where it is common ground that the issue is one of high policy, the judges could decide such cases in a way that preserves the possibility of legislative revisitation. They can do so in a few mutually supportive ways: (a) by relying on the familiar rule of construction that vague laws will not be read so as to infringe human rights (but declining to opine on whether, with proper focus, the policy would be an unjustifiable infringement);[74] (b) by focusing judicial findings on the adequacy of *reasons*, rather than on the constitutionality of specific *policies* or *outcomes*; and (c) by using the techniques of incrementalism detailed in Chapter 10, and specifically the techniques of particularisation, vague legal standards, constitutional avoidance, and revisitation.

B   Primary legislation: ensuring legislative focus

An absence of legislative focus can occur with primary legislation as well. Recall that by absence of legislative focus is meant focus on the rights issue at stake in some dispute. I do not of course mean a focus on the particular individual's case, but rather on the class of dispute that the individual raises. This absence of focus can occur in a few different scenarios. One is where the law adopted clearly infringes or otherwise engages a right, but was adopted at a time when the legislature did not debate the same general concept of the right. This was the case in *McR's Application for Judicial Review* (regarding the equality rights of homosexuals), and in *Bellinger* v. *Bellinger* (rights of transgender people), and *Hirst* v. *UK (No. 2)* (the right to vote).[75] Another is that the statute (perhaps recent) is ambiguous on the point, and there is no evidence that the issue properly came before Parliament. Yet a third situation is where the statute is unequivocal in denying or infringing a right, but it does not appear that the legislature contemplated the particular scenario. If there was no

---

See also J. M. Balkin and S. Levinson, 'Understanding the Constitutional Revolution' (2001) 87 *Virginia Law Review* 1045 (working out the distinction between high and low politics).

[74] *R* v. *Secretary of State for the Home Department, ex parte Simms* [1999] 3 All ER 400, per Lord Hoffmann.

[75] *Hirst* v. *United Kingdom (No.2)* [2005] ECHR 681. The 1983 statute at issue adopted without debate a policy set out in 1870.

mention or discussion of the point on the floor or in a committee, then in my view there has been no legislative focus. In this third case, whether there has been legislative focus is a fact-specific inquiry.

One might argue that if the statute is ambiguous – the second of the scenarios I identified above – then there is no need for any such delicacy because the remedy lies in merely giving a rights-consistent interpretation of the statute under s. 3 of the Human Rights Act 1998 (HRA), which provides that, 'where possible', statutes must be interpreted consistently with Convention rights. Caution is still advised, however. An ambiguous statute may be read in a rights-consistent manner that practically forecloses the possibility of a legislative revisitation of the issue. For example, if a statute can be read to fund or not fund a particular drug, and the court says that the right requires that it be funded, then Parliament will have great difficulty in coming to a different view in fresh legislation.

The remedy for an absence of legislative focus in legislation itself is not entirely straightforward. Some American scholars put forward the idea of a legislative remand,[76] whereby judges could effectively send an issue back to Congress for consideration. The justification for this idea is effectively the same as what is advanced here, but the remedy is a bit exotic for Westminster-style democracies. It is also unnecessary. An English judge who wishes to preserve the possibility of legislative focus would need only to direct her findings against the justifications presented by the government, rather than at the policy. It is consistent with both law and political morality that when the question is whether some policy is necessary in a democratic society, that the legislature be given the chance to express a considered view on the matter. Once it is understood that policies adopted in different ways have different justifications, it becomes rational to say that the same policy can at one time be unconstitutional and at another not be. This is effectively what the European Court of Human Rights found in the *Hirst* judgment,[77] and it is an appropriate judicial technique for the preservation of legislative focus.

---

[76] For an early suggestion of the idea of a legislative remand see A. Bickel and H. Wellington, 'Legislative Purpose and the Judicial Process: The Lincoln Mills Case' (1957) 71 *Harvard Law Review* 1; Farber and Frickey, *Law and Public Choice*, pp. 145–53; Dixon, 'Creating Dialogue about Socioeconomic Rights', 391. See generally, Bickel, *The Least Dangerous Branch*, Chapter 4 (on the 'passive virtues'); C. R. Sunstein, *The Partial Constitution* (Cambridge, MA: Harvard University Press, 1993); W. N. Eskridge Jr, *Dynamic Statutory Interpretation* (Cambridge, MA: Harvard University Press, 1994); Cf. Vermeule, *Judging under Uncertainty*, pp. 132–44.

[77] *Hirst* v. *UK (No. 2)* [2005] ECHR 681, [78]–[79].

There are two important provisos to this approach, both founded on a concern for justice and economy. First, if it is reasonably clear to the judge that the policy at issue would violate the claimant's rights if there were clear legislative focus, and it falls into one of the categories discussed in the next two sections, then the judge will have good reasons to make that view clear. This may pre-empt unfair delay and ping-pong of the issue between the courts and legislature.[78] Second, judges must be aware that the resources of legislative debate are scarce. Debating a major rights issue can be expected to take anywhere from a few hours to a few days or even weeks in both houses.[79] Parliament has much to do, and while focus on rights issues is important, so is everything else, particularly where very much of what is discussed in Parliament ultimately deals directly or indirectly with our social rights.

C   Primary legislation: weak democratic restraint

In this section I discuss those areas in which I argue it is appropriate for judges to give less weight to the idea of democratic legitimacy in judicial review of legislation. The key concern is marginalisation, but there are three further areas in which the democratic case for judicial restraint is weak.

1   Absolute obligations

At the level of constitutional design, a society may wish to commit to rights with varying degrees of intensity or specificity.[80] In the European Convention, for instance, some rights (e.g. Arts. 8, 10, 11) are accompanied by limitations provisions, while others (Arts. 3, 5, 6) are not. In the South African Constitution, for example, some rights – notably the socio-economic rights of children in section 28 – are set out with no qualifications, in contrast with other rights. Representatives at a constitutional convention may wish to impose very onerous obligations in respect of certain rights, indicating a strong presumption that they will be denied only in the rarest of cases. In such cases, a court ought to give stronger protection to the right, because the constitution itself supports

---

[78] See O. Fiss. 'The Perils of Minimalism' (2008) 9 *Theoretical Inquiries in Law* 643 [art. 13], available at: www.bepress.com/til/default/vol9/iss2/art13.

[79] The resulting debate in the UK Parliament prompted by the *Hirst* v. *UK* decision took over five hours of time on the floor of the House of Commons and considerable resources in securing the debate itself. See Hansard, HC, vol. 523, col. 493–586, 10 February 2011.

[80] See the discussion in Chapter 4, section II.B.

that reading. The court may still wish, in certain cases, to defer in such situations on epistemic grounds, or for reasons of expertise or flexibility: a strong constitutional provision is not an order to fumble in the dark. However, *democratic legitimacy* does not provide a sound justification for restraint in such cases, however much it may have at the level of constitutional design. One may argue, as I have in Chapter 4 in respect of broad categories of social rights, against adopting absolute obligations. But once statespersons have elected to include both absolute and qualified rights or obligations in a constitution, it must be acknowledged that there is a doctrinal difference between them.

2   Procedural rights

Democratic legitimacy can often be a weak reason in favour of deference to the legislature on procedural matters. If the remedy given merely allows people to make themselves heard, but leaves the administration or legislature the power to take the same substantive decision, it hardly seems an affront to the democratic process. It may invigorate it, and this is the central insight of Charles Sabel and William Simon's work on democratic experimentalism that I discuss in Chapter 10. For example, in the *Occupiers of 51 Olivia Road* case, the Constitutional Court of South Africa found that, when evicting occupants, the public authorities must engage them meaningfully in a way that went beyond the statutory framework then in force.[81] They still had the right to evict, but only after proper consultation and consideration of a variety of factors.In this sense, it can be viewed as a court-mandated contribution to democratic outcomes.

This claim seems obvious, but in fact it is subject to a few quite important provisos, and I discuss related problems in Chapter 9. For present purposes, it is important to highlight the democratic (not epistemic) problems that lurk in quixotic procedural interventions. Procedural rights can, through delays or increased costs, raise the cost for government of taking social action. Imagine that the cost of introducing a new benefit payment was doubled on account of court-mandated procedural rights (e.g. legal aid-funded appeals up to the Supreme Court). Any responsible government must take account of that cost when deciding upon the regime, and set it off against other alternative items. This is evident in the planning context, where the planning approval process can delay large projects for considerable periods of time, and the use of such

---

[81]   *Occupiers of 51 Olivia Rd v. City of Johannesburg*, 2008 (3) SA 208 (CC).

delays is a major strategic asset.[82] So onerous procedural rights can constrain democratic choice in substantive ways. I address this issue further in Chapters 9 and 10, and in particular a method for recognising procedural rights that is consistent with them contributing to democratic outcomes.

3   Clear or core cases

Most constitutional law cases are hard or penumbral cases, but there may also be clear or core cases. A core case would be a type of case where what is in issue is a breach of the very essence of what the right is and typically was meant to be when adopted, even if the morality of the restriction is hotly contestable. In a core case, to allow the statute to stand would be the total negation of the right, an interpretation of the right that would not be 'reasonable' in the sense used by Waldron. One example of such a clear case was a South African law that banned sodomy even though s. 9(3) of the Constitution's right to equality listed sexual orientation as an unfair ground of discrimination.[83] A similar though less-textually clear example is found in UK cases where a civil procedure deprived a detainee of the right to see the evidence supporting his detention,[84] or the previous practice of allowing the Home Secretary to determine a convict's length of imprisonment.[85] Other cases may include those where, under a limitations analysis, the very purpose of the statute is not pressing and substantial (or legitimate) under the relevant bill of rights.[86] The court's role in such cases is to manifest respect for the basic constitutional principle of the rule of law, and require fidelity to constitutional values.

The use of a judicial review standard such as 'clear case' can be found in American administrative law. In *Chevron*, the Supreme Court held that an agency interpretation of a statute would be set aside only where either (a) the statute spoke clearly to the issue at stake, or (b) the interpretation

---

[82] *R (Alconbury)* v. *Secretary of State for the Environment, Transport and the Regions* [2001] UKHL 23 [69]–[72].

[83] See *National Coalition for Gay and Lesbian Equality* v. *Minister of Justice* (1998) 6 BHRC 127 (CC).

[84] See *Secretary of State for the Home Department* v. *AF (No. 3)* [2009] UKHL 28, [59] (stating the core minimum of Art. 6 ECHR).

[85] *R (on the application of Anderson)* v. *Secretary of State for the Home Department* [2002] UKHL 46.

[86] *Halpern* v. *Canada* (2003) 65 OR (3d) 161 (Ontario Court of Appeal) [114]–[125] maintaining a heterosexual institution of marriage is not a 'pressing and substantial objective' under s. 1 of the Canadian Charter of Rights and Freedoms.

was irrational or arbitrary.[87] In statutory interpretation, as well, a standard of plain meaning is widely used, over the protests of some philosophers.[88] And under the HRA, the judicial choice between s. 3 and s. 4 interpretations turn to some extent upon the question of the ambiguity of the statute.[89] Admittedly, statutes will tend to be more specific than constitutional rights provisions. But the existence of 'clear case' categories in law affirms that this approach can work. Even some of the staunchest American critics of judicial review concede this option at the very least.[90]

Clear cases will sometimes be those that contradict the express terms or implied meaning of the constitutional text, or a higher court case that has given a clear interpretation of the standard. However, I do not wish to suggest that a clear case must contravene the precise wording of the bill of rights. A concept such as equal treatment will in some cases have clear implications. However controversial they may be or have been, I do not, for instance, believe that bans on gay marriage or the requirement of racially segregated educational facilities in post-war America could possibly be reconciled with the conception of equality embedded in most bills of rights. Disagreement on those issues is *not reasonable* – it represents an abdication of the value itself, usually in preference for some extrinsic, non-legal political value such as deference to popular will. It is, in such cases, a political objection to the right itself, not a plausible interpretation of it.

4   Marginalised groups

Judicial review that focuses on protecting marginalised and vulnerable groups in the legislature can provide a proportionate corrective to the problem of marginalisation. One might call this a 'representation-reinforcement' theory, but that would be misleading in part. It is rather a theory that seeks to compensate for the deficiencies of representation by giving members of marginalised groups additional avenues of redress and challenge. Giving people access to enforceable judicial remedies is perhaps not best described as enhancing their representation in some

---

[87] *Chevron USA, Inc.* v. *Natural Resources Defense Council, Inc.* 467 US 837 (1984), 842–3.

[88] Dworkin, *Law's Empire* (Cambridge, MA: Harvard University Press, 1986), Chapter 9; T. A. O. Endicott, *Vagueness in Law* (Oxford University Press, 2000).

[89] But see Kavanagh, *Constitutional Review under the UK Human Rights Act*, pp. 102ff. on why the presumption goes much further.

[90] J. B. Thayer, 'The Origin and Scope of the American Doctrine of Constitutional Law' (1893) 7 *Harvard Law Review* 129; Bickel, *The Least Dangerous Branch*, pp. 35–46; Vermeule, *Judging under Uncertainty*; see also *United States* v. *Carolene Products Co.* 304 US 144 (1938).

assembly. (If we treat courts as a forum for representation, then we must concede that they exclude almost everyone else!) Access to constitutional judicial review compensates for legislative flaws by providing a subsidiary procedure for decision-making. I argue that judges are not required by the principle of democratic legitimacy to show strong restraint on democratic grounds when the claimant has suffered disadvantage that is linked to her membership of a group that is *particularly vulnerable to majoritarian bias or neglect*.

Several works of constitutional theory have used the idea of representation reinforcement to try to cut the Gordian knot of the countermajoritarian difficulty.[91] The basic idea is that judicial review can compensate for the problem of marginalisation, specifically understood as inadequate representation, and in so doing give the courts a democracy-promoting role. I think this general line of argument is correct. However, the variant of it that I adopt is rather different from the most important exposition of this idea, found in the work of John Hart Ely. I will therefore introduce Ely's work, review the critiques of it, and then present arguments for why the standard I present – *particularly vulnerable to majoritarian bias or neglect* – is appropriate and workable.

(a) **Ely's theory** Ely's book, *Democracy and Distrust: A Theory of Judicial Review*,[92] is a both a work of constitutional theory and a systematic interpretation of the constitution of the United States. In Chapter Four of the book, Ely introduces the thesis that the American constitution is best understood as being concerned with 'process writ-large', by which he means the process through which democratic decisions are taken. He introduces the famous footnote four from the case *United States* v. *Carolene Products Co.*, which is worth setting out here in full:[93]

> There may be narrower scope for operation of the presumption of constitutionality when legislation appears on its face to be within a specific prohibition of the Constitution, such as those of the first ten amendments, which are deemed equally specific when held to be embraced within the Fourteenth Amendment ...

[91] L. Lusky, 'Minority Rights and the Public Interest' (1942) 52 *Yale Law Journal* 1; O. Fiss, 'Groups and the Equal Protection Clause' (1976) 5 *Philosophy & Public Affairs* 107; J. Choper, *Judicial Review and the National Political Process* (University of Chicago Press, 1980).

[92] (Cambridge, MA: Harvard University Press, 1980).

[93] 304 US 144 (1938) 152–3.

It is unnecessary to consider now whether legislation which restricts those political processes which can ordinarily be expected to bring about repeal of undesirable legislation, is to be subjected to more exacting judicial scrutiny under the general prohibitions of the Fourteenth Amendment than are most other types of legislation.

Nor need we enquire whether similar considerations enter into the review of statutes directed at particular religious ... or national ... or racial minorities ... whether prejudice against discrete and insular minorities may be a special condition, which tends seriously to curtail the operation of those political processes ordinarily to be relied upon to protect minorities, and which may call for a correspondingly more searching judicial inquiry.

Ely builds on the second and third paragraphs to develop his theory of judicial review, which is that it should be concerned with reinforcing 'the opportunity to participate either in the political processes by which values are appropriately identified and accommodated, or in the accommodation those processes have reached'.[94] Both of these concepts are combined in the idea of representation reinforcement. One of the principal contentions of the book is that such a representation-reinforcing role will allow judges to avoid making the types of substantive value judgments that alternative theories would require.

He develops and applies the theory in subsequent chapters. The most relevant for present purposes is the chapter in which he develops a theory about how to 'facilitate the representation of minorities' (though it is in fact is concerned with how to identify minorities worthy of judicial protection). He finds that definitional standards used to identify minorities that are owed protection, such as those suffering 'disproportionate impact', or which are 'discrete and insular', or simply the object of 'stereotype', or stigma are not rich enough on their own to be sufficient to identify the relevant minorities. To avoid the plain imposition of judicial values, Ely argues that judges must assess whether there was 'unconstitutional official motivation' behind the measure.[95] There may be unconstitutional motivations in respect of race, but also concerning religion (or lack thereof), speech, press and so on. Where such motivations can be discovered (and he discusses how this can be done), then the group is one that will stand in need of additional protection. However, he acknowledges that legislators are not often transparent about their motives. He

---

[94] Ely, *Democracy and Distrust*, p. 77.
[95] *Ibid.*, pp. 136ff.

thus introduces the idea that the doctrine of 'suspect classifications' in equal protection law – which identifies certain particular groups such as racial minorities, aliens, and others – can 'be a way of "flushing out" unconstitutional motivation, one that lacks the proof problems of a more direct inquiry'.[96]

But identifying which groups ought to be included in the list of suspect classifications now raises a similar problem to the one we began with, as Ely frankly acknowledges. So on what principles can classifications other than the race and national origin be identified? (And what, for that matter, of affirmative action on racial grounds?) Here he recognises that immutability of an individual's personal characteristics is not on its own sufficient. And neither is the idea of discreteness and insularity alone, for many such groups will achieve considerable voice in the legislature. He rather settles on the idea of prejudice. The question ultimately is whether there exists 'widespread hostility' against the group.[97] Defining this, he admits, will be difficult. The use of the idea of 'stereotype' without more is not sufficient, as there are all sorts of groups against whom distinctions and generalisations are made justifiably (e.g. criminals). What we ought to be concerned with, he argues, is whether the majority within the legislature was at a high risk of misapprehending the correctness of the relevant generalisation.[98] This is more likely to occur when the majority in the legislature forms part of a group that is likely to favour itself over another group, due to the simple psychological phenomenon of lacking an understanding of the other group's perspective. This leads to the introduction of what can be called 'we–they' distinctions: we (whites) are better than they (blacks) at activity x, and therefore this legislative distinction is justified. By contrast, 'they–they' distinctions between two groups, neither of which correspond to the majority, such as optometrists and dentists, are not likely to be suspicious. And neither are those distinctions premised on a notion that the group disadvantaged is actually superior in some manner (e.g. that Jews are better students), or is at a considerable advantage (e.g. whites in affirmative action programmes). He applies this framework to cases of alienage, homosexuality, poverty, and women.

(b)   **The problems with Ely**   Ely's theory has been enormously influential, but he has scores of critics as well. I will focus on three key criticisms, each of which is illuminating. The first is that it is patently wrong to

---

[96] *Ibid.*, p. 146.   [97] *Ibid.*, p. 154.   [98] *Ibid.*, p. 157.

say that the theory he commends to judges is not substantive in nature.[99] There is a substantive dimension to identifying which groups are subject to prejudice, and a substantive dimension to considering how the problem should be remedied. I think this criticism is entirely correct, but it does not justify the conclusion that Ely's theory collapses into a theory like Ronald Dworkin's.[100] It is his claim that the theory is not substantive that collapses, and rightly so – the claim was unsustainable and was anyway not absolutely integral to his theory. Dworkin is right that the flight from substance must end in substance.[101] But it will end in a lot less substance than Dworkin's own approach, and the prescribed role for judges will correspond roughly to those areas where we have good reasons to doubt the democratic legitimacy of legislative outcomes.

The second problem is with the nature of the 'prejudice' or 'unconstitutional motivation' test that is set out. The high bar he sets renders his theory inconsistent. Ely was right to depart from the mere idea of 'discrete and insular minorities' as found in footnote four of *Carolene Products*. Bruce Ackerman has done the best job of showing how the discrete and insular minorities test in fact leads to some entirely counter-intuitive outcomes that undermine its own rationale.[102] Groups that are discrete and insular minorities may actually gather considerable amounts of lobbying power and influence, while disparate and diffuse groups are the ones for whom the majoritarian political process is most ineffective.

Assuming Ely's use of 'we–they' distinctions is acceptable for cases of bias, the problem is that the proactive dimension of prejudice and unconstitutional motivation in his test fails to deal with situations of neglect. The disabled and elderly are not particularly vulnerable to majoritarian bias, but they are in many cases neglected, seemingly because of the inability of legislative majorities to comprehend and empathise with their situations.[103] This would also be the case for people having rare diseases, those with mental health problems, the homeless, and so on. Indeed, there is no concept of substantive equality or neglect at all in his theory. Clearly Ely avoided this type of criterion in his effort to stay clear of substance.

---

[99] L. H. Tribe, 'The Puzzling Persistence of Process-Based Constitutional Theories' (1980) 89 *Yale Law Journal* 1083; Dworkin, *A Matter of Principle*, pp. 59–69; P. P. Craig, *Public Law and Democracy in the United Kingdom and the United States of America* (Oxford: Clarendon Press, 1990), pp. 91–116.

[100] As Bellamy argues in *Political Constitutionalism*, pp. 107–18.

[101] Dworkin, *A Matter of Principle*, p. 69.

[102] B. A. Ackerman, 'Beyond Carolene Products' (1985) 98 *Harvard Law Review* 713.

[103] No doubt that will change in respect of the elderly as their numbers swell.

For instance, despite showing at several points that the poor lack effective representation, he nonetheless concludes that it would be quite rare to show that their treatment would 'result from a sadistic desire to keep the miserable in their state of misery, or a stereotypical generalization about their characteristics' and that it would rather arise from 'a reluctance to raise the taxes needed to support such expenditures'.[104] Apart from this analysis being manifestly false in respect of proactive bias towards the poor in the United States,[105] his insistence on proactive prejudicial animus has the unjustified effect of excluding groups that more than any other are effectively barred from bargaining in the 'pluralist's bazaar'.[106]

A third and final criticism is that there is no discussion of how the idea of representation reinforcement should condition the relief available to those groups who are at risk of prejudice. Does a statute based on a 'we–they' distinction give the judge a licence to do as she pleases? As Neil Komesar argues, 'he does not observe that the competence of the alternative institution – the judiciary – may be similarly variable.'[107] There is no accounting for the capacity of the judiciary to intervene in complex matters of social policy. This is an odd omission, particularly because of the extent of structural reform litigation in his day, and the widespread criticism of it.[108] Ely's book presented an incomplete theory that focused entirely on the question of institutional legitimacy, and insufficiently on the question of capacity. This book seeks to address both.

(c)   **Particularly vulnerable to majoritarian bias or neglect**   In my view, judges could circumvent all these weaknesses by asking whether, in respect of the challenged policy, the claimant is from a group that is *particularly vulnerable to majoritarian bias or neglect*. If that condition is met, strong democratic restraint would be inappropriate. This is a workable legal standard, and will focus attention on the right issues and ensure to a large extent that judicial review of legislation is aligned with its supporting justification. It will help now to examine each aspect of this

---

[104] Ely, *Democracy and Distrust*, p. 162.
[105] See Ross II and Smith, 'Minimum Responsiveness and the Political Exclusion of the Poor'.
[106] Ely's famous expression, *Democracy and Distrust*, p. 152. For a similar critique of Ely on poverty see Craig, *Public Law and Democracy*, p. 108; Ackerman, 'Beyond Carolene Products'; and Bellamy, *Political Constitutionalism*, p. 116.
[107] N. Komesar, *Imperfect Alternatives: Choosing Institutions in Law, Economics and Public Policy* (University of Chicago Press, 1994), p. 199. See Ely, *Democracy and Distrust*, p. 102.
[108] D. Horowitz, *The Courts and Social Policy* (Washington DC: Brookings Institution, 1977); O. Fiss, *The Civil Rights Injunction* (Bloomington: Indiana University Press, 1978).

definition and address why I have used this standard and how it might be applied in adjudication.

- *Particularly vulnerable:* The requirement that a claimant be 'particularly vulnerable' accommodates three distinct needs. The first is to recognise that some groups may be the object of majoritarian bias but are not particularly *vulnerable* to harm caused thereby. Such minorities might include, for example, the wealthy, corporations, and so on. The second need is to show that a group is *vulnerable*, that is, at *substantial risk* of bias or neglect. One should not have to show that they are actually suffering in a particular way from the bias or neglect. That would set the bar too high, for establishing actual motivations of the legislators will often be well nigh impossible as Ely rightly recognised. The third is that there must be a plausible link between the disadvantage imposed by the policy, and the membership of the group. So a claimant must seek the court's intervention on an issue where there is a link between group status and the risk of harm.

- *Majoritarian bias:* This standard is similar to what Ely identified as prejudice, or what is often called stigma, that is, a form of proactive hostility towards the group, or of disadvantage created by unfair preference for the interests of the majority. It does seem, however, that the painstaking discussion of 'unconstitutional motivation' in Ely's theory was due to the peculiar difficulties on this issue in the American system on the one hand, and Ely's quest to stay clear of substance on the other. The definition of suspect classes of discrimination in most legal systems has not presented anything close to the types of problems that it has in the United States. Such grounds are often enumerated explicitly in modern constitutions, and there is growing agreement as to what kinds of groups are vulnerable. It would not only include those groups enumerated in equality provisions in bills of rights, such as racial, sexual, and religious minorities, but other groups such as asylum seekers, those dependent on benefits, or who come from certain deprived (or otherwise different) regions of a country.

- *Majoritarian neglect:* Paradigm examples of groups who are vulnerable to majoritarian neglect would include the disabled, the elderly, the homeless, (some) social assistance recipients, certain isolated religious minorities, single parents, those with uncommon diseases or disabilities, those with mental health problems, and so on. These are groups who have systemic difficulties overcoming the inertia required to sustain effective political change on their behalf. Such people may or may not suffer proactive prejudice, and it is of course true that the legislature does pay quite laudable attention to many of these groups, in particular the elderly and the disabled. But the problem is that their interests do not align closely enough with those of the majority to ensure that the system of majoritarian politics works sufficiently well in their case. This fact may vary over time, but it is a working presumption of this chapter and is a view for the most part supported by relevant advocacy groups.

- *Identifying the groups in court*: Bias and neglect are in no small part susceptible to proof in fact. In most cases, the vulnerable status of the claimant will not be in dispute and a judge can take judicial notice of the fact. Where it is somewhat controversial, the matter can be proved as a factual question in court. There is no reason to suspect that a judicial forum is a poor one for assessing the evidence relating to the matter. Sources of evidence could include reports of parliamentary committees, such as the Joint Committee on Human Rights, social science studies, expert testimony,[109] public interest interventions, reports by reputable international bodies, and by public bodies such as the Equality and Human Rights Commission (EHRC), and, if needed, by the appointment of an amicus curiae/friend of the court. The involvement of various groups in the process will foster inter-institutional collaboration and the recognition of a group as vulnerable may feed back into the political process in helpful ways.

The main objection to this entire project will of course be that one cannot define what majoritarian bias or neglect are without having some substantive theory of what constitutes equal treatment.[110] And if one has such a theory, the objection goes, then one commits to a richer theory such as the one held by Ronald Dworkin. This argument would be absurd if it is meant to say that the outcome of the process described above would be the same as the outcome of a process in which a judge merely asks herself whether a law violates some facet of equal respect and concern. What is advocated here is far more circumscribed, and is concerned with group or status-based disadvantage. The objection might rather mean something more modest, however, such as that judges will make errors about who is vulnerable to majoritarian bias or neglect, and what should

---

[109] See Chapter 8, section IV.C.3.
[110] See Bellamy, *Political Constitutionalism*, pp. 107–19.

be done about it. That is no doubt true, but answerable. Any procedure at the institutional level will produce errors and error costs. We have good reason to believe that the degree of deviation between judicial determination and actual vulnerable groups, if applying such an approach, would be small enough to render the error costs acceptable in light of the benefits such a procedure would extend, within an overall incrementalist approach, to vulnerable groups.

No doubt the objection to that line of argument will be to ask what benefits will in fact accrue to vulnerable groups, and, by the way, what evidence is there that this approach would keep 'error costs' low (as I put it)? Well, data on that is difficult to marshal, but I showed in Chapter 3 that in fact the evidence supports the claim that there is a modest benefit to adjudication in such contexts. A more focused dossier can be found, however, in the experience of s. 4 declarations under the HRA and of social rights litigation in South Africa, and to a more mixed extent, India. Under s. 4 of the HRA, the British courts have issued declarations of incompatibility in respect of persons sectioned under the Mental Health Act,[111] prisoners,[112] transsexuals,[113] foreign and local persons suspected as terrorists,[114] to foreigners in connection with the receipt of social housing,[115] and to persons subject to immigration control.[116] Those cases in which a declaration was ultimately refused (whether at first instance or on appeal) include challenges by men against legislation extending benefits to widows but not widowers,[117] by property owners against the procedural scheme

---

[111] *R (on the application of H)* v. *Mental Health Review Tribunal for the North and East of London Region, and the Secretary of State for Health* [2001] EWCA Civ 415; *R (on the application of M)* v. *Secretary of State for Health* [2003] EWHC 1094.

[112] *R (on the application of Anderson)* v. *Secretary of State for the Home Department* [2002] UKHL 46; *R (Clift)* v. *Secretary of State for the Home Department* [2006] UKHL 54; *Smith* v. *Scott* [2007] CSIH 9 (Scotland); *R (Thompson)* v. *Secretary of State for the Home Department* [2010] UKSC 17.

[113] *Bellinger* v. *Bellinger* [2003] UKHL 21.

[114] *A and Others; X and Others* v. *Secretary of State for the Home Department* [2004] UKHL 56; *In re MB* [2006] EWHC 1000, subsequently reversed by Court of Appeal ([2006] EWCA Civ 1140), itself reversed by the House of Lords, no declaration issued ([2007] UKHL 46).

[115] *R (Morris)* v. *Westminster City Council and the First Secretary of State* [2005] EWCA Civ 1184; *R (Gabaj)* v. *First Secretary of State* (unreported) (applying *Morris* to a household where the foreign dependent was a pregnant wife).

[116] *R (on the application of Baiai and others)* v. *Secretary of State for the Home Department* [2008] UKHL 53.

[117] *R (on the application of Hooper)* v. *Secretary of State for Work and Pensions* [2005] UKHL 29; *R (on the application of Wilkinson)* v. *Inland Revenue Commissioners* [2003] EWCA Civ 814.

contained in planning legislation,[118] by a pawnbroker against a statutory regulation of his contractual rights,[119] by a navy engineer against Crown immunity from tort liability under a no-fault compensation regime for industrial accidents,[120] and by an NGO that sought to overturn the ban on political advertising on broadcast media.[121] There are a few exceptions to this broad conformity, but none poses particular challenges for the general point being made here.[122] The overwhelming majority of House of Lords/Supreme Court cases, in other words, already reflect the tenor of the advice advanced here.

Precisely the same trend is visible in all the leading social rights cases decided by the Constitutional Court of South Africa, save one. In *Soobramoney* the claimant argued that his right to emergency medical treatment was violated by a policy of allocating scarce kidney dialysis treatment to patients who were not terminally ill over those that were (like him).[123] The Court rejected the claim. At base, there was no reason to believe that Mr Soobramoney was subjected to any majoritarian bias or neglect.

D   Primary legislation: strong democratic restraint

The problem of political marginalisation on the one hand gives a reason for wanting to create supplementary political avenues (e.g. judicial review) for disadvantaged groups in respect of their social rights. Yet it also gives supportive arguments *against* giving the middle classes and the wealthy powers to obtain benefits from the constitutional jurisdiction of courts,

---

[118] *R (Alconbury)* v. *Secretary of State for the Environment, Transport and the Regions* [2001] UKHL 23.

[119] *Wilson* v. *First County Trust Ltd (No. 2)* [2003] UKHL 40.

[120] *Matthews* v. *Ministry of Defence* [2003] UKHL 4.

[121] *R (Animal Defenders International)* v. *Secretary of State for Media, Culture and Sport* [2008] UKHL 15.

[122] *McR's Application for Judicial Review* [2003] NI 1 (a case applying a highly dated statute, which demonstrated a clear absence of contemporary legislative focus); and *International Transport Roth GmbH and others* v. *Secretary of State for the Home Department* [2002] EWCA Civ 158 (where the outcome, if laudable in the case, may be difficult to justify on the approach advocated here and would therefore be rejected). A more difficult case is *R (Wright)* v. *Secretary of State for Health* [2009] UKHL 3, where the Law Lords found a statute that allowed the provisional delisting of care workers, prior to a proper quasi-judicial hearing, to be a violation of the Art. 6 ECHR right to a fair determination of civil rights and obligations. It is arguable that care workers are vulnerable to majoritarian bias. The case also involved the assertion of procedural rights.

[123] *Soobramoney* v. *Minister of Health (KwaZulu-Natal)* [1997] (12) BCLR 1696 (CC).

over and above the unequal influence they already enjoy in the legislature. If the effect is to aggregate more resources for themselves, the poor might be marginalised even further.

Even if courts are not a hollow hope for the poor, it remains true that the middle classes and the wealthy have easier access. This can create acute dangers in social rights adjudication. Each person in society will have extended, pervasive contact with the welfare state, through the health care system, some twenty years of schooling, social security contributions, and ultimately pensions, social care, and palliative treatment before death. The system truly is, in Beveridge's famous words, 'cradle-to-grave'. The civil and political rights adjudication we are familiar with is in an important sense different. Very few of the middle classes will interact with the criminal justice or mental health systems, or have their freedom of expression or religion interfered with, or be subject to state-sponsored discrimination. In other words, the subject-matter of social rights may amplify the distortive threats associated with well-resourced groups in litigation more generally, and it is thus important to consider additional safeguards.

Where a court reviews a statutory provision that reflects legislative focus, and the measure does not fall into one of the categories set out in section IV.C above, my view is that the standard of review for cases involving social rights should be deferential: a failure of rational connection or arbitrariness. The idea of rational basis scrutiny is relatively well developed in the USA for economic due process cases,[124] Canadian law employs a deferential version of the proportionality test,[125] and exists in European Union law, where the 'manifestly inappropriate' standard is used for discretionary legislative choices in conditions of extreme complexity.[126] In each of these cases, the courts use a deferential standard of review but they retain jurisdiction for what may amount to either a clear case, or what would be a measure amounting to a form of irrational law-making that is manifestly unsupported by the legislative objectives. This provides a long stop for those who are not members of marginalised groups, but whose rights are threatened when the state seeks to act in a patently abusive manner. It acknowledges the possibility that some governments will legislate in outright contradiction of the evidential record relevant to the

---

[124] *Minnesota* v. *Clover Leaf Creamery Co*, 449 US 456 (1981) (rational-basis scrutiny under the equal protection clause).

[125] *R* v. *Oakes* [1986] 1 SCR 103 (proportionality test).

[126] *R* v. *Secretary of State for Health, ex parte British American Tobacco Investments Ltd and Imperial Tobacco Ltd* (C-491/01) [2002] ECR I-11453 (ECJ) [123].

measure, or in a way that demonstrates no rational connection to the legitimate aim offered.

It may be argued here that this standard is too deferential, and that non-marginalised groups also have human rights, and so deserve no less judicial protection. Of course everyone has human rights, but it was made clear above that that is no answer to the question of who should define and enforce them. Since I accept the basic argument for the dignity of legislation subject to the flaws I have outlined above, I must admit that apart from corrections to those flaws I am at a loss for a good argument for why courts ought to be able to trump a clearly expressed legislative opinion about the shape of our rights in the countries having the background political conditions outlined in Chapter 1. Further, there is evidence of harm in the United States, where privileged groups have used the courts to great advantage. Even apart from the *Lochner*-era, decisions concerning campaign financing (compatible with Ely's idea that courts can be seen to be 'clearing the channels of political change'),[127] have been in some respects a serious setback for democracy in America.[128]

V   Conclusion

A just democracy depends on the guarantee of social human rights. In any such democracy that guarantee is delivered through a legislative programme of social rights, administered by a responsible executive, and buttressed by the existence of legal accountability. Constitutional judicial review of social rights can complement this process. This chapter has set out one way to do so, by identifying two normative problems with legislative finality, and setting out a role for judicial review that is a proportionate response to those problems. The principle of democratic legitimacy, interpreted this way, would encourage judges to preserve or mandate the possibility of legislative focus, and reserve more searching review either for those cases where review gives effect to unqualified or clear constitutional

---

[127] Ely, *Democracy and Distrust*, Chapter 5.

[128] See *Buckley* v. *Valeo,* 424 US 1 (1976) (financing political campaigns a form of protected political speech); *Citizens United* v. *Federal Election Commission*, 558 US 08–205 (2010). See B. de Blasio, 'Citizens United and the 2010 Midterm Elections' (Office of the Public Advocate of the City of New York, December 2010, available at http://advocate.nyc.gov/files/12–06–10CitizensUnitedReport.pdf (showing 15 per cent of spending in 2010 midterm elections was 'Citizen's United Spending', with surges in anonymous donations and negative advertisements). See also 'The Voters Need to Know', Editorial, *New York Times*, 4 August 2011, A22: ('The Supreme Court did democracy no favour at all when it opened the floodgates to unlimited campaign spending by corporations and unions').

obligations, or reinforces democratic participation through (modest) procedural rights, or seeks to protect the interests of groups who are particularly vulnerable to majoritarian bias or neglect. Claimants operating outside those parameters would, on this justification, be entitled only to a highly deferential form of review reserved for cases of irrationality. This form of constitutional judicial review is not best described as a 'process-based theory', because it is plainly substantive in important respects. It is rather an approach that compensates for the limitations of the legislative process in a manner that is calibrated to the demand for correction.

This conclusion, though, only gets the case for constitutional social rights over the first hurdle. The appropriate role for courts must clear a few more, which relate not directly to the legitimacy of judicial review, but the propriety of it in the light of the epistemic or capacity-based limitations of the judicial role. It is to those problems that the remainder of this part of the book now turns.

7

Polycentricity

I Introduction

The idea that courts should not adjudicate polycentric disputes is the most overrated objection to constitutional social rights. Its popularity in my view stems from the arcane nature of the idea of polycentricity – if people fully understood the implications of the idea rather than chiefly raised its flag in the face of resource disputes, they would realise that its implications would be too strong to square with contemporary adjudication. I have shown elsewhere that polycentricity is a pervasive feature of adjudication, and so it cannot be on its own any conclusive argument against the justiciability of polycentric issues.[1] The task of this chapter is more constructive. It is to demystify the idea introduced to adjudication by Lon Fuller, and refine it so that what is wise in it can be restated as a principle of judicial restraint.

The important tasks are to show what it is, why it is important, when it is relevant to adjudication, and what factors attenuate the weight that it should be given in the adjudication of polycentric cases. While I am in some ways critical of the use of Fuller's idea, I propose three basic refinements to it in this chapter that would get us past the impasse of seeing its relevance on the one hand, but non-conclusiveness on the other. The refinements are to see polycentricity as a property of legal issues and not areas of decision-making (like resource allocation or planning); to argue that polycentricity is relevant to adjudication when the court is asked to make or should make a finding about the substantial and heterogeneous interests of a large number of non-represented persons; and to list and elaborate the factors that attenuate the weight it ought to be given in adjudication. I identify a range of attenuating factors: judicial mandate, degree of polycentricity, access to information, comparative judicial competency, and the nature of the remedy. The exploration of these

---

[1] J. A. King, 'The Pervasiveness of Polycentricity' [2008] *Public Law* 101. I also show at 104–6 how and why its importance as a juristic concept in the United States has waned.

attenuating factors sheds light on the proper role of polycentricity in social rights adjudication.

II   The idea and importance of polycentricity

According to Lon Fuller, a polycentric problem is one that comprises a large network or web of interlocking relationships, such that a change to any one relationship causes a series of complex changes to other factors.[2] Such networks have 'interacting centres' – the points where the strands of the metaphorical web intersect – where different parties interact with each other by means of negotiation, exchange, or in other ways.[3] A network or problem having a profusion of such 'interacting centres' is one that is 'many-centred', hence, polycentric. Fuller used the now well-known image of a spider's web to convey the idea of how pulling on one strand would distribute new and complicated tensions throughout all of the other strands of the web.

The perfect example of a polycentric task is how to set an appropriate price or wage. Setting the price of a commodity or the wage of an employee can affect supply or demand for the commodity or employment, which in turn affects a multitude of other costs and relationships.[4] And each of the separate consequential effects of the price determination (e.g. lay-off, decreased demand for the commodity), in turn affects other networks of relationships (e.g. manufacturing and supply chain contracts, transport, insurance, advertising, and so on).[5]

Fuller derived the idea from natural scientist cum philosopher Michael Polanyi, who used it to explain why he believed the principle of self-coordination in markets is a necessary antidote to the insoluble problems of central planning.[6] Polanyi wrote that in the free market, '[i]ndividuals … evaluate by their independent mutual adjustments the polycentric task of optimum allocation of resources and distribution of products.'[7]

---

[2] L. Fuller, 'The Forms and Limits of Adjudication' (1978–1979) 92 *Harvard Law Review* 353. The paper was a draft published posthumously. As explained on the editor's opening note on the paper, the first draft was written in 1957, and revised in 1959 and 1961. Fuller, as with Polanyi before him, never gave a succinct definition of what a polycentric task was.

[3] *Ibid.*, 397.   [4] *Ibid.*, 394.

[5] *Ibid.*, 394–5 for other examples.

[6] M. Polanyi, *The Logic of Liberty: Reflections and Rejoinders* (New York: Routledge & Kegan Paul, 1951) esp. pp. 170ff.

[7] *Ibid.*, p. 179.

Polanyi's concern demonstrates that polycentric tasks pose difficulties for managers and administrative decision-makers as well. Polanyi's work was essentially libertarian in nature, and he found harmony between his idea and those of Friedrich Hayek, who himself returned the compliment.[8]

For his part, Fuller introduced the idea as part of an overall project aiming to show what kinds of social tasks are best assigned to courts, and those inherently unsuited for adjudicative disposition and thus best left to legislatures, agencies, the market or other mixed forms of adjudication such as arbitration.[9] In so doing, he developed a theory of adjudication:

> This whole analysis [of the optimum and essential conditions for the functioning of adjudication] will derive from one simple proposition, namely, that the distinguishing characteristic of adjudication lies in the fact that it confers on the affected party a peculiar form of participation in the decision, that of presenting proofs and reasoned arguments for a decision in his favor ... Whatever destroys that participation destroys the integrity of adjudication itself.[10]

Thus for Fuller the 'essence' of adjudication is the mode of participation it accords to the affected party.[11]

Issues of participation are intrinsically connected with issues of complexity. Indeed, many feel that polycentricity is foremost about complex subject-matter.[12] But something can be complex without being polycentric: scientific questions can be enormously complex without implicating a network of interconnected variables. But polycentric issues are often 'complex' in the sense of 'understood with great difficulty', because it is difficult to know who will be affected by a change in one relationship in the interlocking scheme. Therefore, it is difficult to know even who should be called to the table to discuss the issue since the network of cause and effect relationships is scarcely comprehended.[13]

Fuller believed that the adjudication of polycentric disputes would (1) give rise to unintended consequences; (2) encourage judges to try unorthodox solutions such as consultations of non-represented parties,

---

[8] King, 'The Pervasiveness of Polycentricity', 104–5; F. A. Hayek, *The Constitution of Liberty* (London: Routledge Classics, 1960), pp. 140–1.

[9] Fuller, 'The Forms and Limits of Adjudication', 354.

[10] *Ibid.*, 364.

[11] *Ibid.*, 365; see also O. M. Fiss, 'The Supreme Court 1978 Term: Foreword: The Forms of Justice' (1978–79) 93 *Harvard Law Review* 1, 40 (calling participation the 'core' of Fuller's theory).

[12] See e.g. the Supreme Court of Canada's decision in *M* v. *H* [1999] 2 SCR 3 [310] (Bastarrache J).

[13] I am indebted to J. W. F. Allison for this point.

guessing at facts and so on; and (3) prompt the judge to recast the problem in a judicially manageable form.[14] These are prescient insights, and all three are visible in some constitutional social rights cases.[15] Unintended consequences arise chiefly because the adversarial adjudicative process limits the information considered by the judge to that provided by represented parties. Abram Chayes described this adversarial structure as 'bipolar', and as an 'organized contest between two individuals ... diametrically opposed, to be decided on a winner-takes-all-basis'.[16] Chayes argued that it was a view of adjudication that failed to account for the emergent American public law litigation paradigm.

Fuller felt that polycentric problems ought to be solved by managerial direction and contract (reciprocity), though not by majority voting.[17] He does not elaborate much on the role of managers, though he does give the example of a baseball manager who handles problems of enormous mathematical complexity through 'a good deal of intuition'.[18] However, true to Polanyi's concern, he believed polycentric issues would often work themselves out through negotiation and mutual self-adjustment in contract,[19] within which he includes parliamentary bargaining and trade-offs.[20]

III   The pervasiveness of polycentricity

Fuller believed that the distinguishing characteristic of adjudication is the mode of participation it gives to the affected party. But it is difficult to imagine a dispute where the people affected by a decision are limited to the parties before the court. Fuller failed to provide examples of bipolar disputes involving discrete issues.[21] Abram Chayes was well aware of this issue and wrote about what he called the 'demise of the bipolar structure'

---

[14] Fuller, 'The Forms and Limits of Adjudication', 395–6, 401. On the last of these, see also J. L. Mashaw, *Bureaucratic Justice* (New Haven: Yale University Press, 1985), p. 6. '[T]here are ... ways of translating many claims for more affirmative protection into a negative, and therefore more judicially manageable form. "Give me a healthful environment" can thus become "Do not proceed without attending to my legislatively validated demand for a more healthful environment."'

[15] See e.g. *Residents of the Joe Slovo Community* v. *Thubelisha Homes and Others,* 2010 (3) SA 454 (CC) and the discussion of its extended context in K. McLean, 'Meaningful Engagement: One Step Forward, Two Steps Back' (2010) 3 *Constitutional Court Review* 1.

[16] A. Chayes, 'The Role of the Judge in Public Law Litigation' (1976) 89 *Harvard Law Review* 1281, 1282.

[17] Fuller, 'The Forms and Limits of Adjudication', 398, 400.

[18] *Ibid.*; see also 403.   [19] *Ibid.*, 399.   [20] *Ibid.*, 400.

[21] J. W. F. Allison, 'Fuller's Analysis of Polycentric Disputes and the Limits of Adjudication' (1994) 53 *Cambridge Law Journal* 367, 372.

in which 'the effects of litigation were not really confined to persons at either end of the right-remedy axis.'[22] Fuller himself acknowledged that 'concealed polycentric elements are probably present in almost all problems submitted to adjudication' and that the true question is one of 'knowing when the polycentric elements have become so significant and predominant that the proper limits of adjudication have been reached'.[23]

The notion of degree does not explain away the problem, though, because as I have shown, highly polycentric problems abound in public and private law.[24] Many unrepresented parties are affected by the most conventional forms of litigation, including contract, tort, employment, criminal, and bankruptcy and insolvency law. Constitutional law questions, human rights, and statutory interpretation routinely involve settling legal questions with sweeping and *relevant* implications for unrepresented persons. Such impact is not only a collateral effect, but a fundamental responsibility of the courts. They are to clarify the applicable law for all to follow, a key difference between the common law and arbitration.[25] Fiss was right in pointing out that Fuller's theory 'would render illegitimate almost all adjudication – both of the common law and the constitutional variety – in which the courts were creating public norms'.[26] There must be something more to it, if it is to be relevant at all.

IV Refinement of Fuller's idea

Three simple refinements to Fuller's idea will help ensure that it is understood and applied correctly. Two are discussed in this section, and the third – the idea and content of the attenuating factors – is discussed in the next.

A A property of issues, not areas

In law, we ought to regard polycentricity as a property of issues or problems and not 'areas' of decision-making such as resource allocation or planning. Fuller wrote of polycentric 'problems' or 'tasks', but the impression created by his work and those accepting his idea is that certain areas of decision-making – resource allocation and planning being leading

---

[22] Chayes, 'The Role of the Judge in Public Law Litigation', 1289–92.
[23] Fuller, 'The Forms and Limits of Adjudication', 398.
[24] King, 'The Pervasiveness of Polycentricity', 109ff.
[25] Fiss, 'The Supreme Court 1978 Term', 1, 43.
[26] *Ibid.*, 43.

examples – are polycentric and thus unsuitable for judicial control. As a matter of fact, both areas are, generally speaking, polycentric *in the sense intended by Polanyi*. Polanyi was concerned with subject-matter because he was concerned with what type of problems a government should attempt to regulate. But a court's role depends not on the 'area' but on how the facts of the dispute fit into the applicable legal framework. The welfare state is comprehensively regulated by a matrix of statutes, regulations, circulars, guidance, and reports of various kinds. These are in turn complemented by a range of public law rules and principles. It is only after the particular facts of a given case are slotted into this framework that one can evaluate whether a legal issue is polycentric. This much is important by way of accuracy, but is entirely consonant with Fuller's paper and so little more need be said on the matter. He was concerned with assigning certain polycentric tasks to courts, and the identification of certain 'areas' as polycentric amounts only to a convenient (but potentially misleading) shorthand for where such tasks will predominate in adjudication. And let there be no doubt in my own message: a vagueness in constitutional social rights adjudication could indeed engender – with or without a sophisticated theory of adjudication – quite polycentric legal disputes. The prescriptions in this book are a response to that fact.

B   *When a legal issue is polycentric*

In *Bush* v. *Gore*,[27] the US Supreme Court had to settle a legal dispute that may arguably have affected the majority of the world's population at the time (through the appointment of George Bush instead of Al Gore as President of the United States), and untold billions into the future. Does that fact alone make it polycentric? It does not, because that impact was not (obviously) relevant to the legal question at stake in the case.

So if impact alone does not make a legal issue polycentric, what does? A brief answer is that the problem is polycentric if the best answer demands comprehension of a highly complex range of cause-and-effect relationships entailed by the potential solutions. Of course policy-makers make decisions under conditions of bounded rationality all of the time. Why be worried about courts? Fuller's concern was that the bipolar adjudicative process necessarily restricts participation in polycentric cases. It also restricts access to information. If we are to give an interpretation of

---

[27]   *Bush* v. *Gore* 531 US 98 (2000).

the relevance of polycentricity that does not fully embrace the libertarian implications that Polanyi and others promoted, then it must lie here.

I would thus argue that polycentricity is relevant in adjudication when the court is *asked to make* or *should make* a finding about the substantial and heterogeneous interests of a large number of non-represented persons. It must contemplate significant numbers of people and heterogeneous interests, because that is what generates the complex network of relationships. It must be substantial interests, because numbers alone might not matter – a trivial matter, such as signs on motorways, might nominally affect millions but nonetheless amount to a trifling aesthetic concern next to road safety policy that would save but a few lives.

True to Fuller's notion that polycentricity is a matter of degree, the greater the number of unrepresented but relevant interests in this sense, (1) the greater the likelihood of a judge making a false assumption about certain interests; (2) the more unknowable the consequences of judicial error; and (3) the graver the potential consequences of that error. But if the legal issue does not require the judge to opine on the interests of unrepresented persons, then whether such persons are affected is not relevant to the dispute and the issue is not polycentric in a legally relevant sense. How the judgment fits into the interlocking scheme would then be for other institutions to worry about.

It is thus necessary (for the sake of analytical clarity) to shed light on when it is that a judge *makes* or *should make* a finding about the rights or interests of a non-represented person, for this will tell us something about the extent to which polycentricity is relevant to the judge's interpretive role. Three basic categories of relevance are discernible, namely, where third-person effects are a primary, secondary, or collateral consideration in interpretation of some legal sources (e.g. statute, precedent, or constitutional standard).

The interests of non-represented persons are a *primary consideration* when the legal test employed by the judge explicitly requires her to balance the interests of non-represented persons against those of a party. This happens, for instance, when judges balance considerations of necessity in pursuit of some public goal when examining the proportionality of limitations of human rights; when they consider policy arguments in civil litigation; when they qualify common law rules or overrule precedents; and whenever they make a finding regarding the public interest or some portion of it. I argue in Chapter 4 that a bill of constitutional social rights ought to make the role of balancing an explicit part of the interpretive approach, and thus a primary consideration, because otherwise judges would be invited to ignore the impact of their rulings.

The interests of non-represented persons are a *secondary consideration* in those cases where they are relevant to the court's determination of a related but logically prior legal issue. The clearest case of this takes place when a court interprets open-textured statutory provisions such as 'fair', 'reasonable', 'accommodation', or 'need'. The lawyers will advance various interpretations, and the impact of each on non-represented persons may become relevant. However, here the effects on non-represented persons arise as a secondary consideration to the logically prior question of what the statute means. Answering that question is the primary task, and polycentricity enters as a secondary consideration only when the ordinary cannons of interpretation are exhausted, and even then only in the space left open by such interpretations. If there were a conflict between such an interpretation on the one hand, and one based on the unpleasant effects of it on the other, it is clear that the conventionally determined 'meaning' should win unless the consequences lead to absurdity. This can be the effect, for instance, when a statute itself offers criteria for defining the term,[28] where the definition offered on the basis of impact is manifestly incompatible with the ordinary usage of the term,[29] or where the consequential effects offered by one party bear little conceptual relationship to the issue of meaning.[30] In other words, although the meaning of the terms are open-textured, there is no licence to engage in the relatively unfettered type of balancing that courts undertake when the effects on other parties are a primary consideration.[31] This point is important, because judges have a history of deferring more at this stage in statutory interpretation than is warranted, relying implicitly on ideas like polycentricity when doing so.[32]

A different approach to whether polycentricity is a secondary consideration might apply when judges apply common law rules,[33] or

---

[28] See e.g. *R* v. *Gloucestershire County Council, ex parte Barry* [1997] 2 All ER 1 (HL) (where the statute offered a list of criteria to decide the meaning of the term 'need').

[29] *R* v. *Hillingdon LBC, ex. parte Puhlhofer* [1986] 1 AC 485 (HL) (where the court found a hotel room to be 'accommodation' for a family of five, later legislatively reversed).

[30] *R* v. *East Sussex County Council, ex parte Tandy* [1998] AC 714 (HL) (quashing a local authority's consideration of available resources in determining the meaning of 'suitable education').

[31] For similar observations on statutes, see R. Dworkin, *Taking Rights Seriously* (Cambridge, MA: Harvard University Press, 1978), p. 109.

[32] King, 'The Pervasiveness of Polycentricity', 418–19.

[33] Dworkin, *Taking Rights Seriously*, pp. 107–11, esp. p. 111.

constitutional standards. One good reason for the more restricted attention to non-represented parties in statutory interpretation is that courts will act with some confidence that Parliament is in fact responsible for, and thus responsible for correcting, any undesirable impact of a particular interpretation.[34] This is a less acceptable assumption under the common law, where the legal standards are judge-made and where judges retain a quasi-legislative mandate to modify them.[35] The constitution, similarly, may have been adopted by 'the People' (though not in the United Kingdom), but the interpretive exercise is different. The provisions are typically more vague, less topically focused, and less guided by the scheme of the overall document by comparison with statutes, and parliamentary correction is almost always out of reach. With the common law and constitutional interpretation, therefore, it is more likely that the impact on non-represented persons is or ought to be a primary consideration, a presumption displaced only when the standard being applied speaks clearly to the resolution of the dispute at issue, which takes it into the third category put forward here.

The interests of non-represented parties can be a *collateral consideration* when the legal standard at issue and the regular standards of interpretation that apply to it appear settled in favour of one interpretation, but to give effect to that meaning produces seemingly absurd consequences. The standard position with statutes is that where the meaning of a provision is relatively settled or plain, the effects on other parties are not ordinarily relevant.[36] As even advocates of purposive interpretation point out, '[t]he primacy of the text is the first rule of interpretation.'[37] Nonetheless, as Michael Zander has pointed out in English law, the evolution of statutory interpretation from the plain meaning rule (emphasising come-what-may literalism), to the golden rule (literalism with an exception for absurd outcomes), to the mischief rule/purposive interpretation (accepting that literalism should give way to purposive interpretation as a matter of course and not exception), has recognised that

---

[34] *R v. Barnet LBC, ex parte Shah* [1983] 2 AC 309 (eligibility of foreign students for student grants under s. 1(1) of the Education Act 1962); amended by the Education (Fees and Awards) Act 1983.

[35] H. L. A. Hart, *The Concept of Law* (2nd edn, Oxford: Clarendon Press, 1997), p. 135.

[36] *Duport Steel* v. *Sirs* [1980] 1 WLR 142, 167. Indeed, historically, apart from judicially noticeable materials such as dictionaries, 'any evidence on the question [of statutory interpretation] is wholly inadmissible': *Camden (Marquis)* v. *Commissioners for Inland Revenue* [1914] 1 KB 641 (CA) 649–50.

[37] Lord Steyn, 'Pepper v Hart: A Re-examination' (2001) 21 *Oxford Journal of Legal Studies* 59, 60.

the 'plain meaning' of statutes cannot justify manifestly absurd results.[38] There have been a number of criticisms of the idea of judges using the notion of 'absurdity' as a ground for giving interpretations that appear at odds with the text, and I have no wish to enter such debates.[39] Insofar as the idea is applied, it means that polycentricity will be relevant only in this collateral sense, meaning that it would be ignored unless it would be completely absurd (or inconsistent with the statutory scheme)[40] to do so. In the common law, the judges will not ordinarily face this situation, though in constitutional law it has arisen a few times and the courts have needed to make embarrassing adjustments.[41]

V   Giving weight to polycentricity: attenuating factors

It has thus far been established that polycentricity of a legally relevant form is pervasive in adjudication. How and why should it be given weight under such circumstances, rather than be dismissed as an incoherent idea? Fuller never managed to answer this question. I argue in this section that once it is established that polycentricity is relevant, factors may attenuate the degree of weight it is to be given in adjudication. The idea of attenuating factors explains the relevance but non-decisiveness of polycentricity. This section presents a non-exhaustive range of such factors that can be given weight in social rights adjudication.

A   Judicial mandate

If the constitution, statute, or the common law provides a clear mandate to adjudicate polycentric issues, then it will be necessary and appropriate

---

[38] M. Zander, *The Law Making Process* (6th edn, Cambridge University Press, 2004), pp. 132–49, 193ff. In the US context, Frank Cross reports that most accept the absurdity doctrine: *The Theory and Practice of Statutory Interpretation* (Stanford University Press, 2009), pp. 108–9.

[39] In the UK, both Zander, *The Law Making Process*, pp. 147–9 and especially Rupert Cross, in J. Bell and G. Engle (eds.), *Cross: Statutory Interpretation* (3rd edn, Oxford University Press, 2005), pp. 88–92 are quite critical of it and believe whatever is useful about it has been absorbed into the practice of purposive interpretation. In the USA, see J. F. Manning, 'The Absurdity Doctrine' (2003) 116 *Harvard Law Review* 2387; A. Vermeule, *Judging under Uncertainty: An Institutional Theory of Legal Interpretation* (Cambridge, MA: Harvard University Press, 2006), pp. 57–9.

[40] Rupert Cross preferred the language of purposive interpretation to the absurdity doctrine; see Bell and Engle (eds.), *Cross: Statutory Interpretation*, pp. 88–92.

[41] *Reference Re Manitoba Language Rights* [1985] 1 SCR 721 (SCC) (ordering temporary validity of unconstitutional legislation); *Robinson* v. *Secretary of State for Northern Ireland* [2002] UKHL 32 (not applying legislatively specified time-limits).

as a matter of democratic legitimacy for courts to do this. There are many instances where this occurs: the increased role of judicial balancing under bills of human rights; the judicial interpretation of vague terms such as 'unfair' in consumer protection law or 'unjust' or 'unfair' dismissal in employment law;[42] inviting courts and tribunals to evaluate whether a proposed merger in competition or anti-trust law is acceptable because it is more efficient;[43] or the adjudication of division of powers problems between federal and sub-federal branches of government. European Union (EU) law provides a wealth of examples of the adjudication of poly-centric problems of mind-boggling proportions. In all such cases the leg-islators no doubt knew that courts would adjudicate highly polycentric disputes. They balanced that cost against the enterprise's benefits. In con-sumer protection and employment law, that cost was balanced against the harm of allowing powerful private institutions to abuse their dispropor-tionate bargaining power. In competition law, they decided that allowing businesses to prove, under significant burdens, the efficiency gains of what appear to be anti-competitive mergers could benefit the public as a whole. In many federal states, disputes over the division of legislative powers are often viewed as requiring the independence and impartiality, as well as other interpretive methods, provided by courts of law. And in EU law, the advantages of closer market and political integration, and the need for impartial adjudication of transnational rules, were balanced against the obvious competence deficit created by inviting a court to evaluate the necessity and propriety of national environmental, economic, and health policies. If such moves achieve a desirable social goal in the best of imper-fect ways, then there is little in what Fuller says that should inhibit it.

The scope of a judicial mandate is entirely dependent on the inter-pretation of the relevant constitutional and statutory scheme, in light of previous jurisprudence and doctrine. Nonetheless, a few general obser-vations might be made. First, if the legal sources are particularly clear in the case at issue, then the *legal issue* will not be polycentric (as I have

---

[42] See the Unfair Terms in Consumer Contracts Regulations 1999 and the Industrial Relations Act 1971 (as modified by the Employment Rights Act 1996).

[43] C. Luescher, 'Efficiency Considerations in European Merger Control – Just another Battle Ground for the European Commission, Economists and Competition Lawyers?' (2004) *European Competition Law Review* 71; *FTC* v. *Butterworth Health Corp and Blodgett Memorial Medical Center*; s. 96(1) Competition Act 1985 (Canada) and *Canada (Commissioner of Competition)* v. *Superior Propane Inc.* [2001] 3 F.C. 185 (Federal Court of Appeal) (reversing the Competition Tribunal's refusal to employ an open-ended bal-ancing test) and *Canada (Commissioner of Competition)* v. *Superior Propane Inc.* [2003] 3 F.C. 529 (Federal Court of Appeal).

shown above), or at best would be so only in a collateral sense. In that case, the mandate is so strong as to ordinarily eclipse the relevance of polycentricity altogether. Second, where the sources confer a general jurisdiction to adjudicate *a class of dispute*, but do not commend any particular outcome in a given case, polycentricity *ought* to constrain the interpretation, but only to the extent it does not undermine the judicial mandate. That would be undemocratic. In other words, it is not open for the European Court of Justice to decline to adjudicate a dispute on grounds of polycentricity if it is centrally within the class of disputes its mandate requires it to address.

A third type of situation is where the judicial mandate to adjudicate a given class of cases is itself what is in question. It is here that considerations of polycentricity blend together inextricably with considerations of democratic legitimacy, in that both weigh heavily. This would be the case in serious constitutional questions, such as whether UK courts have the jurisdiction to refuse to enforce an Act of Parliament;[44] whether the European Court of Justice could decide upon the supremacy of EU law over conflicting national laws;[45] or whether the Supreme Court of Canada can adjudicate the legality of secession given the textual silence of the constitution on the question.[46]

In my view, this is the type of situation now prevailing in respect of reading social rights into the European Convention on Human Rights, the Canadian Charter of Rights and Freedoms, and the Indian and the United States Bill of Rights. In this case, the mandate is limited and the developments in the area of social rights adjudication, in my view, in order to retain legitimacy, will need to be analogous to the organic development of the legal instrument as a whole. In my view, attempts to leverage a *comprehensive* protection of social rights out of an instrument that is chiefly aimed at protecting a class of civil and political rights is not only undesirable, but irresponsible and undemocratic. It is irresponsible because it casts aside the conventions of legal interpretation that give the practice of judicial review its special legitimacy for those who believe in it, a legitimacy that is crucial to answer the objections of its opponents.

---

[44] *Jackson and Others* v. *Attorney General* [2005] UKHL 56 [104]–[128] (Hope LJ) [71]–[103] (Steyn LJ) [142]–[166] (Baroness Hale); the US moment came with *Marbury* v. *Madison* (5 US 137 (1803)), though in an interpretive context making the conclusion more plausible if not less contentious than in *Jackson*.

[45] Case 26/62, *Van Gend en Loos* v. *Nederlandse Administratie der Belastingen* [1963] ECR 1.

[46] *Reference Re Secession of Quebec* [1998] 2 SCR 217 (SCC).

And it is undemocratic of course because the legitimacy of the judicial role depends crucially on the popular mandate accorded to courts via the constitution. Where the judges stray clearly from that role, they lose that legitimacy. Polycentricity, moreover, is a legitimate concern in ascertaining the scope of that mandate, because the mandate itself is what in part licenses the adjudication of such polycentric questions.

To be clear, these comments are by no means meant to reject the *Airey* principle at the European Court of Human Rights, cautiously articulated as follows:

> Whilst the Convention sets forth what are essentially civil and political rights, many of them have implications of a social or economic nature. The Court therefore considers, like the Commission, that the mere fact that an interpretation of the Convention may extend into the sphere of social and economic rights should not be a decisive factor against such an interpretation; there is no watertight division separating that sphere from the field covered by the Convention.[47]

That approach is sound, because it represents the organic growth of the interdependence and permeability of first- and second-generation rights, and recognises the extent to which positive obligations exist to secure first-generation rights. My comments above also mean to detract in no way from the principles of interpretation that recognise dynamic, living tree, evaluative, or purpose interpretation. But such approaches ordinarily respect the organic and incremental development of the law in a manner that respects the dimension of fit with other legal materials, and the context that gives meaning to the abstract principles the legislature enacted upon adoption of the constitution. But my comments here do mean to cast doubt on the possibility of generalising the approach taken in India, where the courts have read far-reaching protection of social rights into a constitution that expressly sets out social rights in a non-justiciable part of the constitution.[48] It would also cast doubt on the arguments advanced by the claimant in the Canadian case of *Gosselin* v. *Quebec* and accepted in the dissenting judgment of Arbour J., to read a state responsibility to provide an existential minimum into the s. 7 guarantee that people not be deprived of their security of the person.[49] These approaches become

---

[47] *Airey* v. *Ireland* (1979–80) 2 EHRR 305 [22].
[48] See Chapter 9, section III.A.3 for a brief discussion of structural relief in India and references to relevant literature.
[49] *Gosselin* v. *Quebec (Attorney General)* [2002] 4 SCR 429 [309] (Arbour's dissent on s. 7).

supporting evidence, in the hands of critics, for arguments that judges will extend their powers beyond the role foreseen for them in bills of rights.

B   Degree

I would argue that, after determining that the legal issue is indeed poly-centric, courts should inquire into the extent of that complexity by con-sidering the number and diversity of interests implicated, and the depth and breadth of the impact. Where the figure is exceptionally high and the impact significant, all else being equal, the issue will be less appro-priately resolved by judges. Clearly, this analysis seems at first blush to be simplistic and impossible, and its conclusion too stark: simplistic because counting heads seems like a crude tool for managing an intricate prob-lem; impossible because the essence of a polycentric problem is that its implications are hard to know; and too stark because so much adjudica-tion is polycentric in exactly this way. Yet this is both a good explanation of how courts proceed in polycentric adjudication, and it is the way that they in fact must proceed in the future.

It is a good explanation because one can see the courts attempting to limit the effects of their decisions on non-represented persons, especially in welfare rights cases. In *ex parte Coughlan*, for instance, the Court of Appeal found that a local authority was bound under administrative law to a promise it made that the home into which it moved an elderly care recipient would be her home for life.[50] The Court found, though, that 'most cases of an enforceable expectation of a substantive benefit … are likely in the nature of things to be cases where the expectation is confined to one person or a few people'.[51] This approach was affirmed in *R* v. *Secretary of State for Education, ex parte Begbie*, where Lord Justice Laws emphasised that this condition would tend to preclude 'wide-ranging issues of gen-eral policy', and that 'the more the decision challenged lies in what may inelegantly be called the macro-political field, the less intrusive will be the court's supervision'.[52]

This idea is also consistent with the public finance cases of *Nottinghamshire County Council v. Secretary of State for the Environment and another another*[53] and *R* v. *Secretary of State for the Environment,*

[50]   *R* v. *North and East Devon Health Authority, ex parte Coughlan* [2001] QB 213 [59] (CA).
[51]   *Ibid.*
[52]   *R* v. *Secretary of State for Education, ex parte Begbie* [2000] 1 WLR 1115 (CA) 1131.
[53]   [1986] AC 240 (HL).

ex parte Hammersmith and Fulham LBC.[54] In the latter case, Lord Bridge refused to treat the claim as raising a justiciable issue because it concerned 'the formulation and the implementation of national economic policy … which can only take effect with the approval of the House of Commons'.[55] Both these cases are indicative of a judicial concern with abstaining from review of cases of 'high policy'.[56] One can also observe a pronounced incrementalist approach in the UK and South African welfare rights cases that avoid sweeping macro-level disruptions,[57] or when they do, the nature of the remedy allows for future adaptation.

While this notion of degree has persuasive explanatory force, it remains difficult to show how judges should determine what is an excessive degree of polycentricity. When administrators address such tasks, as Herbert Simon and Charles Lindblom have made clear, they employ a combination of intuition and heuristics.[58] Judges can use them too. They will first of all use their own intuition about impact, which is not to be underrated as a valid source of expertise. They may also consider: (a) how the issue compares with the balancing undertaken in other cases; (b) whether the decision was taken at a comparatively low or high echelon in the administrative hierarchy and was intended to set a policy for many to follow; (c) whether the case can be decided on narrow grounds, or, by contrast, risks serving as a broadly applicable precedent uncontrollable through sound case management; and (d) whether the remedy can be fashioned in such a way as to leave latitude to the primary decision-maker to adjust to the ruling in a flexible way in future circumstances. Notably, if either of the last two of these questions is answered affirmatively, the polycentric nature of the legal issue will be radically reduced.

C   Access to information: case management and interventions

Access to information, as shown above, is perhaps the key problem for why polycentric issues pose difficulties for adjudication. Fuller's picture of adjudication is no longer, and possibly never was really, an accurate description of the process. There are three reasons, in the present state of English public law, why this picture is flawed: the power of case

---

[54] [1991] 1 AC 521 (HL).   [55] *Ibid.*, 597.

[56] Lord Irvine, 'Judges and Decision-Makers: the Theory and Practice of *Wednesbury* Review' [1996] *Public Law* 65, 67.

[57] See generally Chapter 10.

[58] See Chapter 8, section III and esp. Chapter 9, section II.B.2.

management; the public interest role played by the state; and the growth of third-party interventions.

First, while judges have never really been wholly disinterested in the impact of their rulings on the public interest, their powers of case management under Parts 3 and 26 of the Civil Procedure Rules now reflect the idea that 'ultimate responsibility for the control of litigation should move from litigants and their advisers to the court'.[59] Case management is furthermore a central method for implementing the overriding objective of the new rules.[60] Part 3 empowers judges to direct a separate trial of any issue, decide the order in which issues are to be tried, exclude any issue from consideration, as well as to 'take any other step or make any other order for the purpose of managing the case'.[61] Judges of the administrative court, where most public law cases are heard, do not formally use these case management powers, but they are effectively entitled to use these powers at the permission stage of the litigation, which can be conducted as an oral hearing, and in which process the judge is entitled to make any appropriate directions.[62] Furthermore, the court may make orders on its own initiative, and when doing so may 'give any person likely to be affected by the order an opportunity to make representations'.[63] These powers significantly increase the judge's capacity to ensure that argument is directed to relevant public policy matters and that interventions can be facilitated where appropriate.

Case management need not be limited to the early stages of litigation. In *Howard League for Penal Reform* v. *Secretary of State for the Home Department (No. 1)*, a claimant challenged the legality of the Prison Service Order determination that the Children Act 1989 did not apply to children in prisons.[64] Due to the implications the ruling would have for social services departments, the judge adjourned proceedings and made an order

---

[59] W. Rose (ed.), *Blackstone's Civil Practice 2006* (Oxford University Press, 2006), p. 480. See also S. Sime, *A Practical Approach to Civil Procedure* (9th edn, Oxford University Press, 2006), p. 23.

[60] Civil Procedure Rules (CPR) 1.4.

[61] CPR 3.1(2)(i), (j), (k) and (m).

[62] CPR 54.10. Applicants for judicial review in England and Wales must obtain permission from the Administrative Court before proceeding to the substantive hearing. Permission is usually granted or denied on the papers, but at times with a hearing and judgment.

[63] CPR 3.3(2)(a).

[64] [2002] EWHC 1750 (Admin). For a similar approach to the one taken in this case, see *Shields* v. *E. Coomes (Holdings) Ltd* [1978] 1 WLR 1408 (inviting the Equal Opportunities Commission to assist the court in relation to European discrimination law).

that certain interested parties be invited to file interventions.[65] The case is a model of sound case management for social rights adjudication.

A second reason that it would be wrong to think that the general public's interest is not represented in proceedings is that in public law it is the state's role to do so. In cases against public authorities, the dispute is not between two private citizens. Public authorities are generally well positioned in terms of both mandate and resources to represent the public interest. The state has fulfilled this role in public, regulatory, and criminal law for many years. This public interest function is further recognised in section 5 of the HRA 1998, which entitles the Crown and various public officials to notice and to intervene where a declaration of incompatibility is under consideration. There is admittedly an important concern about the quality of representation of the public interest in such cases.[66] The point being made here is that there is a channel for representing the interests of the public and that the state is *relatively* well positioned for providing it. Critics who make this argument against courts find themselves in an embarrassing cul-de-sac: if one denies that the state takes its role seriously in this regard, then why show restraint on grounds of legitimacy or expertise?

The third and final mode of providing information is by way of third-party interventions. Courts in Canada, the United States, and South Africa have done so for a long time.[67] The same wave has now swept English shores.[68] In *Roe* v. *Sheffield City Council*, Lord Justice Sedley observed that interventions were most valuable where 'aspects of the public interest in a

---

[65] *Howard League for Penal Reform* v. *Secretary of State for the Home Department (No. 1)* [2002] EWHC 1750 (Admin) [3]. The proceedings continued in [2002] EWHC 2497 (Admin); [2003] 1 FLR 484 (QB). It appears from Munby J's observations at [125]–[126] that only one additional party filed a witness statement.

[66] See *Khosa and Others* v. *Minister of Social Development and Others*, 2004 (6) BCLR 569 (CC) [12]–[25] (where the Constitutional Court of South Africa had to actually order the state to defend the legislation adequately).

[67] For some discussion of the Canadian experience, see S. Lavine, 'Advocating Values: Public Interest Intervention in *Charter* Litigation' (1992) 2 *National Journal of Constitutional Law* 27. Cf. J. Welch, 'No Room at the Top: Interest Group Intervenors and *Charter* Litigation in the Supreme Court of Canada' (1985) 43 *University of Toronto Faculty of Law Review* 204.

[68] See CPR 54.177; JUSTICE, *To Assist the Court: Third Party Interventions in the UK* (London: JUSTICE, 2009), and see in particular the statistics on numbers of interventions at [18]–[19] (London: Justice/Public Law Project, 1996); *R (on the application of Northern Ireland Human Rights Commission)* v. *Greater Belfast Coroner* [2002] UKHL 25 (NI); see comment by L. Blom-Cooper, 'Third Party Intervention and Judicial Dissent' [2002] *Public Law* 602–5.

legal issue of general importance may be represented by neither of the two parties before the court. Both NGOs and ministers may play a valuable role here.'[69] In the same case, Lady Justice Hale (as she then was) found that 'where there is likely to be a strong policy element in the decision, the perspective of bodies representative of the differing interests involved may be extremely helpful in enabling the court to strike the right balance between the various policy considerations'.[70] It is worth noting in this connection that public interest groups do not only intervene on behalf of claimants,[71] and the state will, by contrast, on occasion intervene against other public authorities in the claimant's favour.[72]

There has been a healthy debate as to whether third-party interventions really are in the public interest.[73] Sarah Hannett challenges such a view in the English context in a well-researched article.[74] She argues that it is unclear who actually represents the public interest,[75] that interventions can create a perceived bias in the judiciary,[76] that parties may be out-resourced by interveners against their position,[77] and that groups use litigation as a substitute for political campaigning that risks turning the judicial process into a quasi-legislative process.[78] These are important considerations, building on similar observations made earlier by Richard Stewart,[79] but in my view they do not support her conclusion that interventions should be constrained. In short, I believe she overstates the significance of each of them. As concerns the problem of certain organisations dominating the agenda, this is a problem with little evidence. Other groups have ample opportunity to intervene with different views (most barristers take such cases on a pro bono basis and costs are not at issue with interventions). It disregards the fact that without any interventions, the court's view of the problem, on this very reasoning, will be dominated by the parties alone. Groups intervene on behalf of government as well as claimants, and the representative nature of a group is something that courts could require to

---

[69] [2003] EWCA Civ 1 [84].   [70] Ibid., [104].

[71] See Chaoulli v. Quebec (Attorney General) [2005] 1 SCR 791 (SCC).

[72] YL v. Birmingham City Council [2007] UKHL 27.

[73] C. Harlow, 'Public Law and Popular Justice' (2002) 65 Modern Law Review 1.

[74] S. Hannett, 'Third Party Intervention: In the Public Interest?' [2003] Public Law 128; cf. M. Arshi and C. O'Cinneide, 'Third Party Interventions: The Public Interest Reaffirmed' [2004] Public Law 69.

[75] Hannett, 'Third Party Intervention: In the Public Interest?', 135–6.

[76] Ibid., 137–8, 140.   [77] Ibid., 141.   [78] Ibid., 139–40.

[79] R. Stewart, 'The Reformation of American Administrative Law' (1975) 88 Harvard Law Review 1669, 1762–81.

be established if that ever became a real issue. (At any rate this objection leads to a dead end: would the same rationale not support limiting such groups' influence on parliamentary decision-making as well?). The whole objection also underrates the principal role of interveners, which is to present additional *information*, not merely to add another whining voice to the din. The problem of bias in the judiciary, though theoretically a risk, has simply not materialised to any significant extent. The only actual example Hannett adduced was inapposite.[80] The problem of some groups out-resourcing the parties is a real issue,[81] but it is precisely the type of issue the judge is required to attend to under the Civil Procedure Rules. It will be rare for public interest groups (at least in social rights cases) to out-resource the state, and the relatively low number of interventions, and their positive results, support the view that this argument is also exaggerated. And the fact that some interveners oppose a claimant or defendant's claim is not a problem at all; it should rather be welcomed.[82] Hannett's ultimate and best charge is that interventions will turn courts into a substitute political forum, and I answer that argument in my discussion of Richard Stewart and Carol Harlow in a later chapter.[83]

Hannett's observations – as with those of Stewart and Harlow – are valuable. They draw our attention to real pitfalls. Nonetheless, the evidence so far suggests that the benefits of interventions outweigh these drawbacks.[84] Nonetheless, it would be fair to ask, at this point, whether I am not suggesting that an *increased* adjudication of polycentric problems is acceptable, *because* interventions attenuate the problem? Does this not in fact exacerbate the problem for which interventions provide a weak remedy?[85] That would be the wrong tactic, but it is not the one I am advocating. It is wrong to suggest that interventions mitigate all the problems of polycentric adjudication, but right to suggest that it can be a useful part of a package of attenuating factors that a cautious judge could apply to the

---

[80] *R* v. *Bow Street Metropolitan Stipendiary Magistrate and Others, ex parte Pinochet Ugarte (No. 2)* [2000] 1 AC 119. The possibility of Lord Hoffmann's potential bias in favour of Amnesty International in this case was based on his board membership and not Amnesty's frequency of intervention.

[81] See also Stewart, 'The Reformation of American Civil Law', 1767–1768.

[82] See *YL* v. *Birmingham City Council* and *Chaoulli* v. *Quebec AG* for relevant examples.

[83] Chapter 9, section III.A.1.

[84] See JUSTICE, *To Assist the Court: Third Party Interventions in the UK*, p. 13 (showing that between 2005 and 2009 in all cases before the House of Lords, 14 per cent involved interventions by public bodies, 11 per cent by NGOs, and 4 per cent by private persons).

[85] Stewart, 'The Reformation of American Administrative Law', 1789.

whole. With welfare rights claimants, we must recall that we are choosing between imperfect institutional alternatives, a point Richard Stewart accepted as well.[86]

D   Relative competency

In *The Morality of Law*, Fuller spoke of an economic manager who, unlike courts, takes account of 'every circumstance relevant to his decision'.[87] This is a crude understanding of bounded rationality, as the subsequent three chapters demonstrate. Neil Komesar argues that '[t]asks that strain the abilities of an institution may wisely be assigned to it anyway if the alternatives are even worse'.[88] I have already explained in my treatment of judicial mandate why legislatures often decide to assign to courts roles that strain their capacities. Numerous authors have made this point regarding the limitations of the political process for resolving certain polycentric disputes, including Allison,[89] Komesar (indirectly),[90] and Barber,[91] while Fiss provides a particularly eloquent exposition:[92]

> The individual is thrown back to those social processes that are supposed to respect his participatory right – dispute resolution, voting and bargaining. Each of these processes has important roles to play in our social life, but it is hard to believe that any of them enhance the real or effective – as opposed to formal – power of those individuals who are abused by the large-scale organizations of the modern state, the school system, the hospital, the welfare department, or, even worse, the prison.

In the following chapters I show why, for similar reasons, neither expertise nor flexibility justify blanket judicial deference. They falsify the presumption of blanket administrative superiority, just as the last chapter gave reasons to reject legislative finality. Those arguments connect with the point made here. They show why relative competence provides yet another factor that attenuates the weight given to the polycentric character of the dispute: if no other institution is meeting a clear demand for

---

[86] *Ibid.*, 1809; see also 1813.
[87] L. Fuller, *The Morality of Law* (rev. edn, New Haven: Yale University Press, 1969), p. 172.
[88] N. Komesar, *Imperfect Alternatives: Choosing Institutions in Law, Economics, and Public Policy* (University of Chicago Press 1994), p. 6.
[89] Allison, 'Fuller's Analysis of Polycentric Disputes and the Limits of Adjudication', 373–4.
[90] See Komesar, *Imperfect Alternatives*, and accompanying text.
[91] N. Barber, 'A Prelude to the Separation of Powers' (2001) *Cambridge Law Journal* 59, 79.
[92] Fiss, 'The Supreme Court 1978 Term', 43–4.

oversight or accountability, then the task may fall to the courts (assuming they have the jurisdiction to undertake it). The prima facie benefits of legal accountability are among the reasons we may assign such tasks to the courts notwithstanding their polycentric character. Despite the limitations of those benefits, they remain real benefits.[93]

E   Flexibility: remedies and revisitation

Fuller was aware that the extent to which polycentric questions create problems for adjudication is linked to how strictly the doctrine of precedent would be applied. He recommended a relaxation of the doctrine in such cases.[94] Polycentric issues are problematic especially because of the unintended consequences that decisions about them generate. Therefore, the amount of room a judicial remedy leaves for adaptation will be of direct relevance. In Chapter 9 I explore both the importance of flexibility in general, and the various ways in which judges can respect the need for flexibility in their choice of remedy, through interpretive doctrines such as constitutional avoidance, vague legal standards, and constructive uses of silence. In Chapter 10 I argue further that legislature, the executive, and the courts ought to be prepared to revisit a policy after a judicial ruling if new information indicates problems with it. That type of flexibility can attenuate the weight given to the existence of polycentricity in adjudication. If there are grounds for believing that institutions can respond to new information, and that they will do so responsibly, then the extent to which polycentricity should restrain the court will be diminished.

VI   Conclusion

This chapter sought to defang one of the most common objections against constitutional social rights adjudication, but also save that objection from irrelevance given the fact that polycentricity is a pervasive feature of adjudication. I demonstrated that polycentricity needed refinement in order to survive the many counter-examples offered by its critics. The refinement I offered was threefold. First, I clarified that polycentricity is relevant to adjudication as a property of legal issues and not areas of decision-making, such as resource allocation. Second, I showed when a

---

[93] See Chapter 3, section II.
[94] Fuller, 'The Forms and Limits of Adjudication', 398.

legal issue was polycentric. It is so when the court is required to make, or should make, a legal finding as to the substantial and heterogeneous interests of a large number of non-represented persons. Such interests are on a sliding scale of relevance to the judge's role, ranging from where they are a primary consideration in the legal standard applied, to a secondary consideration in the application of an open-textured standard, to a collateral consideration when the legal standard is well settled but its application leads to absurd results.

The key refinement was the idea of attenuating factors. These are the medium through which we both save and use Fuller's idea. They explain why polycentricity is relevant, and how to give weight to it in the adjudication of polycentric disputes. At times, the factors will not be sufficient and there will be proper grounds to defer. At others, they will help sculpt the legal issues such that the degree of polycentricity is manageable, in light of the desirability of legal accountability in that case. The factors include judicial mandate, degree of polycentricity, access to information, relative competency of the courts or its alternatives, and the flexibility of the remedy or possibility for revisitation. These factors would help steer towards the right outcome in social rights cases, and help to explain why polycentric legal issues are already often accepted in adjudication.

8

Expertise

I Introduction

The idea of administrative expertise was a central concept in the most epic battles fought between law and administration. To those acquainted with that history, it is a surprising proposition that courts *increase* their scrutiny of the welfare state in order to promote social justice. Sceptics from both the left and right, though they make odd bedfellows, borrow the idea of expertise for asserting the non-justiciability of resource allocation. The right has been buttressed by the belief that the state generally is a poor substitute for the market in matters of resource allocation. And the left produces a record of conservative opposition to the growth of the welfare state, and situates judicial review as a strong ally in that battle. The *Lochner* era, which I explore in this chapter, and the judicial review of social policy in Britain, back up this progressive brand of scepticism.

It remains the case, however, that the concept plays a role in adjudication, and in particular in public law, and it does not eclipse a role for courts. The question in this chapter is, what weight should it be given as a principle of restraint for social rights adjudication? This question is answered in a number of parts. In section II, I provide a brief historical context for the current debate about law and expertise. I next turn in section III, to introducing a typology of expertise that can assist from the legal point of view. It helps to explain why judicial deference to expertise is variable in accordance with the type of decision-maker under review. In section IV, I outline how judges could give weight to the principle of expertise in the constitutional adjudication of social rights.

The chapter on the whole puts forward three key ideas. First, we must recognise the idea of an expertise–accountability trade-off, namely, that we will rarely defer completely to another's expertise because it leads to unacceptable consequences. We accept an expertise deficit as a trade-off for accountability. Second, it is helpful to consider types of expertise when contemplating the role for courts in public law. When we combine the idea of an expertise–accountability trade-off with different types of expertise, some familiar intuitions about judicial review of expertise are explained. Third, public law must recognise failures of expertise, and these are discernible chiefly in three ways: a failure to apply expertise; a failure evident due to distinctive facts in the record; or when the state's action contradicts a substantial and clear majority of the social science evidence relating to some problem.

II   Law and expertise in historical context

The prescriptive aspects of this chapter must be framed against the experience of those epic battles that were just mentioned. The constitutional and administrative law battles fought in America provide a good backdrop for the more directly relevant British experience.

A   Lesson from America

President Franklin Delano Roosevelt responded to the Great Depression with a New Deal package of expanded government spending and regulation of the economy through administrative agencies. Such agencies included the price-setting National Recovery Administration (1933), the National Labor Relations Board (1935), the Securities and Exchange Commission (1934), Federal Communications Commission (1934), and Social Security Board (1936), among many others. Roosevelt defended these programmes in terms of freedom from want, his vision of America's bill of social rights.[1] However, the agencies, and the economic and social philosophy underpinning them,[2] were vigorously challenged both legally and politically. The legal attack was in both constitutional law and administrative law. The constitutional attack was along three principal lines: first, agencies were challenged as unconstitutional delegations of law-making power from Congress;[3] second, such powers similarly violated the commerce clause, which restricted federal economic regulatory authority to inter-state commerce;[4] and third, the regulatory initiatives

---

[1] C. R. Sunstein, *The Second Bill of Rights* (New York: Basic Books, 2004).
[2] The classic text setting out this justification is J. L. Landis, *The Administrative Process* (New Haven: Yale University Press, 1938).
[3] *Panama Refining Co.* v. *Ryan*, 293 US 388 (1935).
[4] *Hammer* v. *Dagenhart*, 247 US 251 (1918) (federal regulation of child labour); *Railroad Retirement Board* v. *Alton Railroad Co.*, 295 US 330 (1935) (compulsory retirement and pension plan); *ALA Schechter Poultry Corp.* v. *United States*, 295 US 495 (1935)

violated constitutional liberties to contract and to property.[5] This period roughly began with the *Lochner* case in 1905, and continued through the New Deal period until 1937, when the Supreme Court reversed its jurisprudence and upheld key social welfare statutes,[6] some say in response to the President's notorious 'court-packing' plan.[7] Nearly 170 labour statutes were struck down in this period.[8] The same judicial attitudes pervaded the role of courts in administrative law.[9] A number of bodies were established in areas such as water maintenance, labour relations, and inter-state commerce. Regulated entities often sought judicial review, and succeeded on grounds that challenged the legitimacy of the new order.[10]

Administrative expertise provided the 'central rationale' justifying both the expansion of agency government and the case against strong judicial review.[11] This rationale was developed by a number of legal scholars and New Deal luminaries, with John Dickinson, Felix Frankfurter, James McCauley Landis, Walter Gellhorn, and Walter Lippman prominent among them.[12] There were pitched battles fought over the role of courts, in Congress, in the public, and in the courts themselves. It is intriguing that those favouring stronger judicial control of agency decision-making were committed to laissez-faire economics,[13] while those

(striking down the National Industrial Recovery Act 1933, price and wage fixing); *Carter v. Carter Coal Co.* 298 US 238 (1936) (regulation of mining industry).

[5] *Lochner* v. *New York*, 198 US 45 (1905); *Adkins* v. *Children's Hospital*, 261 US 525 (1923).

[6] *West Coast Hotels* v. *Parish*, 300 US 379 (1937) (upholding minimum wage statute); *National Labor Relations Board* v. *Jones & Laughlin Steel Corp.*, 301 US 1 (1937) (upholding the National Labor Relations Act 1935 (the Wagner Act)); *Stewart Machine Co.* v. *Davis*, 301 US 548 (1937) (upholding the Social Security Act 1935).

[7] C. R. Sunstein, 'Lochner's Legacy' (1987) 7 *Columbia Law Review* 873; B. Ackerman, *We the People: Foundations* (Cambridge, MA: Belknap Press, 1993).

[8] W. E. Forbath, *Law and the Shaping of the American Labor Movement* (Cambridge, MA: Harvard University Press, 1991) apps. A, C, pp. 177–92, 199–203.

[9] R. E. Schiller, 'The Era of Deference: Courts, Expertise, and the Emergence of New Deal Administrative Law' (2007)106 *Michigan Law Review* 399.

[10] *Ibid.*; see also F. Frankfurter and N. Greene, *The Labour Injunction* (New York: Macmillan, 1930).

[11] G. E. White, *The Constitution and the New Deal* (Cambridge, MA: Harvard University Press, 2000), p. 100.

[12] J. O. Freedman, *Crisis and Legitimacy: The Administrative Process and American Government* (Cambridge University Press, 1978), p. 45.

[13] E. Freund, *Administrative Powers over Persons and Property: A Comparative Survey* (University of Chicago Press 1928); P. R. Verkuil, 'The Emerging Concept of Administrative Procedure' (1978) 78 *Columbia Law Review* 258, 273; K. C. Davis and W. Gellhorn, 'Present at the Creation: Regulatory Reform Before 1946' (1986) 38 *Administrative Law Review* 511, 525 (remarks of Davis); cf. White, *The Constitution and the New Deal*), p. 122 (claiming that this conventional account is flawed).

supporting Roosevelt's second bill of rights supported strong judicial deference. The American Bar Association, considered a bastion of conservatism at the time, appointed a Special Committee in 1933 to examine the issue of deference to agency expertise, and to propose solutions.[14] The Committee's annual reports were scathing of what they considered to be 'administrative absolutism'. The arguments they advanced are quite similar to the ones advanced today in favour of fundamental rights, including social rights: protection of the rule of law, recourse to independent courts, controlling abuse of power, and protecting individual liberty. These criticisms fed into a vigorous political battle. The Special Committee report became the impetus behind the Walter Logan Act, which was passed in 1940 by both houses of Congress, but vetoed by President Roosevelt for its potential for excessive juridification. President Roosevelt responded by appointing the committee that drafted what became the Administrative Procedure Act 1946. That Act's comprehensive procedural rules and participation rights, and its provision on the scope of judicial review, was viewed at the time ultimately as a compromise document in its balance between agency discretion and judicial oversight.[15] It would later, of course, as I explore in Chapter 9, be accused of leading to undue ossification of regulation of a sort not experienced in Europe or the rest of the Commonwealth.

Although agency government became widely accepted, American scepticism towards agency expertise spread during the 1960s and 1970s. Groups interested in defending consumers, the environment, and the poor began to look to the courts to protect against agency failures. There were several criticisms of blanket deference to expertise. First, there was the problem of 'agency capture' or factionalism.[16] This was the claim that agencies were unduly influenced by the well-organised business interests they regulated. Regulated entities would inundate the agencies with information and slow down its regulatory activity. Second, there were a string of public reports (including one by James Landis) that recognised

---

[14] See e.g. O. R. McGuire, 'Federal Administrative Action and Judicial Review' (1936) 22 *American Bar Association Journal* 492; Schiller, 'The Era of Deference', 421–5.

[15] G. B. Sheperd, 'Fierce Compromise: The Administrative Procedure Act Emerges from New Deal Politics' (1996) 90 *Northwestern Law Review* 1557; White, *The Constitution and the New Deal*, pp. 116–21.

[16] L. Jaffe, 'The Illusion of Ideal Administration' (1973) 86 *Harvard Law Review* 1183, 1187; C. R. Sunstein, 'Constitutionalism After the New Deal' (1987) 101 *Harvard Law Review* 421, 448–9 (preferring 'factionalism' to 'capture'); R. B. Stewart, 'The Reformation of American Administrative Law' (1975) 88 *Harvard Law Review* 1669, 1684–7 (nuanced analysis of 'agency capture theory').

that people were often appointed to agencies for patronage reasons, often serving short terms.[17] Third, it was felt that agencies did not always carry out their statutory mandates. Litigants prompted courts to force agencies to act, rather than to preserve the status quo from state intervention.[18] The absence of organised beneficiaries in the welfare, prison, and public school fields led to a lack of agency responsiveness, and hence an increase in 'public interest litigation'.[19] Fourth, there was basic discomfort with the idea of government by unaccountable experts, largely due to scepticism over a workable distinction between 'subjective/objective' determinations and between fact and values.[20]

The combination of these factors led commentators to agree that the doctrine of blanket deference to administrative expertise had ultimately been defeated.[21] By 1971 the Court of Appeals for the DC Circuit declared the law to be on 'the threshold of a new era in the long and fruitful collaboration between administrative agencies and courts', one in which courts were prepared to do more than 'bow to the mysteries of administrative expertise'.[22]

B   Expertise in British law and administration

One might think that Britain and America simply part ways on the question of public administration.[23] For one, the United Kingdom never faced the scale of constitutional judicial obstruction to its reform of the administrative system. And for another, since as far back as the

---

[17] Freedman, *Crisis and Legitimacy*, p. 49.

[18] Sunstein, 'Constitutionalism After the New Deal', 464, 470–4; R. S. Melnick, *Regulation and the Courts: The Case of the Clean Air Act* (Washington DC: Brookings Institution, 1983), p. 351.

[19] Freedman, *Crisis and Legitimacy*, p. 47; H. W. Jones, 'The Rule of Law and the Welfare State' (1958) 58 *Columbia Law Review* 143; C. Reich, 'The New Property' (1964) 73 *Yale Law Journal* 732; C. Reich, 'Individual Rights and Social Welfare: The Emerging Legal Issues' (1965) 74 *Yale Law Journal* 1245, 1246.

[20] G. Frug, 'The Ideology of Bureaucracy in American Law' (1984) 97 *Harvard Law Review* 1276, 1292–3, 1318ff.; Freedman, *Crisis and Legitimacy*, pp. 46, 48–9, 50–1; Stewart, 'The Reformation of American Administrative Law', 1684; Jaffe, 'The Illusion of Ideal Administration', 1185; C. Reich, 'The Law of the Planned Society' (1966) 75 *Yale Law Journal* 1227, 1235, 1242.

[21] Stewart, 'The Reformation of American Administrative Law', 1711; Sunstein, 'Constitutionalism After the New Deal', 452; Freedman, *Crisis and Legitimacy*, p. 46.

[22] *Environmental Defense Fund* v. *Ruckelshaus*, 439 F.2d 584, 597 (1971); see also *Baltimore OR Co.* v. *Aberdeen & Rockfish R. Co.*, 393 US 87, 92 (1968).

[23] See generally, G. Peele, *Governing the UK* (4th edn, Oxford: Blackwell, 2004).

Northcote-Trevelyan Report of 1854, the Civil Service was mostly purged of patronage. Furthermore, the role of experts in the civil service was for most of its life subordinated to the oversight and management of generalists, who were largely Oxbridge graduates educated in the arts, a situation that was in fact regarded as unduly biased *against* experts until after the report of the Fulton Committee in 1968. And finally, while the American agencies were independent of Congress and were even somewhat independent from presidential powers (apart from the important appointment of bureau chiefs), in Britain departments and their successor executive agencies are headed nominally by a minister who is constitutionally accountable to Parliament for all of its actions. Important regulations are also subject to positive or negative resolution of Parliament before they take effect, stemming the democratic deficit. So the whole constellation seems quite different.

Yet one still finds a very similar set of concerns over expanded executive powers and the need for judges to defer on grounds of expertise. Here, too, the administrative process grew primarily out of the need to regulate the economy and support the welfare state.[24] That process had no shortage of opponents, including Albert Venn Dicey.[25] Lord Chief Justice Hewart, a younger contemporary of Dicey's, published his own polemic against delegated legislation, ouster clauses, and judicial deference, which he called the new despotism.[26] He caricatured the 'creed' of the 'ardent bureaucrat, the amateur of the new despotism', as follows:

1. The business of the Executive is to govern.
2. The only persons fit to govern are experts.

    ...

5. Two main obstacles hamper the beneficent work of the expert. One is the Sovereignty of Parliament, and the other is the Rule of Law.
6. A kind of fetish-worship, prevalent among an ignorant public, prevents destruction of these obstacles. The expert, therefore, must make use of the first in order to frustrate the second.
7. To this end let him, under Parliamentary forms, clothe himself with despotic power, and then, because the forms are Parliamentary, defy the Law Courts.

---

[24] R. G. S. Brown and D. R. Steel, *The Administrative Process in Britain* (2nd edn, London: Methuen & Co Ltd., 1979), pp. 23–33.

[25] C. Harlow and R. Rawlings, *Law and Administration* (2nd edn, London: Butterworths, 1997), Chapter 1.

[26] G. Hewart, *The New Despotism* (London: Ernest Benn Limited, 1929), p. 20.

Hewart here attacks the use of legislation to delegate sweeping discretionary powers to the executive branch. There is no small significance in the Lord Chief Justice of England pitting the idea of administrative expertise against, in point five, the two most fundamental constitutional principles of his time, as of ours. The battle-lines here, too, appeared to be drawn between the expertise needed to expand the welfare state, and a hostile and seemingly conservative judiciary.

However, we must resist the temptation to draw the battle-lines too starkly. For one, Hewart himself was a Liberal MP from 1913 to 1922, a time around which his party was fighting both to expand the welfare state and an ultra-conservative House of Lords on fundamental constitutional questions largely prompted by the redistributive programme.[27] More importantly, Labour Party members and left-wing political theorists were also critical of undue deference to expertise. In a Fabian Pamphlet published only two years after *The New Despotism*, Harold Laski shared his own views:

> [The expert] is an invaluable servant and an impossible master ... He can explain the consequences of a proposed policy, indicate its wisdom, measure its danger. He can point out possibilities in a proposed line of action. But it is of the essence of public wisdom to take the final initiative out of his hands ... For any political system in which a wide initiative belongs to the expert is bound to develop the vices of bureaucracy. It will lack insight into the movement and temper of the public mind.[28]

Of course, Laski was equally critical of courts, and knew well of the American experience through his correspondence with the Supreme Court Justice Oliver Wendell Holmes Jr throughout the *Lochner*-era.[29] Laski carried both strands of scepticism with him when he sat on the Donoughmore Committee on Ministers' Powers, which was set up

---

[27] He also frequently changed his mind. See R. Stevens, 'Hewart, Gordon, first Viscount Hewart (1870–1943)', in *Oxford Dictionary of National Biography* (Oxford University Press, 2004), online edn, Jan 2008, www.oxforddnb.com/view/article/33846, accessed 28 July 2011. Stevens notes that Hewart later joined forces with Prime Minister Lloyd George and that by 1936 'he had decided that *The New Despotism* had been a mistake and, for the welfare state to succeed, civil servants needed wider discretion'.

[28] H. J. Laski, *The Limitations of the Expert* (London: Fabian Society, Fabian Tract No. 235, 1931), p. 10.

[29] H. J. Laski, 'Judicial Review of Social Policy in England' (1925–26) 39 *Harvard Law Review* 836; M. Howe, *Holmes–Laski Letters 1916–1935* (Oxford University Press, 1953).

largely in response to Lord Hewart's tract, but which rejected its conclusions.[30] The concern with unaccountable expertise lived on, however. In 1956 Labour MP Richard Crossman urged socialists to not flinch in facing up to it: '[T]he growth of a vast, centralised State bureaucracy constitutes a grave potential threat to social democracy. The idea that we are being disloyal to our Socialist principles if we attack its excesses or defend the individual against its incipient despotism is a fallacy.'[31] A year later, in the wake of the infamous Crichel Down affair, the Franks Committee on Tribunals and Inquiries adopted its report, which reformed the tribunal system and made it more a part of the machinery of adjudication,[32] and the ombudsman was just around the corner.[33]

Despite these concerns and safeguards, the role of expertise in government and bureaucracy remained significant.[34] Two of the most prominent post-Second World War civil service reforms both pushed in that direction. The Fulton Committee Report contained among its proposals the ideas that the civil service should rely less on generalists and more on experts, and further that it should be increasingly 'hived off' from day-to-day politics. The development of the Next Step agencies under the Thatcher government established the controversial idea that policy and administration could be divorced. Policy questions would go to ministers, and administrative questions to increasingly insulated (often privatised) agencies or bodies. This philosophy, in updated New Labour form, continues to prevail.[35]

The commentary on law and administration is quite clear about the role of expertise as a justification for judicial deference.[36] Deference to expertise is also a frequent stated or unstated premise in much of the curial

---

[30] The Donoughmore Committee, *Report of the Committee on Ministers' Powers*, Cmnd: 4060 (1932).

[31] R. Crossman, *Socialism and the New Despotism* (London: Fabian Society, Fabian Tract No. 298, 1956), p. 6.

[32] See the discussion in Chapter 3, section IV.A.

[33] Parliamentary Commissioner Act 1967; Peele, *Governing the UK*, p. 469.

[34] See generally, Peele, *Governing the UK*.

[35] See P. P. Craig, *Administrative Law* (6th edn, London: Sweet & Maxwell, 2008), Chapters 2 and 4.

[36] Harlow and Rawlings, *Law and Administration*, 2nd edn, pp. 591–8; R. Baldwin, *Rules and Government* (Oxford: Clarendon Press, 1994), pp. 45ff.; J. Jowell, 'Judicial Deference: Servility, Civility or Institutional Capacity?' [2003] *Public Law* 592; D. Dyzenhaus, 'The Politics of Deference: Judicial Review and Democracy', in M. Taggart (ed.), *The Province of Administrative Law* (Oxford: Hart Publishing, 1997), p. 279 (saying 'expertise is the substantive rationale for deference'); T. A. O. Endicott, *Administrative Law* (Oxford University Press, 2009), pp. 221–2.

attitude towards administration,[37] including to statutory tribunals[38] and professional disciplinary tribunals.[39] The Human Rights Act 1998 (HRA) has made the issue even more acute.

The question of expertise has been prominent in discussions concerning judicial restraint, both in the literature offering guidance,[40] and in the decisions of the courts. In *A and Others, X and Others*, for instance, both Lord Bingham and Lady Hale agreed that whether there was 'a threat to the life of the nation' was a question that 'lies outside the expertise of the courts'.[41] As I showed in Chapter 5, some judges in both Britain and Canada have suggested the use of expertise as a factor in a deference analysis, an approach followed on occasion by the Court of Appeal.[42] In Australia some have argued that deference on grounds of expertise has varied in accordance with the political views of the judge.[43]

It is equally obvious that judges find blanket deference to decision-makers and ministers on grounds of their superior expertise to be untenable. Lord Scarman stated this view in a tax case long ago, when the role of courts was at a quite timid stage in public law by comparison to today's standards:

> The courts have a role, long established, in the public law. They are available to the citizen who has a genuine grievance if he can show that it is one in respect of which [a judicial review remedy] is appropriate. I would not be a party to the retreat of the courts from this field of public law merely because the duties imposed upon the revenue are complex and call for management decisions in which discretion must play a significant role.[44]

---

[37] M. Fordham, *Judicial Review Handbook* (5th edn, Oxford: Hart Publishing, 2008) [13.4].

[38] *Cooke* v. *Secretary of State for Social Security* [2002] 2 All ER 279 (Hale LJ, as she then was); *Hinchy* v. *Secretary of State for Work and Pensions* [2005] UKHL 16 [49], [57] (Baroness Hale).

[39] *Council for the Regulation of Health Care Professionals* v. *General Medical Council and Ruscillo* [2004] EWCA Civ 1356 [78]: '[E]xpertise is one of the most cogent arguments for self-regulation'; *Ghosh* v. *General Medical Council* [2001] 1 WLR 1915 (HL) [34].

[40] Jowell, 'Judicial Deference', 592; Lord Steyn 'Deference: A Tangled Story' [2005] *Public Law* 346, 357ff. (endorsing Jowell's approach); A. Kavanagh, *Constitutional Review under the UK Human Rights Act* (Cambridge University Press, 2009), pp. 182–90.

[41] *A and Others; X and Others* v. *Secretary of State for the Home Department* [2004] UKHL 56 [116], [226]. See also Lord Rodger [166].

[42] Chapter 5, section IV.A; see also *Samaroo and Sezek* v. *Secretary of State for the Home Department* [2001] EWCA Civ 1189 [35]; *R (Ponting)* v. *Governor of HMP Whitemoor, and the Secretary of State for the Home Department* [2002] EWCA Civ 224 [27], [112]–[116].

[43] I. Holloway, '"A Bona Fide Attempt": Chief Justice Sir Owen Dixon and the Policy of Deference to Administrative Expertise in the High Court of Australia' (2002) 54 *Administrative Law Review* 687.

[44] *R* v. *Inland Revenue Commissioners, ex parte National Federation of Self-Employed and Small Business Ltd* [1982] AC 617 (HL) [652].

This statement is typical of judicial views in Commonwealth countries. Some deeper analysis of the idea itself therefore seems appropriate.

III   Types of expertise

Bureaucracy and expertise have been studied to death.[45] Max Weber famously set out the notion of a neutral civil servant implementing formal rules determined by the legislative branch *sin ira et studio* ('without hatred or passion').[46] The role of what may now be called expertise played a key, if not supreme role in Weber's scheme:

> Bureaucratic administration means fundamentally the exercise of control on the basis of knowledge. This is the feature of it which makes it specifically rational. This consists on the one hand in technical knowledge, which, by itself, is sufficient to ensure it has a position of extraordinary power. But in addition to this, bureaucratic organizations, or the holders of power who make use of them, have the tendency to increase their power still further by the knowledge growing out of experience in the service.[47]

The vices of bureaucracy and impossibility of Weber's ideal-type are hardly, as Jerry Mashaw put it, 'headline news'.[48] Yet it is still a common tendency in law to speak of 'expertise' in an undifferentiated way: sometimes to speak of technical expertise, at others to speak of bureaucratic experience, and still others when a specialised tribunal has experience of an issue. Yet the differences between them are discernible.

Clearly, the idea of expertise is capable of study from many perspectives, and its implications as a concept stretch well beyond law. The existing studies on expertise are not focused on the role of courts.[49] The focus of

---

[45] See e.g. H. A. Simon, *Administrative Behavior: A Study of Decision-Making Processes in Administrative Organization* (4th edn, New York: The Free Press, 1997); E. Kamenka, *Bureaucracy* (Oxford: Basil Blackwell, 1989); M. Albrow, *Bureaucracy* (London: Pall Mall Press, 1970).

[46] M. Weber *Theory of Economic and Social Organization*, trans. A. R. Henderson and T. Parsons (New York: Free Press, 1947), pp. 329–41.

[47] *Ibid.*, p. 339; see also pp. 335, 337.

[48] J. L. Mashaw, *Bureaucratic Justice* (New Haven: Yale University Press, 1985), p. 51; see generally Chapter 3.

[49] In the scientific context, see H. Collins and R. Evans, *Rethinking Expertise* (University of Chicago Press, 2007); E. Sellinger and R. P. Crease (eds.), *The Philosophy of Expertise* (New York: Columbia University Press, 2006) (though Scott Brewer's excellent chapter does concern the role of judges). For an explanation of why deference to experts can be rational, see J. Raz, *The Morality of Freedom* (Oxford University Press, 1986), Chapter 2.

the present study is on the important aspects of expertise from the point of view of public law. Once focused in this way, five types of expertise emerge as significant, because they differ from one another and, as I argue further below, they call for deference in varying degrees. Before discussing them, however, I will note one significant but intentional omission from that discussion. I omit any suggestion that there exists a form of legislative expertise. My view is that while legislatures are a repository of knowledge about constituent preferences and may serve functionally as an important forum for interest-balancing, they cannot be relied upon as a source of knowledge about general states of affairs (apart from reporting preferences). Of course legislatures do amass and rely upon evidence provided by other sources, and often acquire it through legislative procedures. To the extent they do gather information and evidence, however, it is the expertise embodied in that evidence that would attract deference and not the judgment of the legislature upon it. The risk of non-expert bias is so strong, and any existing professional expertise so random, that it destroys the claim that legislative choices are owed special weight as a source of knowledge. In my view, legislative choices are owed weight on account of their legitimacy, not their accuracy about questions of fact. With that caveat stated, we can continue on to those forms worthy of closer examination.

A   Front-line expertise

This type of expertise is developed through routine exposure to institutional patterns and resource constraints, and to legal and operational guidelines.[50] A typically basic amount of education and training is combined with work experience, and results in an intuitive understanding of the matrix of relevant factors affecting how things are done within the organisation. Intuition has long been recognised in studies on administrative behaviour, and is present in Weber's work, as noted above. Chester Barnard argued that intuition was a highly important non-rational form of task management and decision-making, and that it had distinct advantages of speed and appropriateness to certain tasks.[51] He focused on the non-demonstrable nature of such reasoning, contrasting

---

[50] The classic description is considered to be M. Lipsky, *Street Level Bureaucracy: Dilemmas of the Individual in Public Services* (New York: Russell Sage, 1980); cf. Mashaw, *Bureaucratic Justice*, p. 220 (claiming Lipsky's analysis does not apply to the Social Security Administration).

[51] C. Barnard, *The Functions of the Executive* (Cambridge, MA: Harvard University Press, 1956) (see esp. Appendix A, 'The Mind in Everyday Matters' (1936)).

it with rational processes, including those of courts.[52] Herbert March and James Simon went deeper, finding the idea of recognition to be at the core of intuition: '[M]uch of the behavior we observe in organizations is "intuitive" in the sense that it occurs immediately upon recognition of a situation. The relevant cognitive and organizational processes are recognition and categorization processes more than they are processes of evaluating consequences.'[53] Mashaw speaks of the 'feel or craft', a 'clinical intelligence' that is difficult to communicate explicitly, and which he calls 'intuitive rationality',[54] whereas Halliday describes it as 'professional intuition'.[55] The importance of this phenomenon cannot be overstated.[56] This is why the word 'expert' is appropriate even if it breaks from the narrow topical specialisation sometimes acquainted with the word.

This type of expert is the most frequent target of criticism. The risk of error can be quite high. Due to the volume of work, front-line experts end up adopting routines and rules of thumb,[57] rarely view cases afresh, and are required to 'satisfice' rather than 'optimise' in the face of resource constraints.[58] They are often 'endemically overworked' and may have poor training and low pay,[59] and thus often unsurprisingly constitute a transient workforce.[60] This often results, contrary to what one would hope from their extensive experience, in a poor grasp of the legal matters relevant to their decision-making.[61] Internal audits have demonstrated startling error rates among front-line decision-making.[62] At the tribunal level, some studies show samples of legally represented social security claimants succeeding

---

[52] *Ibid.*, p. 320.
[53] J. March and H. Simon, *Organizations* (2nd edn, Oxford: Blackwell, 1993), p. 13.
[54] Mashaw, *Bureaucratic Justice*, p. 67, 75–6.
[55] S. Halliday, 'The Influence of Judicial Review on Bureaucratic Decision-Making' [2002] *Public Law* 110, 115; see also J. Jowell, 'The Legal Control of Administrative Discretion' [1973] *Public Law* 178, 214; L. Fuller, 'The Forms and Limits of Adjudication' (1978–1979) 92 *Harvard Law Review* 353, 403. *National Labor Relations Board* v. *Seven Up Bottling Co.* 344 US 344, 349 (1953).
[56] Simon, *Administrative Behavior*, pp. 129–37.
[57] K. Hawkins, 'Using Legal Discretion', in K. Hawkins (ed.), *The Uses of Discretion* (Oxford University Press, 1992), pp. 247, 263–5.
[58] Simon, *Administrative Behavior*, pp. xxviii–xxxi, 38–41, 80–1, 240–4.
[59] Harlow and Rawlings, *Law and Administration*, 2nd edn, p. 474.
[60] Halliday, 'The Influence of Judicial Review on Bureaucratic Decision-Making', 118.
[61] *Ibid.*
[62] Harlow and Rawlings, *Law and Administration*, 2nd edn, p. 473; see also Mashaw, *Bureaucratic Justice*, p. 130.

in nearly half their appeals.[63] There are non-expert influences as well. A slight shift at the policy level, as well as regional political variances, can have drastic changes on the way supposedly objective law is implemented.[64] Bias and even racism can be a significant problem.[65] The nature of heuristics and biases in decision-making, which I explore in the subsequent chapter, shows that routinisation leads to predictable, somewhat blameless, but still alarming cognitive biases.[66] And of course it cannot be forgotten that all of the above assumes that front-line experts do carry out their duties in good faith. Experience of bureaucracy often shows that to be false.

B   Managerial expertise

Managerial experts range from mid-level managers to chief executives or officers of local authorities or executive agencies, to senior civil servants, and even, to a much lesser extent, ministers themselves. Such persons are typically experts in public administration. They will typically have developed a rich intuitive understanding of the various competing programme pressures and how to balance them,[67] as well as how to solicit and amalgamate various opinions from within the bureaucracy. In general, there are four arguments in favour of giving strong weight to managerial expertise, and which also show how they differ from front-line experts. First, their decisions are less routine and thus each one is more likely to be given more careful attention, and may be less prone to the cognitive biases and errors that plague front-line experts. Second, the types of decisions taken by them are more likely to set policy and thereby influence a larger number of people, making them more polycentric. One of the core strengths of managerial expertise is determining administrative workability of a proposal. Third, the quality of the decision-maker, her track record, commitment, and experience will normally be more significant and proven than that of a typical front-line decision-maker. This applies with greater force the higher one travels up the internal hierarchy, provided appointments are filled primarily on merit (which is ordinarily the case, at least in the

---

[63]   H. Genn and Y. Genn, *The Effectiveness of Representation at Tribunals* (London: Lord Chancellor's Department, London, 1989), p. 107.

[64]   Mashaw, *Bureaucratic Justice*, p. 163; see also Halliday, 'The Influence of Judicial Review on Bureaucratic Decision-Making', 96–9.

[65]   S. Halliday, 'Institutional Racism in Bureaucratic Decision-Making: A Case Study in the Administration of Homelessness Law' (2000) 27 *Journal of Law and Society* 449.

[66]   Chapter 9, section II.B.2.

[67]   March and Simon, *Organizations*, p. 12.

civil service). Fourth, the higher up the decision-making hierarchy one finds this expert, the more responsive becomes the democratic process at controlling her and her decisions, which can stem the democratic deficit or 'facelessness' associated with the bureaucrats on the front line.

Despite these great strengths, there are also significant problems with strong deference to such decision-makers. The first is the more prominent role played by value choices when managerial decisions are taken. It raises the substantial risk of non-expert influence. One direct influence is in the form of political control. Ministerial responsibility makes the minister constitutionally responsible for any significant policy or operational matters taking place in his or her department or agency. Sometimes the problem is evident at a more micro-level in confrontations between front-line experts and managers.[68] The more noted phenomenon is the influence of political appointments to agencies, particularly in America.[69] Britain has had a different tradition, though there were some fluctuations on the convention of civil service independence during the Thatcher years.[70] But its own home-grown problem was the idea mentioned above that policy and administration could be neatly separated, a key idea behind the Next Step Initiatives used to radically reduce the size of the civil service, and which has been, in turn, fiercely criticised as an unsustainable distinction.[71] It is a well-known problem to which Herbert Simon devoted a chapter of his classic *Administrative Behavior* long ago, criticising the lax usage of the distinction between policy and administration by some leading early American administrative lawyers, also concluding clearly that blanket deference to expertise is unwarranted.[72] Even critics of judicial review rightly acknowledge that setting agency or local authority policy, which

---

[68] Lipsky, *Street Level Bureaucracy*, pp. 18–25; Halliday 'The Influence of Judicial Review on Bureaucratic Decision-Making', 118.

[69] H. Kaufmann, *The Administrative Behavior of Federal Bureau Chiefs* (Washington DC: Brookings Institution, 1981); G. C. Mackenzie, *The Politics of Presidential Appointments* (New York: Macmillan, 1981), p. 244; for a contemporary example, see J. T. O'Reilly, 'Losing Deference in the FDA's Second Century: Judicial Review, Politics, and a Diminished Legacy of Expertise' (2008) 93 *Cornell Law Review* 939–79, 959–62.

[70] Peele, *Governing the UK*, pp. 180–1.

[71] B. W. Hogwood, D. Judge, and M. McVicar, 'Agencies, Ministers and Civil Servants in Britain', in B. G. Peters and J. Pierre (eds.), *Politicians, Bureaucrats and Administrative Reform* (London: Routledge, 2001), p. 35; Peele, *Governing the UK*, p. 171. In local government, see H. Elcock, 'Leading People: Some Issues of Local Government Leadership in Britain and America' (1995) 24 *Local Government Studies* 546, 552 ('the distinction between the political and administrative roles can become so blurred [that] on occasion they become virtually indistinguishable from one another').

[72] Simon, *Administrative Behavior*, pp. 53–6, 70.

may nominally be about implementing law, may often be based more on political doctrine and less on expert advice.[73]

A different problem with deference to managerial expertise cuts the other way, which is that managers are often obscured from public scrutiny. Due to being mid-way up the bureaucratic-political hierarchy, they fall between the accountability of front-line experts who face individuals with bad news, and the accountability of ministers, who face hostile opposition in Parliament. Their remoteness from front-line impact can create a buffer zone between choices and impact, and their remoteness from political accountability means that mistakes may often be unnoticed by ministers. The Crichel Down affair (1954) exposed this type of problem in Britain so notoriously that it led directly to the establishment of the Franks Committee and assisted the establishment of the ombudsman in 1967.[74] Indeed, perhaps the largest problem is the potential for unfairness in the process of decision-making, how it can be monolithic, at times dysfunctional, where absurd policies are perpetuated because the managers are incapable or unwilling to change them, a situation where responsibilities are distributed so diffusely that no one manager has the power to change things, and no minister considers the issue visible. Appeals to expertise in this context of breakdown come across as being in bad faith.

C   Professional expertise

Jerry Mashaw's well-known 'professional treatment' model of justice in decision-making describes this type of expertise in detail.[75] In the Civil Service professional experts are considered to be 'specialists' and are contrasted with 'administrators'.[76] These professional experts typically combine scholarly learning on the topic with professional experience. Included in the category would be doctors, psychologists, engineers, natural scientists, economists, and academics of various sorts. These professionals are proficient in a body of knowledge that is in form and content largely opaque to judges. Other professional experts may have reasoning processes that are less opaque to judges: specialist lawyers, accountants, social workers, bankers, management consultants and so on. It may

[73] Harlow and Rawlings, *Law and Administration*, 2nd edn, p. 21; Mashaw, *Bureaucratic Justice*, pp. 68–9.
[74] Parliamentary Commissioner Act 1967; Peele, *Governing the UK*, p. 469.
[75] Mashaw, *Bureaucratic Justice*, pp. 26–9, 28: 'the professional is master of an arcane body of knowledge and supports his judgment by appeals to expertise.'
[76] Brown and Steel, *The Administrative Process in Britain*, chs. 3–4.

at times be difficult to distinguish professional experts from front-line experts. A useful rule of thumb is whether there is a recognised professional qualification for the role.[77] Social workers are a model example of both front-line and professional experts.

This type of expertise is well known to the legal system, as the individual professional experts are frequently witnesses in civil and criminal proceedings. Although in principle these types of experts are entitled to a great degree of deference, judges and juries routinely reject expert testimony in, for example, asylum, civil, and criminal cases.[78] While it seems ironic that this is so, there are in fact sound reasons for it. Due to the technical, more formally demonstrable nature of inferences drawn by professional experts (by contrast with those of professional intuition), they can be more amenable to falsification through the judicial process. This claim is by no means a suggestion that judges can be cavalier about rejecting expert testimony, especially scientific or social science expert testimony, which I address below. Yet it is also beyond any doubt that judges are to evaluate for themselves the weight to give to expert testimony in, for example, the criminal law, and it is even ordinarily an error of law for them to direct the jury to accept uncontradicted expert testimony.[79] When experts conflict, English law allows judges to reject one or both forms of testimony, provided they give reasons for doing so.[80] This position reflects the fact that at times expertise is needed in adjudication notwithstanding the deficits judges may have in evaluating it.

Professional expertise can be found in individuals or in larger organisations. I call the latter form *collective professional expertise*. In Britain the Monopolies and Mergers Commission and the National Institute on Health and Clinical Excellence (NICE) are good examples of this type of expertise, just as the Intergovernmental Panel on Climate Change and World Health Organisation, both linked to the United Nations, are examples of such expertise at the international level. Deference to agency expertise can often be an instance of deference to collective professional (and managerial, depending on the proposition at issue) expertise. Collective professional expertise need not always be found in public bodies. Private professional associations may also claim collective

[77] Collins and Evans, *Rethinking Expertise*, p. 67 referring to 'credentials' as one of three factors in evaluating expertise, the other two being track record and experience.

[78] G. Edmond (ed.), *Expertise in Regulation and Law* (Burlington, VT: Ashgate, 2004).

[79] *Halsbury's Laws of England* (4th Rev edn, London: Butterworths, 2005) [1494]; *R* v. *Luttrell* [2004] EWCA Crim 1344; *R* v. *Lanfear* [1968] 2 QB 77 (CA).

[80] A. Choo, *Evidence* (Oxford University Press, 2006), Chapter 10.

professional expertise. Predictably, individual and collective professional expertise will conflict.[81]

The chief advantage of collective expertise is that such bodies are established and institutionally designed to strike a balance between various professional opinions. In the ideal scenario, the body's position would seek to amalgamate the views of the body's members as a whole, which greatly reduces the likelihood of error (even if it makes its estimates more conservative). Theoretically, its expertise might perhaps be linked to Condorcet's Jury Theorem, which holds that provided each opinion consulted is more likely than not to be correct, the larger the number of opinions, the more likely it is that the majority result will be correct.[82] Since the members of the body are professional experts, they more plausibly meet the difficult condition of the Theorem, namely, that each be more likely than not of being correct.[83] Studies of group decision-making have shown that the performance of groups in problem-solving where there was a demonstrable answer was vastly superior: in one study, a 75 per cent success rate over an individual rate of about 14 per cent.[84] Such bodies, particularly public ones, often also have some rules or practices concerning procedural safeguards, interest-balancing, public participation, and may have relatively sophisticated legal advice on rule interpretation. Baldwin has explored this in the context of airline regulation.[85] For all these reasons, collective professional expertise is normally entitled to a very great amount of weight.

Despite this, well-known problems remain, and they are similar to those confronting managerial expertise, though more attenuated. Any

---

[81] See e.g. *Barefoot* v. *Estelle*, 463 US 880, 920 (1983) (American Psychiatric Association amicus brief relied upon in dissent to reject trial expert testimony about criminal defendants' 'future dangerousness').

[82] Marquis de Condorcet, *Essay on the Application of Analysis to the Probability of Majority Decisions* (1785); see also C. R. Sunstein, *Infotopia: How Many Minds Produce Knowledge* (Oxford University Press, 2006), Chapter 1.

[83] More plausibly than would the views of a country's citizens on moral questions, which was an important part of the original object of Condorcet's discussion and has been in subsequent use of the idea in democratic theory.

[84] D. Moshman and M. Geil, 'Collaborative Reasoning: Evidence for Collective Rationality' (1998) 4 *Thinking and Reasoning* 231; P. R. Laughlin, 'Collective Induction: Twelve Postulates' (1999) 80 *Organizational Behavior and Human Decision Processes* 50–69; see also B. Mciejovsky and D. V. Budescu, 'Collective Induction Without Cooperation? Learning and Knowledge Transfer in Cooperative Groups and Competitive Auctions' (2007) 92 *Journal of Personality and Social Psychology* 854.

[85] G. Baldwin, 'A British Independent Regulatory Agency and the "Skytrain" Decision' [1978] *Public Law* 57, 79–80.

large organised body is liable to factional influence. Yet to the extent the body is truly composed of experts (especially in a technical domain), it is likely to apply professional standards that are less liable to political interference or member bias, and it is likely to be more formally insulated from government. Despite this, agency capture can remain a problem, and deference to expertise has come under very harsh criticism in the area of environmental regulation (to take one quite technical area), both in the United States and the United Kingdom.[86] Agency capture has not arisen to the same degree in Britain, nor has patronage,[87] but it seems naïve to think that the agencies are immune from it. Further, though agencies may have procedures for consultation, they are as likely to make decisions in a non-transparent fashion. Galligan observes that many aspects of the rule-making process in Britain are 'hidden from the public and resolved without reference to it'.[88] These weaknesses admittedly do not stack up high next to the strengths of collective professional expertise, but they remain relevant to why judges may continue to remain open to persuasion about abuses of power within such bodies.

D   Specialised adjudicative expertise

This is the type of expertise most familiar to courts. Tribunals and ombudsmen are the best examples, but other examples may include arbitration tribunals, university visitors, professional disciplinary committees, and other committees that are functionally if not formally independent of the bodies they review. Such expertise is gained chiefly through adjudicative experience, training and repeated exposure to one area of administrative decision-making (and in some cases through educational or research experience).[89] I discussed both tribunals and ombudsmen in Chapter 3, as well as some of their comparative decisional weaknesses relative to the potential of courts.

---

[86] B. A. Ackerman and W. T. Hassler, *Clean Coal/Dirty Air* (New Haven: Yale University Press, 1980), Chapter 4; E. Fisher, *Risk Regulation and Administrative Constitutionalism* (Oxford: Hart, 2007).

[87] See Craig, *Administrative Law*, 6th edn, pp. 102–6 (discussing the new appointments procedures to agencies).

[88] D. Galligan, *Due Process and Fair Procedures: A Study of Administrative Procedures* (Oxford: Clarendon Press 1996), p. 455.

[89] T. Buck, D. Bonner and R. Sainsbury, *Making Social Security Law: The Role and Work of the Social Security and Child Support Commissioners* (Aldershot: Ashgate, 2005).

By way of summary, some common themes emerge from the foregoing discussion. The first can be called the risk of non-expert influence. This includes factors exogenous to the specialist knowledge, such as bias, indifference, prejudice, patronage, ideology, time constraints, resource scarcity (if irrelevant) and so on. The second is the risk of expert error and the costs associated with verification. Generally speaking, the higher the risk, the more reliable the opportunity for falsification, and the more fundamental the interest, the greater the demand is for oversight and verification. The third concern is lack of popular control, or of self-government, which strikes at the legitimacy of the process. Laski's concern, and the voluminous literature on the undemocratic nature of government by experts, is an important dimension of the issue. Finally, there is a basic concern over procedural fairness, which may be connected instrumentally with all of the above, or stand alone as a dignitarian value concerning the personal autonomy of those whose fate is decided by experts. These various weaknesses in expertise further inform the discussion that now follows about the role for courts.

IV Giving weight to expertise

If the discussion above was at all clear, two important points will have thus far emerged: that expertise is often a good ground for showing judicial restraint, and that different types of expertise confronted by judges will manifest different strengths and weaknesses. We also know that judges will give weight to expertise but will not treat it as a necessary and sufficient condition for showing restraint. They will look past it. This section will attempt to make more sense of that judicial attitude by exploring when it makes sense to give more or less weight to the principle of expertise in adjudication, drawing upon the discussion of types of expertise, but also discussing two other ideas: expertise–accountability trade-offs and failures of expertise.

A Expertise–accountability trade-offs

Expertise cannot be a rationale for complete deference. If it could, we would need to rethink the structure of democratic government. We would have to revise quite radically the nature of public and criminal law, as well as most areas of regulation. We would not do this; the reason for such refusal is that we are prepared to accept, within adjudicatory structures, a trade-off between the need for expertise and the need for accountability and control over abuses of power. One example is the law of unfair dismissal. Some cases, particularly by the Employment Appeals Tribunal, can set important precedents. That employers are *generally* better placed to decide workability issues is beyond doubt. But most states take the view that the consequences of blanket authority to do so are too grave to permit. Another example in Britain is the Unfair Terms in Consumer Contracts Regulations 1999, which gave judges jurisdiction to declare that certain contractual terms, such as certain charges or penalties, are disproportionate and therefore unfair. Criminal procedure is yet another instance: would anyone countenance ousting judicial control of criminal investigation and incarceration? Questions of policing expertise, administrative workability, and even the substantive law (e.g. what defences ought to be available) can and do routinely arise. More broadly, the entire regime of tribunal adjudication and public law is established under the awareness that there ultimately will be some trade-off between the first-hand knowledge of the public authorities and the more detached view of the judge.

The idea of trade-offs helps to explain some familiar intuitions about the role of expertise in adjudication. I will explore some common trade-offs to illustrate the point.

1   Expert intuition and accountability

As discussed above, intuitive judgments play a legitimate and indispensable role in modern administration. Commentators often say that such judgments cannot easily be explained in rational terms. But to be denied an explanation for a decision is often regarded as a hallmark of a cruel, Kafkaesque bureaucracy. It seems to ask too much from the person affected. Reliance on intuition obscures rates of error and non-expert influence. A balance between these risks and the costs of review is desirable, but finding the precise mixture is a tall order.[90] However, it is equally important to recognise that the judge is not stuck between either refusing to question intuition or rejecting it altogether: intuition, or 'judgment', can stand as a source of authority to which she can attach varying degrees of weight under the circumstances.

Those who want more than a mere appeal to intuition are not asking the impossible, but it would be more administratively onerous. There has until recently been tangible judicial reticence in the United Kingdom towards recognising a general common law duty to give reasons, and no attempt to say whether it should be recognised will be

---

[90]   Mashaw, *Bureaucratic Justice*, p. 99.

made here.[91] Yet two points are worthy of note. The first is that most jurisdictions in Europe, as well as the European Community, have recognised a general duty, which strains the plausibility of the strong argument against it. The second is that despite the difficult nature of the balance between expert intuition and accountability, the approach taken by English courts has been precisely the incremental method. They recognise a duty to give reasons in certain categories, ones that slowly (and incrementally) expand over time.[92] Therefore, while English judges can and do give weight to expert intuition, they can nonetheless ask that explanations be provided and sometimes reject them.

2 Expertise and democratic accountability

The tension between deference to expertise and democratic oversight was among the greatest issues in the American literature considering the critique of New Deal policies, and in the writings of Martin Shapiro and others.[93] Given the value-laden determinations made by some technical agencies, there was a demand for, as Shapiro puts it, the idea that judges may sit as 'virtual representatives of the non-expert demos'.[94] The distinction between expertise/science and democracy is also the key theme that is critically examined (and rejected) in Elizabeth Fisher's *Risk Regulation and Administrative Constitutionalism*.[95] The implication of some of the studies considered above is that the role for courts may be strengthened when the value dimension of the issue is more discernible – because technocratic agencies might not claim greater expertise on questions of justice.[96] This type of concern echoes the criticism of the distinction between policy and administration, and the privatisation of policy delivery on the back of it.

Yet the situation is somewhat complicated, so far as the role for courts is concerned. For one, some public agencies are democratically entrusted not just with technical decisions, but ones that are explicitly policy-laden.

---

[91] See Craig, *Administrative Law*, 6th edn, pp. 401–9 (showing the evolution of the case law, also the position in EU law).

[92] *R* v. *Secretary of State for the Home Department, ex parte Doody* [1994] AC 531 (HL); see also *R* v. *Director of Public Prosecutions, ex parte Manning* [2001] QB 330 (CA).

[93] M. Shapiro, '"Deliberative", "Independent" Technocracy v. Democratic Politics: Will the Globe Echo the EU?' (2005) 68 *Law and Contemporary Problems* 341; see also his *The Supreme Court and Administrative Agencies* (New York: Free Press, 1968).

[94] Shapiro, '"Deliberative", "Independent" Technocracy v. Democratic Politics', 341, 345.

[95] (Oxford: Hart Publishing, 2007).

[96] See above, note 20.

A key example is the power of the National Institute of Health and Clinical Excellence to certify a drug as cost-effective. Another is the Monopolies and Mergers Commission's power to take jurisdiction over commerce affecting a substantial part of the UK.[97] Planning inspectorate decisions have much the same flavour.[98] Here the statutory powers of such bodies give them questions that comprise both fact and value dimensions, over *both* of which the agency can claim special competence *and* special jurisdiction. Generally speaking, when the proposition at issue depends heavily on factors relating to both the technical competence of the institution as well as to a value determination it is expressly entrusted with making, there will be no particularly strong argument in favour of judicial oversight on grounds of democratic deficit.

Even in situations where a value dimension arises that is not expressly within the mandate of the body being reviewed, the role of the courts remains delicate. Since the problem concerns a *democratic* deficit, the role of the judge is, though not constrained by the need to defer to expertise, at the same time to be guided by the nature of the problem at hand. In such situations judges can assist in the accountability trade-off by using public law to invigorate the democratic elements of this process. First, a court might enforce procedural rights, to facilitate greater transparency and consideration of different views. Second, where the views of the minister are themselves questionable, either because the minister refuses to consider the issue carefully, or because it is a matter of such importance that the full consideration of Parliament itself seems required (a conceivable scenario particularly when fundamental rights are at issue), then a court could consider a remedy declaring the decision to be illegal absent express legislative approval. This general idea is similar to the principle of legality in UK law,[99] and the power to find delegated legislation to have exceeded the powers authorised by the primary legislation. It occurred, for example, in two English welfare rights cases, one where regulations that attempted to remove any right to extend subsistence support to those who had not filed for asylum promptly were declared *ultra vires*,[100] and in

---

[97] See *R* v. *Monopolies and Mergers Commission, ex parte South Yorkshire Transport* [1993] 1 WLR 23. This body is now called the Competition Commission.

[98] See *R (Alconbury)* v. *Secretary of State for the Environment, Transport and the Regions* [2001] UKHL 23.

[99] *R* v. *Secretary of State for the Home Department, ex parte. Simms* [2000] 2 AC 115 (HL) p. 130 (Lord Steyn) and p. 131 (Lord Hoffmann).

[100] *R* v. *Secretary of State for Social Security, ex parte Joint Council for the Welfare of Immigrants* [1997] 1 WLR 275 (CA).

another where the Secretary of State for Justice sought to introduce court fees for those having no income.[101]

3   Expertise–accountability trade-offs and cost–benefit

Expertise–accountability trade-offs occur when society decides that deference to experts comes at too high a price. We see examples in public law, child protection, decisions about ending life-saving treatment, mental health detentions, and much else. Whenever a state contemplates the extent to which it wants to exercise strong control over the expert's decision, it must make a judgment about the error risks inherent in that supervisory control and weigh them against the benefits of oversight (presumably, prevention of the abuse of power, and assertion of democratic or autonomy rights). So the appropriateness of a trade-off will depend on how this calculus plays out. This cost–benefit approach helps to explain why judges take different attitudes to different experts, something I now turn to explaining.

B   Expertise types and variation of scrutiny

The analysis of expertise types in section II revealed a range of strengths and weaknesses of the various expertise types that are relevant to judicial review. To state a general judicial attitude in respect of each type is difficult outside the context of a given case, but it is possible to make some generalisations about the types.

As for front-line expertise, there is no general posture of deference to front-line experts as a doctrinal matter. Such decisions are standard fare throughout the tribunals. Nearly a million people a year have cases resolved in tribunals, compared to a few thousand claims filed for judicial review.[102] Further, the adjudicators (courts and tribunals) do in fact give considerable weight to the decisions of front-line experts, particularly on matters such as administrative workability and claimant credibility. On the other hand, and importantly, since the decisions of front-line experts are typically localised, the error costs of mistakes on appeal or review are relatively low, and the latitude for bureaucratic adjustment is high. The costs of legal accountability are thus relatively low. Here, the

---

[101] R v. Lord Chancellor, ex parte Witham [1997] 2 All ER 779 (CA).
[102] Department for Constitutional Affairs, 'Transforming Public Services: Complaints, Redress and Tribunals', Cm 6243 (2004) [3.27].

expertise–accountability trade-off has been decided firmly in favour of accountability.

For different reasons, judges can also with modest confidence adopt a generally non-deferential posture towards individual professional experts. This is not because their opinions lack authority, or that judges know better. It is rather because their opinions are falsifiable somewhat reliably and at acceptable costs through the judicial process, and several procedures have been developed for doing this. It is notable here that the falsification I speak of concerns a conflict between experts, or when testimony crumbles upon cross-examination, and not a situation where a judge simply rejects the testimony on the basis of an intuitive mistrust or gut-feeling.

Judges will often defer to managerial expertise, with exceptions, for the reasons discussed above. For those same reasons, the higher up the hierarchical chain the manager is, depending on the legal issue, the more there is a reason to show greater deference. The more people affected, the more substantial the expertise deficit, the greater the risk of harm. Nonetheless, the judicial posture is somewhat deferential but not highly so, because courts and tribunals also gain a sense of administrative workability through their exposure to administration in their day-to-day work. Managerial expertise, like front-line expertise to some extent, is nowhere near as foreign to judges as professional expertise. The reasoning and intuitive factors are less opaque, particularly those who work day to day on administrative law cases. It also means that the judges can understand enough of the basics of the administrative system to carry on a sophisticated conversation with the managerial experts.[103] Furthermore, judges may predictably attribute less weight to the views of managerial experts when there is evidence that political doctrine is a substantial cause for the decision, when the issue concerns a matter of procedural fairness, or where the decision appears from the record to be the product of bureaucratic inertia rather than carefully conceived policy.

Great weight should be and typically is given to collective professional expertise, largely for the epistemic reasons detailed above. The comparative imbalance in epistemic competency, and the fact that such bodies generally set policy for (or provide evidence supporting policy) for a large class of beneficiaries, greatly skews the accountability trade-off towards deference to expertise. In other words, apart from certain

[103] In this connection, see Collins and Evans, *Rethinking Expertise*, on 'interactional expertise'.

questions of legal interpretation, or where there is a failure of expertise (as discussed below), or a problem with procedural fairness, the considered judgments of collective professional expertise ought not to be set aside.

Specialised adjudicative expertise attracts similar deference. The reason is simple: they are the institutional embodiment of an expertise–accountability trade-off. They combine several of the benefits of legal accountability with the professional expertise of the lay-members. So, though they cannot claim epistemic superiority of the same order as collective professional expertise, their findings are entitled to great weight. Having said this, it is clear that courts will engage in review of their decisions much more often than they will of collective professional expertise. When the issue lies less on the borderline of some dispute over benefits, and more about the best interpretation to give to a particular statute, the matter under consideration strays into the core expertise of courts as well. The appellate courts – which are given a statutory role in hearing appeals from tribunals – still now properly acknowledge the expertise of tribunals on this matter.[104] When the matter concerns the interpretation of statutes, courts do retain a special competency even if the subject-matter is complex.

C   *Failures of expertise*

The clearest set of situations where judicial deference to the expertise of another official is inappropriate is where there is evidence showing that there was a failure of expertise. One can distinguish between three subcategories of situations where this occurs.

1   Refusal to apply expertise

Naturally, no deference is owed to a decision where the primary decision-maker has not applied its expertise to the problem. A public authority may be shown to have failed to investigate a problem or to have disregarded the investigation conducted by a relevant official. The failure to apply or heed expertise might be for reasons of simple inertia, a collective action failure, or may even be intentional.

There are a number of examples in administrative law where courts will from time to time compel an authority to apply itself to a particular problem. One example is a finding that an authority has unlawfully fettered its

---

[104] See Chapter 3, section IV.

discretion.[105] Another is quashing decisions for failure to take account of a relevant consideration. In community care law, for instance, there are a variety of statutory duties that require local authorities to carry out assessments of persons who may be in need.[106] Courts may provide remedies for failures to do so. In a representative case, *R (Patrick)* v. *Newham LBC*,[107] a High Court judge held that a local authority had wholly failed to perform a legally required assessment under s. 47 of the National Health Service and Community Care Act of 1990. The claimant had already been found to be intentionally homeless by the authority, but her lawyers argued that, in light of evidence of her physical and mental health difficulties and homeless situation, the medical report they had submitted to the authority ought to have triggered an assessment of her community care needs for urgent accommodation. The judge agreed, finding that there was 'no record of any consideration of the applicant's individual circumstances at all'.[108]

The idea may also be applied under administrative law rationality review. In *R* v. *Secretary of State for the Environment, ex parte Hammersmith and Fulham LBC*,[109] the Minister designated certain local authorities as having set budgets that he deemed 'excessive' under the Rates Act 1984, and he thus greatly reduced their rate support (or funding top-up) grant from central government. The authorities argued, unsuccessfully but not without plausibility, that the principles for designating spending as excessive ought to take account of the spending needs of individual local authorities. The House of Lords regrettably found the Minister's powers to determine the principles were 'unfettered'.[110]

One may also find examples under comparative human rights jurisprudence. The positive duty to investigate the cause of death under Article 2(1) ECHR provides one illustration.[111] The duty to take steps to reasonably accommodate certain groups' differences under equality law is another.[112] Indeed, the very requirement that proportionate limitations of rights be minimally impairing amounts to a general obligation to consider reasonable alternatives. One may also find direct application in social rights cases. In the South African *Grootboom* case, the Constitutional Court

---

[105] *R* v. *Parliamentary Commissioner for Administration, ex parte Balchin (No. 1)* [1997] JPL 917 (QB).

[106] See generally, L. Clements and P. Thompson, *Community Care and the Law* (4th edn, London: Legal Action Group, 2007), Chapter 3.

[107] (2000) 4 CCLR 48 (HC).

[108] *Ibid.*, 51–2.   [109] [1991] 1 AC 521.   [110] *Ibid.*, 546.

[111] See M. Amos, *Human Rights Law* (Oxford: Hart Publishing, 2006), pp. 191–201.

[112] Equality Act 2006, s. 84 (gender); Disability Discrimination Act 2005, s. 49A.

found that the state's statutory regime dealing with responses to homelessness failed inexplicably to provide any plan at all for dealing with persons in desperate, life-threatening circumstances.[113] In its *Jaftha* case, it was found that a debt collection regime that allowed the forced sale of houses in execution of trifling debts, without the mandatory supervision of a court, was a violation of the right to housing.[114] The case found that the accountability expertise of the court in matters of procedural fairness must be applied in that context.

There is a subset of cases in which the decision-maker intentionally disregards a pre-existing and relevant expert opinion on the matter. Such behaviour may be found to be irrational in administrative law. Both statutory guidance and ombudsman decisions can only be disregarded with good cause.[115] In *R v. Warwickshire County Council, ex parte Powergen plc*, a local highway authority's decision to refuse to enter into an agreement with the claimant was held unreasonable because it was based on considerations identical to those that had been rejected by a Planning Inspector on appeal.[116] In the immigration case of *R v. Secretary of State for the Home Department, ex parte Danaei*, the court quashed the Secretary of State's decision to reject the claimant's personal story as a fabrication when considering his application for exceptional leave to remain in the United Kingdom, when the special adjudicator had already accepted the account when it rejected his application for asylum.[117]

Cases where there has been intentional disregard for expertise are also to be found in the resource allocation context. In *R v. North and West Lancashire Health Authority, ex parte A* the claimants succeeded in quashing a health authority's policy of treating gender identity dysphoria as something less significant than an illness in its resource allocation policies.[118] Although the authority's own experts classified the condition

---

[113] *Republic of South Africa v. Grootboom*, 2000 (11) BCLR 1169 (CC) [66] (finding a programme for allocation of state housing unreasonable and unconstitutional if it fails to provide any relief at all for those in desperate need).

[114] *Jaftha v. Schoeman and others; Van Rooyen v. Stoltz and others*, 2005 (2) SA 140 at [47] (CC).

[115] *R (on the application of Munjaz) v. Ashworth Hospital Authority (now Mersey Care NHS Trust)* [2003] EWCA Civ 1036. *R v. Local Commissioner for Administration, ex parte Eastleigh BC* [1988] 1 QB 855 (CA); *R (Bradley and another) v. Secretary of State for Work and Pensions* [2008] EWCA Civ 36.

[116] [1997] EWCA Civ 2280.

[117] [1997] EWCA Civ 2704.

[118] [2000] 1 WLR 977, 992–3.

as an illness, buttressed at trial with overwhelming additional evidence, the authority impliedly rejected this conclusion in its conduct.[119]

Sometimes politics will be a source of non-expert bias. A particularly clear refusal to apply expertise for political reasons is found in the well-known US Supreme Court case of *Motor Vehicle Manufacturers Association* v. *State Farm Mutual Automobile Insurance Co.*, where the agency at issue changed its policy regarding the necessity of mandating motor vehicle safety restraints without adequately considering certain particularly obvious alternatives.[120] The widely accepted explanation was that the incoming agency chief, appointed by President Reagan soon after an election, intended to apply party ideology to the issue and disregard the available alternatives already discovered by the agency. Similarly, in *Canadian Union of Public Employees* v. *Ontario (Minister of Labour)*, the Supreme Court of Canada sustained a union's challenge to have quashed as patently unreasonable the Minister's decision to appoint a labour arbitrator who had no expertise in labour affairs.[121] The Minister was empowered to appoint an arbitrator who was 'qualified to act', and the court interpreted these statutory words as requiring someone with expertise in labour relations, and who was, in accordance with industry practice, of general acceptance in the labour relations community.

More generally, a failure of expertise is a well-recognised principle in American administrative law, and has recently been restated succinctly by the Court of Appeals for the 10th Circuit: 'Deference to the administrator's expertise is inapplicable where the administrator has failed to apply his expertise to a particular decision.'[122] Though this principle will at times be enforceable under administrative law, a constitutional rights jurisdiction will give the court a mandate to apply it in a more assertive manner.

2   Distinctive facts

Although a case may be quite complex, the record may contain a particular, uncontested fact that simply renders far-fetched any claim for deference to expertise. An excellent example of this is the English case *Ex parte World Development Movement*.[123] The Secretary of State in the case

---

[119] *Ibid.*, 992.   [120] 463 US 29 (1983).
[121] [2003] 1 SCR 539.
[122] *Gilbertson v. Allied Signal, Inc.* 328 F.3d 625 (10th Cir. 2003).
[123] *R v. Secretary of State for Foreign Affairs, ex parte World Development Movement* [1995] 1 WLR 386 (QBD).

acted under s. 1 of the Overseas Development and Co-operation Act 1980, which provided the 'power, for the purpose of promoting the development or maintaining the economy of [an overseas] country or territory ... or the welfare of its people, to furnish any person or body with assistance'. A key issue in the case was whether the £316 million disbursement for a hydro-electric dam project (the Pergau Dam) that was economically unsound was illegal for being inconsistent with the Act. Such a polycentric question ordinarily cries out for deference. However, the distinctive fact in the case was that the Secretary of State's own adviser within the Overseas Development Agency advised that the project was uneconomic and not in Malaysia's interests. The Secretary of State disregarded the advice without contradicting it, and decided to take account of Britain's credibility and commercial interests in deciding to approve the disbursement. The Court quashed the decision.

Other examples abound. In the *Ex parte Unilever* case, for instance, the Revenue had tolerated a practice of late filing of tax returns by the applicant company for twenty years, before abruptly enforcing the period against them at a very heavy penalty.[124] The Court quashed the decision on grounds of substantive unfairness. In *R (Bernard)* v. *Enfield LBC*, Sullivan J found that providing a council house to a severely disabled woman which had no wheelchair access to the lavatory, and which effectively confined her to an extremely small space, violated her right to a private and family life.[125] Any call for deference to allocative expertise was considered misplaced, as the council appeared to accept. Similarly, in *R* v. *Governor of HMP Franland, ex parte Russell and Wharrie*, Lightman J quashed the decision of a prison governor to limit an inmate to one meal per day as punishment for refusal to wear prison clothes.[126]

A class of cases that present distinctive facts are those where the decision-maker has acted inconsistently in respect of the particular claim at issue. Such was the finding in the US Supreme Court case of *Immigration and Nationality Service* v. *Cardoza-Fonseca*, where the Board of Immigration Appeals routinely gave a relevant statutory provision a number of different and incompatible meanings.[127] Justice Stevens found that '[a]n agency interpretation of a relevant provision which conflicts with the agency's earlier interpretation is "entitled to considerably

---

[124] *R* v. *Commissioners of Inland Revenue, ex parte Unilever Plc.* [1996] STC 681 (CA).
[125] [2002] EWHC 2282.
[126] (2000) 1 WLR 2027 (QBD) 2037.
[127] 480 US 421 (1987).

less deference"'.[128] Conflicting answers to the same problem cannot be justified by appeal to know-how.[129]

Some may worry that inviting courts to find a failure of expertise based on 'distinctive facts' is to invite an unjustifiable amount of judicial intrusiveness. However, this has been neither the experience in English public law, and nor is it a serious threat within an approach that is incrementalist on the whole.

3   Contradiction of established scientific or social science evidence

Sometimes courts will reject a government's position for being contrary to established scientific or social evidence.[130] Such cases are less rare than one would initially think. Such evidence has been used often in criminal law, and in constitutional rights litigation, most famously in the *Brown* v. *Board of Education* case[131] to show that segregated educational facilities produced feelings of inferiority among children.

Two cases from comparative law show how this power is at once both beneficial and dangerous. In the *Treatment Action Campaign* case, the Constitutional Court of South Africa quashed the government's limitation of the use of the Aids anti-retroviral, nevirapene, in treatment for preventing mother-to-child transmission of HIV.[132] The government insisted on safety grounds that nevirapene be bundled into a 'comprehensive package' of treatment, which also consisted of milk substitutes, counselling, and other items. This was to be piloted at a very small number of locations, rather than be made available upon clinical recommendation.[133] The judgment was multifaceted, but on the issue of the drug's safety, the Court found that there was no evidence to support the state's alleged safety concerns: 'According to the current medical consensus, there is no reason to fear any harm from this particular administration of nevirapene. That is why its use is recommended without qualification for this purpose by the World Health Organization. There is also cogent

---

[128] *Ibid.*, 448 (quoting *Watt* v. *Alaska*, 451 US 259, 273 (1981)).

[129] They might be justified on grounds of intentional experimentation, however.

[130] For a dated but useful survey of such evidence in US litigation, see J. Monahan and L. Walker 'Judicial Use of Social Science Research' (1991) 15 *Law and Human Behavior* 571, and also, by the same authors, *Social Science in Law: Cases and Materials* (5th edn, Westbury: Foundation Press, 2002).

[131] *Brown* v. *Board of Education*, 347 US 483 (1954); see Chapter 3.

[132] *Minister of Health and others* v. *Treatment Action Campaign and Others*, 2002 (10) BCLR 1033 (CC) [10] (Yacoob J).

[133] *Ibid.*, [51], [92ff.].

South African endorsement of the safety of Nevirapene … [including by the General Medical Council]'.[134] The Court therefore ordered that the government remove restrictions.

A similar but more controversial use of social science evidence can be found in the Canadian *Chaoulli* v. *Quebec (AG)* case, discussed in Chapter 4.[135] The Court found that a ban on private medical insurance contracts breached the patient's right to security of the person by subjecting him to long queues in the public health system while simultaneously disallowing recourse to private insurance markets. The key factual question was whether making private medical insurance available would worsen the quality of public health care. A trial judge heard weeks of testimony from nearly unanimous experts and concluded it would, and the Court of Appeal agreed with her finding. But a majority of the Supreme Court rejected the trial judge's findings, as well as a wealth of studies produced in favour of the policy by the government, and declared, instead, that the position was 'arbitrary'. Deschamps J, who sided with three other judges for the majority, found that the evidence was evenly matched, and that Canada was the only country in the Organisation for Economic Co-operation and Development to maintain such a ban.[136] She also rejected some of the expert testimony by holding that it sounded like 'speculation' that 'does not sound … very convincing'.[137] This is a very problematic way to handle expert evidence, one which could ultimately have a profoundly negative impact on the health service.[138] Precisely the same rejection of expert studies on the basis of 'common sense' can be found in the *Lochner* case, where an impressive range of studies appeared to prove that bakers as a group of employees suffered substantially worse than average health complications.

The use of scientific evidence to establish propositions of a highly technical nature is somewhat familiar in the fields of criminal, tort, and family law, and no great elaboration on those methods or their pitfalls is needed here.[139] The more contentious situations where social science is relied

---

[134] *Ibid.*, [60]–[61], see also [63] (showing the doctor's expert testimony to be addressing cost rather than safety considerations).

[135] [2005] 1 SCR 791; see J. A. King, 'Constitutional Rights and Social Welfare: A Comment on the Canadian *Chaoulli* Health Care Decision' (2006) 69 *Modern Law Review* 631, esp. 636–7.

[136] *Chaoulli* v. *Quebec (Attorney General)* [2005] 1 SCR 791, [136]–[137].

[137] *Ibid.*, [64].

[138] King, 'Constitutional Rights and Social Welfare', 631, esp. 636–7.

[139] See L. Blom-Cooper (ed.), *Experts in the Civil Courts* (Oxford University Press, 2006); Choo, *Evidence*, Chapter 10. On the *Daubert* standard, see further below.

upon – having great importance in welfare rights adjudication – concern
the establishment of what Kenneth Culp Davis called 'legislative facts'.[140]
Davis introduced the idea by contrasting it with adjudicative facts, which
are facts about the immediate parties, the 'who did what, where, when,
how'[141] of the case. Legislative facts, by contrast, 'are those which help the
tribunal to determine the content of law and policy and to exercise its
judgment or discretion in determining what course of action to take'.[142]
Donald Horowitz describes social facts (which are basically indistinguishable) as 'facts relating to recurrent patterns of behavior on which
policy is to be based'.[143] The existence of legislative and social facts in legal
reasoning is widespread in both public and private law.[144] Legislative and
social facts were at issue in both *Chaoulli* and *Lochner*.

The interpretation of complex social science evidence puts a strain on
the institutional capacity and integrity of the court. The studies used in
the *Brown* case, for instance, were later attacked for lacking scientific credibility and accuracy.[145] Given the large amount of conflicting data available, there is a substantial risk that judges may cherry-pick from available
studies to support a foregone conclusion, only to be met by bitter dissent
citing contrary studies or contrary conclusions from the same studies.[146]
When the constitutional validity of statutes is at issue, the consequences
of judicial error can be severe.

There is no extensive discussion of legislative facts in English law,[147]
but there is relevant experience of the matter in the United States and

---

[140] K. C. Davis, 'An Approach to Problems of Evidence in the Administrative Process' (1942)
55 *Harvard Law Review* 364.

[141] K. C. Davis, 'Judicial Notice' (1955) 55 *Columbia Law Review* 945, 952.

[142] *Ibid.*, 952.

[143] D. Horowitz, *The Courts and Social Policy* (Washington: Brookings Institution, 1977),
pp. 45–51.

[144] See generally Monahan and Walker, *Social Science in Law*, Chapter 4; K. Burns, 'The
Way the World Is: Social Facts in High Court Negligence Cases' (2004) 12 *Torts Law
Journal* 215.

[145] B. Levin and P. Moise, 'School Desegregation Litigation in the Seventies and the Use of
Social Science Evidence: An Annotated Guide' (1975) *Law and Contemporary Problems*
50, 53–6 (reviewing the academic and judicial controversy stirred by *Brown*'s reliance
upon social scientific evidence to claim social stigma). See also the various sources
reproduced in Monahan and Walker, *Social Science in Law*, pp. 186–204.

[146] *Chaoulli* v. *Quebec* (AG) [2005] 1 SCR 791 [243], [247–8]; *Grutter* v. *Bollinger and Others*,
539 US 306 (2003) (judgment of Thomas J, dissenting).

[147] See A. Henderson, 'Brandeis Briefs and the Proof of Legislative Facts in Proceedings
under the Human Rights Act 1998' [1998] *Public Law* 563 for a short introduction.
However, see A. Carter, 'Proof of Legislative Facts under the Human Rights Act 1998',
M.Phil Dissertation, Faculty of Law, University of Oxford (2011). I have benefitted

Canada. In *Muller* v. *Oregon*,[148] Louis Brandeis submitted a 112-page legal brief detailing foreign law and empirical studies about the effects of long working hours on the health of women, in defence of the constitutionality of Oregon's working time laws, only three years after *Lochner* was decided. It is widely assumed that this type of information – submitted by what is now called a Brandeis brief – helped persuade the court to substitute actual data for *Lochner*-era presumptions about the unconstitutionality of interferences with property and contract rights. This illustrates precisely the allure of encouraging social science evidence. Since social facts already form part of judicial reasoning, the question is what should judges rely upon in deciding: their own assumptions or actual data? It is for this very reason that Davis encouraged the use of Brandeis briefs and social science evidence, and advocated using judicial notice as a method for allowing recognition of legislative facts in conjunction with social science evidence.[149] The acknowledgment of social and legislative facts, and their use by courts, has also been more open in Australia[150] and Canada, whose experience I consider shortly.

The question of how to use social science and other scientific evidence in human rights adjudication is one that has complex civil procedure and fairness ramifications, as well as substantive concerns about the appropriate restraint to be shown. Although a deeper analysis of the question is needed than is possible here, it is necessary to state a view on how such evidence might be used to establish a failure of expertise within the approach taken in this chapter. The following represents the distillation of the principles that I regard as a plausible approach for use in social rights adjudication (and possibly other human rights adjudication).

First, judicial notice will be appropriate for some legislative facts. It was proposed by Davis and is now established in the United States, Canada, and Australia that legislative facts can be noticed in this way, in reliance

greatly from extensive discussions with Ms Carter about the correct approach for proof of legislative facts in English courts.

[148] 208 US 412 (1908).

[149] Davis, 'Judicial Notice'.

[150] A. J. Serpell, *The Reception and Use of Social Policy Information in the High Court of Australia* (Pyrmont, New South Wales: Lawbook Co, 2006); S. Kenny, 'Constitutional Fact Ascertainment' (1990) 1 *Public Law Review* 134; and especially, J. D. Heydon, *Cross on Evidence* (8th Australian edn, Sydney: LexisNexis Butterworths, 2009) and *Thomas v. Mowbray* (2007) 233 CLR 307 (esp. the judgment of Heydon J). I am grateful to Anne Carter for these references and her analysis of them.

on documentary evidence.[151] Traditionally, judicial notice was employed as a technique for efficient decision-making in the courts, used by judges for admitting those 'notorious facts' that were either not reasonably disputable, or were traced to sources of indisputable accuracy.[152] This rule is relaxed in relation to proof of legislative facts. It is common for judges to rely on law reviews, reputable commentary, law commission reports, other reports by public bodies, and those by leading and well-known national and international bodies. These are not just employed for determining the pre-existing content of the law, but also as evidence of legislative facts that bear upon in what direction the law ought to be developed. Government or other publicly commissioned reports as well as evidence not generally in considerable dispute will be particularly appropriate for judicial notice.[153]

Second, there is a need for an approach indicating when evidence ought to be subjected to a more rigorous standard of admissibility. In its examination of this problem, the Supreme Court of Canada has adopted the following rule: the more the legislative or social fact is central to the disposition of the case, the less appropriate will it be for it to be established by judicial notice.[154] This seems appropriate, and judicially manageable.

Third, if the parties have submitted authorities other than those that can be judicially noticed, and they contain conflicting or controversial evidence, or the judge believes it is otherwise helpful or necessary, it will be more appropriate for the evidence to be admitted when accompanied by expert oral testimony as to the reliability of the methods and conclusions used in the tendered studies. This is now the established approach in Canada,[155] and it is particularly sensible. Trial judges may thereby bring their own competence in assessing witness demeanour and by pressing inquiries on blind spots, both with the benefit of cross-examination. Ideally, the question of whether such evidence will form part of the record will be resolved at the very outset of the dispute. Where such evidence is raised on appeal for the first time (e.g. by an intervener), the

---

[151] See generally Davis, 'Judicial Notice'; see also, in Canada, *R v. Edwards Books and Art Ltd* [1986] 2 SCR 713, 802 (LaForest J); *Danson v. Ontario (Attorney General)* [1990] 2 SCR 1086; *Willick v. Willick* [1994] 3 SCR 670, 701–2 (L'Heureux-Dubé J).

[152] In *R v. Spence* [2005] 3 SCR 458, Binnie J for the unanimous Supreme Court of Canada traces the evolution of the idea in US and Canadian law. For the English rule, which uses a vague 'proper to refer to' standard, see *Commonwealth Shipping Representative v. P & O Branch Service* [1923] AC 191 (HL) 212 (Lord Summer).

[153] The approach in *R v. Malmo-Levine* [2003] 3 SCR 571 [27].

[154] *R v. Spence* [2005] 3 SCR 458, [65]. See generally [48]–[69].

[155] *Ibid.*, [68] citing several cases in which this is the preferred approach.

appellate court will have to decide whether to hold a hearing or (more likely) remand the case to trial. The appropriate option will depend on the jurisdiction in question.[156]

Thus far, the question has been about ways of admitting such evidence, but not about the weight it ought to be accorded by reviewing judges in public law (which is the same question as how much restraint such judges should show in review of it). In my view, there is a need for a standard that addresses this question, particularly in respect of social rights adjudication. The Supreme Court of Canada has not established a clear standard. Iacobucci J found on one important occasion, citing earlier authority, that judges ought to show deference in proportionality analyses where they are called upon to examine 'complex and conflicting social science research'.[157] There are similar *dicta* in some of the holdings of the US Supreme Court, which has held that such evidence should not be given great weight when it manifests 'substantial disagreement'.[158]

Some insight is provided in the rules relating to admissibility of scientific evidence in the United States. The test established in the early *Frye* v. *United States* case was that scientific evidence ought not to be admitted unless it had met with general acceptance in the relevant scientific community.[159] This position was overtly relaxed in the *Daubert* case, which based its liberalisation of the rule chiefly on the effect of the Federal Rules of Evidence, which were adopted after *Frye*.[160] Despite its implied criticism of the standard in *Frye*, the Court in *Daubert* retained an important role for the idea of general acceptance in the relevant scientific community: 'Widespread acceptance can be an important factor in ruling particular evidence admissible, and "a known technique which has been able

---

[156] There are some difficulties in applying this approach in the United Kingdom, largely because the Administrative Court only rarely takes evidence other than in documentary form, and does not run trials. However, it is possible under the existing rules (see *Blackstone's Administrative Court Practice* (Oxford University Press, 2006), pp. 140–1) and such rules could be reformed easily.

[157] *M* v. *H* [1999] 2 SCR 3 [79]. However, the dissent in *Chaoulli* did not invoke this notion in their otherwise vigorous critique of the majority's use of social science evidence.

[158] *Washington* v. *Glucksberg*, 521 US 702, 786 (1997) (concurring opinion of Souter J); see further the protestations offered by Thomas J in dissent in *Grutter* v. *Bollinger and Others*.

[159] *Frye* v. *United States*, 54 App. D.C. 46, 293 F. 1013 (1923), 1014.

[160] *Daubert* v. *Merrell Dow Pharmaceuticals* 509 US 579 (1993), pp. 588–9 (Blackmun J, for the Court, also calling the *Frye* standard 'austere'). See also T. S. Renekar, 'Evidentiary Legerdemain: Deciding When *Daubert* Should Apply to Social Science Evidence' (1996) 84 *California Law Review* 1657.

to attract only minimal support within the community," ... may properly be viewed with skepticism.'[161]

It is important to stress that the tests in *Daubert* and *Frye* concerned the admissibility of evidence, and not the weight to be accorded to it. It is possible, in public law litigation in particular, where it is judges rather than juries who give weight to the evidence, to take a liberal view about admissibility, but a more restrained view on the question of weight or judicial restraint. That is precisely the position advocated here. Mindful of that difference, I would propose, within the framework set out in this chapter, that court can find a state's decision to be contrary to established scientific or social science evidence when it conflicts with a proposition that has either (a) met with general acceptance in the relevant scientific community, or (b) is one that is proved by generally accepted methods and there is no real prospect of substantial disagreement within the relevant community as to the result.[162] This standard is one for which both expert testimony and judicial training is well suited. It is one that would have been met in the *Treatment Action Campaign* case, and which would have excluded the results in *Chaoulli* and *Lochner*. When that standard is not met, it is difficult to show with confidence that there has been a failure of expertise and not merely the substitution of opinion on that question. Since the potential for disrupting important functions of the welfare state remains a threat in social rights adjudication, it is appropriate to maintain a high threshold. That is the nature of the expertise–accountability trade-off in this situation. Without such a threshold, there is an invitation, if not a requirement, that judges pick sides in a battle of experts. Until experience of social rights adjudication shows such a threshold to be too restrictive, in my view it remains the only standard that squarely meets the expertise objection.

The reason for such judicial restraint is the court's limited capacity to evaluate such evidence, and the potential consequences of error. It is not at all suggested here that the legislature or executive be bound to show that some proposition is generally accepted or not liable to substantial disagreement. For one, they are given the democratic mandate and have the institutional means to make the difficult judgments about what weight to

---

[161] *Daubert* v. *Merrell Dow Pharmaceuticals* 509 US 579 (1993), p. 594. The Court set out four other factors that are valuable but of less pertinence to this discussion.

[162] This second standard is indicated because some facts or questions may be too specific to make a general acceptance standard appropriate.

accord conflicting evidence. And for another, any rule that forbade them from acting before such consensus would lead to undue constriction of regulatory capacity. It is therefore essential to avoid, for example by shifting an onerous burden of proof onto the state, a situation where the state's regulatory capacity is limited to what it can prove to a court of law on a standard expressly designed to address the court's own institutional limitations.

There is also a question about whether such a standard imposes an unfair cost on the claimants. It may increase costs by requiring expert witnesses and a more substantial forensic search for social science evidence. Yet it does not seem unfair to ask that a claimant seeking to overturn a public decision made by elected or appointed officials actually shows a clear failure of expertise. There are other means for apportioning costs, such as through legal aid, protective cost orders, the role of interveners, and the court's inherent jurisdiction to ensure an equality of arms between the parties. Such techniques may be inadequate at times, but they could be strengthened. Further, the standard set out above may actually reduce costs by comparison with a full-blown battle of the experts, where the question is less about identifying an established proposition, and more about which side can produce a greater volume of expensive expert testimony and documentary evidence.

Lastly, there is the possibility of engaging in some form of institutional reform to facilitate the consideration of such evidence in courts. It might involve using court-appointed assessors or experts, or even the establishment of a research service staffed with social science experts, exclusively for use by the court in such cases.[163] These reforms are not necessary to operate the standard set out here, but there may be good arguments in favour of them, and they would be ripe for serious consideration during a period of constitutional design. What ought to be avoided, however, is a practice whereby a single expert-assessor can substitute judgment for that of the collective professional expertise of some agency. A research service,

---

[163] Such proposals were made early: see K. C. Davis, 'Judicial, Legislative, and Administrative Lawmaking: A Proposed Research Service for the Supreme Court' (1986) 1 *Minnesota Law Review* 1; for a similar contemporary proposal, see P. Yowell, 'Empirical Research in Rights-Based Judicial Review of Legislation', in P. Huber and K. Ziegler (eds.), *Current Problems in the Protection of Human Rights – Perspectives from Germany and the UK* (Oxford: Hart Publishing, 2012). Mr Yowell has contributed greatly to my understanding of this problem.

which would itself be a form of collective professional expertise if well designed, is a different matter, and it is hard to see the case against it.

V   Conclusion

The idea of administrative expertise is a crucial concept in public law, and takes on particular importance in social rights adjudication. The idea that judges lack the competency to adjudicate complex disputes in the modern welfare state is an objection that is partly true and partly false. It is false in view of the extent to which adjudication is woven into the fabric of the welfare state. But it is also true to the extent that administrators and specialists generally enjoy a distinct comparative advantage on how to resolve complex questions under conditions of uncertainty. The goal of this chapter was to shed light on the rationale and limitations of that expertise, and propose a set of considerations that could assist in giving weight to the principle of expertise in social rights adjudication.

I approached this task by first highlighting the historical development of the idea of expertise as a concept in public law and administration. It was shown there that it is a significant factor counselling deference already. But it is further clear that expertise is no conclusive general argument against judicial control. I proceeded in section III to analyse the different forms of expertise. While front-line and individual professional experts ordinarily merit the ordinary degree of deference (which includes giving adequate weight to their views in adjudication), managerial and collective professional expertise will generally be entitled to much greater weight. The latter, in particular, can be all but conclusive absent a failure of expertise or manifestation of some procedural injustice. Specialised adjudicative expertise is, again, something that merits great weight precisely because it combines accountability with subject-matter expertise.

The notion of expertise–accountability trade-off acts like a prism for understanding why these generalisations have appeal. This very idea is necessary because we recognise immediately that such trade-offs pervade adjudication in all areas, and indeed they pervade accountability generally in the welfare and regulatory state. We trade the benefits of unrestricted expertise for those of a mixture of expertise and oversight, and adjudication is no different. This does not provide a green light to courts, but it does explain why judicial review persists. And it also explains why judges rightly review expert decisions even when it is clear that the experts know the relevant field better than they do.

The idea of failures of expertise provides the more determinate set of circumstances for when expertise can be regarded as not meriting deference – even when the result is not incrementalist in the sense identified in Chapter 10. I explored three situations in which they can be found: failure to apply expertise; distinctive facts; and contradiction of established scientific or social science evidence. This last type of failure of expertise raised particularly thorny issues, but if the standard there is observed, then it can be shown that where it is met, there is no reason for judicial restraint on the basis of expertise. These are the occasions on which the myth of expertise that lurks behind so many public decisions gets exposed and shamed by means of the hard accountability that often only public law can provide.

9

Flexibility

I Introduction

Suppose for the sake of argument that in the Canadian health care case *Chaoulli*,[1] as some maintain, neither the Supreme Court nor the government of Canada really knew whether allowing private medical insurance would seriously impair the public health care system. Suppose further that academic and professional opinion substantially leaned against the government's position, or that some leaked memorandum showed that the ministers were basically fumbling in the dark over the issue (a distinctive fact in the legal record). In such a case, expertise offers no justification for judicial deference. Would something else?

The answer is found by asking what would happen if the court turned out to be wrong in assuming that the public health care system would remain unscathed. The court's ability to reverse its earlier position has traditionally been restricted by the doctrine of precedent. It is also limited by the procedural problem that a party must take a case that looks unpromising and shoulder the costs and risks all the way to the Supreme Court. Until that scenario arises, public authorities may have highly limited latitude to adjust. The answer, therefore, is that the need to afford public authorities the latitude to adjust to unforeseen circumstances and mistakes is itself a reason for restraint.

This chapter is concerned with showing why and how judges ought to give prominent consideration to the idea of administrative and legislative flexibility in their adjudication of constitutional social rights. Judges, experts on administration, and legal scholars alike have commented on the need for administrative flexibility in the complex welfare state.[2]

---

[1] *Chaoulli v. Quebec (Attorney General)* [2005] 1 SCR 791.

[2] In addition to the many examined below, see also R. Titmuss, 'Welfare "Rights", Law and Discretion' (1971) 42 *Political Quarterly* 113; H. Street, *Justice in the Welfare State* (London: Stevens & Sons, 1968), pp. 7–8; Lord Bingham, 'Should public law remedies be discretionary?' [1991] *Public Law* 64; P. Sales and K. Steyn, 'Legitimate Expectations In English Public Law' [2000] *Public Law* 564, 573ff.; *Ali v. Lord Grey School* [2006] UKHL

Flexibility can be defined for present purposes as the capacity to adapt to unforeseen circumstances. Flexibility is relevant when circumstances change (e.g. the cost of supplying a drug, or number of applicants for a given benefit or expensive legal procedure), or when a person took a decision based on a proposition that turned out to be false (as in my hypothetical scenario above). I begin the analysis below upon the assumption that it is common ground that flexibility in modern administration is important. I am here concerned to examine the sources of such harmful inflexibility, both judicially imposed as well as those forms adopted within administration and legislative decision-making. I thus examine the forms of inflexibility, and the way in which judges can give weight to the principle that administrative and legislative decision-making should retain the capacity to adapt to new circumstances. Courts can facilitate this flexibility by at times requiring it, and they can adjust their rulings in order to respect it. It emerges, however, that the oft-sought remedy of procedural rights can at times harbour problems for administration that social rights advocates frequently ignore. It is crucial that these problems not be ignored, and this chapter addresses them and proposes manageable ways of overcoming them.

II Forms of inflexibility

There are many forms of constraint upon administrative and legislative action. The present concern is with those relevant to adjudication, either because inflexibility is imposed by judicial oversight or may be corrected by it. Accordingly, I first examine inflexibility that can be imposed by courts and adjudication, and then turn to inflexibility that is imposed consciously or unconsciously by the bureaucracy or legislative process itself.

A Legal forms

1 Agenda control

Agenda control occurs when a court restricts the manner in which a decision-maker can resolve a problem. The breadth of agenda control will depend on the breadth of the holding, and the nature of the remedy. The first and most obvious instance occurs where the court imposes *finality*.

14 [82]–[83] (Lady Hale); *In re Permian Basin Area Rate Cases*, 390 US 747 (1968), 784; *National Labor Relations Board* v. *Hearst Publications Inc.*, 322 US 111, 131 (1944).

Although there is no ultimate legal finality in most legal systems (since either all or most constitutions can be amended), there are various degrees of practical finality. In the United Kingdom, for instance, and depending on the holding itself, it rises in degree from statutory interpretation (in principle reversible by the legislature as mistaken interpretation), to common law holding (reversible but complicated by the question of how the statutory reversal will relate to the common law), to rights-consistent interpretation under s. 3 of the Human Rights Act 1998 (HRA), to a s. 4 declaration of incompatibility/invalidity for violation of human rights, to a holding that a statute is inapplicable by virtue of inconsistency with European Union law. These instances represent rising degrees of inflexibility in that the executive or Parliament's practical latitude to reverse or depart from a court's finding is increasingly restricted. A similar phenomenon will occur depending on the sweep of a particular ruling – the extent to which it lays down a broadly applicable rule with little opportunity for subsequent interpretive adjustment. Of course, any law or accountability will constitute a constraint, and thus a form of agenda control. But that fact does not make the problem of agenda control disappear. If the court rules out a number of options, it is likely that the bureaucracy and responsible politicians will need to work around it.

A second form of agenda control is what Mark Tushnet calls policy distortion. On his definition, this occurs when legislators are constitutionally empowered to articulate their own norms, but instead choose to follow the norms laid down by courts.[3] It is not finality because, legally *and* practically speaking, legislators are not bound to follow the prescription put across by a court. They nonetheless follow the court's lead out of reasons of avoiding risk, misconception as to propriety or legality, or mere expedience. This phenomenon can occur, for example, when a court determines under a proportionality analysis that the government's policy is not necessary in a democratic society because another, less restrictive alternative is available to carry out the same policy.[4] In such cases the state may just take up the court's option because it has been legally ratified.

---

[3] M. Tushnet, 'Policy Distortion and Democratic Debilitation: Comparative Illumination of the Countermajoritarian Difficulty' (1995) 94 *Michigan Law Review* 245–301, 260.

[4] See for example *Chahal* v. *United Kingdom* (1996) 23 EHRR 413 [144] (suggesting that a Canadian model for dealing with terrorism suspects in the immigration context offers better protection to procedural due process rights under Art. 5(4) ECHR), a process later adopted in Britain; see D. Jenkins, 'There and Back Again: The Strange Journey of Special Advocates and Comparative Law Methodology' (2000) 79 *Columbia Human Rights Law Review* 279, 286 ('The Canadian reference in Chahal's *dicta* was neither integral to the Court's reasoning nor necessary for deciding the case.')

Authors writing about judicialisation of politics are also concerned about this type of threat.[5] The basic concern is that through rigorous judicial review, bureaucrats, governments, or even legislatures may become pre-occupied with attending to court-defined policy alternatives, rather than with the broader range open to them.

Policy distortion is a real issue, and it is important for judges, administrative decision-makers, and legislators to be conscious of its potential. But it is implausible to argue that it is an insurmountable problem with rights-based judicial review. It would imply a vastly greater level of rights consciousness among legislators and bureaucrats than what was revealed in the discussion in Chapter 3, which presented evidence that legislatures more often than not tend to evade rather than slavishly adopt the *dicta* or dictates of the courts.

2   Delay

Delay is different though related to agenda control: it slows down rather than formally denies the implementation of a policy. However, and like weaker forms of agenda control, it can have knock-on effects that do constrain substantive choices. The most striking example of this is the phenomenon of regulatory ossification caused by administrative law judicial review in the United States.[6] Some background is important for understanding this phenomenon.

Regulations are adopted in the United States chiefly by administrative agencies, not, as in the UK, by departments of government headed by cabinet ministers, where in most important cases they are laid before Parliament and are subject to a resolution before they take effect.[7] The American system is intentionally at arm's length from the legislative and

---

[5] Titmuss, 'Welfare "Rights", Law and Discretion'; M. Mandel, *The Charter of Rights and the Legalisation of Politics in Canada* (Toronto: Thompson Publishing, 1994); M. Shapiro, A. Stone, and A. Sweet, *On Law, Politics and Judicialisation* (Oxford University Press, 2002); R. Hirschl, *Towards Juristocracy* (New Haven: Yale University Press, 2004).

[6] See e.g. J. M. Mendeloff, *The Dilemma of Toxic Substance Regulation: How Overregulation Causes Underregulation at OSHA* (Cambridge, MA: MIT Press, 1988); J. L. Mashaw and D. L. Harfst, *The Struggle for Auto-Safety* (Cambridge, MA: Harvard University Press, 1990); T. O. McGarity, 'Some Thoughts on "Deossifying" the Rulemaking Process' (1992) 41 *Duke Law Journal* 1385; T. O. McGarity and S. A. Shapiro, *Workers at Risk: The Failed Promise of the Occupational and Safety Health Administration* (New York: Praeger Publishers, 1993); R. J. Pierce, Jr, 'The Unintended Effects of Judicial Review of Agency Rules: How Federal Courts Have Contributed to the Electricity Crisis of the 1990s' (1992) 43 *Administrative Law Journal* 7; R. J. Pierce, Jr, 'Seven Ways to Deossify Agency Rulemaking' (1995) 47 *Administrative Law Review* 59.

[7] On the UK, see E. Page, *Governing by Numbers: Delegated Legislation and Everyday Policy-Making* (Oxford: Hart Publishing, 2001); P. R. Verkuil, 'Comment: Rulemaking

political process. It is therefore less subject to political oversight. This gave rise, as noted in Chapter 8,[8] to a perceived need for compensation. The chosen solution was contained in the statutory framework for adopting regulations, set out in the Administrative Procedure Act 1946 (APA).[9] Regulations are adopted either by informal or formal rulemaking.[10] The former is more commonly employed (partly because the latter is used only when a given statute specifies its use),[11] and it requires publication of a proposed rule followed by a period for the public to provide comments (also called notice and comment rulemaking).

The scope of review of informal rulemaking is found in §706(2) of the APA, and the most common ground for relief is that the rules were adopted in an 'arbitrary and capricious' manner.[12] Review of informal rulemaking under this banner evolved into 'hard look review', in part so-called because courts would carefully examine the administrative record, the relevant law, and the conclusions reached, and determine whether there was a reasonable connection between them.[13] In fact, under the hard look doctrine the courts take a hard look at whether the agency itself has taken a hard look at all the information relevant to the conclusion it has reached. The development of this review by circuit courts was ultimately adopted in spirit if not in name by the Supreme Court in the *State Farm* case, in which courts were admonished to inquire into whether:

> the agency has relied on factors which Congress has not intended it to consider, entirely failed to consider an important aspect of the problem, offered an explanation for its decision that runs counter to the evidence before the agency, or is so implausible that it could not be ascribed to a difference in view or the product of agency expertise.[14]

Ossification – A Modest Proposal' (1995) 47 *Administrative Law Review* 453, 457 (arguing that a model of parliamentary oversight is an alternative to the US model of judicial review).

[8] Sections II.A, and IV.A.2.

[9] Administrative Procedure Act (APA) 1946, 5 USC, Subchapter II.

[10] APA, §553.   [11] *Ibid.*, §553(3)(c); §556; §557.

[12] For an overview of the law and secondary literature, see W. S. Jordan III, 'Ossification Revisited: Does Arbitrary and Capricious Review Significantly Interfere with Agency Ability to Achieve Regulatory Goals Through Informal Rulemaking?' (2000) 94 *Northwestern University Law Review* 393.

[13] *Turpin v. Merrell Dow Pharms Inc.*, 959 F.2d 1349, 1352–3 (6th Cir 1992); *Neighbors Organized to Insure a Sound Env't Inc v. McArtor*, 878 F.2d 174, 178 (6th Cir 1989).

[14] *Motor Vehicle Manufacturer's Association v. State Farm Mutual Auto Insurance Co*, 463 US 29, 43 (1983); earlier cases involving environmental regulation included *Citizens to Preserve Overton Park v. Volpe*, 401 US 402, 415–20 (1971) (the 'substantial inquiry' test).

This statement of considerations appears on its face to non-American lawyers as fairly innocuous, and indeed is not dissimilar (if somewhat more searching) to the grounds of review available under conventional judicial review in the United Kingdom, or elsewhere in the Commonwealth. However, American literature on this phenomenon demonstrates that judicial review under the hard look doctrine has led to a significant delay of regulation, with a very serious impact on the public interest, in areas that include auto safety, consumer protection, environmental protection, occupational health and safety, and utility regulation to name a few.[15] In a comment representative of this literature, one scholar suggests there is mounting evidence that hard look review 'has introduced into the policymaking process delay and resource commitments so great that some agencies have abandoned their efforts at policymaking completely'.[16] The reason is that well-resourced litigants present enormous amounts of information during the notice and comment period, and thereafter charge that the agency's choice of rule, which must be published accompanied by a concise statement of reasoning, fails to respond to a valid point raised. Due to the volume and complexity of the material being submitted, the possibilities for review are manifold. And because of the resource costs and attendant risks of loss or even embarrassment, the agency can be delayed or even dissuaded from carrying out its mandate.

The implications for social rights adjudication ought to be obvious. Social rights may involve an even more assertive, rights-based review of various aspects of the welfare state, including housing regulations, education, social security and pensions, health care, general infrastructure, and possibly much more. Drug approval in health care rationing presents a particular concern. Procedural rights can create delays. Each time an agency like the National Institute on Health and Clinical Excellence (NICE) must reconsider whether to approve a drug as cost-effective, it will increase backlogs, where delays to the process can mean serious harm or even death for those further down the queue waiting for approvals. More substantive judicial review can be more damaging still. A ruling that an expensive drug must be added to the list of funded drugs could complicate the rationing process. There is significant evidence of this in Latin America,[17] but challenges have sought this in the UK as

---

[15] See above, note 6.

[16] R. J. Pierce, Jr, 'The Role of the Judiciary in Implementing an Agency Theory of Government' (1989) 64 *New York University Law Review* 1239, 1264.

[17] See Chapter 3, section III.D.

well. In *Ex parte Pfizer*, the Court of Appeal dismissed a judicial review challenge against NICE to deny National Health Service funding for the Viagra drug.[18] In *Rogers*, the claimant asked the court to order that an expensive breast cancer drug (Herceptin) be provided even though it was pending approval by NICE and the European Medicines Agency.[19] The Court side-stepped that issue and rather quashed the decision for reasons examined below.

Having stated the problem, it is equally important to recognise its limitations. First, the ossification problem, with arguably an exception or two, has not appeared to have bedevilled the United Kingdom, or the European Union.[20] Martin Shapiro, a critic of judicialisation, acknowledges that the problem has been rather judiciously avoided by the European Court of Justice (though he fears the risk is present and that the same causes lead to the same effects).[21] More to the point in welfare rights adjudication, there are no reports of a similar phenomenon in over ten years of South Africa's experience under its bill of social rights, including in its case involving a challenge against the government's refusal to certify AIDS anti-retrovirals for public use (discussed further below). There are a number of institutional and cultural factors that may explain much of the problem in the United States. Second, the ossification literature is itself becoming more divided. Some recent findings show agency objectives to be largely unimpeded,[22] while others suggest that minor doctrinal innovations will accommodate

---

[18] *R* v. *Secretary of State for Health, ex parte Pfizer* [2002] EWCA Civ 1566.

[19] *R (on the Application of Anne Marie Rogers)* v. *Swindon NHS Primary Care Trust, Secretary of State for Health* [2006] EWCA Civ 392.

[20] The exception may be the airways after the Skytrain decision of the Court of Appeal, see G. Baldwin, 'A British Independent Regulatory Agency and the "Skytrain" Decision' [1978] *Public Law* 57; R. Baldwin, *Regulating the Airlines: Administrative Justice and Agency Discretion* (Oxford: Clarendon Press, 1985); for the EU, see P. Craig, *EU Administrative Law* (Oxford University Press, 2006), pp. 134–40; M. Shapiro, 'Judicial Review and Bureaucratic Impact: The Future of EU Administrative Law', in M. Hertogh and S. Halliday (eds.), *Judicial Review and Bureaucratic Impact: International and Interdisciplinary Perspectives* (Cambridge University Press, 2004), p. 251. On Germany, see H. Puender, 'Democratic Legitimation of Delegated Legislation – A Comparative View on the American, British and German Law' (2009) 58 *International and Comparative Law Quarterly* 363.

[21] Shapiro, 'Judicial Review and Bureaucratic Impact'.

[22] Jordan III, 'Ossification Revisited'; A. Joseph O'Connell, 'Political Cycles of Rulemaking: An Empirical Portrait of the Modern Administrative State' (2008) 94 *Virginia Law Review* 889; J. Webb Jackee and S. Webb Jackee, 'Administrative Procedures and Bureaucratic Performance: Is Federal Rule-Making "Ossified"?' (2010) 20 *Journal of Public Administration Research and Theory* 261.

the problem.[23] The literature still leans substantially one way, but the gravity of the threat, especially outside the United States, remains more questionable. Third, and most importantly, the ossification threat will depend in part on how much the court focuses on the protection of vulnerable groups rather than well-organised corporate or middle-class interests. The American experience of ossification has been caused chiefly by well-resourced litigants seeking to delay regulation. The less well off generally have far fewer resources to run strategic or opportunistic litigation.

So it remains the case that although the threat of ossification is real and important, and must be given weight,[24] it is not as significant for the enterprise as a brush with the literature might first suggest.

3   Cost

Resource scarcity is one of the major causes of inflexibility. It often determines the depth of attention an administrative decision-maker can give to a problem. Fewer resources means less time to consider each case in-depth, and thus increases reliance on heuristics and rigid rules.

In an earlier article I distinguished between the judicial review of discretionary allocative decision-making and the allocative impact created by a court ruling.[25] Allocative impact is common, and can come in many forms. The following representative list of types gives some idea of its dimensions: (1) judgment damages and/or immediate costs of administrative compliance; (2) legal representation costs; (3) administrative costs of responding to immediate demands of litigation (e.g. interviews, witness and/or affidavit preparation, document review); (4) increased insurance premiums and related negotiation costs; (5) judgment-required policy alteration costs (e.g. human resources and overhead costs for formulating and disseminating new policy); (6) diversion of resources into liability avoidance behaviour; (7) increased future needs for legal advice; (8) foregone revenue in cases involving revenue law, planning, or regulatory law; and (9) future, unforeseen claims allowed or barred by the judgment, and costs associated therewith.

---

[23] M. Seidenfeld, 'Demystifying Deossification: Rethinking Recent Proposals to Modify Judicial Review of Notice and Comment Rulemaking' (1997) 75 *Texas Law Review* 483; c.f. T. O. McGarity, 'The Courts and the Ossification of Rulemaking: A Response to Professor Seidenfeld' (1997) 75 *Texas Law Review* 525.

[24] As I have elsewhere in addition to here: J. King, 'Proportionality: A Halfway House' (2010) 2 *New Zealand Law Review* 327, 345ff.

[25] See J. A. King, 'The Justiciability of Resource Allocation' (2007) 70 *Modern Law Review* 197, 208ff.

The costs here can be significant. Depending on the scope of the remedial order, this can be tantamount to the creation of what have been called 'unfunded mandates' in the United States, namely, those federal legislative measures that impose requirements on the states or the private sector without any accompanying funding. Worse, the dynamic consequences of allocative impact are extremely difficult to study. Budgeting within local or national authorities is at once too complex and the accounting not adjusted for tracking in any general way the manner in which allocative impact is spread across budget line items within a given authority.[26] In America, the problem with unfunded mandates, without providing funding, led to the Unfunded Mandates Reform Act of 1995,[27] which provided for a set of procedural protections and information-gathering, particularly by requiring the Congressional Budget Office to carry out cost estimates. Nothing similar is available under a judicial review procedure, nor foreseeably so.

Allocative impact is a real problem, but it is also easy to state the problem hyperbolically. One way is to argue that any pound or dollar absorbed by allocative impact may as well be seen as coming from a child's dinner plate. If we took that view, then public accountability would be impossible. Allocative impact is inescapable in public law and administrative justice, particularly if we see any legal accountability as taking some time and resources. There are areas of public and private law where duties are imposed on public authorities that cost money: state liability in tort; enforcement of statutory duties; damages under European Union law or s. 8 of the HRA; tax decisions; tribunal adjudication; ombudsman compensation recommendations and much else. Legal and other forms of accountability have costs: that is the price of modern administration and the cost of rights. The solution is therefore to be found in a delicate balance of considerations, case by case or class by class, where the reality of allocative impact is acknowledged and managed. I discuss how this might occur in Chapter 10.

B   Bureaucratic and political forms

There are a variety of ways in which administrators, policy-makers, and legislators can consciously or unconsciously limit their own capacity to adapt to changing circumstances.

---

[26] Interview with Stuart Fair, Chartered Institute of Public Finance and Accountancy (CPFA), 13 April 2011.
[27] Unfunded Mandates Reform Act, 2 USC (1995).

1   Conscious forms: fettering, ideology, and stereotype

Decision-makers can consciously restrict the way in which they decide a case before them. They may simply act stubbornly, or for bad faith reasons; this is the classic instance of abuse of power. An even more pernicious form is racism or other patently unconstitutional (or rights-antagonistic) stereotype.[28] A more subtle but equally problematic source of inflexibility is ideology. In some cases, policy-makers or elected officials will change the direction of how supposedly neutral institutions are run under the same statutory regime to adapt to the policy ends of the given official.[29] A desire to be bullish about a party policy can lead decision-makers to refuse to consider greater flexibility in their approach. The most obvious instances may be found in administrative law, in cases concerning the fettering of discretion.[30] A second set of instances would include those cases of ideologically motivated interference in relatively technocratic determinations.[31] That it will often be difficult to distinguish ideological inflexibility from legitimate policy discretion is true, but this does not mean that it will always be so. Exceptional cases will and do stand out.

2   Bounded rationality, path-dependence, and heuristics

A far more common form of inflexibility will arise through administrative or legislative decision-making under conditions of uncertainty.

(a)   **Bounded rationality**   This concept was developed by Herbert Simon, in the footsteps of Chester Barnard's work on intuition in organisational behaviour,[32] and has been a prominent feature of organisation theory since he introduced it in the 1940s.[33] Simon contrasted optimisation with bounded rationality:

---

[28] S. Halliday, 'Institutional Racism in Bureaucratic Decision-Making: A Case Study in the Administration of Homelessness Law' (2000) 27 *Journal of Law and Society* 449.

[29] See Chapter 8, section IV.C.1.

[30] Craig, *Administrative Law*, 6th edn, pp. 510–21.

[31] See *Minister of Health and others* v. *Treatment Action Campaign and Others* (*TAC* case), 2002 (10) BCLR 1033 (CC) (concerning the safety of the AIDS anti-retroviral Nevirapene); *Motor Vehicle Manufacturer's Association* v. *State Farm Mutual Auto Insurance Co.*, 463 US 29 (1983) (reversing the apparently ideologically motivated decision to rescind an auto-safety rule).

[32] C. Barnard, *The Functions of the Executive* (Cambridge, MA: Harvard University Press, 1956) (see especially the appendix, including his essay 'The Mind in Everyday Matter').

[33] T. Gilovich, D. Griffin, and D. Kahneman, *Heuristics and Biases: The Psychology of Intuitive Judgment* (Cambridge University Press, 2002), pp. 1–19.

> The task of decision involves three steps: (1) the listing of all the alternative strategies; (2) the determination of all the consequences that follow upon each of these strategies; (3) the comparative evaluation of these sets of consequences. The word 'all' is used advisedly. It is obviously impossible for the individual to know all his alternatives or all their consequences, and this impossibility is a very important departure of actual behavior from the model of objective rationality.[34]

The constraints inherent to searching for alternatives and consequences are what gives us the idea of bounded rationality. The ideal decision-maker would 'optimise' such a search by exploring all possible alternatives. The real decision-maker rather 'satisfices' by setting a target level performance for a search, normally with a bias for a decision premise similar to existing decisions, and then stops searching once a satisfactory decision premise is found.[35]

Search strategies such as satisficing naturally led to incremental forms of decision-making and the use of heuristics or short-cuts. Simon's work was elaborated significantly by Charles Lindblom, who advocated that organisations should adopt a method of successive, limited comparison that amounts to incrementalist decision-making.[36] The study of strategies of decision-making under conditions of bounded rationality has moved on significantly, and there are now two widely acknowledged ways in which those deciding under conditions of bounded rationality tend to manage complex tasks.

(b)   Inertia and path dependence   One common form of deciding is to continue doing what has already been done. Incrementalism already recommended that decisions be taken by selecting among options that differed only marginally from the status quo. While this had positive dimensions as a strategy, the negative possibilities were recognised as well, and this under the banner of what is now called path dependence, a concept borrowed from economics to explain patterns of demand that

---

[34] H. A. Simon, *Administrative Behavior: A Study of Decision-Making Processes in Administrative Organization* (4th edn, New York: Collier Macmillan, 1997). The first edition was published in 1947. For a more recent review of the idea, see R. Selten, 'What is Bounded Rationality?', in G. Gigerenzer and R. Selten (eds.), *Bounded Rationality: The Adaptive Toolbox* (Cambridge, MA: MIT Press, 2001), p. 13.

[35] Simon, *Administrative Behavior*, pp. 118–20.

[36] C. Lindblom, 'The Science of Muddling Through' (1959) 19 *Public Administration Review* 79. See also D. Braybrooke and C. E. Lindblom, *A Strategy of Decision: Policy Evaluation as a Social Process* (New York: Free Press, 1970).

are triggered by earlier events. Defined simply, it is the idea that decisions made concerning circumstances in the past tend to exert great influence on decisions made in the present, even if the relevant circumstances have changed.[37] Decision-makers thus limit the options they consider by adopting a decision strategy that relies heavily on existing practices. Path dependence thus creates inflexibility. The capacity for an individual to prompt changes on her own can be extremely difficult. This is the problem Rosalind Dixon refers to as the 'burdens of inertia'.[38] Clearly, there is a problematic tension between what I assert to be the beneficial effects of incrementalism and the negative, inertial effects of path dependence. The difference is one of emphasis: incrementalism emphasises taking small steps whereas path dependence emphasises non-departure from precedent. There is visible twilight between them, as I argue in Chapter 10, and where I also show that judicial incrementalism can amount to a needed green light for other public authorities to act.

(c)   **Heuristics and biases**   Satisficing was one potential decision-strategy, just as incrementalism was another, and intuition a third (all of these being related). These and other strategies employ heuristics for decision-making. Heuristics are cognitive rules-of-thumb, or techniques of reasoning 'not regarded as final and strict but as provisional and plausible only, whose purpose is to discover the solution of the present problem'.[39] It was acknowledged by Simon, and modern psychologists and organisation theorists that heuristics are needed, but that they also import biases of a less familiar kind than ethnic stereotype and ideology. Behavioural psychologists and other social scientists have identified a plethora of cognitive biases, a representative sample of which is provided in Table 9.1 by way of illustration.

---

[37] For a brief summary, see S. E. Robinson and K. J. Meier, 'Path Dependence and Organization Behaviour: Bureaucracy and Social Promotion' (2006) 36 *The American Review of Public Administration* 241, esp. 244–6.

[38] R. Dixon, 'Creating Dialogue about Socioeconomic Rights: Strong-Form versus Weak-Form Judicial Review Revisited' (2007) 5 *International Journal of Constitutional Law* 391 (on 'blind spots' and 'burdens of inertia').

[39] The quotation is by the originator of the term, George Polya, *How to Solve It* (Princeton University Press, 1945), quoted with explanation in J. Baron, *Thinking and Deciding* (3rd edn, Cambridge University Press, 2000), pp. 49–50. See also T. Gilovich and D. Griffin, 'Introduction – Heuristics and Biases: Then and Now', in Gilovich *et al.*, *Heuristics and Biases*, pp. 1–18.

Table 9.1. *Sample of common heuristics and biases*

Heuristic or Bias	Description
Availability bias	The probability of an event is estimated after an assessment of how easily past examples of the event can be called to mind (e.g. the widely held and erroneous view that murder is a more likely cause of death than suicide).
Framing effect	Tendency to draw different conclusions based on how the same information is presented (e.g. that a product is 90% fat-free instead of 10% fat).
Sunk costs, loss aversion, endowment effect	The tendency to value disproportionately an option into which one has invested time and money. The disutility of parting with an object is valued more greatly than the utility associated with acquiring it (e.g. people may be unwilling to sell a fungible object they own and have no emotional connection to for more than its market value).
Anchoring heuristic	The tendency to give weight to options relative to values proposed by others (e.g. higher claims for damages will predictably lead juries and judges to award higher final sums).
Hyperbolic discounting	The tendency to value earlier payoffs more than later ones, even when later ones are of greater value.
Outrage heuristic	The tendency to exaggerate one's response to a problem due to particularly shocking circumstances.

Source: See generally Gilovich *et al.*, *Heuristics and Biases*; Baron, *Thinking and Deciding*, Chapters 11 and 19; C. Jolls, C. Sunstein and R. Thaler, 'A Behavioural Approach to Law and Economics' (1998) 50 *Stanford Law Review* 1471.

No doubt judges are vulnerable to cognitive biases themselves; Adrian Vermeule reasons from this fact to advocate a strong form of legal formalism and judicial deference in American public law.[40] The use of the anchoring heuristic, for example, is a common ploy for advocates. Nonetheless, there is a way in which judicial control of such decision-making can in fact act to counteract some of these and other biases.

[40] A. Vermeule, *Judging under Uncertainty: An Institutional Theory of Legal Interpretation* (Cambridge, MA: Harvard University Press, 2006), Chapter 6.

Advanced study on the use of heuristics has identified two forms of decision-making under conditions of uncertainty: the intuitive (system I) and reflective (system II).[41] System I thinking provides quick answers to problems requiring judgment (typically with intuition, recognition, and heuristics), while system II acts as a monitoring system that can confirm or override those judgments (by interposing slow, controlled, and self-aware rule application). It is at system II levels that the cognitive biases inherent to intuitive judgments can be identified and hopefully corrected. It would be premature without further research to put great weight on the idea that judges in fact can use system II reasoning to correct system I level biases.[42] But it would not be unreasonable to put some weight on it. Dennis Galligan observed this in his study of discretionary powers, where he claimed that '[t]hose legal actors ... who make decisions relatively infrequently are likely to approach the matter in a more complex way, taking more time and considering more information'.[43] It is precisely the role of public law accountability to re-examine in forensic detail the process behind some type of decision, stripping it of legally irrelevant impurities such as bad faith, and irrelevant considerations, to ensure procedural fairness was adopted and statutory objectives were complied with. The problem with judicial review lies, in my view, not so much in the suggestion that it lies closer to system II, optimific rationality, but that this type of reasoning is resource-intensive and can ignore the role of legitimate heuristics as a tool for decision-making under conditions of scarcity and uncertainty.

Judges are not behavioural psychologists and of course they cannot be expected to diagnose cognitive biases at each turn. However, there are some situations in which all indications suggest that they ought to be particularly vigilant. One is the response to crises. It is here that the availability bias and framing effect will be at their strongest. Crises can

---

[41] See D. Kahneman and S. Frederick, 'Representativeness Revisited: Attribute Substitution in Intuitive Judgment', in Gilovich *et al.*, *Heuristics and Biases*; and S. A. Sloman, 'Two Systems of Reasoning' in Gilovich *et al.*, *Heuristics and Biases* (on associative and rule-based reasoning).

[42] Notably, it was not the approach taken in C. Jolls and C. R. Sunstein, 'Debiasing through Law' (2006) 35 *Journal of Empirical Legal Studies* 199. Adrian Vermeule has also expressed doubts to me on this point, because in his view system II reasoning is engaged quite quickly when the decision-maker acts self-consciously.

[43] D. J. Galligan, *Discretionary Powers: A Study of Official Discretion* (Oxford University Press, 1986), p. 263.

be prompted by all manner of occurrences, such as armed conflict, terrorism, trade, financial, immigration, or public financing issues. Another instance is where media sensationalism on a particular topic becomes strident – a scenario that generates pressures any judge will recognise immediately. This is a concern that is acute in Britain and America. This might include tabloid campaigns highlighting stories such as a purported (but false) upsurge in crime, or immigration, or cases of welfare fraud, problems relating to particular ethnic groups, and so on.

III   Giving weight to flexibility

Flexibility is required because of the need to adjust to unforeseen circumstances. This basic insight generates a corresponding meta-principle that underlies the function of the principle of flexibility: the greater the uncertainty in a given scenario, the more flexibility will play an important role. This principle applies in two ways: the state ought to remain flexible in respect of uncertain future events, and the court ought to ensure that it does not itself contribute unduly to that inflexibility. This section explores the ways in which, in my view, courts could give weight to flexibility in the course of social rights adjudication.

A   *The perils of procedural rights*

Legally enforced procedural rights seem like the perfect solution to the problems of inflexibility. They appear to reserve the lion's share of agenda control for the primary decision-maker, and they have a congenial fit with the influential philosophy of deliberative democracy. I do in fact think that, generally speaking, courts have an institutional competence in the area of procedural rights and that procedural remedies can be a proportionate response to the need for flexibility. However, procedural solutions are not a panacea and the problems with treating them as such become evident upon examination of some experiences detailed below.

1   Interest representation in administrative policy-making

The dangers of ossification have already been explored above in connection with the problem of delay. But what dangers lurk more generally in a general attitude that participation in decision-making ought to be one of the chief ends secured by public law? Some of its dangers were catalogued by Richard Stewart in his seminal article 'The Reformation of American Administrative Law',[44] which, though now dated, contains enough important insights to warrant careful consideration.

The chief goal of the article was to examine how American administrative law attempted to deal with the perceived problems of the growing power of agencies over property, and the failure by agencies to carry out their legislative mandates, chiefly because they are unduly influenced or 'captured' by the entities they regulate. He examined various solutions in law and politics, but his primary aim was to outline and critique the 'interest-representation model' that had been developing in American administrative law during that period. At its core, the model sought to promote participation by expanding rights of standing and intervention, and even by extending rights to force the initiation of agency proceedings. Stewart documents a range of significant problems with this approach, including how to determine what constitutes the public interest.[45] The costs of this interest representation process would include delay; the derivation of informal bargaining power by regulated entities or interest groups due to the agency costs associated with delay; that lawyers may discourage settlement possibilities; and that the process, becoming increasingly multi-partied, moves away from a tractable legal dispute and towards a forum for the balancing of political claims.[46] This is tied – given Stewart's leanings towards the legal process school of jurisprudence – to concerns that have already been covered: '[b]y emphasising the polycentric character of controversies, expanded representation may decrease their tractability to general rules and exacerbate the ad hoc, discretionary character of their resolution.'[47] He further explores the difficulty with which the idea of 'adequate consideration' of an interest can function as a dangerous standard: here judges 'can almost always find some aspect of the controversy that has been overlooked or some contention that arguably has not been given its due'.[48]

Carol Harlow expresses a quite similar critique of the increase of interventions and relaxation of the rules of standing in English administrative law.[49] Her essential claim is that legal process is essentially bipolar – a zero-sum contest between two self-interested parties. Movements that

---

[44] R. Stewart, 'The Reformation of American Administrative Law' (1975) 88 *Harvard Law Review* 1669.

[45] *Ibid.*, 1762–70. For a development of the last point in particular, see 1777–81. I respond to some of these arguments in Chapter 7, section V.D.

[46] *Ibid.*, 1771–2.   [47] *Ibid.*, 1777.   [48] *Ibid.*, 1782.

[49] C. Harlow, 'Public Law and Popular Justice' (2002) 65 *Modern Law Review* 1.

subvert that essential relationship undermine the key values of the legal process: certainty, finality, and independence. Without these values properly respected, the court will lose its legitimacy. She asserts this as the key difference between law and politics. She compares politics to a freeway to which all should have access. Law is a rather more formal discipline in which people present proofs and reasoned arguments for a decision in their favour.

Both authors marshal considerable evidence to show that these risks are not chimerical. I have already explained both why neither the ossification thesis nor expanded rights of intervention are as alarming for the present project as these articles suggest. But more fundamentally, I think that the analyses offered by Stewart and Harlow both suffer from an unduly legal process-oriented understanding of adjudication. One problem is the erroneous assumption that courts are chiefly a forum of principle and reason, and that traditional adversarial litigation is chiefly bipolar. As I showed in the discussion of polycentricity, questions of principle in court have wide-ranging ramifications for other people and this was the impetus for expanded rights in the first place. To privilege the status quo is to ignore the actual third-party impact in favour of the formalist view that principle settles matters in objective and determinate ways. Stewart was well aware that to revert to the status quo ante was simply to continue giving regulated entities disproportionate impact on policy formation both in and out of courts. The second problem with this approach is the compartmentalised view of institutional roles, common both to functionalism (Harlow) and legal process (Stewart). The authors repeatedly claim that courts will become a surrogate political forum. But they *are* political in a sense, and it is alarming to suggest otherwise. The entire common law system relies on courts to decide entire areas of policy on contractual relations, tortious wrongs, property, business relations – not to mention our systems of public law. Parliament often even *relies* on courts to carry out legal reforms or clarifications. Therefore, limiting rights of access means limiting the information available to the court, and participation of groups in the legal policy or law-making process.

There presently appears to be little concrete evidence that expanded interest representation has been problematic in Britain or elsewhere in the Commonwealth. And the claim that expanded interest representation causes courts to lose their legitimacy seems particularly off – there is to my knowledge no evidence of this occurring in Canada since the adoption of its Charter of Rights, and neither has there been any in South Africa. And after over ten years of public interest standing in Britain, it seems that the cases brought thus far have for the most part represented important affirmations (or attempted affirmations) of the rule of law that would otherwise have been unaccountable uses or abuses of power, in many cases for the benefit of vulnerable groups.

This rebuttal does not mean, however, that expanded, unchecked interest representation does not pose some of the threats outlined by Harlow and Stewart. If participation rights were viewed as harmless, the problems would become acute. In this respect, Martin Shapiro is perhaps on better ground when he explains the insidious slide from simple process rights such as rights to reasons, to full blown substantive review of administrative discretion.[50] His illustration of this phenomenon in the jurisprudence of the European Court of Justice is particularly telling. A state duty to give reasons gradually progresses to an individual right to state a defence, and then to a duty of administrative care, and then to a dialogue requirement that involves some agency response to concerns put forward, and even, in one case, to a requirement that the European Commission respond to a claim that a party *might* have put forward if it knew of the proposed action.[51] The courts have rejected a 'strong-dialogue' requirement thus far – apparently due to awareness of the American ossification precedent – but Shapiro is concerned that the tide is swelling, and the levee about to break.

The critiques here can at times border on impressionistic, with the tenor cautioning concern that the law is travelling in a problematic direction. But one often searches in vain for a concrete solution. The need for a cautious, subtle final position emerges at a much less discussed portion of Stewart's monolithic article. He concedes at the very end that the search for a unified theory of administrative law is perhaps untenable, and that:

> the interest representation principle could be viewed, not as a general model for dealing with agency discretion, but as a technique for dealing with specific problems of administrative justice … Occasional judicial resort to … expanded participation rights in order to focus attention on 'underrepresented' interests could be acceptable as a limited part of a more general effort to redress deficiencies in contemporary agency performance … Reliance on judges and public interest litigants to rectify the perceived failings of our administrative system may be indispensable

---

[50] M. Shapiro, 'The Institutionalization of European Administrative Space', in A. S. Sweet, W. Sandholtz, and N. Fliegstein (eds.), *The Institutionalization of Europe* (Oxford University Press, 2001), pp. 94–112.

[51] Shapiro, 'Judicial Review and Bureaucratic Impact', p. 108 discussing *Commission* v. *Sytraval* [1998] ECR I-1719 (ECJ).

> if unorganized interests are to enjoy an acceptable measure of recognition ... [A] central problem becomes how to determine the occasions on which selective judicial effort to promote consideration of ... affected interests should be applied.[52]

Stewart was unwilling to accept the more sweeping implication of his own critique. He realised how important interest representation can be for the poor and marginalised, a point he reaffirms by suggesting that the tasks and policies in welfare administration may call for a different judicial response than those in the regulation of the airways.[53] The more constructive task, which he left unfinished in that article, is what this book seeks to carry out.

2   Trial-like rights in administrative decision-making

The idea of social rights immediately conjures a notion of challenging the way in which housing, social security, health, or education benefits are given or denied to people. However, decisions about what procedures people are entitled to in such situations raise particular problems. In *Begum (Runa)* v. *Tower Hamlets* a majority of the House of Lords was prepared to accept for the sake of argument that certain rights in respect of duties to accommodate the homeless were civil rights within the meaning of Art. 6(1) of the European Convention on Human Rights (ECHR).[54] The more difficult issue was whether Art. 6(1) required a full, judicial-type trial in cases where a person contests a local authority's findings of fact. Runa Begum refused the local authority's offer of accommodation, claiming the area in which it was located was rife with drug use and racism, and that the building was located near her estranged, potentially dangerous husband. Her refusal to accept the accommodation led the Council to deem her as being 'intentionally homeless', and thus not entitled to council housing. This determination was completed internally, and since there was no appeal to a court or tribunal, the factual dimensions of the dispute were regarded as final. The Court of Appeal agreed with Runa Begum that she was entitled under Art. 6(1) to more than internal review by the local

---

[52] Stewart, 'The Reformation of American Administrative Law', 1807–9.

[53] *Ibid.*, 1810.

[54] *Begum (Runa)* v. *Tower Hamlets* [2003] UKHL 5. The Supreme Court (which assumed the judicial functions of the Judicial Committee of the House of Lords in 2009) later, regrettably in my view, rejected that contention and shut the door firmly against such claims in *Ali* v. *Birmingham City Council* [2010] UKSC 8. Shutting the door in this way is not an incrementalist response in my view, and the case is inconsistent with the tenor of *Tsfayo* v. *United Kingdom* [2006] All ER (D) 177.

authority, and held that the local authority could comply with this obligation by engaging an independent fact-finder.[55] However, the House of Lords unanimously allowed the Council's appeal. In the leading speech, Lord Hoffmann found that following the decision of the European Court of Human Rights (ECtHR) in *Bryan* v. *United Kingdom*,[56] an independent and impartial determination would be satisfied by a composite procedure consisting of an administrative decision and the availability of judicial review. The procedure must allow for full 'jurisdiction to deal with the case as the nature of the decision requires'.[57] It is of interest that scholars working closely on homelessness and adjudication thought the House of Lords case was rightly decided. Ian Loveland, for example, argued after the Court of Appeal case that the House of Lords should not endorse the Court of Appeal's finding as it would impede access to justice, and Parliament's clearly expressed view that factual determinations remain with the local authority.[58]

Part of the answer lies in the fact that such authors, in addition to having conducted their own careful studies of homelessness allocations in individual housing authorities, are aware of the American experience on this topic. Charles Reich advanced the influential thesis that government largesse – the system of public benefits, licences and so on – is a form of 'new property' over which, in the modern bureaucratic state, individuals ought to be regarded as having constitutional due process rights.[59] It was one of the leading theses of an active period of welfare rights advocacy in various forms in US Constitutional law.[60] The Supreme Court adopted the spirit of Reich's thesis in the seminal *Goldberg* v. *Kelly* case,[61] in which it ruled that a person is entitled to a full judicial hearing before being deprived of his or her welfare benefits. The previous regime of notice to the claimant and entitlement to submit written comments was held unconstitutional. The expanded rights would include the opportunity to

---

[55] [2002] 1 WLR 2491 (CA).   [56] (1996) 21 EHRR 342.

[57] *Begum* v. *Tower Hamlets* [2002] 1 WLR 249, [37].

[58] I. Loveland, 'Does Homelessness Decision-Making Engage Article 6(1) of the European Convention on Human Rights' (2003) 2 *European Human Rights Law Review* 177. See also I. Loveland, *Housing Homeless Persons* (Oxford: Clarendon Press, 1995). Simon Halliday's similar view was confirmed to me in conversation: see also S. Halliday, *Judicial Review and Compliance with Administrative Law* (Oxford: Hart Publishing, 2004).

[59] C. Reich, 'The New Property' (1964) 73 *Yale Law Journal* 733.

[60] F. I. Michelman, 'Foreword: On Protecting the Poor through the Fourteenth Amendment' (1968) 83 *Harvard Law Review* 7.

[61] 397 US 254 (1970).

cross-examine any witnesses the government relied upon. Notably, the payments that the agency proposed to discontinue would need to continue until such time as the hearing took place and decision was rendered. Six years later, a differently constituted Court found in *Mathews* v. *Eldridge*[62] that the termination of social security disability benefits did not require such stringent procedural requirements. It distinguished *Goldberg* v. *Kelly* on grounds that the position of individuals in the case of welfare was more immediately desperate than that of those on disability benefits. It also introduced a 'balancing test' that became the new standard in due process jurisprudence:

> [T]he identification of the specific dictates of due process generally requires consideration of three distinct factors: First, the private interest that will be affected by the official action; second, the risk of erroneous deprivation of such interest through the procedures used, and the probable value, if any, of additional or substitute procedural safeguards; and finally, the Government's interest, including the function involved and the fiscal and administrative burdens that the additional or substitute procedural requirement would entail.[63]

In *Due Process in the Administrative State*, Jerry Mashaw compiled a withering set of criticisms of both decisions.[64] Of *Goldberg*, he finds the outcome completely wrong. At one point he argued that the Court vastly overestimated the capacity of the bureaucracy to run a hearings system.[65] (However, this claim seems belied – but perhaps only out of pure luck – by the fact that the administration itself had proposed to adopt an even more cumbersome set of procedures.[66]) Of *Mathews* v. *Eldridge*, however, he was extremely critical of the informational needs posed by the balancing test: 'the model of competence has an enormous appetite for data that is disputable, unknown, and sometimes, unknowable.'[67] Mashaw's model of a just, humane, and efficient welfare administration is found in the Veterans Administration, an institution that excludes judicial review in its entirety.[68]

Mashaw does not advocate a total withdrawal of judicial review and process rights. He rather advocated the elimination of an interest-balancing

---

[62] 424 US 319 (1976).   [63] *Ibid.*, 334–5.
[64] J. L. Mashaw, *Due Process in the Administrative State* (New Haven: Yale University Press, 1985), pp. 99–101, 166 (Goldberg); Chapter 3 (Eldridge and Goldberg).
[65] J. L. Mashaw, 'The Management Side of Due Process' (1974) 59 *Cornell Law Review* 772.
[66] As Mashaw himself notes in *Due Process in the Administrative State*, p. 260.
[67] *Ibid.*, p. 115.
[68] *Ibid.*, pp. 264–5. See, however, pp. 212–15 on defending welfare entitlements.

test, and the substitution of a dignitarian values thesis that would require a very thin modicum of consistency and fairness. Above all, he advocated the use of common law rather than constitutional remedies. His stated his main concern thus:

> My aversion to constitutionalizing participation in administrative process … is not based primarily on the fear that constitutionalization may stop innovation that would promote participatory values. It seems to me more likely that the greater danger lies in the opposite direction; that judicial creativity in a constitutional mode will promote and generalize innovations that turn out to be dysfunctional. Promoting participation through structural design is tricky business. Many experiments will require anything from minor modification to complete abandonment.[69]

This reinforces the concern of this chapter. If we accept his concern as valid (and few have studied the question in America as closely as he has), then the question becomes whether we can adopt a mode of constitutional adjudication that does largely preserve this latitude for adjustment. The approach set out below is one that in my view can.

3   Structural injunctions and supervisory jurisdiction

Structural injunctions that command public authorities to carry out institutional reform have been a prominent feature of both American[70] and Indian[71] public law litigation. This is a common option, in particular, when there are positive obligations to reform institutions. In the American model, the judge can appoint an official, typically called a master, to mediate and supervise negotiations between the parties, guiding them towards a jointly agreed solution, and advising the court

---

[69] *Ibid.*, p. 261.

[70] See C. Diver, 'The Judge as Political Powerbroker: Superintending Structural Change in Public Institutions' (1979) 65 *Virginia Law Review* 43; J. Resnik, 'Managerial Judges' (1982) 96 *Harvard Law Review* 374; M. Feeley and E. Rubin, *Judicial Policy Making in the Modern State: How the Courts Reformed America's Prisons* (Cambridge University Press, 2000); C. F. Sabel and W. H. Simon, 'Destabilization Rights: How Public Law Litigation Succeeds' (2004) 117 *Harvard Law Review* 1016.

[71] U. Baxi, 'The Avatars of Indian Judicial Activism', in S. K. Verma and S. K. Kusum (eds.), *Fifty Years of the Supreme Court of India: Its Grasp and Reach* (New Delhi: Oxford University Press, 2000); A. Desai and S. Muralidhar, 'Public Interest Litigation: Potential and Problems', in B. Kirpal (ed.), *Supreme But Not Infallible: Essays in Honour of the Supreme Court of India* (New Delhi: Oxford University Press, 2000); P. Singh, 'Promises and Perils of Public Interest Litigation in Protecting the Rights of the Poor and the Oppressed' (2005) 27 *Delhi Law Review* 8; S. Fredman, *Human Rights Transformed: Positive Rights and Positive Duties* (Oxford University Press, 2008), Chapter 5.

on how to proceed when no solution is forthcoming. The claimants and respondent authorities often do come to agreement on how the institution should be run, and the court will enter a consent decree turning such agreement into a binding public law obligation. The option seems like a clear solution to the need for flexibility and expertise, as well as providing the clear possibility for experimentation. A similar practice prevails in India, though there the courts are empowered to commence investigations on their own initiative, and they may also appoint their own experts who will conduct fact-finding exercises in complex factual scenarios.

However, there are a number of problems and issues that these remedial approaches create. A number of the more serious ones are collected in a book called *Democracy by Decree* by Ross Sandler and David Schoenbrod, both of whom were engaged in such litigation for the Natural Resources Defence Council in the 1970s.[72] These include: (a) lack of broad democratic or popular control over the process; (b) the potential for domination of a bureaucracy by private litigants; (c) manipulation of policy within the bureaucracy itself; (d) long-term management of a public institution by courts and litigants (many injunctions in the USA last over twenty years and comprise twenty or more court hearings);[73] (e) protracted issues of policy resolved through managerial techniques in courts. The evidence suggests a very ambivalent record when looked at on the whole, though the authors themselves propose a reform of rather than elimination of structural reform litigation.[74] The Indian experience has also garnered a mixture of optimism and scepticism by supporters of social human rights.[75]

The clash between such an approach and English legal culture seems radical, a claim underscored by the controversial nature of the *M* v. *Home Office* case, where a Home Secretary was ordered to return a detainee he had removed to Zaire in defiance of a court order.[76] The House of Lords, in a lengthy judgment, found that injunctions of that sort could lie against the Crown, and did in that case. Given how exercised the courts were

---

[72] R. Sandler and D. Schoenbrod, *Democracy by Decree* (New Haven: Yale University Press, 2003); cf. the review by S. Rose-Ackerman, Review of R. Sandler and D. Schoenbrod, *Democracy by Decree* (2003) 118 *Political Science Quarterly* 679–81.

[73] Sandler and Schoenbrod, *Democracy by Decree*, Chapter 9.

[74] *Ibid.*, 198 (for a tidy summary of their proposals).

[75] See works cited in note 72 above, where most authors are somewhat ambivalent, though none condemn the practice.

[76] *M* v. *Home Office* [1994] 1 AC 377. The case also confirmed that contempt proceedings could lie against ministers in their official (though not private) capacities.

over the issue, and the substantive gulf between recalling a deportee and engaging in full-scale structural reform, the issue of cultural fit is obvious enough.

Yet culture can change, and the prescriptions of this book are not intended only for the UK. Given the similarities between British and Canadian legal cultures, the recent experience in Canada is relevant. The Canadian judiciary has historically been very reluctant to recognise supervisory jurisdiction, precisely because of the American experience.[77] Yet in *Doucet-Boudreau*, a bare majority of the Supreme Court for the first time accepted supervisory jurisdiction, over the stringent objections of the minority.[78] In that case a trial judge ruled that the province of Nova Scotia had failed to implement its obligation under s. 23 of the Constitution, which obliges the province to provide minority language schooling when the numbers of eligible children are 'sufficient to warrant' it. It was common ground in the case that s. 23 had been breached. The issue on appeal was whether the trial judge had erred by issuing a vague order (that the province must use 'best efforts'), and more importantly, by retaining a jurisdiction of unspecified duration and requiring the affected parties to report back to the court on progress made. The dissent found that, among other things, the remedy of contempt of court would have provided an adequate remedy for non-compliance in such circumstances, and that the case unnecessarily raised complications with the separation of powers. The case illustrates how even mild supervisory jurisdiction in a case with a clear history of non-compliance prompted strong divisions.

In the *Treatment Action Campaign* case, the Constitutional Court of South Africa formally recognised the possibility of supervisory jurisdiction (what it calls 'structural interdicts'), but declined in that case to issue one.[79] In the *Modderklip* litigation, it did not disturb the Supreme Court of Appeal's criticism of the trial judge's use of supervisory jurisdiction, a criticism that came close to attacking the very idea of it.[80] Yet in *Occupiers*

---

[77] See A. Klein, 'Judging as Nudging: New Governance Approaches for the Enforcement of Constitutional Social and Economic Rights' (2008) 39 *Columbia Human Rights Law Review* 351, 386.

[78] *Doucet-Boudreau* v. *Nova Scotia (Minister of Education)* [2003] 3 SCR 3. See analysis in K. Roach, *Constitutional Remedies in Canada* (Aurora: Canada Law Book, 1994) (suppl. 2001), Chapter 13 and esp. 13.851.

[79] *Minister of Health and Others* v. *Treatment Action Campaign and Others* (*TAC* case), 2002 (10) BCLR 1033 (CC) [107]–[112].

[80] *Modderfontein Squatters, Greater Benoni City Council* v. *Modderklip Boerdery (Pty) Ltd.* (*Agri SA and Legal Resources Centre, amici curiae)*; 2004 (6) SA 40 (SCA) [40] ('Structural interdicts [tend] to blur the distinction between the executive and the judiciary'); cf.

of 51 Olivia Road, the court for the first time 'endorsed'[81] an agreement negotiated between the occupiers and the City of Johannesburg that was meant to give effect to the state's duty, which was established at the Constitutional Court hearing, to engage meaningfully with the occupiers. The judgment came out after the agreement was endorsed. This is tantamount to the 'consent decree' in American litigation,[82] as non-compliance with it would presumably constitute contempt of court.

The obvious concern with this approach is that it is one thing to impose a duty of meaningful engagement on the parties as a general standard of conduct. It is another to require the court, in any given case, to micro-manage and approve each step of the process, and issue rulings that would be appealable to the Constitutional Court in each case. When the Court did make stronger use of this remedy, by issuing an order in the *Joe Slovo* case that specified a timeline for compliance and reporting procedure,[83] the political circumstances changed such that the eviction order would no longer be carried out and the Court had to quietly issue a fresh judgment 'suspending' the effect of its earlier one.[84] Although it is difficult to state a confident view from afar, it would appear in such cases that the better approach is to forego the retention of jurisdiction but be prepared to employ strong remedies, including damages, when a bureaucracy fails to negotiate with the claimants in good faith. A duty to negotiate in good faith is a clearly justiciable standard. Christopher Mbazira examines the issue carefully and states a cautious approach that endorses their use but only as a remedy of last resort.[85] I for the most part agree with his analysis.

The propriety of this remedy is difficult to state in the abstract, as the question depends greatly on context. It is possible, nonetheless, to make some generalisations. The first is that the evidence of the efficacy and propriety of the remedy in India and the United States is distinctly mixed.

President of the Republic of South Africa and Another v. *Modderklip Boerdery (Pty) Ltd.*, 2005 (5) SA 3 (CC).

[81] *Occupiers of 51 Olivia Rd* v. *City of Johannesburg*, 2008 (3) SA 208 (CC) [24]–[30].

[82] See Sandler and Schoenbrod, *Democracy by Decree*, Chapter 3.

[83] *Residents of the Joe Slovo Community* v. *Thubelisha Homes and Others*, 2010 (3) SA 454 (CC) [7].

[84] See the complete discussion in K. McLean, 'Meaningful Engagement: One Step Forward, Two Steps Back' (2010) 3 *Constitutional Court Review* 1.

[85] C. Mbazira, *Litigating Socio-Economic Rights in South Africa: A Choice between Corrective and Distributive Justice* (Pretoria University Law Press, 2009), Chapter 6. Similarly, see K. Roach and G. Budlender, 'Mandatory Relief and Supervisory Jurisdiction: When Is It Appropriate, Just and Equitable?' (2005) 122 *South African Law Journal* 325.

Second, the case for the remedy is most clear where there is a patent breakdown in the principle of inter-institutional collaboration; that is, where the state appears to be acting in bad faith by doing nothing or dragging its feet. Charles Sabel and William Simon, for example, aim their theory at situations involving 'public institutions that have chronically failed to meet their obligations and that are substantially insulated from the normal processes of political accountability'.[86] The case for using the remedy is at its very best when the state patently disregards clear constitutional norms, as in the desegregation and prison reform litigation. The rule of law demands supervisory jurisdiction in such cases. But those cases are not the norm in countries that observe the principle of inter-institutional collaboration. Third, it may be said that when deployed well, structural injunctions in fact lead to a coordination process that is distinctly incrementalist in nature. This is the driving conclusion of Feeley and Rubin in their investigation of prison reform litigation, and it is the tenor of the recommendations made by Sandler and Schoenbrod, as well as Michael Dorf and Charles Sabel.[87] It must be said, though, contrary to Feeley and Rubin, that the outcome of such cases is not always incrementalist in the sense used in this book. Allocative impact can be very substantial.[88] That is why the most that can be said for them here is that they indeed ought to remain a remedy of the very last resort, when the state has patently and chronically ignored its constitutional or other legal obligations, rather than be seen as a panacea for institutional competence problems.

B   Mandating flexibility

Judges can counteract bureaucratic or legislative inflexibility by using legal techniques to require that greater flexibility be observed.

1   Procedural rights

Having explored some of the pitfalls of procedural rights above, we cannot forget their promise. Procedural rights will be more appropriate when

---

[86] Sabel and Simon, 'Destabilization Rights', 1015.
[87] Sandler and Schoenbrod, *Democracy by Decree,* p. 198; Feeley and Rubin, *Judicial Policy Making in the Modern State*, pp. 233–7, 262–3, Chapter 7, pp. 351ff.; and Dorf and Sabel as discussed in Chapter 10, section IV.B.
[88] See *Campaign for Fiscal Equity* v. *State of New York*, 86 N.Y.2d 306 (1995) (confirming that the litigation overall would generate an *annual* allocative impact of $1.93 billion, as this was the 'spending gap'). Many other school finance cases have similarly large levels of allocative impact.

applied in respect of particular, relatively infrequent decisions, or to a general decision-making process where the additional burden is not significant in relation to the process already in place.

A clue to the sustainability of a particular procedural right might appear where another non-adjudicative oversight body has itself recommended the option, as in the case of *Tsfayo* v. *United Kingdom*.[89] The European Court of Human Rights held that the decision of a local authority's Housing Benefit Review Board that the claimant did not have good cause for the late submission of her housing benefit renewal form violated her Art. 6 right to a determination of her civil rights by an independent and impartial tribunal. Elected members of the Fulham Council, also responsible for budgeting, sat on the Board, which was established to determine chiefly factual questions. A distinctive fact in that case was that the Council on Tribunals, an oversight body designed to supervise the tribunals and administrative justice system more generally, had recommended the abolishment of the system in its reports every year for a decade.[90]

A more borderline example in the social rights context may be found in the South African *Occupiers of 51 Olivia Road* case. In that case, the Constitutional Court found that the City of Johannesburg had failed to 'engage meaningfully' with about 400 occupiers of buildings that the city considered unsafe and unhealthy. Yacoob J, for the Court, outlined some of the factors the state must consider to discharge a duty of meaningful engagement:

(a) what the consequences of the eviction might be;
(b) whether the city could help in alleviating those dire consequences;
(c) whether it was possible to render the buildings concerned relatively safe and conducive to health for an interim period;
(d) whether the city had any obligations to the occupiers in the prevailing circumstances; and
(e) when and how the city could or would fulfil these obligations.[91]

These criteria are not on their face particularly onerous, and the Court found in that case there was no attempt to engage at all with the occupiers. The Court stressed how the duty must be tailored to the needs of vulnerable groups, and on concern for their dignity and precarious situation. Yet it also emphasised the importance of flexibility: 'It may in some

---

[89] *Tsfayo* v. *United Kingdom* [2006] All ER (D) 177.
[90] *Ibid.*, [34].
[91] *Occupiers of 51 Olivia Rd* [14].

circumstances be reasonable to make permanent housing available and, in others, to provide no housing at all. The possibilities between these extremes are almost endless.'[92] However, the possibility of the duty being burdensome remained a live issue:

> It has been suggested that there are around 67,000 people living in the inner city of Johannesburg in unsafe and unhealthy buildings in relation to whom ejectment orders will have to be issued and that it would be impractical to expect meaningful engagement in every case. I cannot agree. It is common cause that the implementation of the City's Regeneration Strategy 28 is an important reason that founded the decision to evict. That strategy was adopted in 2003. If structures had been put in place with competent sensitive council workers skilled in engagement, the process could have begun when the strategy was adopted.[93]

It is true that engagement does not have to be extremely time-consuming, but this analysis is very close to the line. While the figure contemplated is minute next to social security or welfare benefits determinations, it is still significant and the terms of meaningful engagement are vague enough to support protracted litigation. Health and safety closures are important not only for the occupiers, but to prevent fire, infestation, and structural damage to other nearby buildings. The key to what makes the judgment work, however, lies in the particular facts on which it is based, which serve as grounds to distinguish it should circumstances be significantly different, and in the *dicta* elsewhere in the judgment clarifying that the state's duty is to act reasonably and in good faith and that the court's role is not to substitute itself for the state in that process.[94]

2 Non-fettering and mandatory consideration

It is a familiar rule in administrative law that a state entrusted with administrative discretion cannot adopt rules that prevent it from considering individual cases on their merits.[95] In the English *Rogers* case, the Court of Appeal found that a policy of funding the drug Herceptin in exceptional cases would be legal only if the authority had some idea of what would constitute an exceptional case.[96] It quashed the decision. The condition had not been met.

---

[92] *Ibid.*, [18]. [93] *Ibid.*, [19].

[94] *Ibid.*, [30] (cases of urgency), [28] (city must respond reasonably to process of engagement), [35].

[95] Craig, *Administrative Law*, 6th edn, pp. 510–21.

[96] *R (on the Application of Anne Marie Rogers)* v. *Swindon NHS Primary Care Trust, Secretary of State for Health* [2006] EWCA Civ 392.

A similar idea is used under human rights law more generally. In the *Ex parte Limbuela* case,[97] the government sought to ban the provision of any support to late-claiming asylum applicants, a policy that rendered such applicants destitute. The House of Lords unanimously found that the policy, which *denied* the very possibility of providing support, amounted to cruel and unusual treatment. The case had a significant impact.[98] Similarly, the Court of Appeal declared certain provisions of housing legislation invalid in *R (Morris)* v. *Westminster City Council*[99] because the provision required the housing authority, when determining whether someone is in 'priority need' for housing, to disregard whether such a person had dependents from abroad. The Court found that the provision discriminated on grounds of national origin, and was not proportionate to the legitimate objective of discouraging benefits tourism. It did not, however, oblige the provision of benefits to them.

The protection afforded in cases of eviction from public housing also led to a protracted litigation saga between the European Court of Human Rights (ECtHR) and the UK courts.[100] Ultimately, the ECtHR made clear that the Art. 8(1) right to protection of the home encompassed a procedural right to have the proportionality of the decision to evict (effected by means of a 'possession order' in the UK) taken into account by a court during the process of decision-making.[101] Early in this litigation saga, the UK courts found that County Courts (lower courts considering simple cases, including possession orders), which consider many such applications, could not consider the question of proportionality of the individual decision. Instead any human rights/proportionality

---

[97] *R* v. *Secretary of State for the Home Department, ex parte Limbuela* [2005] UKHL 66.

[98] A. Donald, E. Mottershaw1, P. Leach, and J. Watson, 'Evaluating the Impact of Selected Cases under the Human Rights Act on Public Services Provision', Report of the Equality and Human Rights Commission, June 2009, 65–77, 143, available at: www.equalityhumanrights.com/uploaded_files/evaluating_the_impact_of_selected_cases_under_the_human_rights_act_on_public_services_provision.pdf.

[99] [2005] EWCA Civ 1184.

[100] Omitting some detail, the key cases are *Chapman* v. *United Kingdom* (2001) 33 EHRR 399; *Connors* v. *United Kingdom* (2005) 40 EHRR 9, [84]; *Kay and others* v. *Lambeth LBC* [2006] UKHL 10; *McCann* v. *United Kingdom* [2008] 2 FLR 899 (adopting the dissenting judgment of Lord Bingham (Lords Walker and Nicholls concurring) in *Kay*, summarised at [39]); *Doherty* v. *Birmingham City* [2008] 3 WLR 636; *Kay* v. *United Kingdom* (App. No. 37341/06) [2010] ECHR 1322; and now *Manchester City Council* v. *Pinnock* [2010] UKSC 45 states the applicable law at the time of writing in a manner that is harmonious with Strasbourg authority.

[101] *McCann* v. *UK*.

challenge had to be directed at the underlying Act of Parliament itself, and thus taken to the High Court by way of an application for judicial review.[102] The effect was to increase the burden on applicants and deprive them of the possibility of raising the claim in individual cases. It also encouraged challenges to the statute, rather than keeping the disputes fact-specific and contextual, to be considered by the judge who was accustomed to considering factual and other circumstances before issuing possession orders. The ECtHR adopted the dissenting judge's reasoning in one of the UK cases, and found that the proportionality issue must be considered in individual cases.[103] This approach mandated flexibility in a manner where there was good reason to believe the solution was administratively workable.

Legislation is often used in an attempt to constrict the beneficial exercise of discretion by administrative decision-makers. A brutal example is the American welfare reform law, the Personal Responsibility and Work Opportunity Reconciliation Act of 1996, which replaced the Aid to Families with Dependent Children Act (AFDC) and instituted Temporary Assistance for Needy Families (TANF).[104] It limited the lifetime amount of benefits that could be claimed to 5 years/60 months. Such an inflexible rule is straightforwardly incompatible with the very idea of social rights and the need for flexibility. A similarly important example of welfare reform was examined by the German Constitutional Court in the *Hartz IV* case,[105] where it found aspects of the reform to be unconstitutional. The reform merged long-term unemployment assistance benefits with social assistance benefits, by replacing both with a single, means-tested basic provision for employable persons and those living with them. It established a standard monthly benefit level for long-term employable people of €345 (the 'Standard Benefit'), together with some social allowance for family dependents such as children. The reform was made by way of the introduction of a new Second Book of the Social Code. The case represents a macro-level resource allocation and law reform case par excellence, and the incrementalist theory in this book must confront it with some trepidation. Importantly, however, the effect of the Court's judgment was not

---

[102] *Kay and others* v. *Lambeth LBC; Leeds City Council* v. *Price and others* [2006] UKHL 10.

[103] *McCann* v. *United Kingdom* [2008] 2 FLR 899.

[104] 42 USC §§ 601–619 (1997); 42 USC § 602 (1935) (AFDC).

[105] BVerfG, 1 BvL 1/09 (9 February 2010). An official English translation with identical paragraph references to the German original is available on the website of the Constitutional Court.

to stop the Hartz reform, so much as condition the way in which it took place.

There were three important holdings in the case. First, the Court declared the Standard Benefit to be unconstitutional. The general statistical approach taken by reference to a survey conducted in 1998 was in basic outline unobjectionable.[106] However, (a) certain reductions in the benefit were based on the (understandable) view that certain goods (furs, tailored clothes) were not necessary, but without determining that the lowest quintile of the relevant income group actually incurs expenditure on such items; and (b) the formula used to up-rate the benefits from the 1998 figures to 2005 were based on pension values, which track wages, salaries and other data that is logically unrelated to the subsistence minimum, rather than on factors such as net income, cost of living, and consumer behaviour.[107] Second, the social allowance for children was determined to be 40 per cent of the Standard Benefit. This meant it fell with the unsound Standard Benefit, but the Court also found that the figure was determined entirely without any empirical or methodological foundation, which should have taken into account children's costs of schooling and living. A schooling supplement of €100 per year was likewise held to be determined without any empirical basis.[108] Third, although the Second Book of the Social Code did make provision for the exercise of discretion to extend benefits to those who had a *non-recurring* special need, there was no category for those who had a *recurring* need of some type that was not elsewhere covered but which nonetheless pertained to basic subsistence needs.[109] The Court ordered that there must be some allowance for extension of benefits in such cases.

Notwithstanding the macro-level issue, the remedy effectively preserved flexibility. The outcome of this case is that all the benefits must be recalculated in a more rigorous and careful manner, catering carefully to the basic needs and dignity of those on social assistance benefits. It could be possible, however, that the figures stay the same, or go up somewhat, or even down if in the recalculation it were found that the original figures went beyond the subsistence level emphasised by the Court and the state was feeling stingy. The exception to this description is the order to make provision for recurring special needs that relate to the subsistence minimum. In this case, the state is obliged to introduce both an assessments procedure and to provide a benefit supplement where circumstances call

---

[106] *Hartz IV*, [162].   [107] *Hartz IV*, [173]ff.
[108] *Hartz IV*, [190]ff., [198].   [109] *Hartz IV*, [150]ff.

for it. But those situations will be rare, as they will by definition be those requiring special needs not covered either by the revised Standard Benefit or by any other benefit within the welfare system as a whole (e.g. disability benefit). Given this background, the requirement remains safely incrementalist and the Court was confident in stating that '[i]n view of its narrowly defined, strict prerequisites, this … claim is likely to arise in rare cases only'.[110]

C   Remedies: respecting flexibility

One very good way for judges to respect the principle of flexibility is to make the idea manifest in their holdings. Again, the South African Constitutional Court is an exemplar in this regard. It has gone out of its way to make this clear in *Treatment Action Campaign*:

> A factor that needs to be kept in mind is that policy is and should be flexible. It may be changed at any time and the executive is always free to change policies where it considers it appropriate to do so. The only constraint is that policies must be consistent with the Constitution and the law. Court orders concerning policy choices made by the executive should therefore not be formulated in ways that preclude the executive from making such legitimate choices. [111]

The flexibility requirement became the basis of a constitutional challenge to the City of Johannesburg's water policy in *Mazibuko v City of Johannesburg*.[112] In Mazibuko, O'Regan J rejected the claim that the government's water allocation policy, which limited free access to six kilolitres a month, was constitutionally unsound due to inflexibility.[113]

Beyond overt recognition of the need for flexibility, there are a number of more specific doctrines that help to preserve flexibility.

1   Constitutional avoidance

Where a claim may succeed on constitutional or non-constitutional grounds (which typically means choosing statutory interpretation or administrative law instead of constitutional remedies), the court should, under circumstances of serious uncertainty, prefer the non-constitutional remedy. I observed in Chapter 6 that there may also be

---

[110] *Hartz IV*, [208].
[111] See the *TAC* case, [114]; see also [68] (quoting *Republic of South Africa* v. *Grootboom*, 2000 (11) BCLR 1169 (CC), [43]).
[112] *Mazibuko and Others* v. *City of Johannesburg and Others* 2010 (4) SA 1 (CC).
[113] *Ibid.*, [90]–[97].

ways to resolve cases that do plainly involve human rights by preserving the possibility of legislative revisitation, including at times through a presumption that statutes are to be read consistently with human rights. Such an approach, if applied properly,[114] preserves flexibility in case the remedy turns out to be problematic. There is nothing novel in this suggestion. There is a virtual sub-genre of literature and case law on the merits of what has been called 'constitutional avoidance'.[115] One might argue that the use of constitutional avoidance limits the expressive and broader enforcement potential available under constitutional adjudication. But while expressiveness may be important, its value compares poorly with the concrete harms identified in section II above. And as to enforcement, it is not always or even normally the case that statutory interpretation or common law rights have less impact than constitutionally declared rights, where both are available. Chapter 3 did nothing if not suggest humility on the expected impact of rights adjudication. Nonetheless, the consequences of avoidance itself must be weighed against the potential implications of uncertainty. It may result in a protracted round of litigation, or leave claimants in a great deal of legal uncertainty as to the scope of their rights. These are the negative factors that weigh against the choice, and which must be considered and weighed alongside the potential harms of a ruling that leaves less flexibility to adjust to unforeseen circumstances.

2   Vague legal standards

Vague legal standards such as 'negotiate in good faith',[116] 'with all deliberate speed',[117] 'reasonableness',[118] 'good faith',[119] 'reasonable adjustment',[120]

---

[114] See Chapter 6, sections IV.A–B.

[115] See *Ashwander* v. *Tennessee Valley Authority*, 297 US 288, 347ff. (1936) (Justice Brandeis setting down the basic tenets of the view); A. Bickel, *The Least Dangerous Branch: Supreme Court at the Bar of Politics* (New Haven: Yale University Press, 1986), Chapter 4; L. A. Kloppenberg, 'Avoiding Constitutional Questions' (1994) 35 *Boston College Law Review* 1003; F. Schauer, '*Ashwander* Revisited' (1995) *Supreme Court Review* 177; C. R. Sunstein, 'Foreword: Leaving Things Undecided' (1995) 110 *Harvard Law Review* 6, 87–8.

[116] *Reference re Secession of Quebec* [1998] 2 SCR 217 (SCC).

[117] *Brown* v. *Board of Education* (*Brown II*) 349 US 294 (1955).

[118] *Republic of South Africa* v. *Grootboom*, 2000 (11) BCLR 1169 (CC). The term is of course also famously used in administrative law, tort law, and disability discrimination law.

[119] R. Zimmermann and S. Whittaker, *Good Faith in European Contract Law* (The Common Core of European Private Law) (Cambridge University Press, 2008).

[120] *Archibald* v. *Fife Council* [2004] UKHL 32 (Lady Hale, interpreting the concept in the Disability Discrimination Act 1995).

'due diligence',[121] 'fairness',[122] 'responsible journalism',[123] and 'meaningful engagement'[124] can be used by judges to maintain flexibility while retaining jurisdiction to intervene in disputes involving the future application of such a standard. The ambiguity of the terms, depending on how they are interpreted, can give both judges and the executive and legislature the interpretive latitude required to make future adjustments. This is the natural position of the English judge in administrative law, as noted by Michael Fordham: '[j]udicial review courts have an aversion to hard and fast rules. They prefer to formulate principles which have an in-built capacity to accommodate the context and circumstances of any given case.'[125] These 'flexi-principles', as he calls them, abound in administrative law.

One may well fear that such standards would invite substantial judicial intrusion into legislative and bureaucratic decision-making. However, if one observes how they are actually used in constitutional and administrative law in the United Kingdom, one can see that they ordinarily are applied in a manner that allows a substantial margin of discretion for the primary decision-makers. Such terms are used quite commonly in litigation. Where more guidance is required, judges may add factors that are relevant to the understanding of such terms, typically noting that such additional factors are non-exhaustive.[126] Such standards, both the vague legal standards and open-ended lists of factors, are used to balance the benefits of jurisdictional control with the need for flexibility and the preservation of the policy-making and standard-setting competency of the primary decision-makers.

3   Flexible remedies and the virtue of silence

Judicial remedies can specify to a greater or lesser degree in a holding what must be done to bring a statute or decision-making process into

---

[121] R. P. Barnidge, 'The Due Diligence Principle under International Law' (2006) *International Community Law Review* 81; *Escott* v. *BarChris Construction Corporation*, 283 F Supp 643 (SDNY 1968) (requiring demonstration of due diligence to establish there was no 'reasonable ground to believe' that there was a material omission or misstatement in a securities registration statement within the meaning of 11(b)(3)(C) of the Securities Act 1933, 15 USC § 77 (k) (1964).

[122] *R* v. *Secretary of State for the Home Department, ex parte Doody* [1994] AC 531 (HL); s. 98(4) Employment Rights Act 1996 (unfair dismissal).

[123] *Jameel* v. *Wall Street Journal Europe Ltd* [2006] UKHL 44.

[124] *Occupiers of 51 Olivia Rd* v. *City of Johannesburg* 2008 (3) SA 208 (CC).

[125] M. Fordham, *Judicial Review Handbook* (5th edn, Oxford: Hart Publishing, 2008), [31.6].

[126] On this, see *Occupiers of 51 Olivia Road*; *Jameel* v. *Wall Street Journal Europe*.

compliance with the constitution. When one speaks with decision-makers and legislators, one often gets the sense that they prefer certainty rather than vagueness or silence from the court. They want to know what they have to do, and may be frustrated by legal or remedial vagueness. But that attitude is insidious, because it can lead to such decision-makers not confronting the problem themselves and applying their own institutional aptitudes and responsibilities.

Sometimes, judges wisely indicate that it is not their role to specify what is required. The Supreme Court of Canada evolved a doctrine whereby it can suspend the effect of any constitutional remedy for a given time in order to give the legislature a chance to adjust to a ruling.[127] This remedial approach was incorporated into the Constitution of South Africa.[128] This approach has found (or would have found) application in certain social rights cases. For example, in the Canadian *Gosselin v. Quebec (AG)* judgment,[129] the Supreme Court upheld a Quebec statute that radically reduced the available welfare benefits to youths under the age of thirty. Four judges would have found the statute to have imposed unjustified discrimination on the basis of age. Bastarache J explained why he would have elected to suspend the effect of the declaration of incompatibility:

> [G]iven the broad impact of this legislation on Quebec society, as well as the wide range of alternatives that might be taken in order to bring complex social legislation such as this into line with constitutional standards, I believe that suspension of the declaration would have been appropriate in this case. Given ... the complexity of the programs at issue, a court should not intrude too deeply into the role of legislature in this field.[130]

In some UK cases judges have opted for the virtue of silence in a similar way. In *R (Wright)* v. *Secretary of State for Health*, the House of Lords found that a statute that allowed the provisional de-listing of care workers for allegations of gross misconduct without giving them a chance to make representations was a violation of their Art. 6 ECHR right to a fair determination of their civil rights.[131] Although she declared the statute to be inconsistent with the ECHR under s. 4 of the Human Rights Act 1998,

---

[127] *Reference Re Manitoba Language Rights* [1985] 1 SCR 721. See generally, Roach, *Constitutional Remedies in Canada.*

[128] Namely, s. 172(1)(b)(ii); see also *Executive Council, Western Cape Legislature, and Others* v. *President of the Republic of South Africa and Others* 1995 (4) SA 877 (CC) [106]–[108].

[129] *Gosselin* v. *Quebec (AG)* [2002] 4 SCR 429.

[130] *Ibid.*, at [292]. For a similar use in a different welfare context, see *Schacter* v. *Canada* [1992] 2 SCR 679, 715–17.

[131] *R (Wright)* v. *Secretary of State for Health* [2009] UKHL 3.

Lady Hale found that so far as the Court was concerned, 'it is not for us to attempt to rewrite the legislation' and that 'it is right that the balance be struck in the first instance by the legislature'.[132] She added, notably, that since legislation was being contemplated at the time to replace the existing scheme, '[n]othing which I have said in this opinion is intended to cast any light on that question.'[133]

This sort of self-conscious attempt to avoid policy distortion and agenda control are appropriate, unless there is a compelling need to do otherwise. The use of declaratory relief, perhaps joined to *dicta* such as this, is an obvious way to do this. Of course, this remedy depends on there being a reasonable belief that the state will absorb and work in good faith with the decisions of the court. That is a principle underlying this book, and where it does not obtain, neither does silence remain a virtue.

IV   Conclusion

This chapter has highlighted the importance of administrative and legislative flexibility in a complex welfare state. Any exercise of welfare rights jurisdiction must account for it. Such jurisdiction appears at first to be an affront to flexibility. As law stifles discretion, it produces inflexibility. Or so the critique runs. In fact, it was shown that bureaucracies and legislatures can themselves be sources of inflexibility, and that public law may provide a palliative to the problem. The routinisation of decision-making, the phenomenon of inertia and path dependence, and the sheer complexity and problem of collective action failures all present difficult scenarios in which individuals can become lost. The capacity to apply to the court for a remedy provides some glimmer of hope to those so affected.

The problem is how to strike a balance between intervention and prudence. We saw from the history of attempts with procedural rights that they have proved a mixed blessing. But the critiques of such initiatives fall short in part. They draw our attention to problems, but we cannot be satisfied with a conclusion that they justify non-justiciability. What is rather needed is a species of justiciability that can accommodate the need for flexibility.

---

[132] *Ibid.*, 39.
[133] *Ibid.* For a similar example of the virtue of silence, see *Bellinger* v. *Bellinger* [2003] UKHL 21, and the astute analysis in A. Kavanagh, *Constitutional Review under the UK Human Rights Act* (Cambridge University Press, 2009), pp. 137–42.

I have tried to advance such an approach, by offering flexibility as a principle of restraint. I drew attention to the need to be cautious about significant uncertainty, agenda control, delay, and costs. Judges can give weight to flexibility by being cautious about imposing onerous trial-like rights in mass administrative decision-making, and by treating structural injunctions as a remedy of last resort rather than a first port of call. They may also do so by respecting flexibility in the process of interpretation and the remedies they give. They can do so by avoiding constitutional questions, employing vague standards, or using the virtue of silence to give the legislature and government the space to develop the standards and policies themselves. All this, of course, assumes that bureaucracies and legislatures will use their flexibility to some good. That conclusion is not only unwarranted at times, but often the very problem at issue is political intransigence or inertia. Here courts can promote flexibility by breaking up inertia and by giving groups an enhanced voice in the policy-making process. Whether this principle of flexibility will strike the right balance is difficult to tell. But that it meets critics half way, as well as puts the problems of procedure up front for advocates of social rights, can hardly be doubted.

PART III

Incrementalism

10

Incrementalism as a general theme

I   Introduction

Incrementalism is the theme that echoes throughout many parts of this book. It is what helps to describe the effect of observing the four principles of restraint set out in Part II of this book, and fits with some of the observations on the epistemic limitations of the judicial process that were discussed in Chapter 5. Judicial incrementalism is an appropriate response to two different demands. One is the practical or managerial demand that enormously complex data be dealt with in a fragmented rather than holistic way. Judges can in this way narrow the particular issues, bracket the set of relevant variables, and thereby decide under better epistemic conditions. Another demand is that courts neither accidentally nor intentionally inhibit the realisation of social rights by other organs of government. We have seen in the chapters on polycentricity, expertise, and flexibility that while certain procedural or other non-intrusive rights or remedies raise no justiciability problems, they may nonetheless stand in the way of other institutions' responsibilities to implement social rights.

This chapter explores judicial incrementalism, outlining a set of techniques that will for the most part capture the tenor of the principles of restraint set out in Part II of this book. It examines the idea of incrementalism as it was introduced in the study of public administration and organisation theory, the specific techniques and general theme of incrementalism, and how it applies, in comparative experience, to social rights adjudication in particular. In section IV I examine the relationship between the model of incrementalism set out in this book and how it fits with some important similar American work in constitutional theory. And in section V I take up some important criticisms of incrementalism, namely, that it is too little, too much, or too unlikely to be observed in practice to make it a worthwhile strategy.

After this discussion, it is appropriate to pan out once again from the focused discussion of incrementalism to consider, in section VI, what prescriptions incrementalism has for some key problems in social rights adjudication (namely, the adjudication of positive obligations and the evaluation of resource scarcity), and, in section VII, what relationship exists between the principles set out in Part II of this book and the theme of judicial incrementalism covered in this chapter. I close out the discussion with a survey of how the entire argument of the book comes together to set out what in my view is the best role for the adjudication of constitutional social rights.

II   Incrementalism and public administration

Charles E. Lindblom most clearly introduced the idea of incrementalism as a method for decision-making for boundedly rational actors acting under circumstances of severe complexity and therefore uncertainty.[1] In his classic article, 'The Science of Muddling Through', he contrasted the 'rational-comprehensive model' with the model of 'successive limited comparison'. He argued that comprehensive theories generated by centralised bureaucracies and rolled out for implementation are neither always the most effective way of planning, nor even always possible. In fact, decisions under uncertainty often lead to means and ends constantly informing each other and therefore changing, and that the analysis of relevant variables is limited in time and scope. Lindblom provided a table that summarised both approaches. The table helps to clarify, succinctly, the essence of his observations, and foreshadows the thinking of much later scholarship and is reproduced in Table 10.1.

The main point of his article was that complex organisations both do and should adopt a model of successive limited comparison for a number of complex tasks. Lindblom revisited his theory as set forth in this paper, but never abandoned it.[2] The later paper amplified certain elements visible in the original paper, such as the use of trial-and-error experimentation, limitation of analysis to some alternatives, and dispersion and fragmentation of analytical work between various participants in decision-making.[3]

---

[1] C. Lindblom, 'The Science of Muddling Through' (1959) 19 *Public Administration Review* 79; see also D. Braybrooke and C. Lindblom, *A Strategy of Decision: Policy Evaluation as a Social Process* (New York: Free Press, 1970); R. Cyert and J. March, *A Behavioural Theory of the Firm* (New York: Prentice Hall, 1963).

[2] C. E. Lindblom, 'Still Muddling, Not Yet Through' (1979) *Public Administration Review* 517.

[3] *Ibid.*, 519. This is very similar to the work of M. Dorf and C. Sabel ('A Constitution of Democratic Experimentalism' (1998) 98 *Columbia Law Review* 267), and it should be

Table 10.1. *Lindblom, incrementalism, and the rational comprehensive model*

Rational Comprehensive Model (Root)	Successive Limited Comparison (Branch)
1a. Clarification of values or objectives distinct from and usually prerequisite to empirical analysis of alternative policies.	1b. Selection of value goals and empirical analysis of the needed action are not distinct from one another but are closely intertwined.
2a. Policy formulation is therefore approached through means–end analysis: first the ends are isolated, then the means to achieve them are sought.	2b. Since means and ends are not distinct, means–end analysis is often inappropriate or limited.
3a. The test of a 'good' policy is that it can be shown to be the most appropriate means to desired ends.	3b. The test of a 'good' policy is typically that various analysts find themselves directly agreeing on a policy (without their agreeing that it is the most appropriate means to an agreed objective).
4a. Analysis is comprehensive; every important relevant factor is taken into account.	4b. Analysis is drastically limited: (i) Important possible outcomes are neglected. (ii) Important alternative potential policies are neglected. (iii) Important affected values are neglected.
5a. Theory is often heavily relied upon.	5b. A succession of comparisons greatly reduces or eliminates reliance on theory.

Source: Lindblom, 'The Science of Muddling Through', 81 (the table is a verbatim reproduction of Lindblom's own).

Lindblom's analysis has had a profound impact on organisation theory, public administration, and on budgeting practice in particular.[4] If we treat judicial decision-making as one branch of public decision-making, it can be seen there too that incrementalism has enormous explanatory

recalled that Lindblom was a contemporary of and collaborator with Robert Dahl, and also believed in the idea of polyarchy.

[4] A. B. Wildavsky, *The Politics of the Budgetary Process* (2nd edn, Boston: Little Brown & Co., 1974); M. Haynes, *Incrementalism and Public Policy* (New York: Longman, 1984).

appeal.[5] The common law ordinarily expands incrementally. Judges prefer not to stray particularly far from the status quo, which is embodied in precedent, industry or communal practice, settled principles of statutory interpretation, and a practice of slow general evolution of common law principles. While many assume that Ronald Dworkin's theory of law as integrity invites judges to engage in wide-ranging theory – and indeed it may have such implications[6] – in fact his claim that eligible interpretations must 'fit' the community's legal practice would ordinarily lead to incremental change, an approach his critics have castigated as an 'extreme case of total faith in analogical arguments'.[7] Even *Brown* v. *Board of Education*, which looks like a revolutionary decision, was to some extent a case that fits (legally) with incrementalism. It was preceded by a range of precedents and practical failures of the separate but equal doctrine, and the remedy in *Brown II* that the states desegregate with 'all deliberate speed' left ample (many say too much) flexibility.[8] In human rights and public law adjudication more generally, judges tend not to adopt comprehensive theories of the state (other than those commended explicitly or implicitly by the constitution), but rather work out the implications of vague principles in a case-by-case way. The intertwining of means and ends analysis, value goals, and empirical analysis is also manifest in constitutional rights adjudication. When judges apply juridical concepts such as proportionality, fairness, and reasonableness, one finds that the analysis in individual cases demonstrates treatment of both practical concerns about consequences, and deontological concerns over justice, equality, and fairness in an inextricable manner. Yet it is important to distinguish between the descriptive claim that judges act incrementally – which in my view definitely does not always hold – with the claim that they ought to, which I endorse as a general heuristic or rule of thumb for social rights adjudication.

---

[5] See M. Shapiro, *The Supreme Court and Administrative Agencies* (New York: Free Press, 1968), pp. 73–91; J. Raz, *The Authority of Law* (Oxford University Press, 1979), Chapter 10, esp. pp. 194–201.

[6] See the brief discussion in Chapter 4, section III.B.

[7] Raz, *The Authority of Law*, p. 205; Raz, *Ethics in the Public Domain: Essays in the Morality of Law and Politics* (Oxford: Clarendon Press, 1994), Chapter 13; Raz, 'Speaking with One Voice: On Dworkinian Integrity and Coherence', in S. Hurley (ed.), *Dworkin and His Critics: With Replies by Ronald Dworkin* (Oxford: Blackwell, 2004), Chapter 15 (and Dworkin's reply at pp. 381–6).

[8] *Brown* v. *Board of Education* (*Brown II*), 349 US 294 (1955). For the same observation, see C. R. Sunstein, 'Foreword: Leaving Things Undecided' (1995) 110 *Harvard Law Review* 6, 50–1.

Two caveats are appropriate. First, Lindblom emphasised that incrementalism is *one form* of strategic analysis, and must be considered in tandem with other strategies. Time-sensitivity can override the allure of incrementalism. The best way to evaluate how to evacuate a ship will depend on whether it is sinking. Political circumstances and great need may combine to generate irresistible demand for something more. William Beveridge's riposte to the opponents of the British welfare state was powerful in both form and content: 'A revolutionary moment in the world's history is a time for revolutions, not for patching.'[9]

The second caveat is that incrementalism is not necessarily an inert strategy, but ought to rather be viewed as a *dynamic* and *searching* process that takes place in a controlled fashion. Lindblom's idea was not conservative in the political sense. He went out of his way to make this clear in his later article, and he was also someone who was noted for his critique of corporate influence in American politics and the conservative, regressive effect of strong property rights as an obstruction to progressive political change.[10] The way that the concept is meant to operate in this book would be best described as *dynamic incrementalism*. It is a strategy for decision-making that can be vigorous and enthusiastic, but in which learning-by-doing, taking feedback, and respect for complexity play an important role.

III   Applying judicial incrementalism

The general theme of incrementalism is that judges should, when adjudicating vague constitutional social rights under conditions of uncertainty, (1) avoid significant, nationwide allocative impact, and either (2) give decisions on narrow, particularised grounds, or (3) when adjudicating a macro-level dispute with significant implications for large numbers of people, decide in a manner that preserves flexibility. Their decision-making should ordinarily proceed in small steps, informed by past steps, and small steps might affect large numbers of people, but in ways that preserve latitude for adaptation.

Before examining the techniques by which this can be done, it is important to state in general terms the limitations of the approach. The

---

[9]   See Beveridge Inter-Departmental Committee, Report on Social Insurance and Allied Services, Cm 6404 (1942) [7]. This report is regarded as the foundation stone of the modern British welfare state.

[10]   See C. E. Lindblom, *Politics and Markets* (New York: Basic Books, 1977); see also Lindblom, 'Still Muddling, Not Yet Through', 520–2.

first and most obvious case is when the legal standard being applied is particularly clear. If the only reasonable interpretation requires an outcome that is not incrementalist, then that is the result that must prevail. Incrementalism and the principles of restraint in Part II of this book are meant to be aids to legal interpretation under conditions of uncertainty in social rights adjudication. They are not meant to undo the law, or provide a non-legal reason for judicial deference. The right *legal* answers to questions often demand awareness of consequences, or awareness of the judiciary's constitutional role vis-à-vis the legislature, and it is there that the role for restraint may come into play.

Second, incrementalism may be inappropriate when there is a great need for clarity as to the legal meaning of a vague legal term, because without it there will be a substantial *and harmful* amount of uncertainty. In this situation, uncertainty is viewed not as an opportunity for other institutions to test different options, but rather as the continuity of chaos and unfairness for those citizens who require a clear statement of their rights. This is the primordial function of courts, and the role must, if social circumstances call for it, be exercised. (Claimants will more often than not, in such a situation, not get the result they desire, so they press the point at their peril.) Third, if the state has demonstrated bad faith in respect of its own obligations under the matter, incrementalism will be less appropriate unless it is the strategy adopted within a framework of more intrusive remedies such as structural injunctions.

A   The techniques of incrementalism

There are specific techniques that can be used to reflect this type of incrementalist approach. When skilfully deployed, they have allowed courts to bring some of the institutional benefits of legal accountability (as discussed in Part I of this book) to a disputed area of decision-making, while also respecting the limits of adjudication and democratic role and institutional potential of other institutions (as discussed in Part II). I now turn to surveying what I consider to be the most useful of these techniques, and how they guide towards the right outcome in social rights cases.

1   Particularisation

According to this idea, judges may attempt, when giving a decision, to accentuate the distinctive features of the case before them. This is a familiar technique of deciding a case on narrow grounds. It provides the material with which the case can be distinguished when a different constellation of facts might call for a different outcome. Particularisation does not need to occur in a way that shuts the door to future cases. Judges can leave open the question of how much more broadly the standard might apply. Leaving the door open is more in line with the incrementalist approach than shutting it prematurely.[11]

A failure to give particularised grounds was the problem in the Latin American cases studied in Chapter 3. Finding that there was a right to life-saving medicine would necessarily lead to unsustainable expansion as the claimants with the sharpest elbows made their way up to the courthouse doors. A similar result is observable in the Canadian *Chaoulli* case,[12] which found that the ban on private medical insurance violated the right to security of the person in the Quebec Charter of Human Rights and Freedoms because there was insufficient evidence that a one-tier regime was necessary to protect the integrity of the public system. This was a very broad ruling that threatened to undermine the national health care regime. However, the dissenting judges found that even if there were a genuine threat to the life of a patient owing to delays, there was a more tailored solution to the problem:

> The safety valve (however imperfectly administered) of allowing Quebec residents to obtain essential health care outside the province when they are unable to receive the care in question at home in a timely way is of importance. If, as the appellants claim, this safety valve is opened too sparingly, the courts are available to supervise enforcement of the rights of those patients who are directly affected by the decision on a case-by-case basis. Judicial intervention at this level on a case-by-case basis is preferable to acceptance of the appellants' global challenge to the entire single-tier health plan. It is important to emphasize that rejection of the appellants' global challenge to Quebec's health plan would not foreclose individual patients from seeking individual relief tailored to their individual circumstances.[13]

This is the right model to follow. It is also evident in the (perhaps unduly) slow but growing jurisprudence in the United Kingdom of recognising positive obligations and welfare interests in 'exceptional' cases under the European Convention,[14] and the Canadian experience

---

[11] Cf. A. Vermeule, *Judging under Uncertainty: An Institutional Theory of Legal Interpretation* (Cambridge, MA: Harvard University Press, 2006), Chapter 6 (for a view outlining misgivings about decision costs that would apply to leaving the door open in this way).

[12] *Chaoulli* v. *Quebec* (AG) [2005] 1 SCR 791.

[13] *Chaoulli*, [264] (Binnie and LeBel JJ, Fish J concurring).

[14] *R(Bernard)* v. *Enfield LBC* [2002] EWHC 2282 (finding the Art. 8 ECHR right to family life was violated due to exceptionally deplorable living conditions); *Anufrijeva and Another* v. *Southwark LBC* [2003] EWCA Civ 1406 [41] (summarising the principles that amount to a cautious approach to positive obligations under the Convention); *N* v. *Secretary of State for the Home Department* [2005] UKHL 31 [62ff.] (where deporting a

of recognising positive equality obligations in cases with relatively contained impact, as opposed to those with complex ramifications and allocative impact.[15]

2   Cautious expansion, analogical reasoning

The idea of cautious expansion is that judicial change should come in relatively small steps, often by reasoning analogically with previous cases. This approach has been thoroughly analysed and theorised by Cass Sunstein and others.[16] Clearly in some cases analogical reasoning will not be appropriate – the interpretation of a new constitution or statute provide notable examples. But the idea of cautious expansion is equally applicable in those situations as well. Forays into new areas should ordinarily be made in relatively small steps, and should provide opportunities for study and feedback that will inform the subsequent developments. At the same time, judges must strike a balance between cautious expansion and the genuine need for the growth that legitimises the incrementalist approach.

3   Vague legal standards

I observed in Chapter 4 that constitutional adjudication inevitably employs vague legal standards, but judges can at times give an interpretation of the standard that effectively imposes a broad rule. This is what happened in the *Goldberg* v. *Kelly* case, where the US Supreme Court

---

person receiving medical treatment for HIV/Aids would violate Art. 3 ECHR only in 'very exceptional circumstances'); *Royal Borough of Kensington and Chelsea* v. *O'Sullivan* [2003] EWCA Civ 371 [82] (courts should stay clear of macro-level resource allocation). However, see *R (Pinnock)* v. *Manchester City Council* [2010] UKSC 45 [51]–[54] (rejecting 'exceptionality' as too narrow but substituting a presumption that amounts to the same). To be clear, I do not here endorse this approach for interpretation of socio-economic rights under the HRA 1998. The best and most nuanced analysis of that issue is E. Palmer, *Judicial Review, Socio-Economic Rights and the Human Rights Act* (Oxford: Hart, 2007).

[15] Contrast *Eldridge* v. *British Columbia (Attorney General)* [1997] 2 SCR 624 (requiring interpretation services in hospitals for the hearing impaired) with *Auton (Guardian ad litem of)* v. *British Columbia (Attorney General)* [2004] 3 SCR 657 (refusing to find a violation in the government's failure to fund Applied Behavioral Therapy for autistic children). The later case in fact, at [38], distinguished *Eldridge* on less tenable grounds. The cost of funding the treatment per child was $45,000–$60,000 per year, and the number of potential claimants nationwide was not made clear.

[16] C. R. Sunstein, *Legal Reasoning and Political Conflict* (New York: Oxford University Press, 1996), Chapter 3, and his *One Case at a Time: Judicial Minimalism on the Supreme Court* (Cambridge, MA: Harvard University Press, 2001), pp. 42–5. See also Raz, *The Authority of Law*, pp. 201–6.

found that an oral hearing was required before the termination of welfare benefits.[17] In the South African case of *Mazibuko*, Justice O'Regan rejected, for the Court, an argument that the Court should declare that the s. 27(1)(b) right to water entitles every person to fifty litres per day, and that the state was required to set its allocation policy on a per-person rather than per-household basis.[18] Justice O'Regan noted the 'extremely burdensome and costly' nature of the proposal, which would be 'expensive and inequitable' in its application.[19] This is surely the right outcome, for the implications of the sought-after policy were complex and unknowable – like the Latin American health cases – and potentially impossible given the transient nature of informal households. On the other hand, the ruling in *Khosa* effectively forbade any distinction between permanent residents and naturalised citizens for the purposes of the right to social security in South Africa.[20] That is a ruling with specific, sweeping implications and which cannot be revisited easily if complications arise.

Vague standards give both judges and legislators and the executive greater room for adaptation to unforeseen circumstances. The successful South African and British cases apply vague standards with some success. The concept of *Grootboom* 'reasonableness', and the right to 'meaningful engagement' in protection from evictions, allows the judges to extend the scope of the right in a flexible manner.[21] Critics of vague standards will argue that such standards may amount to a 'charter for obstruction and delay',[22] depriving claimants of concrete remedies, and inviting foot-dragging as well as protracted litigation. But this critique supposes that judges will foresee and work around the complications of a broad ruling, or that administration will respond appropriately, or the dynamics will work out positively. None of these conditions hold reliably under conditions of serious uncertainty, and any serious judicial incursion into the welfare state will necessarily have complex ramifications. What does remain true, under a vague standard, is that judges can make localised

---

[17] See the discussion in Chapter 9, section III.A.2.

[18] *Mazibuko and Others* v. *City of Johannesburg and Others* (CCT 39/09) 2010 (4) SA 1 (CC) [86]–[97].

[19] *Ibid.*, [88]–[89].

[20] *Khosa and Others* v. *Minister of Social Development and Others*, 2004 (6) BCLR 569 (CC). See section VI.B for a critique of the judgment.

[21] *Republic of South Africa* v. *Grootboom*, 2000 (11) BCLR 1169 (CC); *Occupiers of 51 Olivia Rd* v. *City of Johannesburg*, 2008 (3) SA 208 (CC).

[22] R. Dworkin, *Law's Empire* (Cambridge, MA: Harvard University Press, 1986), p. 391 (a reference to the *Brown II* formula of 'all deliberate speed', though he is (unusually) equivocal in his criticism).

findings and retain jurisdiction to intervene again where fresh circumstances deliver more certainty. Of course vagueness is not always ideal, and all institutions may at times seek greater certainty. But the drive for certainty must be backed by reasonable confidence about the implications of the ruling. That condition is attainable, but most often so when the ruling is either preceded by experience, amounts to a small step, or the arguments of principle are so undeniably compelling – as in a clear or core case[23] – as to make the rule of law prevail over (even unknowable) adverse consequences.

4   Procedural rights

Notwithstanding the problems noted in Chapter 9, procedural rights offer the promise of presenting a range of tools that courts can use to bring the benefits of legal accountability without imposing undue finality or agenda control on an area of decision-making. An approximate range of procedural rights and remedies, ordered roughly in order of increasing judicial control, can be represented as follows:

- (Reasonable) access to information[24]
- Mandatory consideration of a particular interest or factor
- Right to make oral or written representations
- Duty of consultation
- Right to be provided with reasons
- Trial-like hearing, with rigorous evidentiary rights and requirements
- Duty of meaningful engagement
- Duty to negotiate in good faith

This range of duties and remedies shows how judges may adjust the range of responses and the depth of interference with the primary decision-maker's capacity to decide the issue under consideration. Only the last three of these options contain a truly substantive dimension in which judges can compel the decision-maker to do more than listen and respond (in any fashion it desires) to the claimant. But even those three standards give judges and administrators room for accommodation and mutual adjustment. Judges can deploy these various techniques in different cases in order to adjust the extent of judicial control of final decision-making.

---

[23] See Chapter 6, section IV.C.3.
[24] Freedom of information requests can be very onerous, so this remedy can range from a simple transparency measure to a highly onerous one if applied liberally.

The primary issue, seen in Chapter 9, is the *range* of administrative or legislative decision-making that these standards will control. If it is enormous and the imposition administratively onerous (e.g. when it pertains to mass decision-making such as benefits determinations), then the potential for delay and costs is significant. In such cases, where procedural justice demands it, those remedies nearer the top of the scale will be more appropriate. When the decisions are fewer in number and of greater importance, those lying near the bottom of the scale will be more attractive, subject to the proviso that the more macro-level the reform, the more flexible the court's substantive oversight (of the bona fides of negotiation) ought to be.

5   Constitutional avoidance

Having examined the idea of avoidance in Chapter 9, I will here examine some examples of how avoiding constitutional questions can preserve flexibility while doing justice in individual cases. In Britain, the *Rogers* case provides a good example.[25] The claimant asked a local health authority to fund a new breast cancer drug that had not yet been certified by the national and European regulatory agencies that certify drugs as cost-effective. Mindful of the urgency of the issue, the Minister of Health had directed local authorities not to treat cost as crucial to their determinations. The Swindon area health authority adopted a policy of exceptionality – it would fund the drug in exceptional circumstances. The claimant argued that her right to life under the European Convention on Human Rights was violated by the decision, and that the policy was irrational under administrative law grounds. The Court of Appeal found itself in a conundrum. It wanted to find the policy irrational and quash it, but it wanted also to avoid applying the right to life, which raised difficult questions. But the ordinary standard of review in administrative law was notoriously deferential. It cut the cake down the middle, and found that since her rights were *engaged* or *affected*, a more searching standard of review *in administrative law* was engaged. It found the policy irrational because the authority did not have a notion of what an exceptional case would look like. That was judicious constitutional avoidance, because the remedy both left legislative latitude, and left open the more difficult question of the dynamic implications by holding clearly that drug approvals engage the right to life.

[25] *R (on the Application of Anne Marie Rogers) v. Swindon NHS Primary Care Trust, Secretary of State for Health* [2006] EWCA Civ 392.

One can see similar results in some of the South African cases. In *Occupiers of 51 Olivia Rd*, Yacoob J established the 'meaningful engagement' standard for the Court but also refused to entertain a 'general discussion' on the broader reach of s. 26, and in particular the constitutionality of the Prevention of Illegal Eviction from an Unlawful Occupation of Land Act (the PIE Act).[26] Similarly, in *Joe Slovo*, the Court was more prepared to find that the PIE Act required certain procedural and substantive protections for those being evicted from an informal settlement, and was clearer in finding that the requirements of the s. 26 right to housing were satisfied.[27]

One of the better ways to give effect to an avoidance cannon is to give rights-friendly readings to statutes and soft law policies in the welfare state. And a way of extending common law protections is to use a heightened standard of judicial review when constitutional rights are 'engaged', a process that will allow the domestic court to issue a remedy in the case at hand while leaving the question of whether the constitutional rights are 'violated' open for another day.

6   Non-intrusive remedies

Respect for the principle of inter-institutional collaboration means that less intrusive remedies will be appropriate, for it gives a greater role to the executive and legislature as definers of rights and the regulatory regimes that best give effect to them.[28] The intrusiveness of the remedy should be inversely correlated to the extent of respect for this principle by the state. At its best – where the government appears to be acting in good faith, often the case where an old statute or policy comes up for review – declaratory relief with an affirmation of the government's role will be appropriate. At its worst – where there is evidence of governmental intransigence (or the threat thereof) or substantial unfairness to the claimants due to procedural exhaustion – harder remedies, and the last resort of mandatory or structural relief, will be appropriate. Between these two poles, the possibilities are manifold. One underused constitutional remedy is damages. The European Court of Human Rights commonly awards damages, and in the UK ombudsmen typically recommend the payment of compensation. Damages may be a way to give the claimants the expressive victory of

---

[26] *Occupiers of 51 Olivia Rd* v. *City of Johannesburg* 2008 (3) SA 208 (CC), [37]–[38].
[27] *Residents of the Joe Slovo Community* v. *Thubelisha Homes and Others*, 2010 (3) SA 454 (CC).
[28] See Chapter 1, section IV. See also Chapter 9, section III.C.

a ruling in their favour, damages to make it felt in government, and leave the reform of the policy for the state to carry out. The impact of damages awards can in some ways be more easily monitored than complex bureaucratic changes.

7   Revisitation

Revisitation is the idea that judges, administrators, and the legislature should be prepared to revisit a legal holding if new information shows it to have caused significant problems or that it was based on assumptions that are proved to be untrue. The first issue that must be laid aside is the idea that the doctrine of precedent, observed by common law courts, forbids this principle. It is by now clear that courts throughout the Commonwealth have the legal authority to depart from precedent where it is in the interests of justice to do so.[29] Judges naturally feel some reluctance to do so, and this is often for good reasons. But where experience suggests that an earlier ruling has caused some problems not originally foreseen, it is appropriate to revisit the finding.

A good demonstration of this idea can be found in the Canadian constitutional equality law jurisprudence. In *Law* v. *Canada*,[30] the Supreme Court laid down a precedent that was interpreted as requiring that a person must show that differential treatment must impact negatively on the dignity of the individual in order to violate s. 15(1) of the Canadian Charter. Only nine years later, the Court in *R* v. *Kapp* rightly recast its test:

> [S]everal difficulties have arisen from the attempt in Law to employ human dignity as a legal test. [A]s critics have pointed out, human dignity is an abstract and subjective notion that, even with the guidance of the four contextual factors, cannot only become confusing and difficult to apply; it has also proven to be an additional burden on equality claimants, rather than the philosophical enhancement it was intended to be. Criticism has also accrued for the way Law has allowed the formalism … to resurface in the form of an artificial comparator analysis focussed on treating likes alike.[31]

---

[29] See N. Duxbury, *The Nature and Authority of Precedent* (Cambridge University Press, 2008), Chapter 4; see also Shapiro, *The Supreme Court and Administrative Agencies*, pp. 67–73.

[30] *Law* v. *Canada (Minister of Employment and Immigration)* [1999] 1 SCR 497.

[31] *R* v. *Kapp* [2008] 2 SCR 483 [21]–[22]. The Court clarified the standard, which was not in strict terms overruling itself. The effect was the same. For another example of a similar phenomenon in Canadian administrative law, see *Dunsmuir* v. *New Brunswick* [2008] 1 SCR 190.

This is the model of how revisitation ought to work. The United Kingdom House of Lords and Supreme Court have also been notably willing to revisit their findings when it becomes clear that they are inconsistent with the views of the European Court of Human Rights. At times, their Lordships can get testy about it when they believe they are coerced legally rather than prompted to revisit the wisdom of their earlier rulings.[32] But at others, the domestic courts seem to take up the dialogue in good faith and even admit the substantive errors of their previous ways.[33] Sometimes, revisitation is necessitated by changes of circumstances that can render court judgments, especially structural injunctions, obsolete.[34]

Judges can preserve the possibility of revisitation if, as I argued in Chapter 4, they focus generally on the permissibility of justifications rather than on the acceptability of underlying policies. When circumstances change, legislators and administrators may act on the basis of new justifications. It may be difficult for them to do so when such action appears to contradict a clearly established constitutional norm or rule. And such rules will need, from time to time, to be laid down as a remedy for a perceived violation of a right. Constitutional rulings will have inertia in this respect. Yet it can be crucial that legislators and administrators take their responsibility seriously in this regard – that they perceive themselves as being both able and responsible for revisiting the record in court when circumstances call for it. Early guidance from the apex court will be needed on this issue.

Two aspects are likely to play important roles if the idea of revisitation is to be applied effectively when a constitutional norm or rule resists mounting evidence of needed change. The first is the role of government legal advice. Advisers should be aware of the potential and importance of revisitation, and not rule it out as a policy option. Where the legal

---

[32] *Secretary of State for the Home Department* v. *AF (No 3)* [2009] UKHL 28, [70] per Lord Hoffmann: 'I [follow Strasbourg] with very considerable regret, because I think that the decision of the ECtHR was wrong and that it may well destroy the system of control orders which is a significant part of this country's defences against terrorism.'

[33] *Ibid.*, [101] (Lady Hale): 'The ability to make an effective challenge to the case put against the controlled person is the key. However, I did not say so as clearly as, with hindsight, I should have done. And I was also far too sanguine about the possibilities of conducting a fair hearing under the special advocate procedure.' See also *Manchester City Council* v. *Pinnock* [2010] UKSC 45. These judgments are to be welcomed as exemplars of appropriate institutional humility and open-mindedness.

[34] *Residents of the Joe Slovo Community* v. *Thubelisha Homes and Others,* 2010 (3) SA 454 (CC). See the discussion in Chapter 9, section III.A.3.

standard is specific and forbids policies in specific terms, and the government would prefer (rightly) not to engage in constitutional brinksmanship, the appropriate course would be to seek an advisory opinion or declaratory relief from the court. The second is the role of the court. It may either flag, in a judgment, that revisitation may at some time be needed if a new justification arises or they are unsure of the implications of one part of the judgment. That is the brilliance of the South African Court's emphasis on flexibility.[35] On the other hand, where an advisory opinion is sought,[36] the court can use its inherent jurisdiction to ensure that an appropriate friend of the court (*amicus curiae*) is appointed, and that it takes a receptive attitude to interventions from organisations or other public authorities having expertise on the matter.

IV   Incrementalism and its cousins

I was led to incrementalism through a study of public law and the limits of judicial and bureaucratic expertise, which in turn led to organisation theory and in particular the works of Herbert Simon and Charles Lindblom. Yet once atop the shoulders of these giants, affinities with the work of other scholars became apparent. They had incorporated elements of incrementalism into their own proposals, though typically without seeking to link their ideas to those of Lindblom directly. The general approach of this book finds special affinity with these works. Yet it is different in important ways from each of them, and the purpose of this section is to survey those differences and outline some of my misgivings about these companion ideas that, on the whole, I greatly respect.

A   Sunstein's judicial minimalism

The approach advocated in this book finds a strong connection to Cass Sunstein's judicial minimalism, a theory expounded in detail in two books and a number of law review articles.[37] The essence of Sunstein's theory consists of two straightforward prescriptive claims and two straightforward justifications. The prescriptive claims are that judges should decide

---

[35] See Chapter 9, sections III.B and C.
[36] Where this power is not expressly provided for by statute, nor implied within the inherent jurisdiction of the court, it would be wise to provide for it constitutionally or statutorily.
[37] Sunstein, *Legal Reasoning and Political Conflict*; Sunstein, *One Case at a Time*. The theory is set out with greater detail and references in Sunstein, 'Foreword: Leaving Things Undecided'.

cases in a fashion that is *narrow* and *shallow*.[38] The justifications are that these would respect political pluralism and the competence limitations of courts. Narrowness is achieved when judges 'decide the case at hand; they do not decide other cases too, except to the extent that one decision necessarily bears on other cases, and unless they are pretty much forced to do'.[39] I described a similar phenomenon above as particularisation, and it is a familiar technique in the common law. A *shallow* decision-making strategy is one in which courts avoid deep theorisation of the grounds for their views, and prefer to seek agreement with other judges on *outcomes in particular cases*. The two forms identified by Sunstein include (a) agreements on concrete particulars amid disagreements over basic principle, and (b) agreement about abstractions amid disagreements about the application of such abstractions.[40] So, one judge may object to torturing people on Christian grounds, while another may object on utilitarian grounds. But both would prescribe it as an unjustifiable violation of the prohibition on torture. Sunstein explains that shallow decision-making of this sort is in fact pervasive in public law, and also argues that judges ought to follow this practice. It fits together with his theory that constitutional rights and public law norms are incompletely theorised agreements that reflect and indeed permit a broad and relatively stable overlapping consensus. The idea is that at the level of constitutional design, or judicial decision-making, officials can agree on the value of some concept (e.g. free expression) without fully working out its details, or even while overtly having different conceptions.

Narrowness, on the other hand, is justified as a strategy that avoids two types of costs: decision costs and error costs.[41] Decision costs are concerned with what might roughly be described as the transactional costs associated with the litigation process – that is, the degree of activity generated within the courts and by litigants and others affected by the degree of clarity generated by the rulings.[42] It would take considerable time and effort for judges to devise and then agree upon a rule or standard that caters sufficiently for the manifold interests embraced by a wide ruling. And mistakes and incoherencies made could lead to further litigation, while comprehensive rules make judicial agreement less likely. Error costs are those adverse consequences associated with judges having

---

[38]   Sunstein, *One Case at a Time*, pp. 10ff.
[39]   *Ibid.*, p. 10.
[40]   *Ibid.*, p. 11.   [41]   *Ibid.*, pp. 46–50.
[42]   Vermeule, *Judging under Uncertainty*, pp. 166–8, provides a more nuanced definition of decision costs.

made an erroneous supposition in their reasoning, or with those adverse consequences that arise due to a change of circumstances that renders the rationale of the holding obsolete. Error costs are, basically, one of the principal preoccupations of this book.

The affinities are obvious. Sunstein's theory defends a form of judicial incrementalism, inspired also by the problem of bounded rationality and relative institutional competence.[43] He supports his thesis with a plethora of American cases. However, the analysis in this book departs from his theory in a few important ways. The first is that, contrary to Sunstein, I have no *political* aversion to deep theorisation by judges. His view is that the existence of political pluralism generates a demand for shallow decisions. This book nowhere endorses that idea in so strong a form.[44] Rather, the limits on judging legislation set out here stem from the principle of democratic legitimacy (which accepts judicial theorisation subject to the limits set out in Chapter 6), and more generally from epistemic and institutional considerations.

Sunstein is in fact quite equivocal on the implications of pluralism. On the issue of gay marriage, for instance, he has counselled restraint, though not because of respect for pluralism and the fact of disagreement (which would have been wrong in my view), but rather for more sensible consequentialist reasons relating to the problem of backlash.[45] But he has, with that argument, merely evaded the deeper problem, namely, why should not the mere fact of disagreement have counselled restraint according to his theory? Typically, Sunstein will here retreat into claims that judges should avoid deep rulings 'where possible' or unless they are 'necessary'. Yet without evidently allowing a role for theory to back up such judgments, his proposal risks lurching between ad hoc intuitionism (which asks us to trust the judges he also asks us to second-guess), and an invitation to judicial restraint whenever the flag of controversy is raised.[46]

---

[43] Sunstein, *One Case at a Time*, pp. 51–3. In 'Leaving Things Undecided', he appears at times to use 'incremental' as a synonym for 'minimal': see 32, 96, 98, 99.

[44] It does endorse the weaker idea that the judicial review of legislation is open to democratic objection on grounds of equality when the conditions in Chapter 6, sections IV.A–C do not apply.

[45] Sunstein, *One Case at a Time*, Chapter 7, esp. pp. 159–61.

[46] See C. R. Sunstein, 'Virtues and Verdicts: Review of Ronald Dworkin's *Justice in Robes*', *The New Republic*, 22 May 2006 ('Dworkin is quite right to say that analogy is blind without principle, but some principles are more controversial than others. Often it is possible for the Court to rule in a way that avoids the largest controversies').

The other problems stem from the incomplete theorisation of his own approach, and its tendency towards minimalism of an unjustifiable kind. Sunstein is careful to contrast 'minimalism' with 'judicial restraint',[47] and in more recent work is concerned to emphasise the limits of minimalism.[48] But these warning labels do not undo the thrust of his recommendations. He generally advises that judges should avoid broader rulings 'unless they are pretty much forced to do [it]'.[49] This creates a baseline of minimalism, not the searching, dynamic form of incrementalism this book and the theories examined below advocate. Nothing legally 'forces' judges to give a ruling unless there is only one plausible interpretation, an easy case, rarely the stuff of appellate litigation. The idea of 'necessity' is no doubt something richer for Sunstein, but he advances no programme for identifying it, and the minimalist tenor, coupled with respect for value pluralism, leaves the case for extreme restraint more fortified than the case for judicial protection. One passage gives some clues, arguing that judges can be more 'maximalist' when they 'have considerable confidence in the merits of the solution', or that it will 'reduce costly uncertainty', or where it will 'promote democratic goals'.[50] But we are here thrown back upon the instincts of judges when he has given reasons to doubt them, and it privileges judicial consensus when it is both unstable in practice and dubious as a moral goal. It also assumes that judges will be good at promoting democratic goals when there is considerable evidence to the contrary. In short, his theory, its brilliance a given, needs to be less equivocal about the supporting role for interpretive theory, should be shorn of the pluralist trappings that give controversy more weight than is due, and needs more detail than concepts like 'necessary' and 'possible' provide.

B   Democratic experimentalism

The theory of democratic experimentalism put forward by Michael Dorf and Charles Sabel is quite richly theorised.[51] It is an account of governance

---

[47] Sunstein, *One Case at a Time*, p. 28.
[48] C. R. Sunstein, 'Beyond Judicial Minimalism' (2008) 43 *Tulsa Law Review* 825.
[49] *Ibid.*, 10.
[50] Sunstein, *One Case at a Time*, p. 57.
[51] Dorf and Sabel, 'A Constitution of Democratic Experimentalism', 267. See also the precursor article, J. Cohen and C. Sabel, 'Directly Deliberative Polyarchy' (1997) 3 *European Law Journal* 313; C. F. Sabel and W. H. Simon, 'Destabilization Rights: How Public Law Litigation Succeeds' (2004) 117 *Harvard Law Review* 1016.

(for all branches of government) that contains at its core the prescription that institutions of government should promote a localised form of decision-making that respects Robert Dahl's concept of *directly deliberative polyarchy*.[52] The theory is a response to the many problems found to exist with command-and-control conception of governance, which embraced the view of legislatures making the law, the executive applying it, and courts supervising the process for conformity to text, principles of public law, and legislative purposes. In their theory, by contrast, a directly deliberative polyarchy is one in which several agents in a decentralised system participate in the formation of policy through various points of dialogue. The process of forming standards for the determination of satisfactory public goals is in a constant process of renegotiation between various participating actors. This renegotiation, or ongoing development, is particularly important because it gets past the conception of the legislature as the originator of ends and the executive as determiner of means that is instinct in the traditional theory of the separation of powers. Means and ends are in fact constantly evolving in a dynamic process as circumstances change.[53] (This observation reproduces Lindblom's discussion of means and ends noted above.[54]) The absence of a public and legitimating presence in this ongoing process constitutes the chief problem their theory is designed to overcome: the reconciliation of constitutionally limited government with the need for delegated law-making by expert agencies. To ensure adequate participation and goal formation in this process, the directly deliberative polyarchy is focused on fostering participation at the localised level in which such a process takes place.

The role of courts in this system is to facilitate and supervene the process to ensure that the role of local entities is adequately represented in this process of standard-articulation and means-selection.[55] The two key features of judicial decision-making are (a) that courts interpret constitutional and other core values within an approach grounded in the experimentalist understanding, that is that such values are in fact open to renegotiation and redefinition, and (b) the courts defer to political actors' articulation of ends and means only if they have created 'the kind of record that makes possible an assessment of their linking principle and practice'.[56]

---

[52] Dorf and Sabel, 'A Constitution of Democratic Experimentalism', 316ff.
[53] *Ibid.*, 390–5.
[54] The authors do not discuss Lindblom, but they must have assumed the link was obvious.
[55] *Ibid.*, 388ff.   [56] *Ibid.*, 389.

Dorf and Sabel acknowledge the overlapping features between the idea of incrementalism and their own theory of democratic experimentalism, and sought to construct their theory in view of some of the problems they associated with incrementalism, namely, that participation of the vulnerable in a decentralised polyarchy could be weak, and that the approach would be unduly process-oriented.[57]

I agree with much of its pragmatic orientation, the emphasis on incremental methods, the depth of theorisation, and the learned exploration of many illuminating examples. The approach has been developed in respect of social rights by Alana Klein, and is also noted with some approval by Mark Tushnet in his discussion of social rights.[58] I nonetheless have some important misgivings, and the gulf here is greater than that between Sunstein's minimalism and the default approach advocated in this book.

It is necessary first to refine what exactly the role is for judges. As Cohen and Sabel put it elsewhere, it is 'to require that problem-solvers themselves make policy with express reference to both constitutional and relevant policy reasons'.[59] But that result can be reached easily in non-constitutional public law, and Richard Stewart's masterpiece made both that legal fact and its attendant problems quite clear.[60] No doubt, the response is that the authors mean *real* consultation and listening – adequate goals and proper procedures for input. As Dorf and Sabel make clear:

> Experimentalist judging focuses on the permissibility of reasons, and responses to threats to fundamental norms ... experimentalist courts ask whether the parties whose actions are challenged have satisfied their obligation to grant those rights of participation revealed to be most effective by comparison with rolling best practices elsewhere.[61]

This articulation leaves unanswered several hard questions, such as whether reasons are 'permissible', and what standard judges will use to evaluate best practices elsewhere. In my view, the enormous range of examples surveyed shed no further light on this question. One assumes that among the signposts are the ideas of directly deliberative polyarchy,

---

[57] *Ibid.*, 404–18.

[58] A. Klein, 'Judging as Nudging: New Governance Approaches for the Enforcement of Constitutional Social and Economic Rights' (2008) 39 *Columbia Human Rights Law Review* 351; M. Tushnet, *Weak Courts, Strong Rights: Judicial Review and Social Welfare Rights in Comparative Constitutional Law* (Princeton University Press, 2008), pp. 248, 249, 256.

[59] Cohen and Sabel, 'Directly Deliberative Polyarchy', 335.

[60] See the discussion in Chapter 9, section III.A.1.

[61] Dorf and Sabel, 'A Constitution of Democratic Experimentalism', 403.

experimentation, and the localism inherent in both ideas. But that too is unsettling. For example, when the authors do examine a welfare rights issue in that paper, they describe the virtues of experimentation by contrasting (1) a local government policy that uses a variety of institutional mechanisms to stimulate employment, with (2) another in which a local government, 'horrified at the prospect of inducing indolence by providing welfare in the first place, can decide, on the contrary, to provide only minimum training and job placement services'.[62] They then contrast these experimentalist (and thus endorsed) alternatives with those available in 'mass democracies' with their 'central welfare bureaucracies' which sadly 'had the authority to block anything like the second type of solution'.[63] The idea that experimentalism would support disabling national government from requiring local government to provide services is more than a little worrying. It reveals the Pandora's box that the substance of polyarchy and procedure of experimentalism might open. In my view, democratic experimentalism might well have allowed the statutes at issue in *Lochner* and *Chaoulli* to fall, both being attacked for overbreadth and what remained of the underlying regulatory programme liable to be whittled down in subsequent litigation, spurring a deregulatory spiral. And those who opposed the creation of the National Health Service in Britain would have drawn more support from the experimentalist thesis than would the visionary politicians who succeeded in creating it.

There are a few other difficulties. First, it is not quite clear how the idea of participation answers most social rights concerns. Most claimants are not just asking to be heard; they are asking to be given benefits. They are asking that unfair distinctions be removed,[64] that programmes make provision for them,[65] that substantive choices about risk be overturned,[66] that expensive medical treatment be funded,[67] or water provided.[68] One can

[62] *Ibid.*, 406.   [63] *Ibid.*
[64] *Khosa and Others* v. *Minister of Social Development and Others*, 2004 (6) BCLR 569 (CC); *R (Morris)* v. *Westminster City Council and the First Secretary of State* [2005] EWCA Civ 1184.
[65] *South Africa* v. *Grootboom*, 2000 (11) BCLR 1169 (CC).
[66] *Minister of Health and others* v. *Treatment Action Campaign and Others* 2002 (10) BCLR 1033 (CC); *R (on the Application of Anne Marie Rogers)* v. *Swindon NHS Primary Care Trust, Secretary of State for Health* [2006] EWCA Civ 392.
[67] *R (on the Application of Anne Marie Rogers)* v. *Swindon NHS Primary Care Trust, Secretary of State for Health* [2006] EWCA Civ 392; *Soobramoney* v. *Minister of Health (KwaZulu-Natal)* [1997] (12) BCLR 1696 (CC).
[68] *Mazibuko and Others* v. *City of Johannesburg and Others* (CCT 39/09) 2010 (4) SA 1 (CC).

shoehorn these claims into a participatory paradigm, but only with some strain.

Second, the theory starts from the assumption that the features of American constitutionalism, such as the separation of powers and federalism, are in 'crisis': '[n]one functions as originally intended; it is debatable whether any functions at all'.[69] Cohen and Sabel say that the whole theory is 'animated by a recognition of the limits on the capacity of legislatures to solve problems – either on their own or by delegating tasks to administrative agencies – despite the importance of solutions'.[70] I would hope that it is clear by now that the animating idea in this book – for countries having the background political conditions set out in Chapter 1 – is nearly the opposite. The courts, in my view, must work in tandem and in collaboration with these other institutions. The experimentalists agree with that statement, but put the courts in the role of manager, and castigate the political process as dysfunctional. The principle of inter-institutional collaboration, by contrast, means accepting that the various institutions generally seek in good faith to do their own work and cooperate with other branches until it is shown to be otherwise. This is not naïve optimism. All *good* welfare states were built by legislatures, run by administrators, sustained by political consensus, and respected by the courts. A theory that implies otherwise seeks to make a model out of American exceptionalism.

Third, democratic experimentalism does not, in my view, take seriously the epistemic and legitimacy concerns that arise by giving the courts the role of manager of this process of deliberative polyarchy. For one, what gives courts the mandate to impose a theory of governance as rich as that? Recall that the theory of democratic experimentalism is a holistic theory of governance – not a recipe for judges alone. It is an invitation for judges to impose that theory on the other two branches. It is one thing for politicians to do so, but entirely another for a court to do so on the back of a bill of rights. Nor should it be forgotten that judges have to *interpret* laws and cannot, in the ordinary run of things, use legal sources as occasions to improvise new forms of governance.

Lastly, and perhaps of greatest importance, the theory gives less attention to the problems of institutional capacity. The authors apparently believe that the public law litigation paradigm (involving the appointment

---

[69] Dorf and Sabel, 'A Constitution of Democratic Experimentalism', 270.
[70] *Ibid.*, 334.

of masters and supervised negotiation) is a panacea. But it is not,[71] and is not, for the most part, even a possibility in most countries. Polycentricity, expertise, and flexibility present subsets of problems and the solutions to them need to be more carefully tailored than a catalogue of abstract principles backed by a range of exotic structural reform cases.

V   Criticisms of incrementalism

While I regard incrementalism as a theme and not the driving force of the analysis of judicial restraint in constitutional social rights adjudication, it is nonetheless a key unifying theme. Given its importance, therefore, there are some general objections against the view that must be addressed squarely.

A   Inert incrementalism

There have been a number of criticisms of incrementalism in public administration and public policy decision-making.[72] The basic critique is that the strategy is unduly inertial. Whether true or not, the more direct concern here is to distinguish incrementalism as a *judicial* strategy of decision-making. Recall that the New Deal legal luminaries advocated strong social change, and called for strong judicial deference as a way to *facilitate* it.[73] Much of the critique of *political* and *administrative* incrementalism is focused on situations in which inaction will lead to either no public response, or insufficiently rapid public response to a particular problem. In public law, this condition is rarer. Courts constrain the decisions of *other public institutions*. Therefore, in law, the institutional analysis must be more comparative. Judges *not* acting may be tantamount, as the functionalists Harlow and Rawlings hold, to giving the green light to government *to* act.[74] Under such circumstances, one cannot say with any certainty that judicial incrementalism favours the status quo. And

---

[71] See Chapter 9, section III.A.3.
[72] See, notably, R. E. Goodin, *Political Theory and Public Policy* (The University of Chicago Press, 1982), Chapters 1 and 2; Y. Dror, 'Muddling Through – Science or Inertia?' (1964) 24 *Public Administration Review* 153; J. Forester, 'Bounded Rationality and the Politics of Muddling Through' (1984) 44 *Public Administration Review* 23; A. Grandori, 'A Prescriptive Contingency View of Organizational Decision Making' (1984) 29 *Administrative Science Quarterly* 192.
[73] See Chapter 8, section II.
[74] C. Harlow and R. Rawlings, *Law and Administration* (3rd edn, Cambridge University Press, 2009), Chapter 1.

none of the more powerful objections to incrementalism as a strategy for decision-making therefore apply.

Some may argue, though, that judicial incrementalism itself sells legal accountability short. It might be the view is that the role of judges is to give effect to fundamental values, including certain common law constitutional rights or the rule of law. People may regard it as an abdication of the court's role as a guardian of fundamental rights, or agent of transformative constitutionalism.

That vision for courts is partly correct, but also partly romantic and quixotic. The correct aspects are in my view compatible with the approach stated here. The book does, after all, affirm the role of constitutional social rights adjudication. But recognising the principles of restraint is imperative in order to ensure the role of multi-institutional protection of social rights, as set out in Chapter 2. The analysis in Chapter 3 showed that legal accountability can do good, but can also be harmful if not deployed correctly. And if, as I showed in Chapter 2, legislative and administrative action are the key pillars of social rights, then a green light for administration can be incredibly important. Obviously, such avenues do not always work, and the principle of inter-institutional collaboration can break down. Where that is the case, however, incrementalism not only provides a way of getting the process going, but, according to those who have studied structural reform litigation carefully,[75] it is the only way to do so effectively and responsibly.

We would be wise to remember, too, that although we rightly dismiss some old shibboleths about the difference between social and civil rights adjudication, it remains true that, for most traditional civil rights adjudication, rulings regarding police procedure, forbidding discrimination, securing prisoner rights, or allowing free expression tend not to generate complex and unknowable allocative impact or reconfiguration of bureaucracies. When they do, they generate the same kinds of problems diagnosed in this book, and, ultimately, to be effective and good, the courts will adopt incrementalist methods to achieve them. On the other hand, it is much easier for judges to just say 'no' by striking down statutes, regulations, and policies. Here, although the judicial act seems simple and sustainable, the impact would not be incrementalist. And it is here that the damage can be considerable. That is the lesson of the *Lochner* era. I have argued that incrementalism is one way to heed that lesson.

---

[75] See Chapter 9, section III.A.3.

On a more positive note, in my view incrementalism can and ought to be a dynamic, experimental, and searching process. Incrementalism indicates the way that we achieve goals. It is manifestly not an invitation to judges to do nothing. Yet it *is* an invitation to advocates to craft their arguments in a way that respects the principles of restraint and the theme of incrementalism. If so, we can expect the courts' jurisprudence to grow, like a living tree, and for the various affected parties to reach a mutual adjustment as the new legal standards develop over time. Those who seek more radical social change are banging on the wrong door. If the cry is that 'the legislature does not work', then the answer must be that neither is that true historically, and nor is there any evidence of courts generally doing a better job when legislatures are lax. The truth is that constitutional social rights adjudication works best when there is inter-institutional collaboration between all three branches, and respect for the principles of restraint and the theme of judicial incrementalism are the best way to give effect to that principle. The battle must be fought on all fronts at once.

B   Insidious incrementalism

Some will doubtless be more concerned that the acceptance of welfare rights jurisdiction, together with the techniques of incrementalism, will give judges the capacity to issue localised rulings on an ad hoc basis. This may prompt claimants to assert constitutional social rights arguments at every turn. This pattern could have an inflationary effect – a mission or rights creep might set in. A lot of local incrementalism, in other words, might amount to a large aggregate impact. This threat is real, and the concern derives theoretical sophistication from Adrian Vermeule's observations on the problems of judicial coordination.[76] It is what occurred in the Latin American experience of social rights litigation.[77] It is a real threat for our case study too, because, and as I have clarified earlier, everyone has pervasive interaction with the welfare state from the cradle to the grave, and many millions will claim entitlements before tribunals. And, no doubt, if a new social rights instrument is adopted, there will be pressure from the community of advocates to get judges to show that the new constitution makes a difference. The possibility of rights inflation is not to be dismissed.

---

[76] Vermeule, *Judging under Uncertainty*, Chapter 5.
[77] See Chapter 3, section III.D.

Neither should it be exaggerated, though. First, the experience of inflation in South Africa has been notably slight (even absent any doctrine of
incrementalism). There have been only a handful of leading social rights
cases at the Constitutional Court level in the first fifteen years of the new
constitutional order, and only one of them imposed financial burdens of
any considerable size on the government.[78] That is neither a high number of
cases, nor a high amount of allocative impact, and both in a country where
social deprivation and inequality are particularly widespread. I have already
addressed the Latin American hiccup.[79] Second, precisely this fear was
felt with respect to the use of the Human Rights Act 1998, but at least one
empirical study has showed that even though lawyers tended to overuse the
Act, the fears proved unfounded.[80] Neither can it be forgotten that it is hard
for people on low incomes to make frivolous use of judicial review – claims
funded by legal aid usually need to show a reasonable prospect of success.
Third, the techniques of cautious expansion and particularisation already
flag this concern. The issue of whether a particular approach will lead to a
sizeable increase in claims – normally called the 'floodgates' issue – is one
the determination of which lies at the core of judicial expertise. Every new
standard common law judges adopt is done in consideration of this problem. Fourth, if this problem transpires, it is one that can be studied, and the
results fed back into the system by proposing to judges that they apply the
technique of cautious expansion with greater rigour, or the technique of
revisitation to stem the tide. Above all, judges and tribunal members should
stand ready to say 'no' when the gates are being pushed too hard. That is not
(necessarily) an abdication of their role. It is a recognition of their distinct
role in a multi-institutional system of rights protection. On the whole, then,
and given the judicial culture in the United Kingdom and similar countries, it seems that the last of our worries should be the prospect of judges
flinging open the gates of the treasury to the poor.

C   Impossible incrementalism

How can one know for sure that judges will opt for incrementalism or
give weight to the principles of restraint? If the case for constitutional

---

[78] *Khosa and Others* v. *Minister of Social Development and Others*, 2004 (6) BCLR 569
(CC).
[79] See Chapter 3, section III.D.
[80] V. Bondy, *The Impact of the Human Rights Act on Judicial Review: An Empirical Study*
(London: Public Law Project, 2003). See also my discussion of this study in Chapter 3,
section III.B.

social rights depends on it, a lot turns on this point. Adrian Vermeule, for instance, writes about what he calls the 'division fallacy', namely, 'to suppose that an interpretive strategy that would be beneficial if adopted by all judges should therefore be adopted by any particular judge.'[81] He thinks it a common mistake that constitutional theorists prescribe roles for courts without duly considering the difficulty of judges all adopting that role.[82]

That seems to me to be a problem for any theory of judicial review, including Vermeule's advocacy of legal formalism. And the problem of a lack of coordination is one that besets the United States in particular, because there is deep disagreement in the highest court itself about the correct approach to interpretation.[83] That condition does not ordinarily prevail elsewhere. More importantly, there is ample reason to think that the prescription of judicial incrementalism will prevail precisely because the fit with judicial culture is so close that a number of authors think that judges necessarily work incrementally.[84] And it mirrors the approaches taken in South Africa so far, and in Britain.[85] So long as judges recognise that *preventing* government action can itself be a form of non-incrementalism, then it is not unreasonable to have expectations of incrementalism. It is true that this is not the necessary outcome, but there is certainly a strong gravitational pull towards incrementalism. This book seeks to justify that force as well. For those who fail to be persuaded, a still more cautious strategy would be to incorporate interpretive principles that give effect to the basic idea directly in the constitutional text.

VI   Incrementalist answers to familiar social rights problems

Now that the full theory has been set out, it is helpful to revisit a few of the key issues for those who are sceptics of constitutional social rights.

---

[81] Vermeule, *Judging under Uncertainty*, p. 121, and see Chapter 5 generally.

[82] *Ibid.*, pp. 132–5.

[83] A. Scalia and A. Gutmann (eds.), *A Matter of Interpretation: Federal Courts and the Law* (Princeton University Press, 1997).

[84] See authors cited in note 5 above.

[85] On the experience in the United Kingdom, see J. King, 'United Kingdom: Asserting Social Rights in a Multi-Layered System', in M. Langford (ed.), *Social Rights Jurisprudence: Emerging Trends in Comparative and International Law* (Cambridge University Press 2009).

A   Enforcement of positive obligations

The claim that courts do not enforce positive obligations has been a favourite among critics of social rights, especially conservative or libertarian critics. The response of social rights advocates has been to identify cases in which positive rights have been enforced. I showed in Chapter 1 the limitations both of that argument and of the standard reply to it. The reply does not address the risky enterprise argument against social rights – that the magnitude of positive obligations could increase to unsustainable levels.

Incrementalism answers this problem by providing a set of techniques for controlling the expansion of positive obligations. On this approach, such expansion will follow a similar pattern as it has under the European Convention on Human Rights, in Convention rights adjudication in Britain, in Canada, and as it has under the constitution in South Africa. In Britain, in particular, where there is a reasonably well-functioning welfare state, the review will tend to be interstitial and parasitic on existing legal frameworks.

It is fair to assume that if constitutional social rights were adopted, there would be growth in positive obligations. This may be true, but if the prescriptions advocated in this book were followed, it would be steady, predictable, and controlled. It is ultimately for the legislature and the people to decide whether to commit to such a controlled expansion. It would be a decision to elevate, in a vague fashion, the existing commitments within the welfare state to something slightly more robust. The Human Rights Act 1998 has played a similar function in the area of Britain's existing commitments to civil and political rights, and there is little reason to believe that a similar set of commitments towards the welfare state – most of which is already subject to adjudication through tribunals – would be much more of a radical step. To say that a bill of social rights would lead to more positive obligations is therefore no good objection. It would rather be surprising if a bill of social rights did not have that effect. The point here is that the effect would be controlled, and time would be given for the adjustments required, and that the experience is a familiar one.

B   Evaluation of resource scarcity

The constant refrain of social rights sceptics is that courts are not well positioned to evaluate the availability of resources. Now that the principles of restraint and theme of incrementalism are made clear, it is also time to be clear here as well that I generally agree with this claim. But it does not obviate the role for courts in social rights adjudication. Courts, except in the most exceptional of cases, cannot and should not scrutinise line-items in budgets to say that some expenditure should not have been made in preference to some other.[86] But they can and often do say that resource scarcity is *not a permissible reason* for failing to respect some legal principle.[87]

I clarified in an earlier article why allocative impact is justiciable and has been for some time.[88] In that article I distinguished between the judicial review of discretionary allocative decision-making on reasonableness grounds, where scarcity was a relevant consideration, and contrasted it with the allocative impact created by some judgment. The former was traditionally considered non-justiciable in English public law, but the Human Rights Act had changed the situation slightly. What courts were shy of was assessing arguments relating to a public authority's budgeting priorities. This is what the Court of Appeal was effectively being asked to allow in the *Child B* case,[89] a claim rejected for the Court by Sir Thomas Bingham MR. In *Child B*, a father obtained judicial review of a health authority's decision to deny funding for experimental medical treatment for his daughter, who was dying from acute myeloid leukaemia. He had found new doctors who believed that another chance existed for his daughter. The Cambridge Health Authority disagreed. They said that they had to make the best of scarce resources, and they were worried that the treatment would prolong the suffering the girl was undergoing without increasing her chances of living. In the High Court, Justice Laws found that the authority had to do 'more than toll the bell of tight resources' – they had to justify the decision by demonstrating the process of budgeting leading up to the decision.[90] That was too much for the Court of Appeal, in which Sir Thomas Bingham MR, held that a duty to give reasons like that would inevitably invite the courts to begin reviewing and setting aside budgeting decisions. He held that 'difficult and agonising decisions have to be made about how a limited budget is best allocated' and it is not for the court to make such choices.[91]

Lord Bingham, as he later became, was in some views the most outstanding judge of his generation and a great friend of human rights

---

[86] I am in now way suggesting that expert international committees, non-government organisations, inspectors, ombudsman, or other bodies do not have such aptitudes.

[87] J. King, 'The Justiciability of Resource Allocation' (2007) 70(2) *Modern Law Review* 197.

[88] *Ibid.*

[89] *R* v. *Cambridge Health Authority, ex parte B* [1995] 2 All ER 129 (CA).

[90] [1995] 1 FLR 1055 (QB) 1065.

[91] *Ex parte B*, 2 All ER 129 (CA) 137.

(including especially those having a social rights dimension).[92] In one case concerning whether care for the sick, elderly, and disabled was a function of a public nature for the purposes of s. 6 of the Human Rights Act 1998, he held, in dissent, that:

> Historically, the attitude of the state towards the poor, the elderly and the incapable has not been uniformly benign. But for the past 60 years or so it has been recognised as the ultimate responsibility of the state to ensure that [the sick, elderly and disabled] are accommodated and looked after through the agency of the state and at its expense if no other source of accommodation and care and no other source of funding is available. This is not a point which admits of much elaboration. That the British state has accepted a social welfare responsibility in this regard in the last resort can hardly be a matter of debate.[93]

There is no contradiction between the views expressed in the *Child B* case and in this one. In my view, *Child B* remains sound authority in principle as well as law for the proposition that judges should not ordinarily scrutinise budgets. That is a process that takes time, comparison of alternatives, negotiation, compromise, flexibility, and the ability to survey the consequences of any allocation.

This is not to say that information gleaned from budgets should not be put before courts. Budget information can provide important evidence of the extent of allocative impact, for one. This was the strategy taken in both South African and Canadian cases. A Canadian example is *Eldridge* v. *British Columbia*,[94] in which the Supreme Court found that a hospital's failure to provide interpretation services for the hearing impaired was unconstitutional, and that the justification of scarce resources failed. In that case, the allocative impact was projected to be 0.0025 per cent of the provincial health care budget, a mere CND$150,000.[95] This was rightly deemed insufficient to justify the type of unequal treatment that was said to arise from the case. This case is clearly justifiable by reference to the incrementalist principle, and the budgetary evidence of impact contributed to the reasonableness of the finding. It has similarities to but may be contrasted with the South African *Khosa* case,[96] one in which it was found

---

[92] See *R* v. *Secretary of State for the Home Department, ex parte Limbuela* [2005] UKHL 66; *Kay and Others* v. *Lambeth London Borough Council; Leeds City Council* v. *Price and Others* [2006] UKHL 10.

[93] *YL* v. *Birmingham City Council* [2007] UKHL 27 [14]–[15].

[94] [1997] 3 SCR 624 (SCC).   [95] *Ibid.*, [87].

[96] *Khosa and Others* v. *Minister of Social Development and Others*, 2004 (6) BCLR 569 (CC).

that permanent residents had an enforceable right to the same social security payments as naturalised citizens. In *Khosa*, the Court treated the question of resources in a more questionable manner. It found that the expansion of such benefits would, accepting the government's estimation of likely costs, have an allocative impact of about 2 per cent of the social grants budget, a budget that was anyway projected to increase quite substantially.[97] This was considered insufficiently small by the majority, though the dissenting judge felt it was more significant.[98] This result is more difficult to justify. Two per cent might not look like much, but to put it into perspective, 2 per cent of the UK social security spending in 2009–2010 was £4.5 billion, which is roughly the size of the entire budget for prisons in the same year.[99] However much the outcome in *Khosa* looks attractive, it is hard, if not impossible, to square with the principles set out in this book.

So, if judges are not to reorganise budgets, but can look at allocative impact and sometimes treat it as non-decisive, how should they do it? In my view, there are a few signposts that will guide the way. First, a substantive principle such as fairness, equality, or other right may apply so plainly by analogy or necessary implication that it will exclude the relevance of allocative impact. Second, judges may (and intuitively do) use the comparative experience within its own system of adjudication, and perhaps in other similar systems, as a guide to what level of allocative impact is acceptable or workable. So there can be cross-referencing (whether overtly or in chambers) to other areas of the law, such as statutory interpretation, tort liability of public authorities, human rights law and so on. This is precisely how incrementalism works. It is learning by doing, and feeding lessons back into the system. For this to work in ideal fashion, it will be useful and important for public authorities to attempt to keep track of particularly disruptive effects of allocative impact, a task best charged to researchers or auditors, or built into reporting procedures.

Third, and in my view the most important factor in practice, judges will themselves develop an intuitive sense of what sort of resource implications a public bureaucracy can bear. They develop a sense of this through years of day-to-day experience at the Bar and on the bench in dealing with cases having financial repercussions for government. I spent some time discussing the importance of intuitive knowledge in Chapter 8, and it should not

---

[97] *Ibid.*, [62].   [98] *Ibid.*, [129].
[99] HM Treasury, Public Expenditure Statistical Analyses 2011, Cm 8104 (2011), p. 69 (Table 5.2).

be forgotten that judges possess such knowledge as well, and that due to the appellate structure, their expertise may also be treated as an instance of collective judicial expertise. Surely, judges may make mistakes here, but some mistakes are a feature of public decision-making. The techniques of incrementalism and application of the principles of restraint will contain them, and legal and social commentary will point them out. Fourth, there will be an evolution of legal practice in which arguments by counsel, nudged by cautious precedent, will coalesce around doctrines and claims in which allocative impact is contained. Lastly, and for all the reasons given above, substantial macro-level impact not generated clearly by legal obligations ought ordinarily to be avoided. The greater the scope of interests covered by the decision-making that is challenged, the more courts will and ought to gravitate towards less intrusive remedies, such as declaratory relief, vague standards, procedural remedies, non-constitutional remedies and so on.

VII   Incrementalism and the principles of restraint

Incrementalism remains a heuristic and a general theme, and is not offered as a complete substitute for the principles set out in Part II of this book. It is rather offered as a default position. The principles of restraint remain relevant for the analysis of particularly difficult issues that arise in social rights cases (e.g. social science evidence, claims by non-marginalised groups, structural injunctions) or when a claimant asks the court to depart from an incrementalist approach in a given case.

The idea of incrementalism can help by shaping and guiding the way in which the principles are to be applied. It can serve as the default position to be adopted when the principles themselves involve too complex an analysis, or deliver an unclear message because different principles themselves send different or unclear messages. There will, nonetheless, be cases in which the principles of restraint require a more interventionist outcome than the incrementalist ethos would suggest. Incrementalism will have little to say about how failures of expertise should be identified or handled. In the English *ex parte World Development Movement* case,[100] the Court quashed a minister's decision to provide funding for a hydro-electric dam in Malaysia on the grounds that it was not for the purposes of development in the country. The disbursed sum at stake was very substantial – £316 million. Yet the minister's failure to heed his own

---

[100]   *R v. Secretary of State for Foreign Affairs, ex parte World Development Movement* [1995] 1 WLR 386 (QBD).

expert's assessment of the Pergau Dam's benefits provided the distinct-ive fact in the case that proved the exercise of his statutory power was illegal. This was not an incrementalist remedy, but a wholly justified one. Similarly, in the *Treatment Action Campaign* case,[101] the determination that the government's position contradicted the established scientific evi-dence justified more searching review of the government's nationwide HIV/Aids strategy and its regulation of the availability of anti-retroviral drugs. Recall that the government's programme of pilot test sites in that case *was* incremental. So were the odious grade-a-year plans for racial integration that were invalidated in America during the civil rights era.[102] Incrementalism also fails to account for judicial expertise as well. In the South African *Jaftha* case,[103] the Constitutional Court insisted that courts must supervise the process by which trifling debts are executed by seizure of the debtor's home and eviction of the occupants. This too involved a question that affected a regime of security for lending as well as of tenure. The Court's own expertise in overseeing such proceedings, and know-ledge of the costs of doing so, was relevant to its confidence in mandating the court procedure.

The principle of democratic legitimacy may sometimes require more or less judicial restraint than the idea of incrementalism alone. When the court adjudicates an absolute or unqualified right, it may claim a mandate to exercise greater scrutiny of the measure being challenged. Further, the category of clear or core cases in Chapter 6,[104] and of clear legal mandates in Chapter 7,[105] recognises that sometimes legal interpretation will lead to only one conclusion: that the legal sources will only, properly con-strued, bear one interpretation and that the content of the right would be negated if the state's obligation is not enforced. Incrementalism and the principles of restraint, on this view, cannot dispense with the rule of law. They remain a supplementary guide to its interpretation.

On the other hand, where the individual challenging a legislative meas-ure is not particularly vulnerable to majoritarian bias or neglect, and does not come within the other classes of exception, the court ought to review on a more deferential standard of rationality review. A small step can be too big in such circumstances. Furthermore, as was noted in the analysis

---

[101] *Minister of Health and others* v. *Treatment Action Campaign and Others* (*TAC* case), 2002 (10) BCLR 1033 (CC).

[102] See M. Klarman, *From Jim Crow to Civil Rights: The Supreme Court and the Struggle for Racial Equality* (New York: Oxford University Press, 2004), p. 361.

[103] *Jaftha* v. *Schoeman and others, Van Rooyen* v. *Stoltz and others*, 2005 (2) SA 140 (CC).

[104] Section IV.C.3.   [105] Section V.A.

of democratic legitimacy, this principle of democratic legitimacy is relevant to the exercise of judicial restraint in cases involving executive action as well. Incrementalism fails on its own to make such distinctions.

The idea of flexibility and incrementalism share the closest conceptual connection. It is, however, an open question whether incrementalism alone puts sufficient emphasis on the nature of the problems affecting the recognition of procedural rights. (Notably, Sunstein's judicial minimalism and Dorf and Sabel's democratic experimentalism clearly do not emphasise this problem.) There is a less overt attention given to the issues of agenda control, costs, and delay in these more general theories, and it may be that a more direct focus on the principle of flexibility is important.

All told, then, it seems that the idea of incrementalism provides a useful set of techniques for addressing the various situations in which there is uncertainty in the application of the various principles of restraint. It is a natural tool to use in conditions of uncertainty. But it can only serve as a rough rule of thumb or heuristic that must work against a more sophisticated backdrop of principles to which an appeal may be made in particularly challenging social rights cases.

VIII   Conclusion

This section stands as the conclusion of this chapter as well as a summary of the entire book. It is helpful to retrace the steps traversed to see the conclusion towards which they all lead.

In Part I of the book, I introduced the case for constitutional social rights. That case comprises four chapters. In Chapter 2, I began by introducing different moral and legal interpretations of the term 'social rights', and set out a defence of the idea that all persons have a human right to a social minimum. I examined different political theories that support that view, each arriving at a consensus that any just society ought to protect a social minimum. That political conclusion complements the analytical structure of human rights discourse, because it explains the normative importance of the human interests that the structure of rights is meant to identify, and in respect of which it specifies certain state duties. I sought further to specify the content of the bundle of resources that would constitute the social minimum, and examined the nature of a state's obligations to secure it to the holders of such rights. Importantly, I examined how various state institutions can and ought to give effect to such obligations, and in particular, the role of legislatures, the executive, of adjudicative institutions outside of constitutional law, and of the constitution and constitutional adjudication. The conclusion was that constitutional social rights can play an important role in protecting the social minimum, but that it is a subsidiary role and must be understood in that way.

In Chapter 3, I expanded on the claim that courts can provide a worthwhile avenue for protecting social human rights by responding to a number of important challenges to that claim. I addressed a number of studies that suggest courts might be a hollow hope for social change, and also that other mechanisms of accountability deliver whatever benefits are sought from legal accountability in a cheaper and more accessible manner. The case for constitutional social rights meets these challenges successfully, and the analysis helps to shed better light on the propriety of judicial incrementalism as a strategy for social rights.

Chapter 4 began to address the specifics of constitutional adjudication itself, including the form of constitutional text, and the nature of the judge's role in constitutional social rights adjudication. Although I show in Chapter 2 that there is a substantive core to the idea of social rights, it is in Chapter 4 that it emerges that the main function of the court, in the ideal system, is to adjudicate vague constitutional obligations, by assessing the justifications put forward by the state for compliance with such obligations. I argue there that it is more appropriate to state constitutional rights obligations in a qualified rather than absolute manner. Adjudicating qualified obligations, however, means adjudicating vague constitutional obligations, and focusing less on the nature of the human interest in receiving certain resources. This role is familiar in contemporary rights adjudication. It generates inescapable vagueness, and with it, some powerful objections to constitutional review in the modern welfare state. It creates a need for a theory of judicial restraint, a need, as I demonstrated, that is not sufficiently addressed by other existing theories of interpretation.

The task of Part II of the book was to set out that theory of restraint. I commenced, in Chapter 5, by reflecting on different approaches to judicial restraint. I settled on what I call a contextual institutional approach that involves taking a broad view of justiciability, but commends judicial reasoning with principles of restraint. That chapter dealt with the form that a doctrine of restraint would take, whereas Chapters 6–9 addressed its content. In those subsequent chapters, the format is largely similar in each case. I explored the principles of democratic legitimacy, polycentricity, expertise, and flexibility. In each case, the analysis explains and confirms what is wise in these objections, and acknowledges the need to accommodate them within an approach to social rights. The manner in which the four chapters seek to accommodate each concern is similar. I state the problem and its force, but also its limitations, and how courts have adjusted to these familiar concerns in a variety of cases. The key contribution here was to propose a role for judges in which they could give weight to the nuanced principle so identified. The aim was to examine arguments and provide guidance concerning where greater restraint is indicated, or, by contrast, where judges either owe no restraint, or could make use of their legal role to ensure that the idea is respected. That latter role might involve compensating for *democratic* inadequacies in parliamentary decision-making, or ensuring that expertise is applied or not disregarded, or mandating greater flexibility in administrative and legislative decision-making.

Part III of the book consists of the present chapter only. It is a crucial chapter, though, as it draws out the general implications embedded within the complex analysis of the preceding five chapters. Due to epistemic and in some cases legitimacy concerns, the role for judges in constitutional social rights adjudication[106] ought ordinarily to proceed incrementally. Judges, on this view, ought to take small steps either by particularising their judgments, or, when reviewing policies that apply to a broad or macro-level set of interests, would impose constraints to the decision-making process that leave substantial room for future adaptation. This approach is a dynamic, searching process, one that seeks out feedback and takes new steps based on the wisdom culled from previous steps. This approach accords well with studies of organisational behaviour, it fits with the culture of judging in the countries this book is chiefly concerned with, and there are a set of clear and familiar techniques that would commend incrementalist results in a pragmatically reliable way. Judicial incrementalism provides a useful and normatively defensible rule of thumb that captures the essence of the principles of restraint outlined in Part II. It is not, however, a substitute. It would be too crude a substitute for the lengthier analysis, for one. But more importantly, it is not a substitute because at times the principles themselves will suggest a different approach to a social rights case.

---

[106] It is an open question how much that prescription applies beyond social rights cases. It appears to me that civil and political rights adjudication in Britain, Canada, and elsewhere in Europe ordinarily does proceed incrementally within the sense used here, though less so in the United States.

The conclusion of the entire study is that constitutional social rights can be an important medium for protecting social human rights. The best way to ensure that result, in countries having the background political conditions set out in Chapter 1, is for courts to enforce such rights in a manner that is ordinarily incrementalist. That role may appear restrained to some. People will want more from the courts, and even accuse judges of denying the promise of a new constitution. Yet the true concern of any advocate of social rights must be that people are secured their social human rights and social citizenship rights in the best of available ways. Legal avenues can only work effectively if they complement and ultimately collaborate with other institutions, even if that involves prodding those institutions into action. If social justice is the true concern, then judicial incrementalism is in fact an ambitious constitutional strategy. It will provide not a panacea, nor a hollow hope, but rather an important additional avenue of accountability and participation for those vulnerable persons whose moral claims to equal treatment ought to be our highest priority.

Appendix 1

The scope of economic and social rights under international law

Global

- Universal Declaration of Human Rights (1948), Arts. 22–28
- International Covenant on Economic, Social and Cultural Rights (1966/1976)[1]
- Optional Protocol to the ICESCR (2008/ (not yet in force))
- International Convention on the Elimination of All Forms of Racial Discrimination (1965/1969), Arts. 1, 2, 5(e)
- Convention on the Elimination of All Forms of Discrimination Against Women (1979/1981), Arts. 1, 10–14
- Convention on the Rights of the Child (1989/1990), Arts. 23, 24, 26–29, 31
- International Convention on the Protection of the Rights of All Migrant Workers and Members of their Families (1990/2003)
- Convention on the Rights of Persons with Disabilities (2006/2008), Arts. 4(2), 9–11, 13, 16–20, 24–30

Regional

- European Social Charter (1961/65)
- Revised European Social Charter (1996/1999)
- Additional Protocol to the European Social Charter Providing for a System of Collective Complaints (1995/1998)
- European Union Charter of Fundamental Rights and Duties (2007), Parts III, IV, V

Excluding International Labour Organisation Conventions, and other relevant but non-human rights conventions deposited with the Secretary-General of the United Nations. Citation data is provided in the Table of Authorities.
[1] = Adopted/In Force

- American Declaration of Human Rights and Duties of Man (1948), Arts. VIII, IX, XI–XVI
- American Convention on Human Rights (1969/1978), Art. 26
- Additional Protocol to the American Convention on Human Rights in the Area of Economic, Social and Cultural Rights Protocol of San Salvador (1988/1999)
- African Charter of Human and Peoples' Rights (1981/1986), Arts. 9, 10, 15–18
- African Charter on the Rights and Welfare of the Child (1990/1999), Arts. 4, 11, 12, 13, 14, 15, 16, 23
- Draft Protocol to the African Charter on Human and Peoples' Rights on the Rights of Women (2003/2005), Arts. 12–16
- Arab Charter on Human Rights (1994/not in force), Arts. 29–34, 36–39

BIBLIOGRAPHY

Abraham, A., 'The Ombudsman and Individual Rights' (2009) 61 *Parliamentary Affairs* 370.

'The Ombudsman and "Paths to Justice": a Just Alternative or Just an Alternative?" [2008] *Public Law* 1.

Ackerman, B. A., 'Beyond Carolene Products' (1985) 98 *Harvard Law Review* 713.

We the People: Foundations (Cambridge, MA: Belknap Press, 1993).

Ackerman, B. A. and Hassler, W. T., *Clean Coal/Dirty Air* (New Haven: Yale University Press, 1980).

Adler, M., 'A Socio-Legal Approach to Administrative Justice' (2003) 25 *Law and Policy* 323.

'Substantive Justice and Procedural Fairness in Social Security, UK', in Robson, P. and Kjønstad, A. (eds.), *Poverty and the Law* (Oxford: Hart Publishing, 2001).

Adler, M. and Asquith, S. (eds.), *Discretion and Welfare* (London: Heinemann Educational, 1981).

Adler, M. and Bradley, A. (eds.), *Justice, Discretion and Poverty: Supplementary Benefit Appeal Tribunals in Britain* (London: Professional Books, 1975).

Afonso da Silva, V. and Vargas Terrazas, F., 'Claiming the Right to Health in Brazilian Courts: The Exclusion of the Already Excluded?' (2011) *Law & Social Inquiry* 825.

Albrow, M., *Bureaucracy* (London: Pall Mall Press, 1970).

Alcock, P., *Understanding Poverty* (3rd edn, London: Palgrave-Macmillan, 2006).

Alexy, R., *A Theory of Constitutional Rights*, trans. J. Rivers (Oxford University Press, 2002).

All Souls/Justice, *Administrative Justice: Some Necessary Reforms* (Oxford University Press, 1988).

Allan, T. R. S., 'Human Rights and Judicial Review: A Critique of "Due Deference"' (2006) 65 *Cambridge Law Journal* 671.

Allison, J. W. F., 'Fuller's Analysis of Polycentric Disputes and the Limits of Adjudication' (1994) 53 *Cambridge Law Journal* 367.

Alston, P. and Quinn, G., 'Nature and Scope of States Parties Obligations' (1987) 9 *Human Rights Quarterly* 156.

Alston, P. and Scott, C. M., 'Adjudicating Constitutional Priorities in a Transnational Context: A Comment on Soobramoney's Legacy and Grootboom's Promise' (2000) 16 *South African Journal of Human Rights* 206.

Álvarez-Díaz, Á., González, L., and Radcliff, B., 'The Politics of Happiness: On the Political Determinants of Quality of Life in the American States' (2010) 72 *The Journal of Politics* 894.

Amos, M., *Human Rights Law* (Oxford: Hart Publishing, 2006).

Archibold, R. C. and Goodnough, A., 'California Voters Ban Gay Marriage', *New York Times*, 5 November 2008 (available at www.nytimes.com/2008/11/06/us/politics/06ballot.html).

Arden, A. *et al.*, *Local Government Constitutional and Administrative Law* (2nd edn, London: Sweet and Maxwell, 2008).

Arden, A., Hunter, C., and Johnson, L., *Homelessness and Allocations* (7th edn, London: Legal Action Group, 2006).

Arshi, M. and O'Cinneide, C., 'Third Party Interventions: The Public Interest Reaffirmed' [2004] *Public Law* 69.

Arts, W. A. and Gelissen, J., 'Models of the Welfare State', in Castles, F. G. *et al.* (eds.), *The Oxford Handbook of the Welfare State* (Oxford University Press, 2010).

Baldwin, G., 'A British Independent Regulatory Agency and the "Skytrain" Decision' [1978] *Public Law* 57.

Baldwin, J., Wikeley, N., and Young, R., *Judging Social Security: The Adjudication of Claims for Benefit in Britain* (Oxford: Clarendon Press, 1992).

Baldwin, R., *Regulating the Airlines: Administrative Justice and Agency Discretion* (Oxford: Clarendon Press, 1985).

  Rules and Government (Oxford University Press, 1995).

Baldwin, R. and Hawkins, K., 'Discretionary Justice: Davis Reconsidered' [1984] *Public Law* 570.

Balkin, J. M. and Levinson, S., 'Understanding the Constitutional Revolution' (2001) 87 *Virginia Law Review* 1045.

Barber, N., 'A Prelude to the Separation of Powers' (2001) *Cambridge Law Journal* 59.

  'Professor Loughlin's Idea of Public Law' (2005) 25 *Oxford Journal of Legal Studies* 157.

Barnard, C., *The Functions of the Executive* (Cambridge, MA: Harvard University Press, 1956).

Barnidge, R. P., 'The Due Diligence Principle under International Law' (2006) 8 *International Community Law Review* 81.

Baron, J., *Thinking and Deciding* (3rd edn, Cambridge University Press, 2000).

Barry, B., 'Political Accommodation and Consociational Democracy' (1975) 5(4) *British Journal of Political Science* 477.

Baxi, U., 'The Avatars of Indian Judicial Activism', in Verma, S. K. and Kusum, S. K. (eds.), *Fifty Years of the Supreme Court of India: Its Grasp and Reach* (New Delhi: Oxford University Press, 2000).

Beitz, C. R., *On Political Equality: An Essay in Democratic Theory* (Princeton University Press, 1990).

The Idea of Human Rights (Oxford University Press, 2009).

Bell, J., *Policy Arguments in Judicial Decisions* (Oxford University Press, 1983).

Bell, J. and Engle, G. (eds.), *Cross: Statutory Interpretation* (3rd edn, Oxford University Press, 2005).

Bellamy, R., *Political Constitutionalism: A Republican Defence of the Constitutionality of Democracy* (Cambridge University Press, 2007).

Beveridge Inter-Departmental Committee, Report on Social Insurance and Allied Services, Cm 6404 (1942).

Bickel, A., *The Least Dangerous Branch* (2nd edn, New Haven: Yale University Press, 1962).

Bickel, A. and Wellington, H., 'Legislative Purpose and the Judicial Process: The Lincoln Mills Case' (1957) 71 *Harvard Law Review* 1.

Bilchitz, D., *Poverty and Fundamental Rights: The Justification and Enforcement of SocioEconomic Rights* (Oxford University Press, 2007).

Bingham, T., 'Should Public Law Remedies Be Discretionary?' [1991] *Public Law* 64.

Blackburn, R. and Kenyon, A., *Griffith and Ryle on Parliament: Functions, Practice and Procedures* (2nd edn, London: Sweet & Maxwell, 2003).

Blackstone's Administrative Court Practice (Oxford University Press, 2006).

Blasio, B. de, 'Citizens United and the 2010 Midterm Elections' (Office of the Public Advocate of the City of New York, December 2010, available at http://advocate.nyc.gov/files/12–06–10CitizensUnitedReport.pdf.

Blom-Cooper, L., 'Third Party Intervention and Judicial Dissent' [2002] *Public Law* 602.

Blom-Cooper, L. (ed.), *Experts in the Civil Courts* (Oxford University Press, 2006).

Bogg, A., *Democratic Aspects of Trade Union Membership* (Oxford: Hart, 2009).

Bohman, J., 'Deliberative Democracy and Effective Social Freedom: Capabilities, Resources, and Opportunities', in Bohman, J. and Rehg, W., *Deliberative Democracy: Essays on Reason and Politics* (Cambridge, MA: MIT Press, 1987).

Bohman, J. and Rehg, W., *Deliberative Democracy: Essays on Reason and Politics* (Cambridge, MA: MIT Press, 1987).

Bondy, V., *The Impact of the Human Rights Act on Judicial Review: An Empirical Study* (London: Public Law Project, 2003).

Bondy, V. and Sunkin, M., 'Settlement in Judicial Review Proceedings' [2009] *Public Law* 237.

Bondy, V., Mulcahy, L. *et al.*, *Mediation and Judicial Review: An Empirical Research Study* (London: Public Law Project, 2009).

Booth, C. and Squires, D., *The Negligence Liability of Public Authorities* (Oxford University Press, 2006).

Braybrooke, D. and Lindblom, C. E., *A Strategy of Decision: Policy Evaluation as a Social Process* (New York: Free Press, 1970).

Bridges, I. (ed.), *Blackstone's Police Operational Handbook 2010: Law* (Oxford University Press, 2010).

Brown, L. N. and Bell, J. S., *French Administrative Law* (5th edn, Oxford University Press, 1998).

Brown, R. G. S. and Steel, D. R., *The Administrative Process in Britain* (2nd edn, London: Methuen & Co Ltd., 1979).

Brussiere, E., *(Dis)entitling the Poor: The Warren Court, Welfare Rights, and the American Political Tradition* (University Park, PA: Pennsylvania State University Press, 1997).

Buck, T., *Judicial Review and Social Welfare* (London: Pinter, 1998).

'Judicial Review and the Discretionary Social Fund: The Impact on a Respondent Organisation', in Buck, T., *Judicial Review and Social Welfare* (London: Pinter, 1998).

'Precedent in Tribunals and the Development of Principles' (2006) 25(4) *Civil Justice Quarterly* 458.

Buck, T., Bonner, D., and Sainsbury, R., *Making Social Security Law: The Role and Work of the Social Security and Child Support Commissioners* (Aldershot: Ashgate, 2005).

Burns, K., 'The Way the World Is: Social Facts in High Court Negligence Cases' (2004) 12 *Torts Law Journal* 215.

Calabresi, G. and Bobbit, P., *Tragic Choices* (New York: W. W. Norton & Co, 1978).

Cane, P., *Administrative Law* (4th edn, Oxford University Press, 2004).

Administrative Tribunals and Adjudication (Oxford: Hart Publishing, 2009).

Canon, B. C. and Johnson, C. A., *Judicial Policies: Implementation and Impact* (2nd edn, Washington DC: Congressional Quarterly Inc., 1999).

Carter, A., 'Proof of Legislative Facts under the Human Rights Act 1998', M.Phil Dissertation, Faculty of Law, University of Oxford (2011).

Chapus, R., *Droit administratif général* (12th edn, Paris: Editions Monchrestien, 1998).

Chayes, A., 'The Role of the Judge in Public Law Litigation' (1976) 89 *Harvard Law Review* 1281.

Choo, A., *Evidence* (Oxford University Press, 2006).

Choper, J., *Judicial Review and the National Political Process* (University of Chicago Press, 1980).

Choudry, S., 'Worse than Lochner?', in Flood, C., Roach, K., and Sossin, L. (eds.), *Access to Care, Access to Justice* (University of Toronto Press, 2005).

Christiano, T., *The Constitution of Equality: Democratic Authority and Its Limits* (Oxford University Press, 2008).

Citro, C. and Michael, R., *Measuring Poverty: A New Approach* (Washington DC: National Academies Press, 1995).

Clayton, R., 'Principles for Judicial Deference' [2006] *Judicial Review* 109.

Clements, L., *Community Care and the Law* (3rd edn, London: Legal Action Group, 2004).

Clements, L. and Thompson, P., *Community Care and the Law* (4th edn, London: Legal Action Group, 2007).

Cohen, G. A., *Self-Ownership, Freedom and Equality* (Cambridge University Press, 1995).

Cohen, J., 'Procedure and Substance in Deliberative Democracy', reprinted in Bohman, J. and Rehg, W., *Deliberative Democracy: Essays on Reason and Politics* (Cambridge, MA: MIT Press, 1997).

'The Economic Basis of Deliberative Democracy' (1989) 6 *Social Philosophy and Policy* 25.

Cohen, J. and Sabel, C., 'Directly Deliberative Polyarchy' (1997) 3 *European Law Journal* 313.

Cohen, M. (ed.), *Ronald Dworkin and Contemporary Jurisprudence* (London: Duckworth, 1984).

Collins, H. and Evans, R., *Rethinking Expertise* (University of Chicago Press, 2007).

Condorcet, Marquis de, *Essay on the Application of Analysis to the Probability of Majority Decisions* (1785).

Craig, P. P., *Administrative Law* (5th edn, London: Sweet & Maxwell, 2004).
Administrative Law (6th edn, London: Sweet & Maxwell, 2008).
EU Administrative Law (Oxford University Press, 2006).
Public Law and Democracy in the United Kingdom and the United States of America (Oxford: Clarendon Press, 1990).

Craig, P. and Tomkins, A. (eds.), *The Executive in Public Law* (Oxford University Press, 2006).

Cranston, M., *What are Human Rights?* (London: Bodley Head, 1969).

Craven, M., *The International Covenant on Economic, Social and Cultural Rights: A Perspective on its Development* (Oxford University Press, 1995).

Creyke, R. and McMillan, J., 'The Operation of Judicial Review in Australia', in Hertogh, M. and Halliday, S. (eds.), *Judicial Review and Bureaucratic Impact: International and Interdisciplinary Perspectives* (Cambridge University Press, 2004).

Cross, F., *The Theory and Practice of Statutory Interpretation* (Stanford University Press, 2009).

Crossman, R., *Socialism and the New Despotism* (London: Fabian Society, Fabian Tract No. 298, 1956).

Cyert, R. and March, J., *A Behavioural Theory of the Firm* (New York: Prentice Hall, 1963).

Dahl, R. A., *A Preface to Democratic Theory* (Expanded edn, University of Chicago Press, 1956).

Democracy and its Critics (New Haven: Yale University Press, 1989).

How Democratic is the American Constitution? (2nd edn, New Haven: Yale University Press, 2003).

On Democracy (New Haven: Yale University Press, 1998).

Daniels, N., *Just Health Care* (Cambridge University Press, 1985).

Daugherity, B. J. and Bolton, C. C. (eds.), *With All Deliberate Speed: Implementing Brown* v. *Board of Education* (Fayetteville: University of Arkansas Press, 2008).

Davidov, G., 'The Paradox of Judicial Deference' (2001) 12 *National Journal of Constitutional Law* 133.

Davis, K. C., 'An Approach to Problems of Evidence in the Administrative Process' (1942) 55 *Harvard Law Review* 364.

Administrative Law Treatise (St Paul, MN: West Publishing Co, 1958).

'Judicial, Legislative, and Administrative Lawmaking: A Proposed Research Service for the Supreme Court' (1986) 1 *Minnesota Law Review* 1.

'Judicial Notice' (1955) 55 *Columbia Law Review* 945.

Davis, K. C. and Gelhorn, W., 'Present at the Creation: Regulatory Reform Before 1946' (1986) 38 *Administrative Law Review* 511.

Davis, M. F., *Brutal Need: Lawyers and the Welfare Rights Movement, 1960–1973* (New Haven: Yale University Press, 1993).

Department for Communities and Local Government, *Allocation of Accommodation: Choice Based Lettings Code of Guidance for Local Housing Authorities* (London: TSO, 2008).

Homelessness Code of Guidance for Local Authorities (London: TSO, 2006).

'Local authority revenue expenditure and financing England: 2010–11 Budget (Revised)', Statistical Release (17 February 2011) available at: www.communities.gov.uk/documents/statistics/pdf/1846276.pdf.

Department for Constitutional Affairs, 'Transforming Public Services: Complaints, Redress and Tribunals', Cm 6243 (2004).

Department of Health, *Code of Practice: Mental Health Act 1983* (London: TSO, 2008).

Desai, A. and Muralidhar, S., 'Public Interest Litigation: Potential and Problems', in Kirpal, B. (ed.), *Supreme But Not Infallible: Essays in Honour of the Supreme Court of India* (New Delhi: Oxford University Press, 2000).

Dicey, A. V., *Introduction to the Law of the Constitution* (8th edn, London: MacMillan, 1915).

Dillon, R. S. (ed.), *Dignity, Character, and Self-Respect* (New York: Routledge, 1995).

Diver, C., 'The Judge as Political Powerbroker: Superintending Structural Change in Public Institutions' (1979) 65 *Virginia Law Review* 43.

Dixon, R., 'Creating Dialogue about Socioeconomic Rights: Strong-Form versus Weak-Form Judicial Review Revisited' (2007) 5 *International Journal of Constitutional Law* 391.

Donald, A., Mottershaw, E., Leach, P., and Watson, J., 'Evaluating the Impact of Selected Cases under the Human Rights Act on Public Services Provision', Report of the Equality and Human Rights Commission, June 2009 (available at: www.equalityhumanrights.com/uploaded_files/evaluating_the_impact_of_selected_cases_under_the_human_rights_act_on_public_services_provision.pdf).

Donelly, J., 'Natural Rights as Human Rights' (1982) 4 *Human Rights Quarterly* 391.

Donoughmore Committee, Report of the Committee on Ministers' Powers, Cmnd 4060 (1932).

Dorf, M. and Sabel, C., 'A Constitution of Democratic Experimentalism' (1998) 98 *Columbia Law Review* 267.

Dror, Y., 'Muddling Through – Science or Inertia?' (1964) 24 *Public Administration Review* 153.

Dryzek, J., *Deliberative Democracy and Beyond: Liberals, Critics and Contestations* (Oxford University Press, 2000).

Duguit, L., *Manuel de Droit Constitutionnel: Théorie générale de l'État* (3rd edn, Paris: Boccard, 1918).

Duxbury, N., *Patterns of American Jurisprudence* (Oxford University Press, 1992).
The Nature and Authority of Precedent (Cambridge University Press, 2008).

Dworkin, R., *Freedom's Law: The Moral Reading of the American Institution* (Cambridge, MA: Harvard University Press, 1996).
Justice for Hedgehogs (Cambridge, MA: Belknap Press, 2010).
Justice in Robes (Cambridge, MA: Harvard University Press, 2006).
Law's Empire (Cambridge, MA: Harvard University Press, 1986).
A Matter of Principle (Cambridge, MA: Harvard University Press, 1985).
Sovereign Virtue: The Theory and Practice of Equality (Cambridge, MA: Harvard University Press, 2000).
Taking Rights Seriously (Cambridge, MA: Harvard University Press, 1978).
Taking Rights Seriously (2nd edn, London: Duckworth, 1996).

Department for Work and Pensions, 'The Law of Social Security – The Blue Volumes', Supplement No. 93 (10 December 2011) 'List of Statutes – All Volumes', available at www.dwp.gov.uk/publications/specialist-guides/law-volumes/.

Dyzenhaus, D., 'Law as Justification: Etienne Mureinik's Conception of Legal Culture' (1998) 14 *South African Journal of Human Rights* 11.
'The Politics of Deference: Judicial Review and Democracy', in Taggart, M. (ed.), *The Province of Administrative Law* (Oxford: Hart Publishing, 1997).

Eckhoff, T., 'Guiding Standards in Legal Reasoning' (1976) 29 *Current Legal Problems* 205.

Edmond, G. (ed.), *Expertise in Regulation and Law* (Burlington, VT: Ashgate, 2004).

Edwards, R., 'Judicial Deference under the Human Rights Act' (2002) 65 *Modern Law Review* 859.

Elcock, H., 'Leading People: Some Issues of Local Government Leadership in Britain and America' (1995) 24 *Local Government Studies* 546.

Elster, J., *Sour Grapes: Studies in the Subversion of Rationality* (Cambridge University Press, 1985).

Ely, J. H., *Democracy and Distrust: A Theory of Judicial Review* (Cambridge, MA: Harvard University Press, 1980).

Endicott, T. A. O., *Administrative Law* (Oxford University Press, 2009).

  Vagueness in Law (Oxford University Press, 2000).

Epp, C. R., 'Law as an Instrument of Social Reform', in K. E. Whittington, R. D. Kelemen, and G. A. Caldeira (eds.) *The Oxford Handbook of Law and Politics* (New York: Oxford University Press, 2010).

  Making Rights Real: Activists, Bureaucrats, and the Creation of the Legalistic State (University of Chicago Press, 2010).

  The Rights Revolution: Lawyers, Activists and Supreme Court in Comparative Perspective (University of Chicago Press, 1998).

Equality and Human Rights Commission, *Human Rights Inquiry: Report of the EHRC* (London: EHRC, 2009).

Erkulwater, J. L., *Disability Rights and the American Social Safety Net* (Ithaca: Cornell University Press, 2006).

Eskridge Jr, W., 'Book Review: The Circumstances of Politics and the Application of Statutes' (2000) 100 *Columbia Law Review* 558.

  Dynamic Statutory Interpretation (Cambridge, MA: Harvard University Press, 1994).

Esping-Anderson, G., *The Three Worlds of Welfare Capitalism* (Cambridge: Polity Press, 1990).

Fabre, C., *Social Rights Under the Constitution: Government and the Decent Life* (Oxford University Press, 2001).

Farber, D. A. and Frickey, P. J., *Law and Public Choice: A Critical Introduction* (University of Chicago Press, 1991).

Feeley, M. M., 'Hollow Hopes, Flypaper, and Metaphors' (1993) 17 *Law and Social Inquiry* 745.

  'Implementing Court Orders in the United States: Judges as Executives', in Hertogh, M. and Halliday, S. (eds.), *Judicial Review and Bureaucratic Impact: International and Interdisciplinary Perspectives* (Cambridge University Press, 2004).

Feeley, M. and Rubin, E., *Judicial Policy Making in the Modern State: How the Courts Reformed America's Prisons* (Cambridge University Press, 2000).

Feinberg, J., *Social Philosophy* (Englewood-Cliffs: Prentice-Hall, 1973).

Ferraz, O., 'Brazil: Health Inequalities, Rights and Courts: The Social Impact of Judicialization of Health', in Yamin, A. and Gloppen, S. (eds.), *Litigating Health Rights: Can Courts Bring More Justice to Health?* (Cambridge, MA: Harvard University Press, 2011).

    'The Right to Health in the Courts of Brazil: Worsening Health Inequities?' (2009) 11 *Health and Human Rights: An International Journal* 33.

Finkelman, P., 'Book Review: Civil Rights in Historical Context: In Defense of *Brown*' (2008) 118 *Harvard Law Review* 973.

Fisher, E., *Risk Regulation and Administrative Constitutionalism* (Oxford: Hart, 2007).

Fiss, O., 'Against Settlement' (1984) 93 *Yale Law Journal* 1073.

    'Groups and the Equal Protection Clause' (1976) 5 *Philosophy & Public Affairs* 107.

    The Civil Rights Injunction (Bloomington: Indiana University Press, 1978).

    'The Perils of Minimalism' (2008) 9 *Theoretical Inquiries in Law* 643.

    'The Supreme Court 1978 Term: Foreword: The Forms of Justice' (1978–79) 93 *Harvard Law Review* 1.

Forbath, W. E., *Law and the Shaping of the American Labor Movement* (Cambridge, MA: Harvard University Press, 1991).

    'Not so Simple Justice: Frank Michelman on Social Rights, 1969–Present' (2004) 39 *Tulsa Law Review* 597.

Fordham, M., *Judicial Review Handbook* (5th edn, Oxford: Hart Publishing, 2008).

Forester, J., 'Bounded Rationality and the Politics of Muddling Through' (1984) 44 *Public Administration Review* 23.

Frank, J. P., 'Statement of Essential Rights', in *American Law Institute, Seventy-Fifth Anniversary 1923–1998* (American Law Institute, 1998).

Frankfurter, F. and Greene, N., *The Labour Injunction* (New York: Macmillan, 1930).

Franks Committee, Report of the Committee on Administrative Tribunals and Inquiries, Cmnd 218 (1957).

Fraser, D., *The Evolution of the British Welfare State* (3rd edn, London: Palgrave, 2003).

Fredman, S., *Human Rights Transformed: Positive Rights and Positive Duties* (Oxford University Press, 2008).

Freedman, J. O., *Crisis and Legitimacy: The Administrative Process and American Government* (Cambridge University Press, 1978).

    'Defining Taxpayer Responsibility: In Support of a General Anti-Avoidance Principle' [2004] *British Tax Review* 332.

Freeman, D. C., 'Note: The Poor and the Political Process: Equal Access to Lobbying' (1969) 6 *Harvard Journal on Legislation* 369.

Freund, E., *Administrative Powers over Persons and Property: A Comparative Survey* (University of Chicago Press, 1928).

Frug, G., 'The Ideology of Bureaucracy in American Law' (1984) 97 *Harvard Law Review* 1276.

Fuller, L., 'The Forms and Limits of Adjudication' (1978–1979) 92 *Harvard Law Review* 353.

   The Morality of Law (rev. edn, New Haven: Yale University Press, 1969).

Fuller, L. and Randall, J. D., 'Professional Responsibility: Report of the Joint Conference' (1958) 44 *American Bar Association Journal* 1159.

Galanter, M., 'Words and Deals: Using Negotiation to Teach about Legal Process' (1984) 12 *Journal of Legal Education* 268.

Galligan, D. J., *Discretionary Powers: A Study of Official Discretion* (Oxford University Press, 1986).

   Due Process and Fair Procedures: A Study of Administrative Procedures (Oxford: Clarendon Press, 1996).

Gargarella, R., Domingo, P. and Roux, T., *Courts and Social Transformation: A New Institutional Voice for the Poor?* (Aldershot: Ashgate, 2009).

Gauri, V. and Brinks, D. M., 'A New Policy Landscape: Legalizing Social and Economic Rights in the Developing World', in Gauri, V. and Brinks, D. M. (eds.), *Courting Social Justice: Judicial Enforcement of Social and Economic Rights in the Developing World* (Cambridge University Press, 2008).

   'Introduction: The Elements of Legalization and the Triangular Shape of Social and Economic Rights', in Gauri, V. and Brinks, D. M. (eds.), *Courting Social Justice: Judicial Enforcement of Social and Economic Rights in the Developing World* (Cambridge University Press, 2008).

Gauri, D. and Brinks, D. (eds.), *Courting Social Justice: Judicial Enforcement of Social and Economic Rights in the Developing World* (Cambridge University Press, 2008).

Gearty, C., *Principles of Human Rights Adjudication* (Oxford University Press, 2004).

Gearty, C., and Mantouvalou, V., *Debating Social Rights* (Oxford: Hart Publishing, 2011).

Genn, H., *Hard Bargaining: Out of Court Settlement in Personal Injury Actions* (Oxford: Clarendon Press, 1987).

Genn, H. and Genn, Y., *The Effectiveness of Representation at Tribunals* (London: Lord Chancellor's Department, 1989).

Genn, H. *et al.*, *Paths to Justice: What People Do and Think About Going to Law* (Oxford: Hart Publishing, 1999).

Giddens, A., *The Third Way: The Renewal of Social Democracy* (Cambridge: Polity Press, 1998).

Gilovich, T. and Griffin, D., 'Introduction – Heuristics and Biases: Then and Now', in Gilovich, T., Griffin, D., and Kahneman, D., *Heuristics and Biases: The Psychology of Intuitive Judgment* (Cambridge University Press, 2002).

Gilovich, T., Griffin, D., and Kahneman, D., *Heuristics and Biases: The Psychology of Intuitive Judgment* (Cambridge University Press, 2002).

Glennon, R. J., 'The Role of Law in the Civil Movement: The Montgomery Bus Boycott, 1955–1957' (1991) 9 *Law and History Review* 59.

Goodin, R. E., *Political Theory and Public Policy* (University of Chicago Press, 1982).

    Reasons for Welfare (Princeton University Press, 1988).

    Utilitarianism as a Public Philosophy (Cambridge University Press, 1995).

    'Welfare, Rights and Discretion' (1986) 6 *Oxford Journal of Legal Studies* 232.

Goodin, R. E., Headey, B., Muffels, R., and Dirven, H.-J., *The Real Worlds of Welfare Capitalism* (Cambridge University Press, 1999).

Grandori, A., 'A Prescriptive Contingency View of Organizational Decision Making' (1984) 29 *Administrative Science Quarterly* 192.

Greenawalt, K., 'Discretion and Judicial Decision: The Elusive Quest for the Fetters that Bind Judges' (1975) 75 *Columbia Law Review* 359.

    'Dworkin's Rights Thesis' (1976) 74 *Michigan Law Review* 1167.

    'Policy, Rights, and Judicial Decision' (1977) 11 *Georgia Law Review* 991.

Griffin, J., *On Human Rights* (Oxford University Press, 2008).

    Well-being (Oxford: Clarendon Press, 1986).

Griffith, J. A. G., 'The Political Constitution' (1979) 42 *Modern Law Review* 1.

Guest, S., *Ronald Dworkin* (2nd edn, Edinburgh University Press, 1997).

Gutman, A. and Thompson, D., *Democracy and Disagreement* (Cambridge, MA: Harvard University Press, 1996).

Haakonssen, K., 'Republicanism', in Goodin, R., Pettit, P., and Pogge, T. W. J., *A Companion to Contemporary Political Philosophy* (2nd edn, Oxford: Blackwell, 2007).

Habermas, J., *Between Facts and Norms*, trans. W. Rehg (Cambridge: Polity Press, 1996).

Halliday, S., 'Institutional Racism in Bureaucratic Decision-Making: A Case Study in the Administration of Homelessness Law' (2000) 27 *Journal of Law and Society* 449.

    Judicial Review and Compliance with Administrative Law (Oxford: Hart Publishing, 2004).

    'The Influence of Judicial Review on Bureaucratic Decision-Making' [2002] *Public Law* 110.

Halsbury's Laws of England (4th rev edn, London: Butterworths, 2005).

Hammond, A. H., 'Judicial Review: The Continuing Interplay between Law and Policy' [1998] *Public Law* 34.

Hannett, S., 'Third Party Intervention: In the Public Interest?' [2003] *Public Law* 128.

Hansard, HC Deb., vol. 734, col. 51, 18 October 1966.

    HC Deb., vol. 421, col. 1502–1518, 25 May 2004.

HC Deb., vol. 421, col. 1537–1538, 25 May 2004.

HC Deb., vol. 523, col. 493–586, 10 February 2011.

Hardin, R., *Morality within the Limits of Reason* (University of Chicago Press, 1988).

Hare, R. M., *Freedom and Reason* (Oxford University Press, 1963).

Harlow, C., 'Public Law and Popular Justice' (2002) 65 *Modern Law Review* 1.

Harlow, C. and Rawlings, R., *Law and Administration* (2nd edn, London: Butterworths, 1997).

Law and Administration (3rd edn, Cambridge University Press, 2009).

Pressure through Law (London: Routledge, 1992).

Hart, H. L. A., *The Concept of Law* (2nd edn, Oxford: Clarendon Press, 1994).

Hart Jr, H. M. and Sacks, A. M., *The Legal Process: Basic Problems in the Making and Application of Law* (Westbury, NY: Foundation Press, 1994).

Harvey, T. and Kenner, J., *Economic and Social Rights in the EU Charter of Fundamental Rights* (Oxford: Hart Publishing, 2003).

Hawkins, K., 'Using Legal Discretion', in Hawkins, K. (ed.), *The Uses of Discretion* (Oxford University Press, 1992).

Hayek, F. A., *The Constitution of Liberty* (London: Routledge 1960).

Haynes, M., *Incrementalism and Public Policy* (New York: Longman, 1984).

Held, D., *Models of Democracy* (3rd edn, Cambridge: Polity Press, 2006).

Henderson, A., 'Brandeis Briefs and the Proof of Legislative Facts in Proceedings under the Human Rights Act 1998' [1998] *Public Law* 563.

Hertogh, M., 'Coercion, Cooperation, and Control: Understanding the Policy Impact of Administrative Courts and the Ombudsman in the Netherlands' (2001) 23 *Law and Policy* 54.

Hertogh, M. and Halliday, S. (eds.), *Judicial Review and Bureaucratic Impact: International and Interdisciplinary Perspectives* (Cambridge University Press, 2004).

Hewart, G., *The New Despotism* (London: Ernest Benn Limited, 1929).

Heydon, J. D., *Cross on Evidence* (8th Australian edn, Sydney: LexisNexis Butterworths, 2009).

Heywood, M., 'Debunking Conglomo-talk: A Case Study of the Amicus Curiae as an Instrument for Advocacy, Investigation and Mobilisation' (2001) 5 *Law, Democracy and Development* 133.

'Preventing Mother-to-Child HIV Transmission in South Africa; Background, Strategies and Outcomes of the Treatment Action Campaign Case against the Minister of Health' (2003) 19 *South African Journal on Human Rights* 278.

Hickman, T. R., 'Constitutional Dialogue, Constitutional Theories and the Human Rights Act 1998' [2005] *Public Law* 306.

Public Law after the Human Rights Act (Oxford: Hart Publishing, 2010).

Hills, J., *Inequality and the State* (Oxford University Press, 2004).

Hirschl, R., *Towards Juristocracy* (New Haven: Yale University Press, 2004).

HMRC, 'Employment Income Manual', EIM76100 and EIM76101 (available at: www.hmrc.gov.uk).

HM Treasury, Public Expenditure Statistical Analyses 2011, Cm 8104 (2011).

Hogg, P. W., Thornton, A. A. B., and Wright, W. K., 'Charter Dialogue Revisited – Or "Much Ado About Metaphors"' (2007) 45 *Osgoode Hall Law Journal* 1.

Hogwood, B. W., Judge, D., and McVicar, M., 'Agencies, Ministers and Civil Servants in Britain', in Peters, B. G. and Pierre, J. (eds.), *Politicians, Bureaucrats and Administrative Reform* (London: Routledge, 2001).

Holloway, I., '"A Bona Fide Attempt": Chief Justice Sir Owen Dixon and the Policy of Deference to Administrative Expertise in the High Court of Australia' (2002) 54 *Administrative Law Review* 687.

Holmes Jr, O. W., *The Common Law* (Boston: Little Brown, 1881).

Horowitz, D. L., *Ethnic Groups in Conflict* (Berkeley: University of California Press, 1985).

  The Courts and Social Policy (Washington DC: Brookings Institution, 1977).

Howe, M., *Holmes–Laski Letters 1916–1935* (Oxford University Press, 1953).

Htun, M., 'Is Gender like Ethnicity? The Political Representation of Identity Groups' (2004) 2 *Perspectives on Politics* 439.

Hunt, M., 'Sovereignty's Blight: Why Contemporary Public Law Needs the Concept of "Due Deference"', in Bamforth, N. and Leyland, P. (eds.), *Public Law in a Multi-Layered Constitution* (Oxford: Hart Publishing, 2003).

Irvine, Lord, 'Judges and Decision-Makers: The Theory and Practice of Wednesbury Review' [1996] *Public Law* 65.

Ishay, M. R., *The History of Human Rights: From Ancient Times to the Globalization Era* (Berkeley: University of California Press, 2008).

Jaffe, L., 'The Illusion of Ideal Administration' (1973) 86 *Harvard Law Review* 1183.

Jenkins, D., 'There and Back Again: The Strange Journey of Special Advocates and Comparative Law Methodology' (2000) 79 *Columbia Human Rights Law Review* 279.

Joint Committee on Human Rights, 'A Bill of Rights for the UK?' (Twenty-Ninth Report of Session 2007–2008), 10 August 2008.

  'The International Covenant on Economic, Social and Cultural Rights' (Twenty-First Report of Session 2003–2004), 10 October 2004.

Jolls, C. and Sunstein, C. R., 'Debiasing through Law' (2006) 35 *Journal of Empirical Legal Studies* 199.

Jolls, C., Sunstein, C. R. and Thaler, R., 'A Behavioural Approach to Law and Economics' (1998) 50 *Stanford Law Review* 1471.

Jones, H. W., 'The Rule of Law and the Welfare State' (1958) 58 *Columbia Law Review* 143.

Jones, R., *Mental Health Act Manual* (8th edn, London: Thomson Reuters, 2008).

  Mental Health Act Manual (London: Sweet & Maxwell, 2010).

Jordan III, W. S., 'Ossification Revisited: Does Arbitrary and Capricious Review Significantly Interfere with Agency Ability to Achieve Regulatory Goals Through Informal Rulemaking?' (2000) 94 *Northwestern University Law Review* 393.

Joseph O'Connell, A., 'Political Cycles of Rulemaking: An Empirical Portrait of the Modern Administrative State' (2008) 94 *Virginia Law Review* 889.

Joubert, P., 'Grootboom dies homeless and penniless', *Mail and Guardian*, 14 August 2008.

Jowell, J., 'Judicial Deference and Human Rights: A Question of Competence', in Craig, P. and Rawlings, R. (eds.), *Law and Administration in Europe: Essays in Honour of Carol Harlow* (Oxford University Press, 2003).

'Judicial Deference: Servility, Civility or Institutional Capacity?' [2003] *Public Law* 592.

Law and Bureaucracy: Administrative Discretion and the Limits of Legal Action (New York: Dunellen Pub Co, 1975).

'The Legal Control of Administrative Discretion' [1973] *Public Law* 178.

Jowell, J. and Oliver, D., *The Changing Constitution* (4th edn, Oxford University Press, 2000).

JUSTICE, *To Assist the Court: Third Party Interventions in the UK* (London: JUSTICE, 2009).

Kagan, R. A., *Adversarial Legalism: The American Way of Law* (Cambridge, MA: Harvard University Press, 2003).

Kahneman, D. and Frederick, S., 'Representativeness Revisited: Attribute Substitution in Intuitive Judgment', in Gilovich, T., Griffin, D., and Kahneman, D., *Heuristics and Biases: The Psychology of Intuitive Judgment* (Cambridge University Press, 2002).

Kamenka, E., *Bureaucracy* (Oxford: Basil Blackwell, 1989).

Kaufmann, H., *The Administrative Behavior of Federal Bureau Chiefs* (Washington DC: Brookings Institution, 1981).

Kavanagh, A., *Constitutional Review under the UK Human Rights Act* (Cambridge University Press, 2009).

'Deference or Defiance? The Limits of the Judicial Role in Constitutional Adjudication', in Huscroft, G. (ed.), *Expounding the Constitution: Essays in Constitutional Theory* (New York: Cambridge University Press, 2008).

'Participation and Judicial Review: A Reply to Jeremy Waldron' (2003) 22 *Law and Philosophy* 451.

Keck, T. M., 'Beyond Backlash: Assessing the Impact of Judicial Decisions on LGBT Rights' (2009) 43 *Law and Society Review* 151.

Kennedy, D., *A Critique of Adjudication: Fin de Siècle* (Cambridge, MA: Harvard University Press, 1997).

Kennedy, R., 'Martin Luther King's Constitution: A Legal History of the Montgomery Bus Boycott' (1989) 98 *Yale Law Journal* 999.

Kenny, S., 'Constitutional Fact Ascertainment' (1990) 1 *Public Law Review* 134.

King, J. A., 'Constitutional Rights and Social Welfare: A Comment on the Canadian *Chaoulli* Health Care Decision' (2006) 69 *Modern Law Review* 631.

'Constitutions as Mission Statements', in Galligan, D. J. and Versteeg, M., *The Social and Political Foundations of Constitutions* (Cambridge University Press, forthcoming).

'Institutional Approaches to Judicial Restraint' (2008) 28 *Oxford Journal of Legal Studies* 409.

'Poverty and Fundamental Rights, by D. Bilchitz (Oxford University Press 2007)', [2008] *Public Law* 820.

'Proportionality: A Halfway House' (2010) 2 *New Zealand Law Review* 327.

'The Justiciability of Resource Allocation' (2007) 70(2) *Modern Law Review* 197.

'The Pervasiveness of Polycentricity' [2008] *Public Law* 101.

'The Value of Legal Accountability', in Bamforth, N. and Leyland, P., *Accountability in the Contemporary Constitution* (Oxford University Press, forthcoming).

'United Kingdom: Asserting Social Rights in a Multi-Layered System', in Langford, M. (ed.), *Social Rights Jurisprudence: Emerging Trends in Comparative and International Law* (Cambridge University Press 2009).

King Jr., M. L., *Why We Can't Wait* (New York: Signet, 2000 [1964]).

Kirkham, R., 'Auditing by Stealth? Special Reports and the Ombudsman' [2004] *Public Law* 740.

'Challenging the Authority of the Ombudsman: The Parliamentary Ombudsman's Special report on Wartime Detainees' (2006) 69 *Modern Law Review* 792.

Klarman, M., *From Jim Crow to Civil Rights: The Supreme Court and the Struggle for Racial Equality* (New York: Oxford University Press, 2004).

Klashtorny, N., 'Comment: Ireland's Abortion Law: An Abuse of International Law' (1996) 10 *Temple International and Comparative Law Journal* 419.

Klein, A., 'Judging as Nudging: New Governance Approaches for the Enforcement of Constitutional Social and Economic Rights' (2008) 39 *Columbia Human Rights Law* Review 351.

Kloppenberg, L. A., 'Avoiding Constitutional Questions' (1994) 35 *Boston College Law Review* 1003.

Kluger, R., *Simple Justice: The History of Brown v. Board of Education and Black America's Struggle for Equality* (New York: Vintage USA, 2004).

Knight, J. and Johnson, J., 'What Sort of Equality does Deliberative Democracy Require?', in Bohman, J. and Rehg, W., *Deliberative Democracy: Essays on Reason and Politics* (Cambridge, MA: MIT Press, 1987).

Komesar, N., *Imperfect Alternatives: Choosing Institutions in Law, Economics and Public Policy* (University of Chicago Press, 1994).

Law's Limits: The Rule of Law and the Supply and Demand of Rights (Cambridge University Press, 2001).

Kritzer, H. M., 'To Lawyer or Not to Lawyer? Is that the question?' (2008) 5 *Journal of Empirical Legal Studies* 875.

Krook, M. L., 'Quota Laws for Women in Politics: Implications for Feminist Practice' (2008) 15 *Social Politics* 345.

Kumm, M., 'The Idea of Socratic Contestation and the Right to Justification: The Point of Rights-Based Proportionality Review' (2010) 4 *Law and Ethics of Human Rights* 141.

Kymlicka, W., *Contemporary Political Philosophy: An Introduction* (Oxford University Press, 2002).

Kyritsis, D., 'Principles, Policies and the Powers of Courts' (2007) 20 *Canadian Journal of Law and Jurisprudence* 1.

'Representation and Waldron's Objection to Judicial Review' (2006) 26 *Oxford Journal of Legal Studies* 733.

Landis, J. L., *The Administrative Process* (New Haven: Yale University Press, 1938).

Langford, M. and King, J., 'The Committee on Economic, Social and Cultural Rights', in Langford, M. (ed.), *Social Rights Jurisprudence: Emerging Trends in Comparative and International Law* (Cambridge University Press, 2009).

Laski, H. J., 'Judicial Review of Social Policy in England' (1925–26) 39 *Harvard Law Review* 836.

The Limitations of the Expert (London: Fabian Society, Fabian Tract No. 235, 1931).

Laughlin, P. R., 'Collective Induction: Twelve Postulates' (1999) 80 *Organizational Behavior and Human Decision Processes* 50.

Lavine, S., 'Advocating Values: Public Interest Intervention in Charter Litigation' (1992) 2 *National Journal of Constitutional Law* 27.

Law Commission, 'Public Services Ombudsmen', Law Com No. 329, 13 July 2011.

Law, D. S., and Versteeg, M., 'The Evolution and Ideology of Global Constitutionalism' (2011) 99 *California Law Review* 101.

Lawrence, S. E., *The Poor in Court: The Legal Services Program and Supreme Court Decision Making* (Princeton University Press, 1990).

Lester, A. and Pannick, D. (eds.), *Human Rights: Law and Practice* (2nd edn, London: Lexis-Nexis, 2004).

Levin, B. and Moise, P., 'School Desegregation Litigation in the Seventies and the Use of Social Science Evidence: An Annotated Guide' (1975) *Law and Contemporary Problems* 50.

Levitas, R., 'The Concept and Measurement of Social Exclusion', in Pantazis, C., Gordon, D., and Levitas, R. (eds.), *Poverty and Social Exclusion in Britain: The Millennium Survey* (Bristol: Policy Press, 2006).

Lindblom, C. E., *Politics and Markets* (New York: Basic Books, 1977).
  'The Science of Muddling Through' (1959) 19 *Public Administration Review* 79.
  'Still Muddling, Not Yet Through' (1979) *Public Administration Review* 517.
Lindholm, T., 'Article 1: A New Beginning', in Eide, A. *et al.* (eds.), *The Universal Declaration of Human Rights: A Commentary* (Oslo: Scandinavian University Press, 1992).
Lipjhart, A., *Democracy in Plural Societies* (New Haven: Yale University Press, 1977).
  Patterns of Democracy: Government Form and Performance in Thirty-Six Countries (New Haven: Yale University Press, 1999).
Lipsky, M., *Street Level Bureaucracy: Dilemmas of the Individual in Public Services* (New York: Russell Sage, 1980).
Lister, R., *Poverty* (Cambridge: Polity Press, 2004).
Local Government Ombudsman, 'Annual Report 2009–2010: Delivering Public Value' (Commission for Local Administration in England) (available at www.lgo.org.uk/publications/annual-report/).
Loughlin, M., *The Idea of Public Law* (Oxford University Press, 2003).
  Legality and Locality: The Role of Law in Central–Local Government Relations (Oxford University Press, 1996).
  Public Law and Political Theory (Oxford: Clarendon Press, 1992).
Loveland, I., 'Does Homelessness Decision-Making Engage Article 6(1) of the European Convention on Human Rights' (2003) 2 *European Human Rights Law Review* 177.
  Housing Homeless Persons (Oxford University Press, 1995).
Lowe, R., *The Welfare State in Britain Since 1945* (Basingstoke: Palgrave Macmillan, 2005).
Luba, J. and Davies, L., *Housing Allocation and Homelessness: Law and Practice* (2nd edn, Bristol: Jordan Publishing Limited, 2010).
Luescher, C., 'Efficiency Considerations in European Merger Control – Just another Battle Ground for the European Commission, Economists and Competition Lawyers?' (2004) *European Competition Law Review* 71.
Lukemeyer, A., *Courts as Policymakers: School Finance Reform Litigation* (New York: LFB Scholarly Publishing, 2003).
Lusky, L., 'Minority Rights and the Public Interest' (1942) 52 *Yale Law Journal* 1.
Lyons, D., 'Between Utility and Rights', in Waldron, J. (ed.), *Theories of Rights* (Oxford University Press, 1985).
MacCormick, N., *Legal Reasoning and Legal Theory* (Oxford University Press, 1978).
Mack, K. W., 'Rethinking Civil Rights Era Lawyering and Politics in the Era before Brown' (2005) 115 *Yale Law Journal* 256.
Mackenzie, G. C., *The Politics of Presidential Appointments* (New York: Macmillan, 1981).

Mæstad, O., Rakner, L., and Ferraz, O. L. A., 'Assessing the Impact of Health Rights Litigation: A Comparative Study of Argentina, Colombia, Costa Rica, India and South Africa', in Yamin, A. and Gloppen, S. (eds.), *Litigating Health Rights: Can Courts Bring More Justice to Health?* (Cambridge, MA: Harvard University Press, 2011).

Mandel, M., *The Charter of Rights and the Legalisation of Politics in Canada* (Toronto: Thompson Publishing, 1994).

Manning, J. F., 'The Absurdity Doctrine' (2003) 116 *Harvard Law Review* 2387.

March, J. and Simon, H., *Organizations* (2nd edn, Oxford: Blackwell, 1993).

Marlier, E. *et al.*, *The EU and Social Inclusion: Facing the Challenges* (Bristol: Policy Press, 2006).

Marshall, G., 'Justiciability', in Guest, A. G. (ed.), *Oxford Essays in Jurisprudence* (Oxford University Press, 1961).

Marshall, T. H., 'Citizenship and Social Class', in Marshall, T. H. and Bottomore, T., *Citizenship and Social Class* (London: Pluto Press, 1992).

Martin, R., *A System of Rights* (Oxford University Press, 1997).

Mashaw, J. L., 'Bureaucracy, Democracy and Judicial Review: The Uneasy Coexistence of Legal, Managerial and Political Accountability', in Durant, R. F. (ed.), *The Oxford Handbook of American Bureaucracy* (New York: Oxford University Press, 2010).

Bureaucratic Justice (New Haven: Yale University Press, 1985).

Due Process in the Administrative State (New Haven: Yale University Press, 1985).

Greed, Chaos and Governance: Using Public Choice to Improve Public Law (New Haven: Yale University Press, 1997).

'The Management Side of Due Process' (1974) 59 *Cornell Law Review* 772.

Mashaw, J. L. and Harfst, D. L., *The Struggle for Auto-Safety* (Cambridge, MA: Harvard University Press, 1990).

Mbazira, C., *Litigating Socio-Economic Rights in South Africa: A Choice between Corrective and Distributive Justice* (Pretoria University Law Press, 2009).

McCann, M., 'Litigation and Legal Mobilization', in K. E. Whittington, R. D. Kelemen, and G. A. Caldeira (eds.) *The Oxford Handbook of Law and Politics* (New York: Oxford University Press, 2010).

'Reform Litigation on Trial' (1992) 17 *Law and Social Inquiry* 715.

Rights at Work: Pay Equity Reform and the Politics of Legal Mobilization (University of Chicago Press, 1994).

McCann, M. and Silverstein, H., 'Rethinking Law's Allurements: A Relational Analysis of Social Movement Lawyers in the United States', in Sarat, A. and Scheingold, S. (eds.), *Cause Lawyering and the State in a Global Era* (New York: Oxford University Press, 1998).

McGarity, T. O., 'Some Thoughts on "Deossifying" the Rulemaking Process' (1992) 41 *Duke Law Journal* 1385.

'The Courts and the Ossification of Rulemaking: A Response to Professor Seidenfeld' (1997) 75 *Texas Law Review* 525.

McGarity, T. O. and Shapiro, S. A., *Workers at Risk: The Failed Promise of the Occupational and Safety Health Administration* (New York: Praeger Publishers, 1993).

McGuire, O. R., 'Federal Administrative Action and Judicial Review' (1936) 22 *American Bar Association Journal* 492.

Mciejovsky, B. and Budescu, D. V., 'Collective Induction without Cooperation? Learning and Knowledge Transfer in Cooperative Groups and Competitive Auctions' (2007) 92 *Journal of Personality and Social Psychology* 854.

McLean, K., 'Housing', in Woolman, S. and others (eds.), *The Constitutional Law of South Africa* (2nd edn, Cape Town: Juta & Co., 2007).

'Meaningful Engagement: One Step Forward, Two Steps Back' (2010) 3 *Constitutional Court Review* 1.

Melnick, R. S., *Between the Lines: Interpreting Welfare Rights* (Washington DC: Brookings Institution Press, 1994).

Regulation and the Courts: The Case of the Clean Air Act (Washington DC: Brookings Institution, 1983).

Mendeloff, J. M., *The Dilemma of Toxic Substance Regulation: How Overregulation Causes Underregulation at OSHA* (Cambridge, MA: MIT Press, 1988).

Michelman, F. I., 'Foreword: On Protecting the Poor through the Fourteenth Amendment' (1968) 83 *Harvard Law Review* 7.

'Law's Republic' (1988) 97 *Yale Law Journal* 1493.

'Welfare Rights in a Constitutional Democracy' (1979) *Washington University Law Quarterly* 659.

Mill, J. S., 'Considerations on Representative Government', in *On Liberty and Other Essays*, ed. J. Gray (Oxford University Press, 1991 [1861]).

Minnow, M., *In Brown's Wake: Legacies of America's Educational Landmark* (New York: Oxford University Press, 2011).

Monahan, J. and Walker, L., 'Judicial Use of Social Science Research' (1991) 15 *Law and Human Behavior* 571.

Social Science in Law: Cases and Materials (5th edn, Westbury: Foundation Press, 2002).

Morsink, J., *Inherent Human Rights: The Philosophical Roots of the Universal Declaration* (Philadelphia: University of Pennsylvania Press, 2009).

The Universal Declaration on Human Rights: Origin, Drafting, Intent (Philadelphia: University of Pennsylvania Press, 2000).

Mowbray, A. R., *The Development of Positive Obligations under the European Convention on Human Rights by the European Court of Human Rights* (Oxford: Hart Publishing, 2004).

Moshman, D. and Geil, M., 'Collaborative Reasoning: Evidence for Collective Rationality' (1998) 4 *Thinking and Reasoning* 231.

Newell, C., Calvert, J., and Krause, S., 'Insight: "I'm like a cab for hire, at £5,000 pounds a day"', *The Sunday Times*, 21 March 2010.

Nickel, J. W., *Making Sense of Human Rights* (2nd edn, Oxford: Blackwell Press, 2007).

Nozick, R., *Anarchy, State and Utopia* (Oxford: Basic Books, 1974).

Nussbaum, M., *Women and Human Development* (Cambridge University Press, 2000).

O'Brien, N., 'Social Rights Adjudication and the Ombudsman' [2009] *Public Law* 466.

O'Neill, O., 'The Dark Side of Human Rights' (2005) 81(2) *International Affairs* 427.

O'Reilly, J. T., 'Losing Deference in the FDA's Second Century: Judicial Review, Politics, and a Diminished Legacy of Expertise' (2008) 93 *Cornell Law Review* 939.

Ogus, A., 'Bureaucrats as Institutional Heroes' (1987) 7 *Oxford Journal of Legal Studies* 305.

Otsuka, M., *Libertarianism without Inequality* (Oxford University Press, 2003).

Pacek, A. and Radcliff, B., 'Assessing the Welfare State' (2008) 6 *Perspectives on Politics* 267.

Page, E., *Governing by Numbers: Delegated Legislation and Everyday Policy-Making* (Oxford: Hart Publishing, 2001).

Palmer, P., *Judicial Review, Socio-Economic Rights and the Human Rights Act* (Oxford: Hart, 2007).

Pantazis, P., Gordon, D., and Levitas, R. (eds.), *Poverty and Social Exclusion in Britain: The Millennium Survey* (Bristol: Policy Press, 2006).

Parijs, P. van, *Real Freedom for All* (Oxford University Press, 1995).

Paris, M., *Framing Equal Opportunity: Law and Politics of School Finance Reform* (Stanford University Press, 2010).

Parliamentary Commissioner for Administration, Annual Report for 1993, HC 290 (1993/4).

    Principles of Good Administration (London: TSO, 2007).

Peay, J., *Tribunals on Trial: A Study of Decision-Making under the Mental Health Act 1983* (Oxford: Clarendon Press, 1989).

Peele, G., *Governing the UK* (4th edn, Oxford: Blackwell, 2004).

Peiser, G., *Droit administratif général* (23rd edn, Paris: Dalloz, 2006).

Pettit, P., *Republicanism: A Theory of Freedom and Government* (Oxford University Press, 1997).

Peysner, J. and Seneviratne, M., *The Management of Civil Cases: The Courts and Post-Woolf Landscape* (DCA Research Series 9/05, 2005).

Pierce, Jr, R. J., 'Seven Ways to Deossify Agency Rulemaking' (1995) 47 *Administrative Law Review* 59.

'The Role of the Judiciary in Implementing an Agency Theory of Government' (1989) 64 *New York University Law Review* 1239.

'The Unintended Effects of Judicial Review of Agency Rules: How Federal Courts Have Contributed to the Electricity Crisis of the 1990s' (1992) 43 *Administrative Law Journal* 7.

Pieterse, M., 'Health, Social Movements, and Rights-based Litigation in South Africa' (2008) 35 *Journal of Law and Society* 364.

Platt, L., Sunkin, M., and Calvo, K., 'Judicial Review Litigation as an Incentive to Change in Local Authority Public Services in England and Wales' (2010) 20 *Journal of Public Administration Research and Theory* 243.

Pleasence, P. and Balmer, N. J., 'Caught in the Middle: Income, Justiciable Problems and Use of Lawyers' in M. Trebilcock, A. Duggan, and L. Sossin (eds.), *Middle Income Access to Justice* (University of Toronto Press, 2012).

Pleasence, P., Balmer, N., and Buck, A., *Causes of Action: Civil Law and Social Justice* (2nd edn, London: Legal Services Research Centre, 2006).

Pleasence, P. and Balmer, N., Patel, N. and Denvir C., *Civil Justice in England and Wales 2009: Report of the 2006–2009 English and Welsh Civil and Social Justice Survey* (London: Legal Services Commission, 2010).

Pogge, T. (ed.), *Freedom from Poverty as a Human Right* (Oxford University Press/ UNESCO, 2007).

Polanyi, M., *The Logic of Liberty: Reflections and Rejoinders* (New York: Routledge & Kegan Paul, 1951).

Polya, G., *How to Solve It* (Princeton University Press, 1945).

Posner, R. A., *How Judges Think* (Cambridge, MA: Harvard University Press, 2008).

'Review of Jeremy Waldron, Law and Disagreement' (2000) 100 *Columbia Law Review* 582.

Post, R. and Siegal, R., 'Roe Rage: Democratic Constitutionalism and Backlash' (2007) 42 *Harvard Civil Rights–Civil Liberties Law Review* 373.

Pound, R., 'Mechanical Jurisprudence' (1908) 8 *Columbia Law Review* 605.

Prosser, T., 'Poverty, Ideology and Legality: Supplementary Benefit Appeals Tribunals and their Predecessors' (1977) 4 *British Journal of Law and Society* 44.

Test Cases for the Poor: Legal Techniques in the Politics of Social Welfare (London: Child Poverty Action Group, 1983).

Puender, H., 'Democratic Legitimation of Delegated Legislation – A Comparative View on the American, British and German Law' (2009) 58 *International and Comparative Law Quarterly* 363.

Rawls, J., *A Theory of Justice* (Cambridge, MA: Harvard University Press, 1971; rev. edn 1999).

Justice as Fairness: A Restatement (Cambridge, MA: Harvard University Press, 2001).

Political Liberalism (New York: Columbia University Press, 1996).

Raz, J., *The Authority of Law* (Oxford University Press, 1979).

'Disagreement in Politics' (1998) 43 *American Journal of Jurisprudence* 25.

Engaging Reason: On the Theory of Value and Action (Oxford University Press, 1999).

Ethics in the Public Domain: Essays in the Morality of Law and Politics (Oxford: Clarendon Press, 1994).

'Human Rights Without Foundations', in Besson, S. and Tasioulas, J. (eds.), *The Philosophy of International Law* (Oxford University Press, 2010).

The Morality of Freedom (Oxford University Press, 1986).

'Speaking with One Voice: On Dworkinian Integrity and Coherence', in Hurley, S. (ed.), *Dworkin and His Critics: With Replies by Ronald Dworkin* (Oxford: Blackwell, 2004).

Rebell, M. A. and Block, A. R., *Equality and Education: Federal Civil Rights Enforcement in the New York City School System* (Princeton University Press, 1985).

Reich, C., 'Individual Rights and Social Welfare: The Emerging Legal Issues' (1965) 74 *Yale Law Journal* 1245.

'The Law of the Planned Society' (1966) 75 *Yale Law Journal* 1227.

'The New Property' (1964) 73 *Yale Law Journal* 732.

Renekar, T. S., 'Evidentiary Legerdemain: Deciding When *Daubert* Should Apply to Social Science Evidence' (1996) 84 *California Law Review* 1657.

Resnik, J., 'Managerial Judges' (1982) 96 *Harvard Law Review* 374.

Richardson, G., 'Impact Studies in the UK', in Hertogh, M. and Halliday, S. (eds.), *Judicial Review and Bureaucratic Impact: International and Interdisciplinary Perspectives* (Cambridge University Press, 2004).

Ridell, T. Q., 'The Impact of Legal Mobilization and Judicial Decisions: The Case of Official Minority-Language Education Policy in Canada for Francophones Outside Quebec' (2004) 38 *Law and Society Review* 584.

Rivers, J., 'Proportionality and the Variable Standard of Review' [2006] *Cambridge Law Journal* 174.

Roach, K., *Constitutional Remedies in Canada* (Aurora: Canada Law Book, 1994) (suppl. 2001).

Roach, K. and Budlender, G., 'Mandatory Relief and Supervisory Jurisdiction: When Is It Appropriate, Just and Equitable?' (2005) 122 *South African Law Journal* 325.

Roberts, D., *Victorian Origins of the British Welfare State* (New Haven: Yale University Press, 1960).

Robertson, D., *The Judge as Political Theorist* (Princeton University Press, 2010).

Robinson, S. E. and Meier, K. J., 'Path Dependence and Organization Behaviour: Bureaucracy and Social Promotion' (2006) 36 *The American Review of Public Administration* 241.

Rose, W. (ed.), *Blackstone's Civil Practice 2006* (Oxford University Press, 2006).

Rose-Ackerman, S., 'Review of R. Sandler and D. Schoenbrod, *Democracy by Decree*' (2003) 118 *Political Science Quarterly* 679–81.

Rosenberg, G., *The Hollow Hope: Can Courts Bring About Social Change?* (University of Chicago Press, 1991; 2nd edn, 2008).

Ross II, B. L. and Smith, T., 'Minimum Responsiveness and the Political Exclusion of the Poor' (2009) 72 *Law and Contemporary Problems* 197.

Ruedin, D., 'Ethnic Group Representation in Cross National Comparison' (2009) 15 *Journal of Legislative Studies* 335.

Sabel, C. F. and Simon, W. H., 'Destabilization Rights: How Public Law Litigation Succeeds' (2004) 117 *Harvard Law Review* 1016.

Sager, L. G., 'Fair Measure: The Underenforcement of Constitutional Norms' (1978) 91 *Harvard Law Review* 1212.

Sainsbury, R., 'Administrative Justice: Discretion and Procedure in Social Security Decision-Making', in Hawkins, K. (ed.), *The Uses of Discretion* (Oxford University Press, 1992).

Sajo, A., 'How the Rule of Law Killed Hungarian Welfare Reform' (1996) 5 *East European Constitutional Review* 31.

Sales, P. and Steyn, K., 'Legitimate Expectations in English Public Law' [2000] *Public Law* 564.

Sandler, R. and Schoenbrod, D., *Democracy by Decree* (New Haven: Yale University Press, 2003).

Sarat, A. and Scheingold, A. (eds.), *Cause Lawyers and Social Movements* (Stanford University Press, 2010).

Scalia, A. and Gutmann, A. (eds.), *A Matter of Interpretation: Federal Courts and the Law* (Princeton University Press, 1997).

Schauer, F., '*Ashwander* Revisited' (1995) *Supreme Court Review* 177.

Scheingold, S., *The Politics of Rights: Lawyers, Public Policy and Political Change* (New Haven: Yale University Press, 1974).

Scheinin, M., 'Protection of Economic, Social and Cultural Rights in Finland – A Rights-Based Variant of the Welfare State', in Scheinin, M. (ed.), *The Welfare State and Nordic Constitutionalism in the Nordic Countries* (Copenhagen: Nordic Council of Ministers, 2001).

Schiller, R. E., 'The Era of Deference: Courts, Expertise, and the Emergence of New Deal Administrative Law' (2007) 106 *Michigan Law Review* 399.

Scott, C. and Macklem, P., 'Constitutional Ropes of Sand or Justiciable Guarantees? Social Rights in a New South African Constitution' (1992) 141 *University of Pennsylvania Law Review* 1.

Seidenfeld, M., 'Demystifying Deossification: Rethinking Recent Proposals to Modify Judicial Review of Notice and Comment Rulemaking' (1997) 75 *Texas Law Review* 483.

Sellinger, E. and Crease, R. P. (eds.), *The Philosophy of Expertise* (New York: Columbia University Press, 2006).

Selten, R., 'What is Bounded Rationality?', in Gigerenzer, G. and Selten, R. (eds.), *Bounded Rationality: The Adaptive Toolbox* (Cambridge, MA: MIT Press, 2001).

Sen, A., 'Elements of a Theory of Human Rights' (2004) 32 *Philosophy & Public Affairs* 315.

Inequality Reexamined (Oxford: Clarendon Press, 1992).

'Poor, Relatively Speaking' (1983) 35 *Oxford Economic Papers* 135.

The Idea of Justice (London: Penguin, 2009).

Sen, A. and Nussbaum, M. (eds.), *The Quality of Life* (Oxford: Clarendon Press, 1993).

Seneviratne, M., *Ombudsmen: Public Services and Administrative Justice* (London: Butterworths, 2002).

Serpell, A. J., *The Reception and Use of Social Policy Information in the High Court of Australia* (Pyrmont, New South Wales: Lawbook Co, 2006).

Shapiro, I., *The State of Democratic Theory* (Princeton University Press, 2003).

Shapiro, M., '"Deliberative", "Independent" Technocracy v. Democratic Politics: Will the Globe Echo the EU?' (2005) 68 *Law and Contemporary Problems* 341.

'Judicial Review and Bureaucratic Impact: The Future of EU Administrative Law', in Hertogh, M. and Halliday, S. (eds.), *Judicial Review and Bureaucratic Impact: International and Interdisciplinary Perspectives* (Cambridge University Press, 2004).

'The Institutionalization of European Administrative Space', in Sweet, A. S., Sandholtz, W., and Fliegstein, N. (eds.), *The Institutionalization of Europe* (Oxford University Press, 2001).

The Supreme Court and Administrative Agencies (New York: Free Press, 1968).

Shapiro, M., Stone Sweet, A., *On Law, Politics and Judicialisation* (Oxford University Press, 2002).

Shelton, D., *Remedies in International Human Rights Law* (2nd edn, New York: Oxford University Press, 2006).

Sheperd, G. B., 'Fierce Compromise: The Administrative Procedure Act Emerges from New Deal Politics' (1996) 90 *Northwestern Law Review* 1557.

Shuck, P. R., 'Public Law Litigation and Social Reform' (1993) 100 *Yale Law Journal* 1763.

Shue, H., *Basic Rights: Subsistence, Affluence, and US Foreign Policy* (2nd edn, Princeton University Press, 1980).

Sime, S., *A Practical Approach to Civil Procedure* (9th edn, Oxford University Press, 2006).

Simon, H. A., *Administrative Behavior: A Study of Decision-Making Processes in Administrative Organization* (4th edn, New York: The Free Press, 1997).

Simhony, A. and Weinstein, D. (eds.), *The New Liberalism: Reconciling Liberty and Community* (Cambridge University Press, 2001).

Singh, P., 'Promises and Perils of Public Interest Litigation in Protecting the Rights of the Poor and the Oppressed' (2005) 27 *Delhi Law Review* 8.

Sloman, S. A., 'Two Systems of Reasoning' in Gilovich, T., Griffin, D., and Kahneman, D., *Heuristics and Biases: The Psychology of Intuitive Judgment* (Cambridge University Press, 2002).

Smith, M., *Political Institutions and Lesbian and Gay Rights in the United States and Canada* (New York: Routledge, 2008)

Smith, S. A. de, *Judicial Review of Administrative Action* (4th edn, London: Stevens, 1980).

Sossin, L., *Boundaries of Judicial Review: The Law of Justiciability in Canada* (Toronto: Carswell, 1999).

'How Judicial Decisions Influence Bureaucracy in Canada', in Hertogh, M. and Halliday, S. (eds.), *Judicial Review and Bureaucratic Impact: International and Interdisciplinary Perspectives* (Cambridge University Press, 2004).

Stevens, R., 'Hewart, Gordon, first Viscount Hewart (1870–1943)', in *Oxford Dictionary of National Biography* (Oxford University Press, 2004); online edn, Jan 2008 [www.oxforddnb.com/view/article/33846, accessed 28 July 2011].

Stewart, R. B., 'The Reformation of American Administrative Law' (1975) 88 *Harvard Law Review* 1669.

Steyn, Lord, 'Deference: A Tangled Story' [2005] *Public Law* 346.

'Pepper v Hart: A Re-examination' (2001) 21 *Oxford Journal of Legal Studies* 59.

Street, H., *Justice in the Welfare State* (London: Steven & Sons, 1968).

Summers, R., 'Justiciability' (1963) 26 *Modern Law Review* 530.

Sumner, L. W., *The Moral Foundations of Rights* (Oxford University Press, 1986).

Sunkin, M. and Pick, K., 'The Changing Impact of Judicial Review' [2001] *Public Law* 736.

Sunstein, C. R., 'Beyond Judicial Minimalism' (2008) 43 *Tulsa Law Review* 825.

'Beyond the Republican Revival' (1988) 97 *Yale Law Journal* 1539.

'Constitutionalism After the New Deal' (1987) 101 *Harvard Law Review* 421.

'Foreword: Leaving Things Undecided' (1995) 110 *Harvard Law Review* 6.

Infotopia: How Many Minds Produce Knowledge (Oxford University Press, 2006).

Legal Reasoning and Political Conflict (New York: Oxford University Press, 1996).

'Lochner's Legacy' (1987) 7 *Columbia Law Review* 873.

One Case at a Time: Judicial Minimalism on the Supreme Court (Cambridge, MA: Harvard University Press, 2001).

'Preferences and Politics' (1991) 10 *Philosophy & Public Affairs* 3.

The Partial Constitution (Cambridge, MA: Harvard University Press, 1993).

The Second Bill of Rights (New York: Basic Books, 2004).

'Virtues and Verdicts: Review of Ronald Dworkin's Justice in Robes', *The New Republic*, 22 May 2006.

Sunstein, C. R. and Vermeule, A., 'Institutions and Interpretation' (2003) 101 *Michigan Law Review* 885.

Supperstone, M. *et al.*, 'ADR and Public Law' [2006] *Public Law* 299.

Tasioulas, J., 'Are Human Rights Essentially Triggers for Intervention?' (2009) 4 *Philosophy Compass* 938.

Thayer, J. B., 'The Origin and Scope of the American Doctrine of Constitutional Law' (1893) 7 *Harvard Law Review* 129.

Thomas, E. W., *The Judicial Process* (Cambridge University Press, 2005).

Titmuss, R., *Essays on the Welfare State* (London: Allen and Unwin, 1958).

'Welfare "Rights", Law and Discretion' (1971) 42 *Political Quarterly* 113.

Tomkins, A., *Our Republican Constitution* (Oxford: Hart Publishing, 2004).

Townsend, P., *Poverty in the United Kingdom: A Survey of Household Resources and Standards of Living* (London: Penguin Books, 1979).

Toynbee, P. and Walker, D., *The Verdict: Did Labour Change Britain?* (London: Granta, 2010).

Traynor, I. 'Four and No More: Swiss Referendum Bans Muslims from Building Minarets', *The Guardian* (London), 30 November 2009.

Tribe, L. H., 'The Puzzling Persistence of Process-Based Constitutional Theories' (1980) 89 *Yale Law Journal* 1083.

Tribunal Service, Quarterly Statistics, 3rd Quarter, 2010–2011, 1 October 2010–31 December 2010 (Ministry of Justice, 31 March 2011).

Tushnet, M., 'Policy Distortion and Democratic Debilitation: Comparative Illumination of the Countermajoritarian Difficulty' (1995) 94 *Michigan Law Review* 245.

Red, White, and Blue: A Critical Analysis of Constitutional Law (Cambridge, MA: Harvard University Press, 1988).

Weak Courts, Strong Rights: Judicial Review and Social Welfare Rights in Comparative Constitutional Law (Princeton University Press, 2008).

Twining, W., *Karl Llewellyn and the Realist Movement* (London: Weidenfeld and Nicolson, 1973).

Vanhala, L., *Making Rights a Reality? Disability Rights Activists and Legal Mobilization* (Cambridge University Press, 2011).

'Social Movements Lashing Back: Law, Social Change, and Intra-Social Movement Backlash in Canada' (2011) 54 *Studies in Law, Politics and Society* 113.

Veenhoven, R., 'Well-Being in the Welfare State: Level Not Higher, Distribution Not More Equitable' (2003) 2 *Journal of Comparative Policy Analysis* 91.

Verhovek, S. H., 'The 2000 Campaign: The Ballot Questions; "Oregon Ballot Full of Voter Initiatives Becomes Issue in Itself"', *The New York Times*, 25 October 2000.

Verkuil, P. R., 'Comment: Rulemaking Ossification – A Modest Proposal' (1995) 47 *Administrative Law Review* 453.

'The Emerging Concept of Administrative Procedure' (1978) 78 *Columbia Law Review* 258.

'The Ombudsman and the Limits of the Adversary System' (1975) 75 *Columbia Law Review* 845.

Vermeule, A., *Judging under Uncertainty: An Institutional Theory of Legal Interpretation* (Cambridge, MA: Harvard University Press, 2006).

Virally, M., 'L'introuvable acte de gouvernement' (1952) *Revue de Droit Publique* 317.

Waldron, J., 'Homelessness and the Issue of Freedom', in Waldron, J. (ed.), *Liberal Rights: Collected Papers 1981–1991* (Cambridge University Press, 1993).

Law and Disagreement (Oxford: Clarendon Press, 1999).

'The Core of the Case Against Judicial Review' (2006) 115 *Yale Law Journal* 1347.

Weaver, M., 'Is a General Theory of Adjudication Possible? The Example of the Principle/Policy Distinction' (1985) 48 *Modern Law Review* 613.

Webb Jackee, J. and Webb Jackee, S., 'Administrative Procedures and Bureaucratic Performance: Is Federal Rule-making "Ossified"?' (2010) 20 *Journal of Public Administration Research and Theory* 261.

Weber, M., *Theory of Economic and Social Organization*, trans. A. R. Henderson and T. Parsons (New York: Free Press, 1947).

Welch, J., 'No Room at the Top: Interest Group Intervenors and Charter Litigation in the Supreme Court of Canada' (1985) 43 *University of Toronto Faculty of Law Review* 204.

Wellman, C., *The Moral Dimensions of Human Rights* (Oxford University Press, 2010).

Wesson, M., 'Grootboom and Beyond: Assessing the Socio-Economic Jurisprudence of the South African Constitutional Court' (2004) 20 *South African Journal of Human Rights* 284.

White, G. E., *The Constitution and the New Deal* (Cambridge, MA: Harvard University Press, 2000).

White, S., *Social Minimum* (Stanford Encyclopedia of Philosophy, 2004), available at: http://plato.stanford.edu/entries/social-minimum (accessed 1 July 2011).

The Civic Minimum: On the Rights and Obligations of Economic Citizenship (Oxford University Press, 2003).

Whittington, K. E., Kelemen, R. D., and Caldeira, G. A. (eds.), *The Oxford Handbook of Law and Politics* (New York: Oxford University Press, 2008).

Wikeley, N., *The Law of Social Security* (5th edn, London: Butterworths, 2002).

Wildavsky, A. B., *The Politics of the Budgetary Process* (2nd edn, Boston: Little Brown & Co., 1974).

Wilkinson, R. and Pickett, K., *The Spirit Level: Why Equality is Better for Everyone* (London: Penguin, 2010).

Wolfrum, R. and Groter, R. (eds.), *Constitutions of the Countries of the World*, Loose Leaf (New York: Oxford University Press, 1971 (with updates)).

Woodhouse, D., 'Ministerial Responsibility', in Bogdanor, V. (ed.), *The British Constitution in the Twentieth Century* (Oxford University Press, 2003).

Woolf, H., Jowell, J., Le Sueur, A. P., and De Smith, S. A., *Principles of Judicial Review* (London: Sweet & Maxwell, 1999).

Woolf, Lord, *Access to Justice: The Final Report* (London: TSO, 1996).

Work of the Scrutiny Unit, 'Liaison Committee Annual Report', HC 419 of 2004–05.

Yamin, A. E. and Gloppen, S. (eds.), *Litigation Health Rights* (Cambridge, MA: Harvard University Press, 2011).

Young, K., 'The Minimum Core of Economic and Social Rights: A Concept in Search of Content' (2008) 33 *Yale Journal of International Law* 113.

Yowell, P., 'Empirical Research in Rights-Based Judicial Review of Legislation', in Huber, P. and Ziegler, K. (eds.), *Current Problems in the Protection of Human Rights – Perspectives from Germany and the UK* (Oxford: Hart Publishing, 2012).

Zander, M., *The Law Making Process* (6th edn, Cambridge University Press, 2004).

Zimmermann, R. and Whittaker, S., *Good Faith in European Contract Law* (The Common Core of European Private Law) (Cambridge University Press, 2008).

INDEX